PERIURBAN CARTOGRAPHIES

PERIURBAN CARTOGRAPHIES

KOLKATA'S ECOLOGIES AND SETTLED RURALITIES

Victoria Jane Marshall

ORO

ORO Editions
Publishers of Architecture, Art, and Design
Gordon Goff: Publisher

www.oroeditions.com
info@oroeditions.com

Published by ORO Editions

Author: Victoria Marshall
Project Manager: Jake Anderson

Book design: CircularStudio / Pablo Mandel, Micaela Carraro (typesetting)
Typeset in Minion Pro and Avenir

10 9 8 7 6 5 4 3 2 1 First Edition

ISBN: 978-1-957183-78-7

Color Separations and Printing: ORO Editions Inc
Printed in China

ORO Editions makes a continuous effort to minimize the overall carbon footprint of its publications. As part of this goal, ORO Editions, in association with Global ReLeaf, arranges to plant trees to replace those used in the manufacturing of the paper produced for its books. Global ReLeaf is an international campaign run by American Forests, one of the world's oldest nonprofit conservation organizations. Global ReLeaf is American Forests' education and action program that helps individuals, organizations, agencies, and corporations improve the local and global environment by planting and caring for trees.

CONTENTS

Acknowledgments

Periurban Cartographies is a revised version of a mid-career PhD in geography completed at the National University of Singapore in 2021. In that journey, I was expertly guided by my supervisor Jane M. Jacobs, then at Yale-NUS. As I stepped into cultural geography, I was able to keep one foot in landscape architecture and urban design through my collaboration with the ETH Singapore Future Cities Laboratory. Thank you to Stephen Cairns for inviting me to join in and to continue on as a co-investigator in the Agropolitan Territories of Monsoon Asia laboratory. Many of my teachers, advisors, classmates, and friends have now left the National University of Singapore but their impact persists. I thank Jessica Clendenning, Miya Irawati, Annu Jalais, Pareena Lawrence, Jonathan Rigg, Tracey Skelton, Chitra Venkataramani, and Syeda Jenifa Zahan. Also, at the National University of Singapore, I acknowledge the Department of Architecture and the social cultural geographies group in the Department of Geography. This forms my hybrid, intellectual community in Singapore and I am grateful to be part of it.

From Kolkata, am grateful to the resident respondents from Ward 13, for they offered an open mind and sweet Bengali hospitality. I thank my research assistants Dipanwita Manna and Swastika Bhattacharya, and audio translator and transcriber Mandalika Sanyal. Their playful guidance made my fieldwork not only informative but pleasurable. In Maheshtala, I thank Chairman Dulal Das of Maheshtala Municipality for providing access to his staff and the Ward 13 Councillors. I visited many archives in Kolkata, and I thank the librarians at The National Library, The Asiatic Society, State Archives of West Bengal, West Bengal Forest Department library, Biren Roy Trust library, and the library of A.K. Ghosh at the Centre for Environment and Development. There are many individuals who made introductions for me and for this I would like to thank Bonani and Pradeep Kakkar at People United for Better Living in Calcutta (PUBLIC), Damayanti Lahiri from the Modern Academy of Continuing Education (MACE), Partha Mukhopadhyay at the Centre for Policy Research (CPR), New Delhi, Pratiti Iti Sarkar from Calcutta International Modern Art (CIMA), and V Ramaswamy. Thank you to Sumit Dabriwala from the Hiland

Group for describing real estate in Kolkata from the inside. I am obliged to Amites Mukhopadhyay at Jadavpur University, who kindly agreed to be my temporary supervisor in India. Finally, I acknowledge Shubhra and Pavan Mukherjee who hosted me at their beautiful New Alipore homestay for seven months.

From New York, I acknowledge those who have shaped my intellectual path. Thank you to my teacher at the University of Pennsylvania, mentor and friend, Grahame Shane from Columbia University. He prompted me to do a PhD and then regularly sent cheerful emails along the way. Yeah Vic! Similarly, I thank my colleague Brian McGrath from Parsons School for Design for his ongoing support and friendship. Many people ask me, how did someone from Sydney, who was living in New York, end up studying Kolkata from Singapore? To answer this question, I must acknowledge the India China Institute at The New School. My 2010-2012 India China Institute Fellowship broadened my design research practice and expanded my academic network. Most importantly, the fellowship gave me the unforgettable experience of witnessing the post-1990's transformations of urbanisation and environment in India and China first hand.

From Greece and Australia, I address those who have known me the longest. I thank my dear friend Karolos Hanikian from Greenways who gave me the perfect gift. Over several years, I have intermittently revised and edited this book from his peaceful, beachside village near Athens. Lastly, from Newcastle, Australia, I acknowledge David and my mother Sue, as well as Kate and my father George with love.

—Victoria Jane Marshall

INTRODUCTION

IN INDIA, as elsewhere, urban edges are often positioned in a developmentalist framework, which assumes a preexisting rural is in transition towards something that inevitably becomes urban. Recent scholarship has started to question such teleological assumptions and offer more complex renderings of notions of urban edges. This book takes up this challenge. In doing so, it pushes back on practices and assumptions that insist on a dichotomous reading of an idealized urban in relation to an idealized periurban, like developed versus undeveloped, complete versus incomplete, or privileged versus disenfranchised. Instead, this book argues that hybrid urban-rural conditions, and urban edges more generally, are best thought of as emplaced.

The book is an up-close study of a one-kilometer-square area of periurban Kolkata, in Gangetic West Bengal, India.[1] Specifically, it focuses on periurbanization in southwest Kolkata through an in-depth study of a settlement area in Maheshtala Municipality. This study area sample was selected precisely because of the absence of spectacular or unusually rapid change: there are no megaprojects here, no stories of sudden eviction. In the absence of that type of change there is, nevertheless, the emergence of a particular "kind of urban" condition, remarkable in its characteristic of slow urban-rural hybridization.

Many parts of Gangetic West Bengal, as with Monsoon Asia more broadly, encompass built landscapes created from dense interactions between humans, nonhumans, and their diverse agencies. The current periurbanization processes both rupture and confirm those preexisting logics in spatially and ecologically diverse ways. For instance, the households and institutions in the case study area are embedded in an incrementally changing context that is neither fully rural nor fully urban. For them, the transition from a rural to a post-rural condition has taken a lifetime and encompasses a range of simultaneous changes across a number of generations. The book describes and accounts for the dimensions of these processes through the lenses of governance, livelihoods, ecologies, and infrastructure.

Additionally, the book takes a radically literal approach to emplaced scholarship of contemporary settlement conditions. The assumption that urban edges are not much more than "becoming urban" is stitched into place by normative thinking about where and how transcendent urban theory and good urban practice emerge. Core principles of urbanization often derive from Global North experiences. This book participates in thinking anew about such assumptions. Geographer Jennifer Robinson (2002) maintains that cities in the Global South have long been rendered "off the map" of widely circulating approaches to contemporary urbanization. In response, I purposefully shift attention from the "almost urban" toward a larger, collective, and comparative project of learning from multifaceted "kinds of urban." The book is offering more than just another instance, another isolated case study. It is a situated contribution toward a newly invigorated urban comparativism. As geographer Jane M. Jacobs (2012) reasons, complex, emplaced renderings of urbanization are needed for comparativism to be meaningful.

While it is important to engage the term *periurban*, it is also necessary to move away from it. I engage the sense of uncertainty that an urban transition implies and delve into "actual socio-spatial and political ecological processes by which specific forms of urbanism come into being," including the periurban (Friedmann, 2016, p. 163). I do so to better understand the logics and consequences of such conditions, with the ultimate goal of better understanding situated future possibilities. This includes better understanding a range of intersecting questions, including: Are there distinct, "place-specific" periurban phenomena that generate their own dynamics, including dynamics specific to Asia (Friedmann, 2016)? And, thinking specifically about India, to what extent are the urban and the agrarian "co-produced" (Gururani & Dasgupta, 2018) in such edge conditions? The book contributes to this body of scholarship. Central to grasping the temporal and spatial aspects of change and transformation in the case study area is a methodological commitment to the visualization of process.

Rural and Urban in India

The terms *urban* and *rural* are social constructs as much as they are lived experiences or land uses. They are categories that are used politically, and this political framing of the rural and the urban is an important context for understanding the transitional assumptions behind the concept of periurbanization, both generally and in India specifically (Leaf, 2016; Shatkin, 2016). As Friedmann (2016, p. 163) notes of India, it is a nation in "catch-up" with respect to urbanization, with the central government deliberately aiming (as policy) to have 50 percent of the population living in cities by 2050. Becoming urban, however, requires massive quantities of land suitable for construction and the obstacle in the way is that most of this land is already dedicated to other uses. In India most land is dedicated to other, nonurban uses: "a variety of human settlements, from indigenous villages to the tens of thousands of 'irregular' settlements that dot the periurban landscape, as well as smaller urban centers and farming communities" (Friedmann, 2016, p. 163).

At the same time, India has compelling examples of rapidly growing megacities, with populations of over ten million people. It currently has five such cities (New Delhi, Mumbai, Kolkata, Bengaluru, and Chennai) and is projected to have seven by 2030, with the addition of Hyderabad and Ahmedabad (UN Habitat, 2016). In most instances, these Indian megacities incorporate the densely settled, rural-urban, "metropolitan" periphery, and these extended metropolitan regions are, in part, products of changing state-level definitions of the urban. Such urban regions are often "urban" only by categorization for the purpose of the Census, but do not have the appropriate policy, administrative, or finance structures. Any effective plan-making for such extended "metropolitan" regions is either missing or ineffective (Ahluwalia, 2019, p. 86; see Sivaramakrishnan, 2015). The part of Gangetic West Bengal/Kolkata that forms the focus of this study is an illustrative example of a rural-urban condition that has been nominally designated and imaginatively envisioned as "urban", and so incorporated into the development framework of the extended Kolkata Metropolitan Area.

Yet this new emphasis on the urban rests on a longer history in which there has been a political bias in favor of the rural sector, at the expense of the urban. For example, the urban population is underrepresented in both national and state legislatures, and until recently there has been an assumption that "urban areas can take care of themselves" (Ahluwalia 2019, p. 86). Such assumptions no longer hold in India, and this is manifest in both political and infrastructure development reforms that have, with various degrees of success, placed new emphasis on the urban. The most pertinent political reform relates to the Constitution of India which, through a commitment to decentralization, now places the responsibility for urban governance on poorly prepared substate local bodies, like Maheshtala Municipality, creating an enduring problem that is still not rectified. The most pertinent economic and infrastructural reform was the launch of the Jawaharlal Nehru National Urban Renewal Mission (JnNURM) in December 2005, and further targeted, "mission-mode" initiatives that aimed to support both sustainable urban development and the "urban growth machine" (Molotch, 1976).

Turning first to the political reform of decentralization: the 74th Constitutional Amendment, enacted in 1992, brought in a commitment to decentralization of governance, and as part of this there was formal recognition of urban local bodies as the "third tier" of government in India (Ahluwalia, 2019, p. 84). Under its 12th Schedule, the Amendment mandated that state-level governments transfer to local-level governments a set of specified functions, including town planning functions such as the regulation of land use and infrastructure construction (buildings, roads, and bridges), as well as public health functions, such as the provision of water, sanitation, and solid waste management. Although such responsibilities now rest with urban local bodies, this is not backed by either adequate finances or local capacity in planning and management. Many urban local bodies are in a quandary, as they are unable to deliver the services to residents that are their constitutional responsibility. Maheshtala Municipality, as a formerly rural area that switched to urban local governance in 1993, immediately after the 74th Constitutional Amendment was formally recognized, manifests an explicitly developmentalist version of this troubled condition, wherein becoming urban is often embraced as an aspiration by political institutions that do not have the capacity to realize that vision.

Turning next to the economic and infrastructure reforms: in 1991—and reversing course from a heavily protected and highly regulated policy regime—the Government of India, like many other countries in Asia, launched a process of wide-ranging economic reform. The intention was to create room for market forces and to open the economy to foreign trade and investment (Ahluwalia, 2019, p. 87). Two results of these initiatives relevant to this study are first, the rapid escalation of land prices and the efforts by state governments to capture this value; and second, the initiative of national "missions" for urban renewal, which encouraged urban local bodies to capture the funds and opportunities made possible through these initiatives. Various missions have generated a lot of action on the ground, including preparation of comprehensive City Development Plans, incentivizing private-public partnerships, and the identification and realization of infrastructure and service delivery projects. Urban renewal missions have also encouraged intercity rivalry in India, as different cities vie for recognition for attaining the best progress in various sectors in national government-sponsored competitions (Ahluwalia, 2019, p. 96).

Across India, these fast-track, mission-sponsored infrastructure investments produced "global" projects, reflecting what geographer Eric Shephard et al. term "mainstream global urbanism" (2013, p. 895). A survey of mission-sponsored infrastructure investments revealed a preference for "big visions" like the construction of large-scale infrastructure projects (Kundu, 2014; Mahadevia, 2011). The impulse to invest in impressive "mega" projects has meant that peripheral urban local bodies, such as Maheshtala Municipality, have not necessarily seen any direct benefit. Instead, as this book will show, mission-sponsored investment is arriving slowly, in fragmented packages that build toward a vision of universal coverage of "basic" services and Sustainable Development Goals.

Yet the municipal authority's revenues and responsibilities are not matched. The revenue of local urban bodies in India is limited, as it is largely dependent on a single tax—property tax—and the tax itself is not fully collected. In addition, the total "basket of revenues" available to municipal authorities has been described as "narrow, non-buoyant, inflexible, and grossly inadequate" (Mohanty, 2014, p. 130). Nevertheless, in Maheshtala Municipality, much-needed, smaller-scale public services such as street lighting, paved local roads, solid waste management, and the provision of reliable and healthy drinking water are slowly being built. Such infrastructure is being delivered as separate projects, one after the other, and much later than anticipated. As this study shows, the condition of impoverished local urban bodies "muddling through" their service delivery responsibilities is often impacting negatively on the lives and livelihoods of long-term residents, testing the patience of newcomer residents, and contributing to the ruining of the cultivated landscape. At the same time, the condition of impoverished local urban bodies muddling through draws society within the bureaucracy itself, and does so in emplaced ways.

Being Ordinary

The book looks at an ordinary urban local body within an extra-ordinary city and delta region. In what follows, I explain what I mean by the term *ordinary*, drawing on the notion of the "ordinary city" as called for by geographer Jennifer Robinson (2005). But first, I must explain various territorial boundaries and briefly situate Maheshtala within the expansion of Kolkata over time. Maheshtala Municipality lies on the southwestern edge of Kolkata. It is an urban local body located within the Kolkata Metropolitan Area, but outside of the jurisdiction of the Kolkata Municipal Corporation, which has planning and development responsibility for the core "city" area. In terms of population, Maheshtala Municipality is the largest urban local body of the Kolkata Metropolitan Area, after Kolkata and Howrah.[2] This reflects the fact that the planned expansions of metropolitan Kolkata have, until recently, been to the less populated north (in the 1950s), then toward the east and west (since the 1990s), bypassing the historically densely settled southwestern area. Why the southwest has been long settled is a complex of historical and ecological factors. Maheshtala sits, in part, on the levee of the Hooghly River, which is higher ground relative to the surrounds. Since the 1800s, the area has included riverfront industries and port facilities and has been populated by migrant groups seeking refuge following famine, the partition of India and Pakistan, and war. In the words of a local official, "growth" has never been planned toward the south because "we are already urban" (Maheshtala Municipality Officer, personal communication, December 2018). Meaning he didn't see the need for the southwest to be built up in a planned way, because the area is already densely settled, deeply linked to the city, and long connected to the river and the delta.

Calling the types of changes that do and do not happen in Maheshtala Municipality as "growth" is already assuming something about the development trajectory of the area. By the 1990s, the area may well have been urban in kind, but the formal specification of the Maheshtala Municipality in 1993 offered a framework for planned urban growth in the southwest; albeit growth that is mainly incremental and led by small landholders and entrepreneurs, along with some elite residential high-rise enclaves and related infrastructure development.[3] These kinds of periurban changes seen in Maheshtala Municipality stand in stark contrast to contested and politically damaging state-level-led land development projects in the outer western and eastern edges of metropolitan Kolkata, such as Singur, Nandigram, and New Town. Furthermore, not all change is in the direction of increased population density, but is informed by diverse nonhuman agencies, as subsequent chapters will show. When rural local governance is changed by political fiat to urban local governance, it does not mean that irrigation networks, paddy cultivation practices, plantations, and productive home gardens and ponds immediately disappear. Sometimes, such recategorization lags behind public infrastructure provision and livelihood changes, such that it confirms an already-present urban condition. In other areas, it may herald a hopeful transition yet to be realized. The temporality and directionality of such governance change can vary greatly from place to place, and within places. In areas like Maheshtala Municipality, periurbanization is taking place in a jumbled fashion, where areas that are closer to the few main roads are much more congested and connected than (often nearby) areas that are linked by narrow or unsealed roads, lanes, and pathways.

Many of the characteristics of slow, incremental periurban transformation are overlooked, even though stasis and extended temporalities have long been noted in relation to agrarian transformation, as small landholders struggle to meet their escalating needs from farming ever smaller landholdings (Rigg et al., 2016, p. 128). Slow, incremental periurban transformation is also vast, in the sense that, when considered collectively, unspectacular rural-urban hybridization is significantly bigger in extent than the type of city created by spectacular "mega" developments (see Sahana et al., 2018). Most importantly, incremental change is lived, and may even be experienced as a slow violation of existing livelihoods or aspired-to lives (Christian & Dowler, 2019; Dillon, 2012). Longtimer and newcomer residents live in this "doubling" for an extended period of time, even a lifetime.

The major conflicts in periurban areas in India are often created by tensions arising from activism by the "new" middle class to exclude others, and this often takes the form of a "bourgeois environmentalism" (Shaw, 2018, p. 106; see Baviskar, 2004). There is, however, an under-studied dimension of periurban middle-class life in India which is the existence of a "peripheralized middle class" (Shaw, 2018, p. 104). Geographer Malini Ranganathan (2011, p. 172) distinguishes between lower middle-class groups who "do not distance themselves from the working-class poor and who are different from the English-speaking middle-class." In fact, like the poor, Shaw (2018, p. 106) says, the lower middle class also make claims on the state for regularization of their settlements through legal and extralegal means. The one-kilometer-square study area is sited in such a peripheralized middle-class community, which is characterized by many microconflicts where long-timers and newcomers continuously find ways to get by and get along amicably.

Robinson (2005, p. 1) argues that an ordinary-cities approach takes the "world of cities" as its starting point and attends to the diversity and complexity of all cities. Instead of seeing only some cities as the originators for theories of the urban and dividing them up according to levels of development, she argues that "ways of being urban and ways of making new kinds of urban futures are diverse and are the product of the inventiveness of people everywhere" (2005, p. 1). This book is committed to this claim: it also seeks to extend its veracity by thinking beyond a city-scale view toward subcity categories and processes, most notably the category of periurban and the process of rural-urban hybridization everywhere. By starting with periurbanization, this book contributes to scholarship that refuses and decenters city-centrism. This is why I frame the study area as becoming a particular "kind of urban," one that is not simply defined by being on the edge of Kolkata, or even in the municipality. This ordinary, area is also located in ecologically defined territories such as Gangetic West Bengal and the Ganges Brahmaputra Meghna Delta. As will be clear, the monsoon and delta context influences power and agency in the study area, just as the municipal and local bodies exert juridical and planning power, but they do not define it.

Maheshtala Municipality, like other newly formed urban local bodies of India, is simultaneously newly empowered by the 74th Constitutional Amendment and profoundly disempowered. Yet Maheshtala Municipality, manages to make things happen and "muddle through." Planning, regulation, and financial management happens, despite shortfalls in capacity and routine procedural detours. Planner Neha Sami (2017, p. 107) talks of the way in which urban governance by such newly formed, urban local bodies is attained through "learning by doing." In the context of her study in Bangalore, this local learning happened in conversation with arriving experts and through procurement partnerships, a process noted in other Indian cities (see Ghertner, 2011, 2017; Weinstein et al., 2014). In ordinary Maheshtala Municipality there is nothing of a scale or cost from which to garner such external expertise, or to incentivize a model of private-public urban planning and development.

The muddling through evident in the study area is not "planning failure." As planner Ananya Roy (2009) notes, planning failure in the Indian urban context is often characterized by three explanations. The first is the narrative of the chaotic Third World megacity that defies all planning controls and forecasts. The second is the explanation that places the onus of fault on incompetent Indian planners who consistently underestimate infrastructure and service needs. The third is the explanation that blames failure on the forces of neoliberal capitalism and unchecked liberalization. Roy offers an alternate reasoning for why Indian cities cannot plan, which is to argue that India's mode of planning is poorly understood. She redefines it as an "informalized entity" that proceeds through systems of deregulation, unmapping, and exceptionalism (2009, p. 86). She says, "these systems are neither anomalous nor irrational; rather they embody a distinctive form of rationality that underwrites a frontier of metropolitan expansion" (2009, p. 86). My study avoids the romanticism evident in Roy's alternative typology but I do draw on the idea of alternative rationalities. I argue that the local culture of governance in my study area confirms the presence of an alternative, informal state rationality, and that this rationality is grounded in "learning by doing" in a context that is undeniably framed by neoliberalization of development, and most notably the pressure on underresourced local urban bodies to capitalize on the opportunities of urban-like development.

The Study Area

In this section I offer a concise historical and statistical account of the study area with relevant contextual details about urban local governance.[4] Maheshtala Municipality, in the district of South 24 Parganas, was formally constituted on December 21, 1993 (West Bengal Legislative Assembly [WBLA], 2016, p. viii). It was previously self-governed by an assortment of *panchayati raj* (village rule) institutions, including twenty-one *gram panchayats* (village councils) and forty partial and total *mouzas* (rural administrative districts) (2016, p. viii).[5] The area was settled long before British colonization, however it is said that the area was named "Maheshtala" for Shri Mahesh Suri, who was given the role of *lambadar* (land-tax collector) by Shri Ramkanta Banerji, a local *zamindar* (landholder) who had been nominated by Lord Clive, the governor of Bengal Province under the East India Company (WBLA 2016, p. viii). Relative to surrounding areas, Maheshtala's municipal status arrived late. For instance, the two municipalities bordering Maheshtala were designated earlier, as they were anchored in colonial trading towns within long-settled bazaar towns, centers of learning, and ports. Budge-Budge Municipality, which is on the Hooghly River and directly to the south of Maheshtala, was established as a municipality as early as 1900 (Bureau of Applied Economics and Statistics, 2009). Similarly, Rajpur-Sonarpur, located nearby on the Adi-Ganga (the old main channel of the Ganges) toward the east of Maheshtala, was established as a municipality in 1876.

For Maheshtala to be designated as a municipality it had to meet three criteria, as outlined in the West Bengal Municipal Act 1993 (Government of West Bengal, 2017, p. 14). First, it had to contain a population of "not less than 30,000 inhabitants." Second, it had to have a population density of "not less than 750 inhabitants per square kilometer." Finally, it had to have an "occupational pattern in which more than 50% of the adult population [were] chiefly engaged in pursuits other than agriculture." By the time it gained its municipal status, Maheshtala exceeded all these measures significantly. In 1991 the total population was 211,352 inhabitants, the "urban" population was 83 percent, and the "rural" population was 17 percent (Bureau of Applied Economics and Statistics, 2009). By 2001 the entire population of Maheshtala—385,266 inhabitants—was categorized as "urban" (Census Organization of India, 2001). Across a municipal area of 42 square kilometers, the population density of Maheshtala was 9,260 people per square kilometer in 2001. As noted earlier, Maheshtala's population density and urbanity is derived from colonial and post-independence industry. The riverfront is comprised of large factories, and the main artery road, Budge-Budge Trunk Road, continues to be lined with small and medium enterprises. In addition, clothing manufacturers, the nearby Port of Kolkata at Khidirpur, and the industrial area of Taratala have been longtime employment centers for the residents of Maheshtala. The main occupational pattern of the area is described by the state-level government as "non-agricultural," and the recognized occupations are tailoring, leather works, fireworks, and "a major workforce of unorganized sectors" (West Bengal Legislative Assembly, 2016, p. 1).

As noted earlier in this introductory chapter, being classified as urban or rural in India is a politically motivated nominal and statistical outcome. Although Maheshtala displayed various signs of urbanity in 1993, the 2001 Census also shows that some agricultural cultivation persisted in the area, as evidenced in a close reading of the various categories of "non" or "other" workers. In 2001, of a total of 385,266 inhabitants, some 265,612 (68.9%) were categorized as nonworkers, most likely home-based women but also possibly informal cultivators. Some 119,654 (31.1%) inhabitants were classified as workers, most likely men, with 358 (0.3%) of this worker category described as cultivators and 417 (0.4%) as agricultural laborers (2009; 2001). Some 11,619 (9.7%) inhabitants were described as household or industrial workers, and 107,260 (89.6%) were classified as "other" types of workers.

Maheshtala was also included in the animal census in 2003, which indicated that there were some 3,645 cattle, 1,909 buffalo, 106 sheep, 935 goats, 4,781 pigs, 2,302 dogs, 51,081 poultry birds, as well as 1,006 persons engaged in fishery (Directorate of Animal Resources and Animal Health, 2003). In Ward 13, the specific case study site, there were 308 cattle, 24 buffalo, 0 sheep, 18 goats, 104 dogs, 3,727 poultry birds, as well as 53 persons engaged in fishery in 2001. With an area of 3.12 square kilometers, Ward 13 is the largest ward of the thirty-five wards that comprise the municipality (total area 44.18 square kilometers) and it is the third most populated with a total of 18,829 persons (Maheshtala Municipality, 2015). While the Ward is located adjacent to the southwestern boundary of the Kolkata Municipal Corporation, or "the city," the density of Ward 13 is 6,034 person per square kilometer, which is less than the average of 10,172 person per square kilometer in the municipality.

What this brief historical and statistical account of the case study area offers is a glimpse into its characteristics of slow urban-rural hybridization. What this account also offers is a reminder of the need to move beyond a dichotomous reading of rural and urban, even if planning and census taking insist on reproducing such terms. To undertake this rethinking, I draw inspiration from urban political ecology, which is an established field of scholarship that seeks to analyze emergent socio-spatial formations and their political-ecological effects. In particular, I draw on a subset thread of urban political ecology scholarship that emphasizes the value of being situated (Lawhon et al., 2014). In the periurban area at the heart of this study nonhumans and their diverse agencies are entangled with society, in situ ecologically, via event-linked situations, and through enduring situated institutional and infrastructural formations. It is thus appropriate to place this study in the broader field of relevant scholarship. That scholarship comprises, firstly, work on periurbanization, both within urban geography and wider urban studies, which I address in chapter 8. Secondly, it comprises urban political ecological and related scholarship that helps to break the binary and teleological assumptions linked to understanding periurbanization, by further deconstructing categories such as rural and urban, society and ecology, as well as human and nonhuman agency. It is this scholarship on urban political ecology that I turn to next.

Parsing Urban Political Ecology

Urban political ecology focuses on unsettling traditional understandings of "cities" as ontological entities separate from "nature," and on how the production of settlements is metabolically linked with humans, nonhumans, and their diverse agencies, like flows of capital (Tzaninis et al., 2020). The approach is central to this study, however not all parts of the field apply evenly. I am selective in how I engage the urban political ecology, which is itself not settled or formalized. In what follows, I parse the field, and in the final section of this chapter I show how the approach informs the organization of the book. In short, I retain the core concept of "metabolism" while advancing emerging concepts about the agency of nonhumans in the context of the unique histories and trajectories of Southern urbanism. I use the term nonhuman agencies in a broad way, encompassing institutions with their official documents and reports, infrastructural and architectural legacies, as well as the forceful agencies of heat, humidity, wind, water, vegetative decay and growth, and the life of animals.

Metabolism

As argued by geographers Erik Swyngedouw and Maria Kaika (2014), the field of urban political ecology emerged in response to late twentieth-century urban theory and practice, which was "strangely silent" about nature. They observe that urban thought at that time said little about the "socio-natures" that underpinned capitalist urbanization processes or about how urbanization processes produced increasingly problematic environmental conditions (2014, p. 464). The field of urban political ecology, they say, also emerged in the Northern context of the increased deterioration of the environment in the 1970s, the "specter of immanent scarcity in nature," and environmental movements that propelled environmental matters to the top of the urban policy agenda (2014, p. 465). In response to this silence about a troubled nature, Swyngedouw (1996, p. 69) developed a "new language," which was soon recognized as a productive analytical approach for understanding society and nature (Heynen et al., 2006; Swyngedouw, 2006). Swyngedouw revisited nineteenth-century Marxian social theory, which addressed nature in a historical-materialist and dialectical ontology, and he combined this with work on "cyborgs" (Haraway, 1991) and "quasi-objects" (Latour, 1993). The concept of "metabolism" developed by Swygedouw was the analytical "entry-point" for theorizing and analyzing "socio-natural things" (2006, p. 106; also see Keil & Boudreau, 2006). Since then, the field of urban political ecology has emerged as a rapidly expanding body of thought in nature-society scholarship and the dimensions of this continue to be well documented (Collard et al., 2018; Heynen, 2013, 2016, 2018; Keil, 2003, 2005; Zimmer, 2010).[6]

Environmental sociologist Jason Moore (2017, p. 286), has argued that metabolism "has become a plastic category that can be molded to serve diverse analytical objectives." Nonetheless, it has become especially useful to Marxian-inspired scholars who seek to understand the "rupture" in the interaction between humanity and "the rest of nature" that has resulted from capitalist production (Foster, 1999). Metabolist thinking has helped move conceptualization away from the dualism of Humanity and Nature to the dialectics of humanity-in-nature (Moore, 2017, p. 288). Geographer Matthew Gandy (2004, p. 364) argues that the metabolist "dialectical" is especially relevant to urban environments, noting that it points to:

> a mutually constitutive conception of relations between nature and culture in urban space: nature is not conceived as an external blueprint or template but as an integral dimension to the urban process, which is itself transformed in the process to produce a hybridized and historically contingent interaction between social and bio-physical systems.

"Hybridity" is also emphasized by Swyngedouw (1996, p. 69) who conceptualized socio-natural things as hybrids (subjects and objects, material and discursive, natural and social) "from the very beginning." He says, central to dialectical metabolism is to recognize the social, cultural, and political power of socio-natural relations, and to understand such relations as "techno-natural imbroglios" (Swyngedouw, 2006, p. 113). In thinking through metabolism, Swyngedouw and Kaika's (2014, p. 459) concern is not with the presence of nature in the city but, as they put it, the urbanization of nature, "the process through which all forms of nature are socially mobilized, economically incorporated and physically metabolized/transformed in order to support the urbanization process." In this sense, their interest in "imbroglios" is much more than coincident assemblages or entanglements of social and natural elements, it is invested in understanding a socio-spatial process whose functions are predicated upon ever longer, often globally structured, socio-ecological metabolic flows that not only fuse objects, nature and people together, but do so in socially, ecologically and geographically articulated, but depressingly uneven, manners (2014, p. 462). Historical-geographical insights into these ever-changing configurations are thus necessary for the sake of considering future political-ecological urban strategies (Swyngedouw and Heynen 2003, p. 898). While my research does not adopt a specifically historical-materialist perspective, it does delve into the agency of documents and socio-spatial processes. Such situated geography is highly localized, often being formed amidst policies and aspirations created in comparison with other cities.

Nonhuman Agency

Metabolism is an urban political ecology idea that aims to conceptually consider nature in society. However, this is not always well realized. Geographer Noel Castree (2002, p. 131) argues that much urban political ecology "erases nature altogether in the guise of making non-dualistic theoretical space for it." Castree (2002, p. 131), who positions himself as writing from a "nonorthodox Marxist perspective," argues that Marxian-inspired urban political ecology often bestows on capitalism "all the power in the society-nature relation," such that nature is always ultimately assumed to be outside and subject to the exploitations, constructions, and manipulations of capitalism. Concurring, geographer Bruce Braun (2008, p. 668) suggests that the concept of metabolism can actually "reinstate a separation between nature and society" because it retains "the economy" as a pre-given ontological category.

It is in part this problem that led urban political ecology to engage with actor network and vitalist perspectives that more emphatically emphasize nonhumans and their diverse agencies. The work of Sarah Whatmore (2002, p. 4) was an early lead in this respect, drawing both on concepts of hybridity in actor network theory and feminist science studies "to accommodate nonhumans in the fabric of the social" and "redistribute … agency." For example, Paul Robbins's (2007, p. 13) pertinent study *Lawn People* accounts for the interaction between suburban lawns and suburban people. It offers an urban political ecology that sees the lawn not as an "ecological product" of human action, but as an "environmental actor" that forces behaviors and adjustments in individuals and institutions. As he notes, "The rhythms and behaviors of these neighborhoods, although enforced by human communities, are dictated by the pattern, pace, and specific ecological needs of other species" (2007, p. 116). The present study does not engage directly with these epistemological debates, but it does emphasize the need to think about capital, humans, nonhumans, and their diverse agencies altogether. Furthermore, the study remains inspired by Whatmore's commitment to "the spatialities of everyday life" and how these "constitute a mode of dwelling in the world." Accordingly, this study seeks to better understand periurban "nature-culture hybrids" and how "their interferences [are] resisted and accommodated in the intimate fabric of social life" (Whatmore, 2002, p. 5; see also Ingold, 1995; Thrift, 1996).

There are a range of nondualistic approaches that emphasize the liveliness of nonhumans and their agencies. Post-human or "more-than-human" geographies (Whatmore, 2002, 2006) include relational approaches (see Haraway, 1991; Latour, 1993; Massey, 2004)[7] and vitalist approaches (see Deleuze & Guattari, 1988). Importantly, post-human ontologies are distinct from the dialectical ontology of metabolism. According to Castree (2002, p. 121), a "relational" ontology is a view of the world where the liveliness of nonhuman agencies is considered on equal status with humans—they are "co-constitutive." Similarly, a "vitalist" ontology brings a focus on life as an "immanent, vital, and emergent force" (Wylie, 2007, p. 202). Relational and vitalist ontologies are often described as conceptually "flat" or nonhierarchical, and they break the dualist habit of thinking that determines either nature or society/capital to be structuring agents.

A flat ontology such as this offers the possiblity for symmetrical agency. So, while Marxian-inspired metabolist thinking can ultimately erase nature in pursuit of its critical perspective on capitalism and uneven development, post-human approaches open out to a diverse field of liveliness and agency. While not directly political, such approaches are productive in their potentiality. For example, consider "multispecies studies," which aim to think about sociability within "socio-natures." As outlined by anthropologists Eben Kirksey and Stephan Helmreich (2010), multispecies studies bring forward "creatures previously appearing on the margins of anthropology—as part of the landscape, as food for humans, as symbols," and show that they have "legibly biographical and political lives" (2010, p. 545). Multispecies studies reveal that it is possible to put nature in society without erasing the notion of nature as something that changes of its own accord (see also de la Bellacasa, 2017; Haraway, 2016; Tsing, 2014).[8] Another example, and one that I engage later in this study, is work on the agency of paper documents, like maps. Anthropologist Matthew Hull (2012, p. 21) argues that documents, or what he terms "graphic artefacts," build associations. They do this through circulation and recontextualization of the graphic artefacts themselves, and through human "involvement in the enactment of the objects [the graphic artefacts] talk about" (2013, p 25).

In sum, Marxian-linked metabolist thinking is a dialectical ontology that has usefully offered a framework for examining society and nature as entangled. However, its explanatory default can still privilege the determining agency of capitalist processes, ultimately pacifying nonhumans and their diverse agencies. Post-human approaches, in contrast, bring nonhuman agencies and social action together through relational and vitalist ontologies, although there can be some loss of explicit political dimensions. In this study, I do not overly commit to one position or the other. There is a place for metabolist thinking as proposed by Swyngedouw and others, particularly when the uneven nature of development is starkly evident. However, my interest in ordinary, periurban conditions that are shaped amidst the graphic artefacts of bureaucratic institutions and a monsoon and delta environment, reveals the need to see diverse nonhuman agencies as powerful. Similar approaches have been pursued by those advocating a "situated" urban political ecology, something that is especially pertinent to conditions of urbanization in the Global South. It is to this special notion of urban political ecology that I now turn.

Southern Urbanism

There have been a number of calls for urban political ecology scholarship to more fully account for the diversity of forms and contexts of urbanism globally. Geographer Yaffa Truelove (2016, p. 4), for example, argues that a "situated" approach to urban political ecology can better account for a range of distinctions, including the unique histories and trajectories of urbanism in Southern cities (Lawhon et al., 2014; Silver, 2016; Zimmer, 2010); the diversity of intra-urban environments in any one city (McFarlane et al., 2017); as well as the diversity across city dwellers in terms of everyday practices and politics (Birkenholtz, 2010; Graham & McFarlane, 2014; Loftus, 2012; Truelove, 2011). Similarly, geographer Mary Lawhon, et al. (2014) aspire to "provincialize" urban political ecology. They show that, for example, African urban political ecologies can inform wider theoretical conceptualizations, thereby influencing associated research methods and policy practice (2014, p. 497). This approach aligns with my interest in shifting the focus from seeing periurban areas as not just "becoming urban" but as emplaced, "kinds of urban."

Lawhon et al. (2014, p. 497) suggest that a situated, urban political ecology should start with everyday practices, be attuned to discerning diffuse forms of power, and open the way for a politics of change based on practices of "radical incrementalism." These analytical steps resonate with conditions and possibilities in periurban Gangetic West Bengal/Kolkata and directly inform the way that I have staged urban political ecology in this study.

First, Lawhon et al. (2014, p. 506) observe that there has been a tendency in urban political ecology scholarship to overly link metabolist ideas of "techno-natural imbroglios" to formal infrastructure. However, this does not translate smoothly to ordinary periurban contexts in the Global South where there is a relative paucity of formal or "basic" infrastructure. In such contexts, to focus on modern infrastructure development, for example, can provide only a partial understanding of urbanization. Indeed, the techno-natural imbroglios of water, energy, and waste (and even transport, housing, and broadband), in the Global North are very different from those in the Global South, where there is extreme poverty and extensive informality (see Bhan, 2019; Derickson, 2014; McFarlane et al., 2017; Ranganathan, 2014; Roy, 2009; Simone, 2004; Zimmer, 2010). Inspired by Simone's (2004) idea of people as infrastructure, Lawhon et al. (2014, p. 506) argue that it is better to recognize "people as the central means through which materials flow in many cities" of the Global South. On this basis, they argue for an "epistemological reorientation" in urban political ecology more generally, as seen in the second and third analytical steps.

Second, a situated, urban political ecology begins with a conception of power as diffuse and relational. Building on feminist critiques of urban political ecology (Rocheleau et al., 2013; Truelove, 2011), Lawhon et al. (2014, p. 508) call attention to the limitations of understanding power as created and operating primarily through the process of capital accumulation and class relations. In response, they suggest the need to "reformulate our understanding of power as relationally constructed and enacted." They operationalize an understanding of power that includes other social categories besides class, such as race and gender, as well as discursive power and associated knowledge claims. This approach has much in common with the work of geographer John Allen (2016; 2010) who argues, in relation to everyday governance, that power has a newfound "reach." Allen questions the idea that power is simply extended across a given territory or network, and that it is something only related to institutional size and organizational capacity. Instead, he (2016, p. 43) focuses on the way that power as a practical tool is mutable, and thus can be practiced in many ways while remaining the same (2016, p. 61). In this study I look closely at "quieter registers" of power, as well as diffuse power as expressed in everyday life as suggested by the feminist critiques noted above.

Third, a situated, urban political ecology makes the connection between theory and practice explicit. Lawhon et al. (2014, p. 502) observe that neo-Marxian recommendations for change largely "fail to respond" to the radical or revolutionary provocation of their arguments (see Swyngedouw, 2018). In response, they argue for a more multifaceted approach for progressive change "rooted in the realities and possibilities of everyday urban practices" (2014, p. 510). This is because, as they put it, "the everyday opens up new spaces through which to derive alternatives for understanding and creating change" (2014, p. 510). For instance, learning from the work of sociologist Edgar Pieterse (2008), they observe how everyday practices can be a foundation and impetus for effecting incremental change, especially in contexts where formal mechanisms are weak, nonexistent, or partisan (Lawhon et al., 2014, p. 511). Others have called this "recursive empowerment" (Ernstson et al., 2014; Silver, 2014). For instance, Simone (2014, p. 36), in describing what he calls the "urban majority of the ordinary" asks:

> If residents once made significant accomplishments in building districts that worked for them, then what now? How are their practices of autoconstruction related to the unwillingness or inability of municipal institutions to conduct basic planning and delivery of services, which only dedicated institutions with clear authority and capacity can do at the scale necessary? What has to be considered in order for these accomplishments not to exist as mere relics or shadows of themselves, but constitute a source of influence on subsequent events? What kind of institutional assumptions are prevalent about who residents are and what they can reasonably or legitimately do? What does urban policy attempt to do as an instrument of relating to the residents of the city?

Consistent with this ethos, the research reported upon in this study draws on thick description of everyday life and diffuse power in periurban Gangetic West Bengal/Kolkata. It does so in the hope of enriching our understanding of incremental modes of political empowerment and the futures they make. My intention is to not just communicate the transformations at work in creating a particular "kind of urban," but also to point to connections that make us rethink the ways in which change happens. I offer the cartographic practice created in this study as yet another circulation of the many documents that I analyze. Furthermore, the study makes a conceptual contribution to periurban scholarship through an urban political ecology approach. This study is not simply a look at a novel and singular periurban condition in and of itself but uses that singularity to better understand periurbanism generally and urban political ecologies particularly. The review of the current scholarship in urban political ecology reminds us of some of the enduring tensions in this field around the conceptualizations of socio-natures, agency, and practice. The urban political ecology approach that I have outlined here offers a way of moving past some of these tensions.

Book Outline

In chapter 1, I begin with urban policy and the search for an appropriate mode of planning by the national Government of India. To do this, I succinctly review the urban reform initiatives that have been launched since the 1990s. I bring a special focus on the 74th Constitutional Amendment for empowering local government and the "mission-mode" projects focused on urban infrastructure. I show how, despite the agenda to empower local government, the central and state governments continue to retain power at the local level, albeit in new ways.

Chapter 1 then shifts to an account of the urban policy and planning initiatives of the State of West Bengal. By way of official visualization strategies, I illustrate how periurban Kolkata has been rendered since the 1990s. I present a close reading of three metropolitan planning documents: the *2011 Perspective Plan;* the *2025 Vision Plan;* and the *2030 State Plan.* The first two plans focus on spatial planning, that is, the planning of "centers" and connective infrastructure. In these earlier plans, the study area is rendered blank, neither being a major center, nor a beneficiary of major infrastructure. The later plan abandons spatial planning altogether, opting for an indicator mode of governance . In this indicator mode, the effects of growth can be read in a digital interface and modulated indefinitely, according to up-to-the-minute urban reform initiatives. What I demonstrate is that situated spatial needs and distinct futures of periurban municipalities do not register on such official maps.

In chapter 2 I situate local-level policy and planning initiatives since the 1980s, revealing the imperfect realization of urban-linked development aspirations. In this chapter, I explain the land use and spatial layout of the municipality and I visualize how Maheshtala was rendered as a "city in the making" in its local development plans. The chapter also offers a brief overview of party politics, an important factor in the local governance cultures of West Bengal.

In chapter 3 I seek to speak back to the many assumptions (about, for example, land, livelihoods, and development trajectories) of the official visualizations discussed in chapters 2 and 3. I do so by generating alternative visual materials that are built from the experiences of residents and from my observational work as a researcher in the field. The visual logic of my methodology spans all phases of the research process, from using visual assessments of land cover and land use to select the case study area, through to the analysis and presentation of findings.

Chapters 4, 5, 6, and 7 are linked, as all three chapters are focused on lived accounts of periurban transformations in the one-kilometer-square study area, in Ward 13, Maheshtala Municipality. In chapter 5, I also look back further in time and highlight the characteristics of the long-settled-rural through a close reading of colonial maps and reports of Gangetic West Bengal from the 1800s to the mid-1900s. In particular, I look at colonial "drainage works" projects, and the colonial project of establishing cultivated and uncultivated land. In all instances, I map the one-kilometer-square study area into various visualizations, modern and colonial. What I reveal are the ways that big spatial ideas, like the colonial "permanent settlement," have been built upon, and have shaped, the settled-rural of Gangetic West Bengal.

In chapter 4, I begin what I term "re-rendering" Ward 13, and I introduce the first of three techniques for recognizing the study area anew. I describe the elements and characteristics of drainage and fields in chapter 4, jungle and land in chapter 5, "village" property in chapter 6, and the "urban" land market in chapter 7. That is, I first look at preexisting, periurban infrastructures of tree-lined garden ponds and plantations along with an interlinked waterway and canal system. I then look at the emergence of newly built settlement colonies and a land market amidst preexisting, but now "jungly" rice paddies. The presentation of perspectives on these imbroglios is in chronological order, however, they should also be thought of as occurring simultaneously.

Overall, the empirical chapters (4-7) seek to unfold, or disentangle, how changes were made and the forces which are at work to either diminish or consolidate their presence. I show how the periurban is a condition that is uniquely realized in the context of Gangetic West Bengal specifically, and Monsoon Asia more generally. In chapter 8, I step back and reflect upon the case study in relation to scholarship on periurbanization over time and from India. I argue that the book is a contribution to work being done on urban theory-building from elsewhere than the Global North, specifically from Asia and periurban Gangetic West Bengal/Kolkata. Lastly, the concluding chapter reflects on what this instance of emplaced periurbanization has to say to wider studies about nonhuman agency, territory, and cartographic practice.

Endnotes

1 Following Friedmann (2016) I use periurban, rather than peri-urban.

2 Maheshtala Municipality has the third-highest population in the Kolkata Metropolitan Area (448,317) after Kolkata (4,496,694) and Howrah (1,077,075) Municipal Corporations (Census Organization of India, 2011).

3 Growth towards the southeast of the Kolkata Metropolitan Area is similarly incremental and led by small landholders and entrepreneurs, however, it has been enhanced by the construction of a bypass and the in-progress relocation of the South 24 Parganas district governance headquarters from Alipur to Baruipur.

4 The study is an in-depth look at a one-kilometer-square area within Ward 13, of Maheshtala Municipality, the reasoning for this dimension and its location is defined in detail in chapter 2.

5 With the founding of Maheshtala Municipality, the twenty-one gram panchayats and forty partial and total mouzas were reassigned into thirty-five wards. Maheshtala Municipality is designated as an "urban local body," a term I use throughout this chapter, and as interchangeable with the term "municipality."

6 A narrow critique of urban political ecology argues that it is failing to live up to its promise of constructively examining urbanization as a global process because the city remains central. Geographers Hillary Angelo and David Wachsmuth (2015, p. 16) argue that urban political ecology has "become bogged down in methodological cityism--an overwhelming analytical and empirical focus on the traditional city to the exclusion of other aspects of contemporary urbanization processes." Recently, this assessment of "methodological cityism" has been refuted by geographer Creighton Connolly (2018, p. 63), who points out that urban political ecology has always moved beyond the city to consider "the various metabolisms and circulations of humans and non-humans connecting cities with places outside of their borders at a variety of scales." The metabolisms Connolly (2018, p. 69) offers as examples of this claim are: rural-urban metabolisms; landscape; urban agriculture; work on eco and smart cities; and infrastructure. This book, which looks at the metabolism of periurbanization in Gangetic West Bengal/Kolkata, thus aligns within Connolly's revision of methodological cityism.

7 Swyngedouw also engages this post-human approach.

8 Multispecies studies also reveal the limits of the term "nonhuman nature" because it is, after all, a dualist concept.

1/

"QUIETER" STATE POWER

The urban policy frameworks relevant to the study area have changed over time. For they have situated and resituated how periurban areas are understood, and how their futures are imagined. This chapter charts this path with a special emphasis on power and cartographic representation. India has three levels or "tiers" of government: central government, state government, and "local bodies." While local cultures of governance are comprised of a combination of all three tiers, for reasons of clarity, this chapter focuses on the changing institutional and policy settings for central and state levels of governance. The local level of governance is addressed in chapter 2.

Before proceeding, it is important to grasp some aspects of these three tiers. At the broadest scale is the national Government of India, what is often referred to as the first tier. On the second tier the authority for regional planning is the State Public Policy and Planning Board, which guides the Department of Planning, Statistics and Program Monitoring. Also at the second tier, but from a statutory planning perspective, the relevant authority is the Kolkata Metropolitan Development Authority, which sits within the state-level West Bengal authority known as the Department of Urban Development and Municipal Affairs. The third tier is the local level, and in relation to periurban Kolkata specifically, the relevant governance entities include both urban local bodies as well as village *panchayat* (rural local bodies).

The term "local bodies" is a technical term and can be thought of as local government. The urban local bodies can include geographically quite extensive municipal corporations as well as municipalities and "notified areas," which are rural areas earmarked as "transitional" with respect to urbanization (Government of India, 1949). The Kolkata Metropolitan Area (hereafter metropolitan Kolkata) comprises the following local bodies; two Municipal Corporations (Kolkata, Howrah); thirty-nine Municipalities (urban local bodies) of which Maheshtala Municipality, the focus of this study, is one; seventy-four Census Towns (rural local bodies); seven Outgrowths; one Cantonment Board; and one Industrial Township (Census Organization of India, 2011).

The urban policy frameworks at all three tiers cannot be disconnected from recent trends of governance reform in Asia. In India, as elsewhere in Asia, reforms were made in pursuit of two main goals (Laquian, 2005). First, to provide efficient delivery of urban infrastructure and services through coordinated region-wide governance. Second, to support decentralization of government to improve local autonomy and greater public participation in decision-making. As discussed in the introductory chapter, this process of reform began in India in 1992, with the 74th Constitutional Amendment, which formally recognized urban local bodies as the third tier of government. Unfortunately, the 74th Constitutional Amendment has engendered a mode of urban policy implementation that forges a strong connection between local bodies and the central government, without a devolution of power or creation of meaningful spaces of inclusion in decision-making. In analyzing how such supralocal policy relevant to Indian urbanization fits amidst existing governance cultures in the periurban context of Maheshtala Municipality, I draw inspiration from a topological approach to power, as outlined by geographer John Allen (2016).

Allen argues (2016, p. 153) that power is no longer simply related to older measures of authority and domination, which relied on institutional size or organizational capacity and were articulated through territorial scope. Instead, power is reproduced differently now through a more adaptable mix of practices. Notably, he says, "quieter registers" of power are assuming greater significance. For example, institutional arrangements manipulate outcomes, offer the lure of inducement, and use the art of persuasion or inviting gestures of seduction (2016, p. 153). What this means is that authority does not become diffuse with distance; rather, it can gain intensity through a special mix of pointed practices that are "actively leveraged" (Allen 2016, p. 155). It is not geography but the leveraging of practices that "composes the distances" of power, placing "people and ideas within reach or beyond reach."

Allen (2016, p. 75) elaborates his argument with reference to the widespread adoption of market-oriented urban policies, something that I report on in this chapter. He considers such policy adoption a more "tenuous achievement" than many straightforward domination scripts would acknowledge. The "seductive combination" of viable growth strategies and rewards for compliance pave the way for policy imitation and emulation across cities. While the promise of growth and rewards acts as leverage, the ability of policies to move and take hold relies on a network of international advisors, private consultants, think tanks, urban policy professionals, and managers. Their authority over policy-adopting officials and city authorities is, however, not direct: they exercise powerful influence through "quiet advice." This field of influence translates neoliberal policy solutions from one city to another, with various inducements "suggest[ing] some futures while others are held back" (Allen 2016, p. 76).

In sum, there are now more and quieter ways that power may be leveraged to register a durable influence. Adaptable mixes of practices such as those outlined above, are in play today, and they show up in the slow, incremental, and imperfect realization of the process of reform and implementation of market-oriented urban policies, as this chapter and the following show.

Mutable Agendas

Technically, the national Government of India does not have the power to pass specific legislation on urbanization and urban planning, but nonetheless it does influence urban development. In practice, much of what happens at the local scale in urban development and policy in India comes from national-level government directives. This occurs even though in the Indian Constitution, urban policy and planning are specified as state government responsibilities. The state governments are empowered with respect to urban planning, and more so since the central government made commitments to decentralization. However, the regional planning apparatus is missing or ineffective. As Shaw (2004) explains, this contradiction arises because, although empowered to make urban policy, very few state-level authorities take initiatives in this area. Those states that do make regional urban policy do it sporadically or reluctantly. More commonly, state governments have undertaken other types of periurban development strategies, particularly strategies aiming to attract external investors and reach voters, as I describe later in the discussion of second tier initiatives. In what follows, I detail key urban policy directives that have been endorsed by the national Government of India, showing how they have changed over time. This provides a broader context for understanding first tier urban policy implementation in periurban, Gangetic West Bengal/Kolkata today.

From Direct Control to a Troubled Agenda

The current powerful role of the central government in directing policy on urbanization and urban planning is the most recent iteration of three different modes for intervening in urbanization since independence (Shaw, 2004). The initial post-independence (1945 to mid-1960s) path was for urban policy making to be subsumed within top-down economic policy (2004, p. 58). During this phase, the role of local institutions and nongovernment initiatives was overlooked or underestimated. This was followed by a second path (mid-1960s to 1980s) in which fiscal incentives and disincentives were replaced by a disproportionate use of direct controls. For example, controlling land use and freezing land prices for reasons of halting growth in some areas, and master planning multicentered cities for reasons of dispersing urbanization into other areas. These troubled policymaking practices culminated in the late 1980s with the National Commission on Urbanization that described the situation with respect to the quality of Indian cities as one of "deep crisis" (A. Kundu, 1989, p. 1185). Since the 1990s, national urban policy has been concentrated on the decentralization of governance and the implementation of neoliberal economic policy, which was mandated in 1991.[1] That is, urban policy is now directed toward empowering the authority and capacity of local urban bodies and encouraging less dependence on the national Government of India for finance and expertise.

There have been mixed scholarly reactions to decentralization. The sociologist Liza Weinstein (2014, pp. 49, 55) sees decentralization as a significant break from the earlier "reactive set of responses", and a move toward a "purposive agenda." Weinstein (2014, p. 56) argues that the urban reforms that have emerged from decentralization have addressed in a more systematic way than previously the realization of a more entrepreneurial mode of governance. This entrepreneurial mode includes the establishment of legal autonomy for urban local bodies and the provision of incentives for administrative and political devolution. Alongside such changes, the central government has established a framework for corporate and civil society participation in governance and incentivizing public-private partnerships. In contrast, political scientist Govind Gopakumar (2015, p. 89) views the changes more negatively, suggesting that they are an unwelcome shift in the intensity of interference by the central government in more localized urban authority. He sees decentralization as a "deeply invasive" process of urban transformation, whereby the national sphere now has greater reach into local urban politics and development than before through systems of monitoring, assessing, and evaluation of state-level and local-level institutional performance. I will return to this theme later, when I discuss local-level governance and planning in Maheshtala Municipality in chapter 2.

The goal of decentralization is to bring government closer to residents, and it cannot be understood without consideration of a parallel and somewhat contradictory trend. This is the trend for government entities to provide services in partnership with both the private sector and civil society groups. Sociologists Baud and de Witt (2008, p. 30) show that the move to public-private partnerships can exclude groups even though decentralization aims to be inclusive. They found that public-private partnerships in India do not proceed smoothly, and that frequent gaps occur between the responsibilities, which are delegated, and the required mandates and finances, which are not always in place. In addition, they observe that local urban institutions are reluctant to allow "humble" residents a greater say in determining urban affairs. This is particularly so in instances where the middle class becomes more vociferous about its preferences, which are often accommodated as a result. Baud and de Witt (2008, p. 32) conclude that rather than strengthening participatory arrangements in India, the current urban policy agenda is being used as "a mechanism of contestation and exclusion." This chimes with the observation of Weinstein et al. (2014, p. 60) that decentralization policy agendas in Asia are often a push by state actors, particularly at the central level, to "create opportunities for the influence of elite collective action in shaping urban space."[2]

The contradictory arrangements attempting to create both greater empowerment of local-level government and greater involvement of the central government sets the scene for more specific, national Government of India urban initiatives. This is exemplified by the Jawaharlal Nehru National Urban Renewal Mission and the follow-on "mission-mode" policy directives, discussed next.

The JnNURM and Related Urban Reforms

The Jawaharlal Nehru National Urban Renewal Mission was envisaged as an initiative that would strengthen the 74th Constitutional Amendment. It was meant to put into action the vision for inclusive economic development, efficiency in provision of urban infrastructure and services, community participation, and better accountability by urban local bodies to citizens (Ministry of Urban Development, 2005, p. 2). The JnNURM and follow-on missions have however, received widespread criticism.[3] One point of concern was that they consolidated uneven development by exacerbating intracity, intercity, and interstate inequalities. For example, Kundu and Samanta (2011, p. 60) have shown that the Mission had a "big city bias." Small towns and poorer states struggled to take advantage of the program because of their limited capacity to understand and implement reforms, as well as to prepare the various documents needed to qualify for funds (D. Kundu, 2014). Even within particular urban contexts, as Mahadevia (2011, p. 62) notes, there was often a bias in favor of large-scale infrastructure projects, such that the program was susceptible to "big visions" and "elite capture."

Another criticism was that JnNURM and follow-on missions obscured the more generalized reality that urbanizing areas are grounded in gradual improvements made "with or without the JnNURM" (2011, p. 63). Mahadevia (2011, p. 63) explains that such gradual improvements can occur through both "people's own investments in housing and basic infrastructure at the local level", as well as "urban local body or State governments' investments in trunk [i.e., roads, water supply, street lighting, drainage, and sewerage] and settlement-level infrastructure." We will see some of these localized outcomes through my study area where basic services are being built in small increments, and municipal services are similarly slowly delivered step by step.

For others, the limited success of JnNURM and follow-on missions in strengthening the 74th Constitutional Amendment is attributed to the politicized link between project financing and policy reform. As Kundu (2014, p. 619) observes about JnNURM, ongoing financing was approved without evidence of reform implementation along the way. At the same time, urban local bodies did not demand autonomy because they are effectively "creatures" of state governments (Mohanty, 2016; Mukhopadhyay, 2006). When there was collaboration between local and state-level institutions it was often pursued instrumentally, to satisfy technicalities to draw funds from the centrally funded Mission. In addition, urban local bodies were not properly empowered, as they were not backed by either adequate financing or the capacity for building needed to improve planning and management, which reduced their ability to operate autonomously and in ways appropriate to local needs. As I show later, my study area is no exception to these more widely observed trends, even though the State of West Bengal is often applauded for its advanced reform efforts, such as the early setup of functioning wards and municipalities as well as establishing the first Metropolitan Planning Commission (M. Chatterjee, 2013).

From Infrastructure "Under Strain" to Infrastructure Assets

Through JnNURM and follow-on missions, infrastructure development has become a significant part of India's urban policy agenda. So much so that, as I show in future chapters, this is also what residents on the ground talk about when asked about changes in their locality. In this section I delve more deeply into the emphasis on infrastructure (defined as basic services) within urban reform, focusing specifically on differences between the *Eleventh Five-Year*

Plan (2007 to 2012) (Government of India, 2008) subtitled "inclusive growth" and the follow-on *Twelfth Five-Year Plan* ((2012 to 2017) (Government of India, 2013) subtitled "faster, more inclusive and sustainable growth".

From the point of view of the central-level Planning Commission, infrastructure was initially seen as an indicator of a larger problem. From the *Third Five-Year Plan* (1961 to 1966) onwards, there was a preoccupation with finding ways to halt the growth of very large, densely inhabited cities and to disperse urbanization elsewhere (Shaw, 2004, p. 50). In the eleventh plan, this preoccupation with size persisted. For example, large cities themselves were blamed for urban deterioration including "problems of traffic congestion, pollution, poverty, inadequate housing, crime, and social unrest" (Government of India, 2008, p. 395). Infrastructure was identified as the aspect most "under strain" and accordingly, specific types of urban infrastructures, notably water supply, sewerage and drainage, uncollected solid waste, parks and open spaces, and transport are identified as requiring "extra effort" and "special attention" (2008, p. 395).

By the time of the twelfth plan, large cities are no longer framed in wholly negative terms. What are described as "urbanized conglomerations" are seen to be inevitable and with a more positive spin (Government of India, 2013b, p. 108). For example, the twelfth plan emphasizes the potential of such areas to generate entrepreneurship, employment, and urban livelihoods. Instead of infrastructure being positioned as something under pressure from, or inadequate for, the intensity of urbanization, it is argued that investment in infrastructure has the potential to make Indian cities more "inclusive" and "sustainable." The twelfth plan outlines the importance of infrastructure investment, specifying electricity, roads and bridges, telecommunications, railways, irrigation, water supply and sanitation, ports, airports, storage, and oil-gas pipelines (Government of India, 2013a, p. 26). Both a McKinsey Global Institute report entitled *India's Urban Awakening: Building inclusive cities, sustaining economic growth*, and the *Report on Indian Urban Infrastructure and Services*, by the central-level High Powered Expert Committee for Estimating the Investment Requirements for Urban Infrastructure Services, highlight the potentials of infrastructural investment (High Powered Expert Committee [HPEC], 2011).

The twelfth plan not only opened the way for an infrastructure growth period, but it was also distinctive as it looked beyond the megacity (Government of India, 2013a, p. 109). This partly reflects an alignment to new, internationally set (World Bank) guidelines for measuring urban agglomerations (Uchida & Nelson, 2009). In the case of India, the stringent definitions of what is considered "urban" has not been updated in the past fifty years, creating a statistical artefact increasingly out-of-step with the realities of urbanization on the ground. For instance, the World Bank (2013, p. 24) pointed out that in India, while 2,774 additional settlements exhibited urban characteristics between 2001 and 2011, only 147 had official urban status. The rest had urban characteristics, but due to the outdated criteria were not considered urban for policy purposes, even though rapid growth of metropolitan edges was the most striking feature of India's spatial transformation.

The twelfth plan clearly absorbed this newly prescribed international way of conceptualizing urbanization for it also includes a vision for rural development. Noting that there must be a "synergistic relationship" between rural prosperity and the "continuum of urban development" from small towns through to extended urban areas (World Bank, 2013, p. 108). Lastly, in the twelfth plan, infrastructure provision was not only reframed in a positive light and as necessary in both urban and rural areas, but it was also newly reframed in line with a wider field of change, where the emphasis is on replacing public investment in infrastructure with private investment. International financial institutions such as the World Bank and the Asian Development Bank, have played an important role in fostering the ideological basis for this policy shift (Baindur and Kamath, 2009).

This section has accounted for key aspects of the urban policy endorsed by the national Government of India since the 1990s. These policies have aimed to shape urban destinies like that of Maheshtala Municipality. What is apparent is that national development agendas are increasingly made evident through topological, rather than topographical (territorial or sectorial) logics of power. These "quieter" (Allen, 2016) forms of disciplinary power do not see existing, settled-rural infrastructure as valuable, thus creating a barrier to equitable change. While there is some acknowledgement of the urban-rural mixing found in the periphery of cities, and in urbanizing towns and urban-rural regions, the urban policy for such areas is missing. Competitively attained, mission-funded development initiatives bring an emphasis on big, privately funded, infrastructure. There is however, no acknowledgement of the significant accomplishments made by residents in building periurban localities that work for them. To ignore the agency of incremental practices of post-rural settlement limits the imagination of possible urban futures. It means that there is no space for serious consideration of the best type of investment in these hybrid areas and for those that will emerge in the future.

Paper Tools

As noted in the introduction to this chapter, policy frameworks since the 1990's have situated and resituated how periurban areas are understood, and how their futures are imagined. In this section I chart how this has occurred in Gangetic West Bengal through a close reading of key second tier planning documents and associated reports. I am particularly interested in the spatial and cartographic imagination reflected in these reports, as they reveal a range of assumptions, aspirations, and capacities about how to shape the future of Kolkata and the role of periurban areas in this.

The reports have a further role in this book. As anthropologist Matthew Hull (2012a, p. 251, 2012b) notes, documents are not simply instruments of bureaucratic organizations, but rather are "constitutive of bureaucratic rules, ideologies, knowledge, practices, subjectivities, objects, outcomes, even the organizations themselves." Documents not only have a role in coordination and control, but they also have the capacity to "make things come into being" (2012, p. 259). Thus, viewing the reports materially as "paper tools" (Jardine, 2017) not only reveals how the renderings on the page circulate and render actual landscapes but it also does work to situate my re-rendering of the one-kilometer-square study area in this book. The spatial and cartographic imaginations presented in this study are intended as another instance of the circulation of documents and as a re-rendering of territory—one that assists in the re-rendering of actual landscapes.

There is no single entity or department at the state level that deals with urban affairs, and the distribution of responsibility has also changed over time with various restructurings—the picture is complicated. However, for the purposes of what follows I focus on two key state-based entities with responsibility for planning and monitoring of urban conditions in West Bengal: The Department of Planning, Statistics and Program Monitoring (DoPSPM); and the Department of Urban Development and Municipal Affairs (DUDMA).

The first entity, DoPSPM, was formed in 2016 by way of a merger of two previously independent entities, the Department of Statistics and Program Implementation and the Department of Planning (itself formerly known as the Development and Planning Department). Urban and general settlement questions come into the orbit of concern for this sphere of state-level government because they are responsible for preparing and monitoring long- and short-term plans for comprehensive development of the State of West Bengal, often in consultation with other departments of the state government.

They are also meant to coordinate District Planning Committees. In addition, in 2016 the Government of West Bengal set up a State Public Policy and Planning Board (SPPPB) under the DoPSPM. The SPPPB functions as a policy think tank for the state government and is mandated to prepare a vision mission and long- and short-term perspective plan for the state and districts.

The second entity is DUDMA. Since 1932 with the passing of the Bengal Municipal Act, there has been state-legislated and coordinated municipal government in West Bengal. The 74th Constitutional Amendment Act in 1992 thus strengthen ed existing municipal governance and DUDMA is tasked with helping old and new municipalities perform their functions more efficiently. Entities like the Kolkata Municipal Corporation and the Kolkata Metropolitan Development Authority are established and authorized by, and accountable to, the DUDMA, even though the territorial scope of their effort is at the city scale.

The three plans that I look at in detail are:

(1) *A Perspective Plan for Calcutta, 2011* (the 2011 perspective plan), which was a statewide plan issued in 1990 by the State Planning Board, Development and Planning Department, Government of West Bengal.

(2) *Vision 2025, Perspective Plan of KMA* (the 2025 vision plan), which is a perspective plan prepared by the Kolkata Metropolitan Development Authority through DUDMA in 2005. The 2025 vision plan partially adopts some outcomes of a *Comprehensive Mobility Plan 2001-2025* (the 2025 mobility plan), prepared by the Kolkata Metropolitan Development Authority through DUDMA in 2006.

(3) *State Vision, Mission, Short and Long Term Perspective Plan* (the 2030 state plan), is a statewide plan in preparation at the time of writing by the State Public Policy and Planning Board and the global professional services company Deloitte through the DoPSPM. The 2030 state plan is aligned with United Nations Sustainable Development Goals[4] and thus shares a target date of 2030 with incremental targets of 2020, 2025.

The three plans have been selected because they are the key state-level documents addressing matters of urbanization in West Bengal. As plans and visions, each has a strong focus on future thinking, and shuttles between fact and aspiration. Furthermore, as planning documents, all of them have extensive visual registers, especially dependent on mapping, a form of cartographic idiom, historically and currently conventional in spatial planning (Huxley, 2007, 2008; Legg, 2007). As Crampton (2004, 2010) has argued, mapping is performative and political. That is, a primary and important source of spatial knowledge is produced in mapping practices, and accordingly, mapping is necessarily part of our engagement with space and thus also part of our political concern (2004, p. 3). Moreover, planning documents have long played a part not only in describing spatially what is there but also in mapping imagined futures through the planning process (Blomley & Sommers, 2019 [1999]; see also Greenhalgh, 2018; Perkins & Dodge, 2012). Furthermore, and as Rose-Redwood (2006) argues following the Foucauldian-inspired work of Nikolas Rose (1999), maps play a particular role in the production of "governmental rationalities," and the authority those rationalities can garner. Although, as we shall see below, the capacity of the State of West Bengal to fully stabilize maps in the service of their rationalities of planning is precarious. These three distinct planning visions, and the spatial rationalities they rely upon, seek to promote, and manage urbanization, however they create challenges for effective municipal governance.

The three plans must also be understood in another way. In the mid-1990s it was noted that the planning process in Kolkata, which was never very open, had become more secretive (Chakravorty, 1996). By the mid-2000s, a senior planner in the Kolkata Metropolitan Development Authority noted that "there is no need" for planning documents to be presented to the public as they are "prepared by elected representatives" (Pal, 2008, p. 48).[5] In my experience, lack of transparency and accountability around planning has persisted. For example, I obtained a well-thumbed printed copy of the 2011 perspective plan from the private library of a planning consultant which was not otherwise available.[6] I was unable to obtain a printed copy of the 2025 vision plan, the 2025 mobility plan, or the 2030 state plan from the relevant government department officials, but eventually sourced them online, although not through the official departments authorized with respect to their development, where they are not available for download.[7]

My presentation of the visualizations used in these reports expresses my experience of receiving them as communicative information that was hard to obtain and with poor visual resolution. I do not retouch the maps to make them clearer because I am as much interested in the materiality of the document as I am in the content of the maps. For example, I do not apologize for a well-thumbed report comprised of poorly drafted and badly reproduced images (as for the 2011 perspective plan). I retain this, as it communicates something of the experience of how these reports might be received. I also do not attempt to clarify or improve the quality of poorly designed maps, or maps that are hard to read because they are overly complicated (as in the 2025 mobility plan). Nor do I adjust very low-resolution images, which are scans of poorly photocopied, seemingly hand-colored maps (as in the 2025 vision). The only adjustment I make is to draw onto these maps the location of my study area of Maheshtala Municipality, the one-kilometer-square area within Ward 13 and add notation symbols. In later chapters I include my newly produced maps of the study area.

The 2011 Perspective Plan

In 1990, the three-hundredth anniversary of the founding of Kolkata, the West Bengal State Planning Board launched *A Perspective Plan for Calcutta, 2011* (Government of West Bengal, 1990). In the 2011 perspective plan (1990, p. 87), the board envisaged an expansive coordination role for itself with the objective of "orderly" development. Reflecting the national Planning Commission's preoccupation with the need to "halt [the] growth" of megacities, the 2011 perspective plan offered a "comprehensive approach" for "reorienting growth." The direction of that reorientation was not only in the core of Kolkata and its far edges, but also the region beyond, including other cities and small towns of West Bengal.

An extended regional approach had been long-discussed in Kolkata (see M. Chatterjee, 1970; Dasgupta, 1991), especially after the bi-nodal development concept articulated in the Ford Foundation–sponsored *Basic Development Plan for the Calcutta Metropolitan District, 1966-1986* (1966 plan) (Calcutta Metropolitan Planning Organization, 1966), which was influential in broadening the planning culture in Kolkata (see Banerjee, 2005, 2009; Banerjee & Chakravorty, 1994). The regional approach promoted in the 2011 perspective plan was also gestured towards in the Calcutta Metropolitan Development Authority's *Development Perspective Plan* of 1976, as well as the *Perspective Plan and Action Program* of 1981. However, it was the 2011 perspective plan that offered the first "comprehensive, detailed, and analytical" regional planning document since the 1966 basic development plan (Chakravorty, 1996, pp. 422–23). A regional approach to managing growth was also a party agenda. The Left Front coalition, led by the Communist Party of India-Marxist, had been the governing party of West Bengal from 1977 until 2011. Up until 1990, the focus of the Left Front had been rural areas (Das, 2015, p. 200), including rural land reforms and decentralization via the *panchayati raj* (the system of local self-government operating in rural areas). In this political context it is unsurprising that the 2011 perspective plan emphasized regional (urban-rural) development over city-centric development.[8]

Central to the 2011 perspective plan was the definition of four nested regional zones (1990, p. 70), which altogether covered an area of 23,310 square kilometers, some 26 percent of the state (see Figure 1.01). The largest of these zones is the Calcutta Metropolitan Region, which extends some 100 kilometers from the center of Kolkata and was determined by what was called the city's "zone of daily influence." This included, for example, the territorial limit of daily "suburban" train commuters as well as the extent of the hinterland of production for Kolkata's daily consumption goods like vegetables, fish, etc. (1990, p. 69).[9] The Calcutta Metropolitan Region zone was later described by McGee (1991) as an example of an Emerging Metropolitan Region surrounding Kolkata (see chapter 8). Within the Calcutta Metropolitan Region is the next planning zone, the Intermediate Metropolitan Region (75-kilometer radius), then the Inner Metropolitan Region (50-kilometer radius), and then the Central Metropolitan District, which is coextensive with the, somewhat confusingly, later termed Calcutta/Kolkata Metropolitan Area. The Central Metropolitan District (shown in yellow on the map) is what I mean when I refer more generally to metropolitan Kolkata (which is the area under the authority of the Calcutta/Kolkata Metropolitan Development Authority). The largest zone of the Calcutta Metropolitan Region (thick red line on the map) is what I mean when I refer to the Kolkata metropolitan region.

Drawing on census data from 1981, the 2011 perspective plan identified the main problem of the extended Kolkata region to be the presence of what it described as a "discontinuous" gradient of big to small settlements (Government of West Bengal 1990, p. 74). To counter this problem, the plan advocated the spatial decentralization of built-up areas, in line with directives outlined both in the World Bank–sponsored *Third Calcutta Urban Development Project 1983-1988* (World Bank, 1983) and the *National Commission on Urbanization* (Government of India, 1988). The goal was an idealised spatial hierarchy of settlements that would dissipate the polarized imbalance of a large, singular urban agglomeration, surrounded by impoverished rural areas. The preferred spatial logic had a "megacity" like Kolkata as one node in a more balanced sizing of settlements across a "rural-urban continuum" (1990, p. 74). This more orderly urban/town hierarchy was meant to ensure a regional settlement pattern in which rural town development was supported alongside that of the large urban centers (Institute of Town Planners, India, 1991).

The 2011 perspective plan communicated the problem of settlement discontinuity in a series of maps. The maps are, on the one hand, shaped by categorization and spatial ordering common in the modern cartographic conventions of planning. On the other hand, they are often hard to read, and appear to assume a professional readership proficient in map-reading, familiar with the region, and willing and able to do the work required to

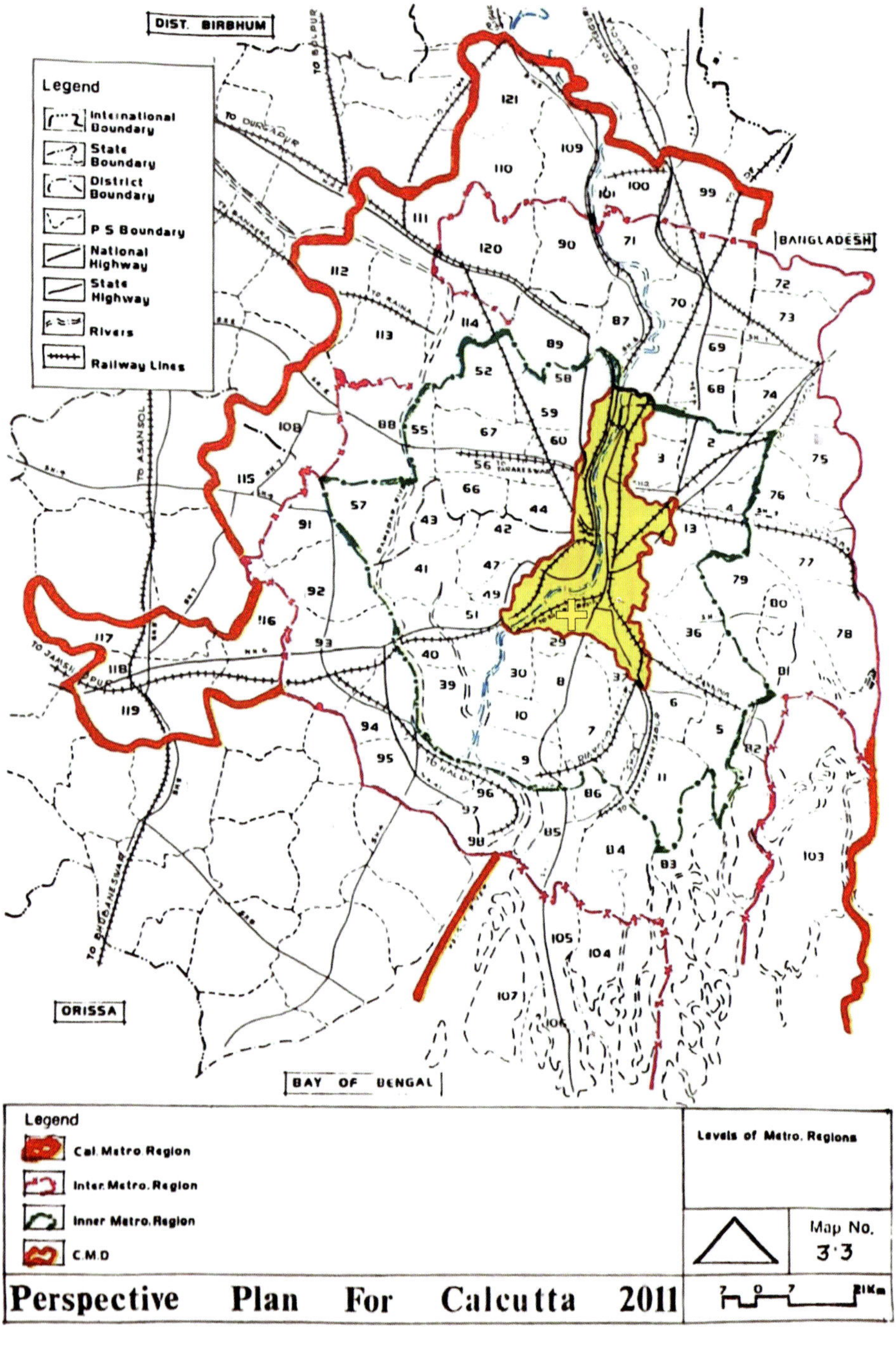
DIST. BIRBHUM
Legend
International Boundary
State Boundary
District Boundary
P S Boundary
National Highway
State Highway
Rivers
Railway Lines
BANGLADESH
ORISSA
BAY OF BENGAL
TO ASANSOL
TO BOLPUR
TO DURGAPUR
TO BANKURA
TO RAINA
TO TARAKESWAR
TO JAMSHEDPUR
TO BHUBANESWAR
Legend
Cal. Metro Region
Inter Metro. Region
Inner Metro. Region
C.M.D
Levels of Metro. Regions
Map No.
3·3
Perspective Plan For Calcutta 2011
7 0 7 21Km

understand what is being supposedly communicated. For example, Figure 1.02 shows the distribution of towns by class (size of population) for the territorially extensive Calcutta Metropolitan Region. The less extensive core of the Calcutta Metropolitan District is barely visible, but is marked out with a thin, black, dashed line in the center of the map and is not specified at all in terms of class of settlement. If it were, it would presumably appear as a very big red dot in the middle of the map. In other words, on this map, metropolitan Kolkata is a "blank" space, and the map is drawing attention to the hierarchy of settlement size for everything other than the Calcutta Metropolitan District, which is shown on a completely separate map. With the Calcutta Metropolitan District missing, the map implies that the existence of an extremely polarized hierarchy of settlement distribution is two separate problems—that of the region as shown on one map, and that of the core as shown on another (see Figure 1.03).

Figure 1.01. Map showing the spatial ambition of *A Perspective Plan for Calcutta: 2011*. The 2011 plan aimed to discipline urban growth within a region defined by four nested zones. Beginning with the largest, the zones are entitled the Calcutta Metropolitan Region (thick red line), the Intermediate Metropolitan Region (pink dashed line), the Inner Metropolitan Region (green dashed line), and the Calcutta Metropolitan District (yellow area with red outline). Also shown, as an overlay, is the Ward 13 study area (yellow symbol).

(Source: Government of West Bengal, 1990. *A Perspective Plan for Calcutta: 2011*. Map 3.3. Kolkata, State Planning Board, Development & Planning Department, Government of West Bengal.)

Figure 1.02. Map entitled Hierarchy of Urban Settlements, sited in the Calcutta Metropolitan Region zone. The highly populated Calcutta Metropolitan District (CMD) zone is merely a faintly outlined void in the center of the map shown as a dashed, thin, black line. The specifics of the CMD is presented in another map, allowing this map to communicate a clustering of Class IV (10,000-19,999) and V (5,000-9,999) settlements around the missing CMD. The cluster of small settlements around the cartographic void that is Calcutta reinforces the argument about the potential of the Kolkata "hinterland" to fix the concentration problem of "giant urban sprawl" and a "chaotic urban agglomeration" (Government of West Bengal 1990, p. 67). Such "central villages and small and medium size towns" are intended to receive "selective concentration of socio-economic activities and related infrastructure" and to "play their role in absorbing new migrants, reducing the cost of urbanization and energy consumption, as well as maintain a desirable rural-urban continuum" (1990, p. 67). Also shown, as an overlay, is the Ward 13 study area (yellow symbol).

(Source: Government of West Bengal, 1990. *A Perspective Plan for Calcutta: 2011.* Map 3.4. Kolkata, State Planning Board, Development & Planning Department, Government of West Bengal.)

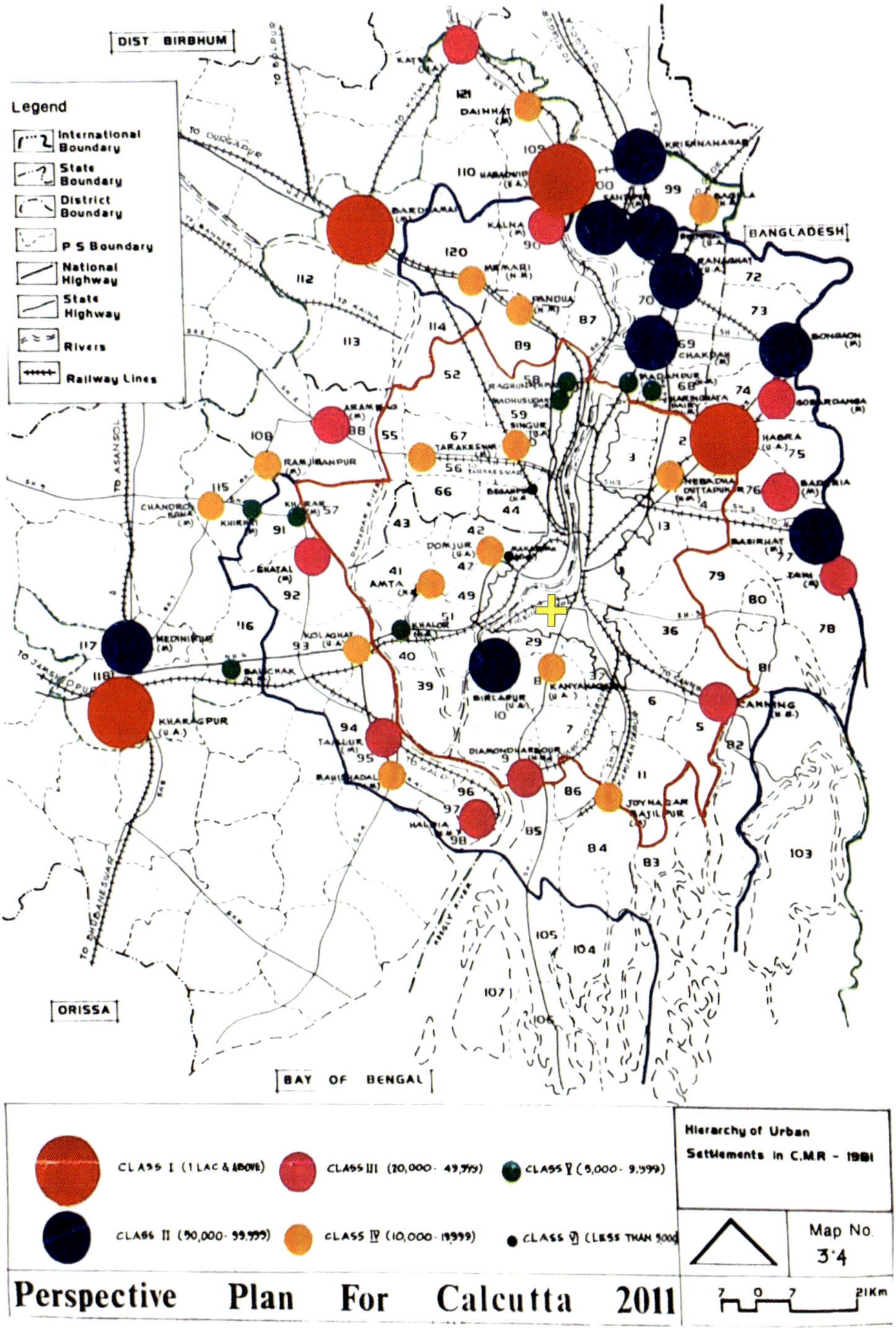

DIST BIRBHUM
Legend
International Boundary
State Boundary
District Boundary
P S Boundary
National Highway
State Highway
Rivers
Railway Lines
BANGLADESH
ORISSA
BAY OF BENGAL
TO ASANSOL
TO DURGAPUR
TO DHUBANESWAR
KHARAGPUR (U.A)
MEDINIPUR (M)
BARDHAMAN
KALNA (M)
DAINHAT (M)
KRISHNANAGAR
BONGAON (M)
HABRA (U.A.)
BASIRHAT (M)
CANNING (N.A.)
BIRLAPUR (U.A)
DOMJUR (U.A)
AMTA
TARAKESWAR
RAMJIBANPUR
GHATAL (M)
KOLAGHAT (U.A)
CHAKDAH (M)
CLASS I (1 LAC & ABOVE)
CLASS II (50,000 - 99,999)
CLASS III (20,000 - 49,999)
CLASS IV (10,000 - 19999)
CLASS V (5,000 - 9,999)
CLASS VI (LESS THAN 5000)
Hierarchy of Urban Settlements in C.M.R - 1981
Map No. 3·4
Perspective Plan For Calcutta 2011
7 0 7 21Km

Figure 1.03. Map of the existing settlement hierarchy that comprises the more territorially constrained Calcutta Metropolitan District zone. Again, we can see the 2011 plan's interest in charting and communicating a story of "unbalanced" development in term of population size and hierarchical growth. The "old core" of Kolkata dominates but the Calcutta Metropolitan District comprises a string of sixteen other Class I (100,000 +) settlements, as well as 17 Class II (50,000-99,999) settlements. The visualization choices of the map imply settlement/non-settlement, whereas on the ground, metropolitan Kolkata is a field of mixed settled and developed conditions, mostly urban but also including agrarian and water uses. Also shown, as an overlay, is the Ward 13 study area (yellow symbol).

(Source: Government of West Bengal, 1990. *A Perspective Plan for Calcutta: 2011.* Map 3.5, 1:100,000. Kolkata, State Planning Board, Development & Planning Department, Government of West Bengal.)

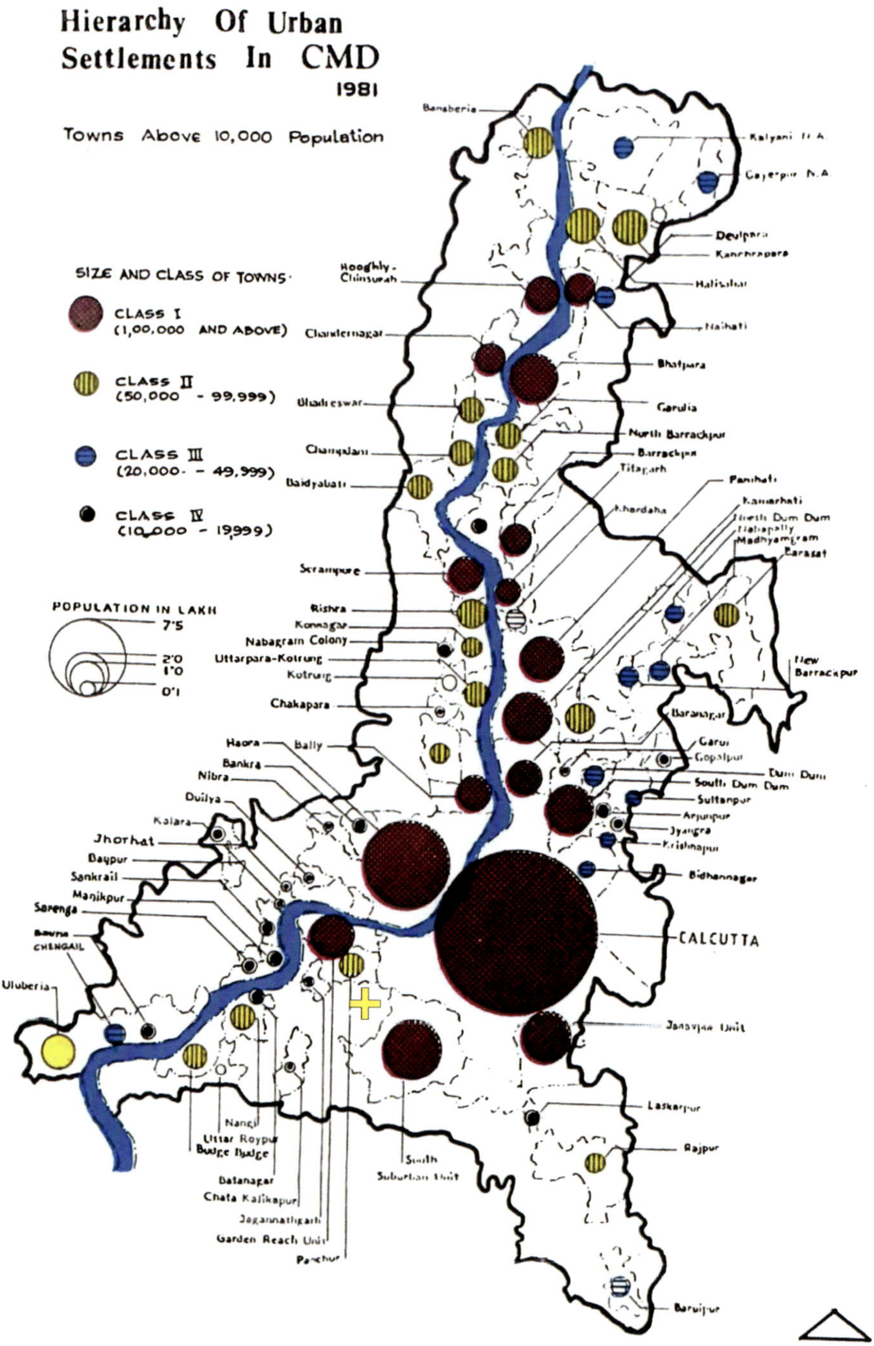

Perspective Plan For Calcutta 2011 | 2 0 4 km. | Map No. 3.5

The text accompanying these maps makes clear that the aspiration in the 2011 perspective plan is to reduce the problems of both extreme congestion and sprawl through a multicentered regional framework comprised of many more middle-sized towns imagined as "partially self-contained units" (Government of West Bengal 1990, p. 66). The 2011 perspective plan also recommends growth for smaller settlements, proposing that some become "district towns" that could act as "magnets" for economic activities, others become so-called "block or service towns" that could cater to their "rural hinterlands," and yet others stay as "basic villages" that catered to "basic needs" (1990, p. 87). Another planned action with respect to this goal was to support the development of two industrial-based, "metro-centers" of two million-plus inhabitants, located at Uluberia-Bagnan, on the west bank of the Hooghly River, and at Barrackpore-Barasat, an area on the east bank of the Hooghly River (1990, pp. 88-90). As a scaffold for this transformation of the problematic settlement gradient, the 2011 perspective plan proposed the development of "strong transportation corridors of movement" between all new nodes, as well as to and from the core of Kolkata (1990, p. 66), a matter picked up on in later plans discussed below. Overall, the obsession of the 2011 perspective plan was the matter of unbalanced population density, underscored by a Christaller-inspired (1966), hierarchical growth model of urbanization. The 2011 perspective plan was thus performative of an ambitious, coordinated vision of metropolitan Kolkata in West Bengal that was "complete" within its limited, internal logic, but difficult to implement. Indeed, although some key spatial concepts of the plan are current today, as I shall show, the 2011 perspective plan was considered "dead" by the mid-1990s (Chakravorty, 1996, p. 423).

The 2025 Vision Plan

The Kolkata Metropolitan Development Authority was set up in 1970 and it was made a statutory body in 1979 with the power of the West Bengal Town and Country (Planning and Development) Act, 1979. It was established as the agency of implementation for the Ford Foundation–sponsored 1966 basic development plan. Throughout the 1990s and supported in part by central investment through the Mega City Program, the authority was engaged in active planning, reflected in a range of linked reports, including the 2025 vision plan. Like the predecessor reports, the 2025 vision plan focuses on improving infrastructure, both within and beyond metropolitan Kolkata. However, unlike the predecessor reports, the 2025 vision plan reflects central-level urban reform initiatives for decentralization and public-private-partnership-led infrastructure development.

Before I introduce the visualizations found in the 2025 vision plan, I must first explain the characteristics of the document itself as it came to me as a researcher in the field. My 221-page PDF copy of the 2025 vision plan was not given to me by the authorities nor was it locatable in any public record office or library. I eventually found the (incomplete) version used for this study using a Google keyword search. The 2025 vision plan search result appeared as an ambiguously labelled file entitled "book 9" and linked to an officially correct URL of the KMDA. Second, the maps in the found 2025 vision plan are extremely low quality, due as much to the quality of cartographic drafting as well as the low-resolution reproduction of the report itself. This is even though this plan is an official statement about how future growth of metropolitan Kolkata would be shaped for the next two decades. Third, this "public" version of the 2025 vision plan is a PDF scan of a printed copy. There are pages missing and there is no index page. Tables that are referenced in the text are occasionally missing or found out of order elsewhere in the report. Finally, maps are numbered inconsistently, if at all.

The 2025 vision plan reports that from 1991 to 2001 the rate of urban population growth of metropolitan Kolkata declined relative to the very high population growth from 1951 to 1961, and from earlier in the century (Kolkata Metropolitan Development Authority, 2005, p. 24). Nevertheless, the 2025 vision plan aims to manage a projected population of more than 21 million by 2025, a significant increase from 13.2 million in 2001 (2005, p. 103). While this may seem to be a problem of too many people in and of itself, the 2025 vision plan views the growth positively and frames the "metropolis" as having moved "from conditions of crisis to that of confidence" over the past decades. The issue with this growth is not that it is coming, but that it will meet an "infrastructure deficit" and there is thus a need to distribute new infrastructure rationally (2005, p. 103). "There is still a huge backlog of accumulated deficits in the infrastructure facilities and services that will have to be wiped out". The second issue with this growth is that there is an "overfill problem" - it needs to go somewhere other than the inner core, which is positioned in a parochial move as "full." The plan therefore envisages "a massive program ... to channelize the new population growth outside the [inner core of Kolkata and Howrah] and even to centers outside the boundaries of Kolkata Metropolitan Area" (2005, p. 103).

The proposed new centers are simply designated, being located in nearby areas with fewer people than the inner core of Kolkata and Howrah. They are targeted to absorb increased populations and so extend the urban continuum outwards. These outer areas are positioned as the solution to the "crowding, congestion, squalor, and deprivation" evidenced in the inner core of Kolkata and Howrah (2005, p. 103). The proposed centers are effectively intensity nodes in a planned continuous densification of existing, lower density settlements, yet on the maps they are represented in the language of centrality—a series of colored dots and names (see Figure 1.04). The existing "metro-centers" of Kolkata and Howrah are complemented with fifteen new "major centers" and five new "trans-metro centers." Confusingly, there are three other maps which locate thirteen new "townships," seventeen new industrial growth centers, and a set of truck terminals/wholesale trading centers.[10] Lastly, one map shows existing and proposed regional centers beyond the Kolkata Metropolitan Area (see Figure 1.05). Astonishingly, there is no synthetic plan that brings all the centers together in one visualization, either at the scale of the metropolitan area or of the region. The reader is thus left with the task of mentally collapsing the maps together in a vision of their own making. One is left dazzled by dots and the impression that everything else that is on the map, or missing from the map, is irrelevant or secondary. This experience unfolds because red- or yellow-colored dots or squares are sometimes scaled to be large or small to communicate information about population size, but in other cases, dots are simply just marks that show locations on a map.

Figure 1.04. Map showing the proposed, spatial distribution of centers within the now-titled Kolkata Metropolitan Area (KMA) zone. The proposed, periurban "major centers" (red dots) and "trans-metro centers" (yellow dots) are intended to absorb a projected population increase. In 2005, they have lower population than the "metro-center" (larger red dot) and the "metro sub-center" (black dot) and are thus "visioned" as available for further densification toward 2025. A "major center" is projected into Maheshtala Municipality. The text at the bottom of the map notes that the base map is sourced from the *Master Plan for Traffic and Transportation in KMA* (2001-2025), which shows proposed expressways (red lines) proposed arterial roads (purple lines), the newly designated (2002) East Kolkata Wetlands (black hatched area), and New Town (red hatched area). Also shown, as an overlay, is the Ward 13 study area (yellow symbol).

(Source: Government of West Bengal, 2005. *Vision 2025, Perspective Plan of KMA*. Kolkata, Kolkata Metropolitan Development Authority through the Department of Urban Development and Municipal Affairs, Government of West Bengal.)

METROPOLITAN STRUCTURE
SPATIAL DISTRIBUTION OF CENTRES - 2025

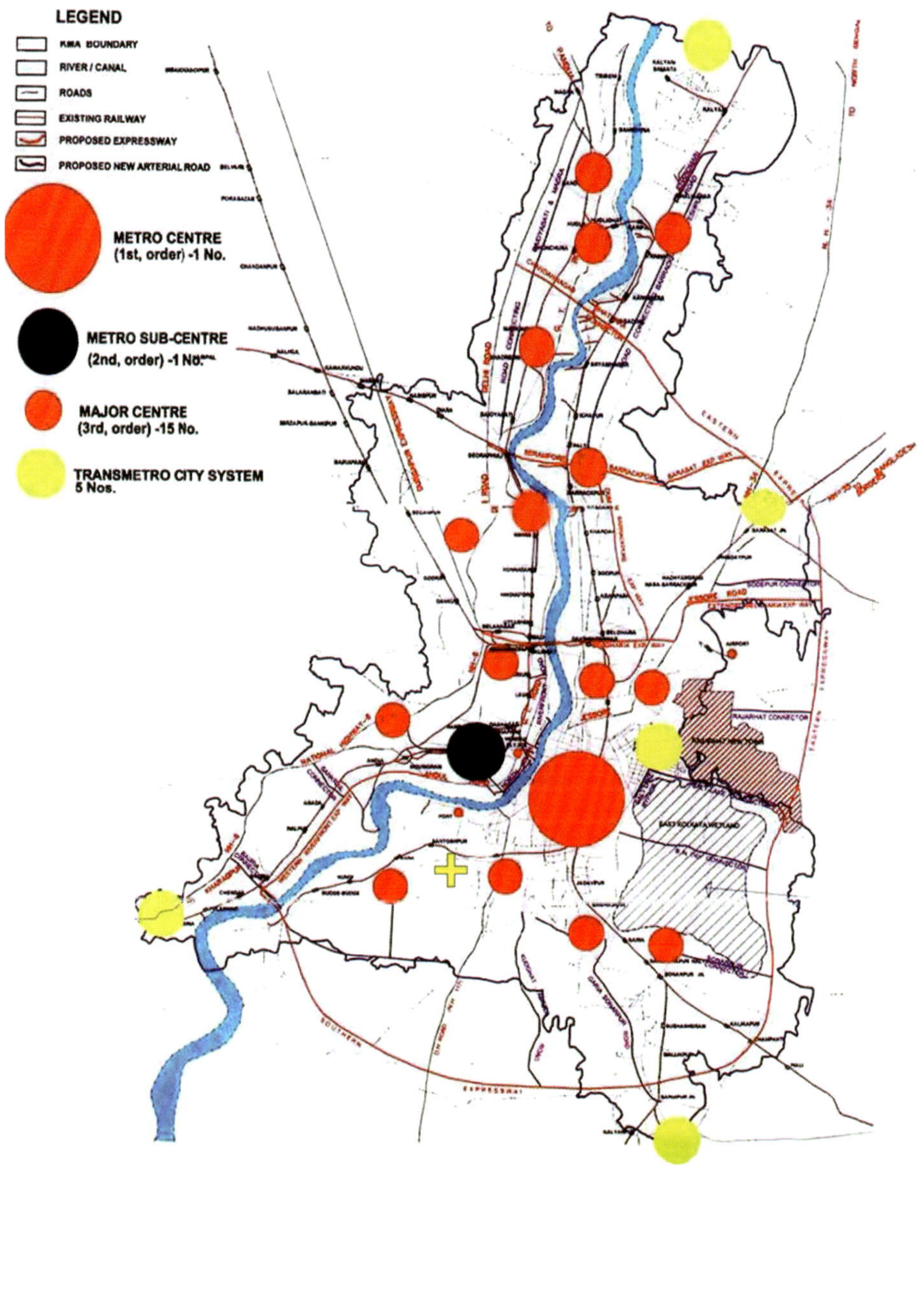

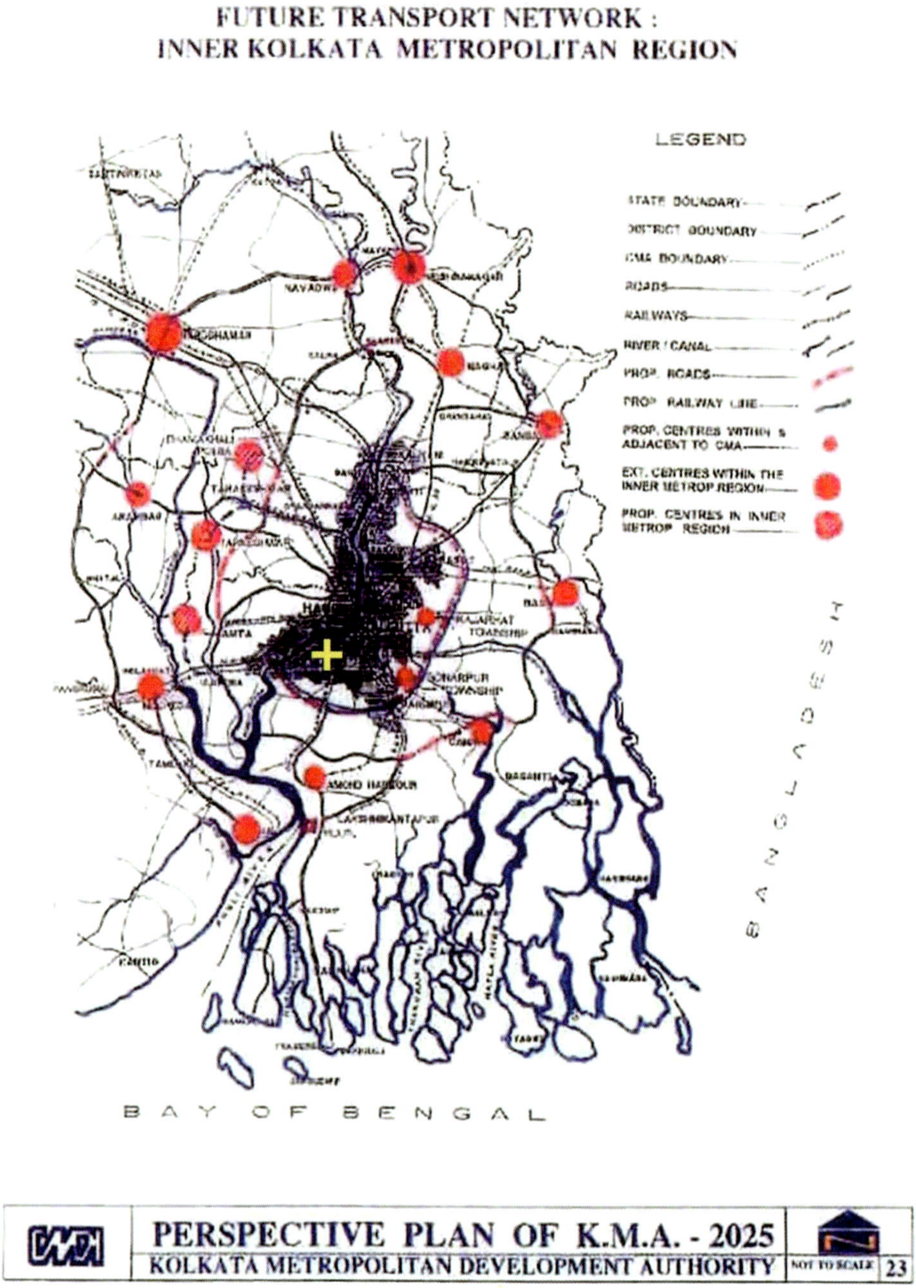
FUTURE TRANSPORT NETWORK :
INNER KOLKATA METROPOLITAN REGION
LEGEND
STATE BOUNDARY
DISTRICT BOUNDARY
CMA BOUNDARY
ROADS
RAILWAYS
RIVER / CANAL
PROP. ROADS
PROP. RAILWAY LINE
PROP. CENTRES WITHIN & ADJACENT TO CMA
EXT. CENTRES WITHIN THE INNER METROP REGION
PROP. CENTRES IN INNER METROP REGION
BANGLADESH
BAY OF BENGAL
PERSPECTIVE PLAN OF K.M.A. - 2025
KOLKATA METROPOLITAN DEVELOPMENT AUTHORITY
NOT TO SCALE
23

Figure 1.05. The low-resolution, poorly rendered map showing the vision for the Inner Metropolitan Area zone. The future transport network is based on "ring roads," which emphasizes centrality. Confusingly, the red dots showing the proposed centers are similar in color to the red dots showing existing centers. In addition, the proposed centers within the Kolkata Metropolitan Area (KMA) are not shown (see Figure 1.04). Instead, the KMA is inexplicably shown as a black zone, a color choice that blends with the dark blue lines of rivers, islands and creeks. Existing towns that are located between the dots, connective lines, and water bodies are shown as not settled and "off the map." Overall, this garbled image communicates the impact of central-level urban reforms which places emphasis on State-led management of population growth across a region. Also shown, as an overlay, is the Ward 13 study area (yellow symbol).

(Source: Government of West Bengal, 2005. *Vision 2025, Perspective Plan of KMA*. Map no. 23, not to scale. Kolkata, Kolkata Metropolitan Development Authority through the Department of Urban Development and Municipal Affairs, Government of West Bengal.)

The maps published in the 2025 vision plan communicate important changes for urban and rural local bodies, but they have had very limited circulation. As noted above, they are poorly drafted and hard to read, and so do not allow local government officials nor residents in localities to see how they will be affected. All this communicates something additional about these maps, and the vision they are part of. One immediate message is that this vision and its maps are directed to certain kinds of official readers and users with the appropriate interest and skill (government and private partner readers), as opposed to a wider public audience. This would be consistent with what planner Tridib Banerjee (2005, p. 145) argues is the long-standing "paradox" of the planning cultures of Kolkata. On the one hand, he argues, Kolkata is a political city, "if not the most political city of India." For Kolkata residents played an important role in the struggle for independence and have a long-standing preference for left party rule. Yet, he says, from a planning point of view, there has been very little systematic resident involvement in planning for local and metropolitan space. Banerjee (2005, p. 161) argues that, for historical reasons, the possibility of local government being close to the people it serves is "totally absent" from the minds of Kolkata residents. The legacy of a distant and insular colonial planning apparatus managed through elaborate bureaucratic inscription practices established a culture that did not change after independence (also see Hull, 2012, p. 6-11). In such a context, it is possible to read the blurry maps of the 2025 vision plan not simply as technical shortfalls, but as obfuscating effects created by governing entities that do not feel the need to be accountable to wider publics. As Banerjee (2005, p. 162) elaborates, the concepts of citizenship, civil society, and civic engagement, which are usually taken for granted in contemporary theories of planning in Western liberal democracies, are not necessarily present in Kolkata. Instead, in the minds of Kolkata residents, planning is seen as "permanently embedded in the thicket of bureaucracy, professional expertise, and administrative practices, never to appear in the consciousness of ordinary citizens" (2005, p. 151). A "general cynicism" exists among Kolkata residents who think that planning can never be changed or influenced (2005, p. 161), and the voices of residents explicate this in the chapters to follow.

The analysis thus far has already flagged that the plans see an infrastructure deficit as problematic. On the matter of distributive infrastructure, the 2025 mobility plan is illuminating.[11] The plan clearly shows the aspirations with respect to investing in an "integrated transport network." For example, twenty major arterial roads are proposed along with the metropolitan highway system, which includes a Southern-Eastern Expressway or ring road (see Figure 1.06). Another map reveals a proposal for five new bridges across the Hooghly River. In all, there are thirteen maps that show proposals for highways, arterial roads, widening of arterial roads, bridges, ferry, bus terminal, MRT extension, rail network extension, light rail, truck terminals, congestion trouble spots, flyovers and underpasses, and an elevated ring road. As with the study of centers, there is no map that shows all these elements together as a promised "integrated" transportation network.

The set of urban continuum centers and network infrastructure maps in the 2025 vision plan deliver what geographer Sudeshna Mitra (2018b) terms the "optics of connectivity". Mitra (2018b, p. 58) argues that as territorial strategies, road projects represent expensive and substantive infrastructure interventions that signal clear state intent regarding transforming periurban areas. Among other things, they are a form of "state guarantee" to real estate interests in areas that are made accessible and given connection. At the same time, she argues, they are "flexible," as they are operationalized through a range of governance and financing modalities, including Special Purpose Vehicles (an institutional arrangement) and public-private partnerships (2018b, p. 58). The transport systems represented in the 2025 vision plan are an expression of the state government's agenda to market West Bengal as an investment destination that is "surging ahead" (Government of West Bengal, 2020b). Realizing that this networked vision is already a challenge, the outer ring road project for Kolkata was put in "cold storage" in 2010 (Bandyopadhyay, 2010), while the proposed new bridge across the Hooghly River, which was announced in 2017, has not been built to date (Press Trust India, 2017). This suggests that a successful territorial development strategy for Gangetic West Bengal remains elusive.

The poorly drafted and hard-to-access maps of the 2011 perspective plan and the 2025 vision plan also allow us to see what the state creators want their maps to do, as physical and digital artefacts. The maps convey an official spatial strategy for the economic development of a region, but they do so obscurely. The obscurity is created in their graphic incomprehensibility (weak design and drafting), their informational disconnection (many poorly linked maps), and their ambition (maps with too much information). The obscuring effect is intensified, rather than alleviated, by their being digitally processed. While maps and plans are made available online, they arrive there not as elements of crisply designed web pages, but as blurry, over-reproduced PDFs. Finally, the obscurity of the vision is amplified by the ways in which various elements come and go from the maps, leaving the impression that none of the spatial elements are serious propositions and that every spatial element is negotiable. It is very likely that these obscuring cartographic conventions are a symptom of the

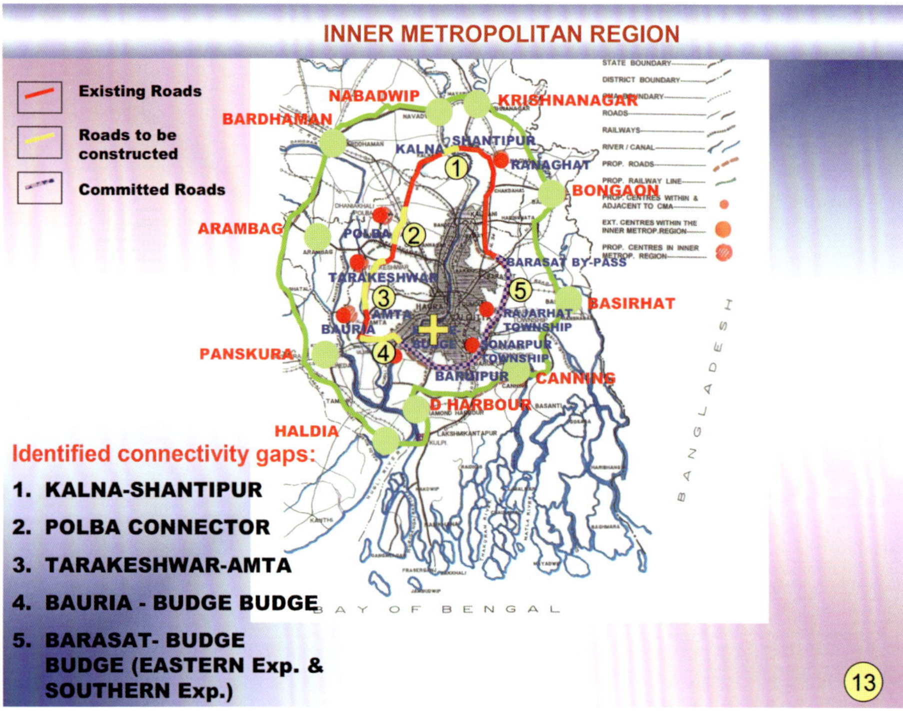

Figure 1.06. Map showing the distribution of proposed arterial roads within the Inner Metropolitan Area (left) and the Kolkata Metropolitan Area (KMA) (right) zones. Note the shift from a visual language of dots and centering in the earlier plans toward an emphasis on lines and multidirectional flows. These two maps are from a set of 50 maps from a PowerPoint presentation and accordingly, are diagram-like to rapidly communicate the Plan to an audience. In the KMA map, pink lines show proposed arterial roads and green lines show existing arterial roads. The new arterial roads connect the inner core toward the north-east, where New Town and the airport are located, and the south-east, which is a growth area and a proposed, relocated district government center. The longest red line, which is

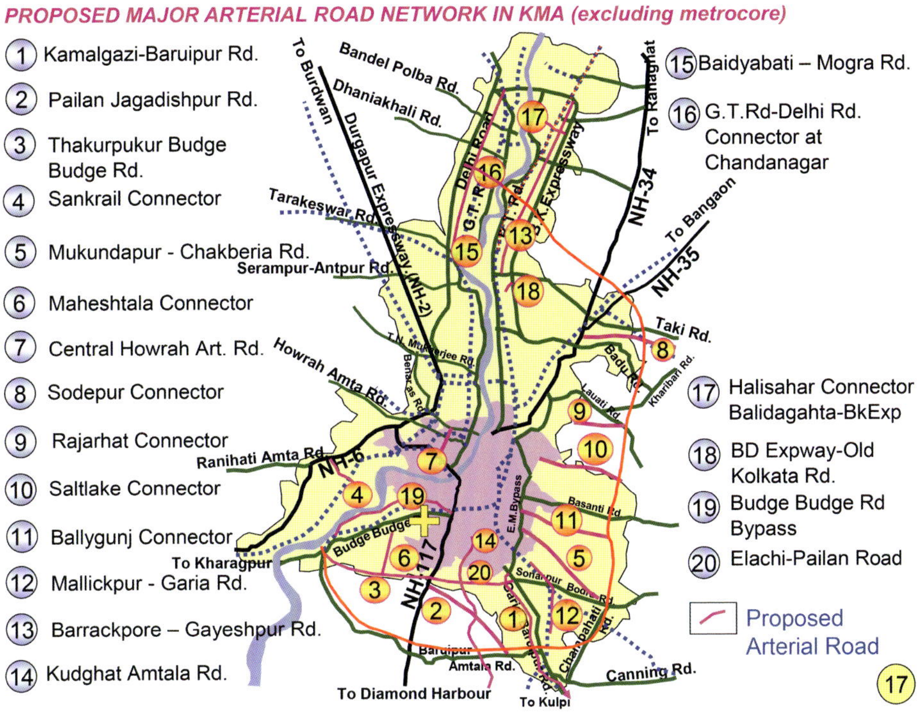

difficult to discern as is it looks like a pink line, is the proposed expressway (shown along the eastern edge of metropolitan Kolkata). The East Kolkata Wetlands area is not shown in this map and the proposed expressway is shown as going through them. This might be thought of as an example of "unmapping" (Roy, 2003) whereby the East Kolkata Wetlands are visioned as "undeveloped land". Also shown, as an overlay, is the Ward 13 study area (yellow symbol).

(Source: Government of West Bengal, 2006. *Comprehensive Mobility Plan 2001-2025*. Map no. 13 and 17. Kolkata, Kolkata Metropolitan Development Authority through the Department of Urban Development and Municipal Affairs, Government of West Bengal.)

"informalized entity" that is planning in Kolkata (Roy, 2009). This mode of map-making articulates how the urban agencies of the Government of West Bengal, like other state entities in India, are clear in their aspirations for "Urban India," but unclear about their role in carving out the route to that future. The state agencies that map these urban futures are increasingly in the hands of private partnerships and the political elite.

The 2030 State Plan

The 2030 state plan guides DoPSPM and district-level action plans across the State of West Bengal (Department of Planning, Statistics & Program Monitoring, 2018a, 2018b). It is produced by the West Bengal State Public Policy and Planning Board, which functions explicitly as a "think tank," often translating central government directives into state-level initiatives and visions (Government of West Bengal, 2020a). Many national-level initiatives are framed in "mission-mode," meaning they are limited-timeframe projects that implement novel, central-level policy directives, themselves often responsive to obligations such as the United Nations' Sustainable Development Goals. The Board engaged the "knowledge partner," Deloitte in creating the 2030 state plan. Such partnerships are encouraged by the central government, as well as external funding agencies, and firms like Deloitte have extensive expertise and transferable frameworks of knowledge production based on such consultancies.

There is an important difference between the earlier reports and the 2030 state plan, which is the implementation of "quieter registers" of disciplinary power than the topographical (territorial or sectorial) logics expressed in the 2011 perspective plan and the 2025 vision plan. First, the 2030 state plan includes an agenda to continuously "seek resources" (human, financial, physical) from external partners to achieve a sustainable development goal (SDG) vision by 2030 (Department of Planning, Statistics & Program Monitoring, 2018a). Second, and most centrally, it rewards compliance by departmental and district levels of government in meeting West Bengal development goals, which are themselves reflections of the SDGs. Overall, West Bengal's SDG compliance is visualized in an online interface, comparing it with all the other Indian state measures (see Figure 1.07) (NITI Aayog, 2020). A reward system requires that compliance be measured, and this is done by evaluating numerically how departmental and district levels meet key performance indicators (KPI). The KPI data is gathered and coordinated by way of an "aggregator platform," which includes a geographical information system (GIS) representing KPIs and other data points geospatially to support "easy visualization and decision making."

The aggregator platform includes what are called "drill down" options that display KPIs at district and subdistrict level (Department of Planning and Statistics, 2018).

The 2030 state plan is a disciplinary mechanism guided by what Davis et al. (2012) call "governance by indicators," where standards and pathways of development are realized in and through classification and ranking systems (see also Merry et al., 2015; Rottenberg et al., 2015). What is at stake in governance by indicators is that KPI benchmarking can play out unevenly, as those districts that comply with accountability measurement will become advantaged with respect to the parameters set up by competitive frameworks of reward and distribution. This raises questions about the uneven geographies that may arise when many municipalities (like Maheshtala Municipality) are underequipped to enter the data-driven framework for distribution of resources.

The new reliance on indicator governance means that performance and data enumeration extend the reach of the central government, both in terms of what is accountable and who is responsible for the accounting. For example, a number of existing missions or local schemes have had their performance frameworks reset to reflect the SDGs (Department of Planning and Statistics, 2018). Economic competition between Indian cities, including the desire of Kolkata to be a global or world city, has been much written about (see Bose, 2015). The 2030 state plan extends that sphere of competition to both the district and locality level. For instance, the implementation of the 2030 state plan has a required phase of "sensitization programs"—awareness and training sessions designed to build capacity in data collection and performance indication among a range of local rural entities, like panchayat institutions, "self-help" groups, and the boards of village level cooperatives. This extended reach is consistent with what sociologist Sailen Routray (2013, p. 150) refers to as a new "regime of tactility" (meaning tactics) and space in which hitherto unreached communities of so-called backward regions and districts are "targeted." Similarly, tactility is also an expression of a shift toward populist practice in the everyday "people-party-policy interplay" by "party" political leaders within the Government of West Bengal (Nath, 2017, 2018).

At the second tier, West Bengal is only able to adjust to a topological modality of governance if it too makes capacity adjustments. The "knowledge partner" of Deloitte is central to the vision articulated in the 2030 state plan. The partnership and vision is with and for West Bengal, but the tools and concepts that Deloitte brings to the table are tried and tested instruments used by them in a global market of partnerships (Datta & Young, 2011).

Figure 1.07. Sustainable Development Goals India Index for West Bengal. Note the shift from "vision" plan-making into a completely different spatial register. Numerous, measured sustainable development goals are represented in a circle graph, which is continuously updated and thus, forms a dynamic image. In this indexical mode, the objective is to fill in the white space near the edge of the circle - to color in the circle with future sustainable development practices. In a comparative index across all Indian States, West Bengal is given a rank of 13 and a marginal increase in score from 2018-2019. "Front runner" States are Andhra Pradesh, Chandigarh, Goa, Himachal Pradesh, Karnataka, Kerala, Puducherry, Sikkim, Tamil Nadu, Telangana. "Performer" States are Andaman & Nicobar Islands, Arunachal Pradesh, Assam, Bihar, Chhattisgarh, Dadra and Nagar Haveli, Daman and Diu, Delhi, Gujarat, Haryana, Jammu & Kashmir and Ladakh, Jharkhand, Lakshadweep, Madhya Pradesh, Maharashtra, Manipur, Meghalaya, Mizoram, Nagaland, Odisha, Punjab, Rajasthan, Tripura, Uttar Pradesh, Uttarakhand, and West Bengal. There are no "achiever" or "aspirant" States.

(Source: SDG India index for West Bengal for 2019-2020, 2020. NITI Aayog. https://sdgindiaindex.niti.gov.in/#/.)

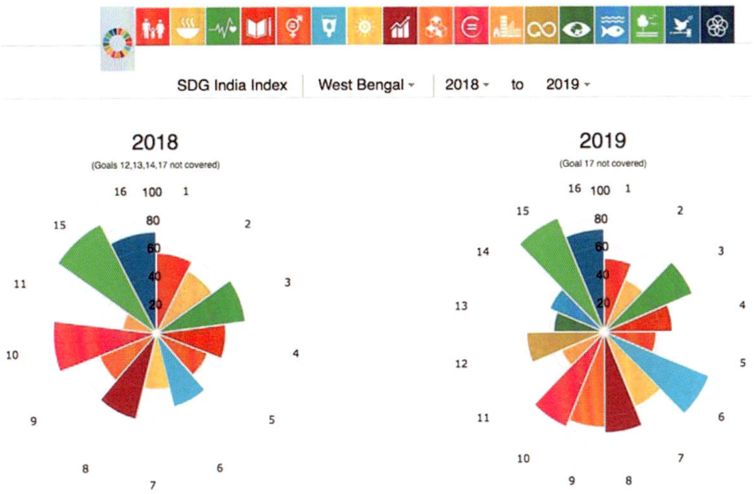

The numbers indicate the following.

SDG 1 No poverty

SDG 2 Zero hunger

SDG 3 Good health and well-being

SDG 4 Quality education

SDG 5 Gender equality

SDG 6 Clean water and sanitation

SDG 7 Affordable and clean energy

SDG 8 Decent work and economic growth

SDG 9 Industry, innovation, and infrastructure

SDG 10 Reduce inequalities

SDG 11 Sustainable cities and communities

SDG 12 Sustainable consumption and production

SDG 13 Climate action

SDG 14 Life below water

SDG 15 Life on land

SDG 16 Peace, justice, and strong institutions

SDG 17 Partnerships for the goals

For example, the visualizations appear in any number of reports by other entities Deloitte has partnered with. Planner David Sadoway (2018), looking specifically at the legacy of JnNURM, notes that the reliance on "mobile policy ideas, best practices, and norms" generates tendering procedures that in turn favor the services of third-party consultancies. Indeed, he argues, the consultant infrastructures (such as the SDG targets shaped by Deloitte) serve as a kind of "echo chamber" for governments, civil society organizations, businesses, and international finance institutions, providing lucrative benefits for consultancies (2018, p. 77). These various institutions and individuals inform further governance process and planning practices and serve their own interests in particular sociocultural and political contexts, such as West Bengal. Some scholars go even further, arguing that policy implementation in India today is a site for private capital investment (Gopakumar, 2015, p. 90). That is, mission-mode planning and implementation by way of indicators is not only a disciplinary mechanism but is also its own arena of economic activity. It is important to note here that this second tier arena sits in relation to emplaced local cultures of governance and investment. As geographer Asher Ghertner (2017) notes, a topological approach to power is already the reality of everyday life for the poor. Although rules, plans, and institutional hierarchies' matter, one of the defining features of the state in postcolonial India is the extent and depth of bureaucratic negotiability. This phenomenon has historically allowed lower-level officials to reinterpret the mandates they are given to service the needs of the local clients, with whom they share close ties (also see Corbridge et al., 2005; Kaviraj, 1984).

Conclusion

The focus of this chapter has been the interrelated emergence of "quiet" power in the urban and regional planning practices of the national Government of India and the Government of West Bengal. Such changes in India, as the economist Joel Ruet (2009, p. 271) notes, have produced a "multiplicity of modes of interaction with the state" (cf. Corbridge & Hariss, 2002; Sellers, 1997). As I have shown, the Government of West Bengal planning documents help materialize the urban policy directives of the national Government of India. The three plans are the 2011 perspective plan, which aimed to control the problematic megacity through the planning of a hierarchical network of centers across Gangetic West Bengal; the 2025 vision plan which aims to promote urban economic growth across an urban continuum through public-private partnership–led infrastructure development in metropolitan Kolkata;

and the 2030 state plan, which aims to modulate the effects of ("sustainable") urban growth through indicator compliance across the State of West Bengal.

My close reading of these planning documents, and in particular their visualization strategies, show how urban politics is in the nonhuman entities of paper documents, as well as digital interfaces and databases. I have historicized this materiality itself by examining the ways in which these graphic entities and the associations they build have "flickered into view and out again" (Jardine, 2017, p. 57). In the meantime, the situated spatial needs and distinct futures of the periurban municipalities are out of view altogether, being simply rendered as white, "blank space". Also missing are commitments to building institutional capacity through decentralized ("inclusive") models of governance, and the need to think about how urban development and rural prosperity might be more synergistic and complementary. This sets the ground for understanding periurbanization in Maheshtala Municipality, and it is this third tier of governance that I turn to in chapter 2.

Endnotes

1 The central government–led "new economic policy" includes deregulation of domestic industry and promotion of foreign direct investment; liberalization of the trade regime; reform of domestic interest rates coupled with measures to strengthen capital markets and institutions; and initiation of public enterprise reform (World Bank, 1991, p. i).

2 Many of the outcomes of this troubled agenda are well documented. For instance, Vidyarthi (2014), considering the case of Jaipur, shows how required participation in urban local body planning processes is used by established and emergent elites to promote and expedite their preferred spatial projects and growth initiatives. And, in the context of urbanizing Bangalore, Sami (2017) has documented the role of external experts or consultants in urban planning practices, including the enduring influence they have had on shaping the politics of planning processes over time. Similarly, Sundaresan (2019) has examined the relationship between land use violations and the urban planning process in Bangalore, demonstrating how elite associational networks capture planning power. Lastly, Mitra (2018a, p. 79), also building on Chatterjee's (2004) concept of "political society," argues that it is necessary to accept such intervention "as is," highlighting how planning in India evolves in, and as part of, a wider and disaggregated "politicized terrain."

3 In 2014, JnNURM was replaced by a range of sub-missions that similarly proceeded in a framework of apparent decentralization. A broad-based, Clean India (Swachh Bharat) campaign with an explicit urban component was announced first. This was followed by the announcement in 2015 of three new national urban missions: Atal Mission for Rejuvenation and Urban Transformation; Housing for All by 2022; and the Smart Cities Mission.

4 The SDGs and targets aim to stimulate action in the following areas: poverty, hunger, education, health and well-being, education, gender equality, water and sanitation, energy, economic growth and decent work, infrastructure, industry and innovation, reducing inequalities, sustainable cities, consumption and production, climate action, ecosystems, peace and justice, and partnership (United Nations, 2020a).

5 Roy (2003) also reflects upon her inability to secure planning documents in Kolkata.

6 A.K. Ghosh of the Centre for Environment & Development, Kolkata.

7 The URL for the 2025 vision plan is: http://kmdaonline.org/home/land_cell_book9. In my search for the 2030 state plan, only two PDFs of PowerPoint presentations from the URL of the consultancy firm Deloitte appeared in the Google search results.

8 This kind of state-level planning ambition nowadays sits within the political context of a West Bengal All India Trinamool Congress, and, since 2014, a Bharatiya Janata Party in the central government.

9 There are many studies that contributed to the official definition of the Kolkata region (see M. Chatterjee, 1991, p. 180).

10 My understanding is that "townships" are privately developed, high-rise enclaves, including the dot located at Calcutta Riverside, Batanagar, within Maheshtala Municipality.

11 The 2025 vision plan and the 2025 mobility plan draw on the *Master Plan for Traffic and Transportation in KMA: 2001-2025*, including using some of its visualizations.

2/

BECOMING MUNICIPAL

Even when urban policy visions are ambitious, and when periurbanization as a whole can be rapid and extensive, periurban transformations can often be incremental. Central level policy works through long-settled areas where the agency of longtime and newcomer residents, municipalities, and nonhumans are enlivened in imbroglios. In the study area, the shift from post-rural to periurban livelihoods and toward an integrated urban infrastructure often takes a lifetime, quite literally. This slow reality of incremental change is quite different from some of the very early post-independence visions for the area that was ultimately to become Maheshtala Municipality. For example, in 1958 it was to this southwestern hinterland of Kolkata that the then Chief Minister for the State of West Bengal, Bidhan Chandra Roy, turned when planning a "New Calcutta City" (S. Roy, 2001, p. 102) (see Figure 2.1.). Planned as a response to the perceived congestion of Kolkata and its "over-populated and outdated" urban form, the new city was to be adjacent to the busy settlement of Budge Budge, just south of the contemporary Maheshtala Municipality (2001, p. 100). This was a concept for a modern city with distinct functional zones (industrial, government, residential). It was to be built on an elevated "plinth" made from silt dredged from the Hooghly River, and would completely fill up the low-lying agricultural areas that the city was sited upon (2001, p. 100). New Calcutta City was never built, but was a precursor to Salt Lake (Bidhannagar), a new town built in the early 1960s on the eastern edge of Kolkata. New Calcutta City was also a precursor to the "bi-nodal" proposal put forward in the Ford Foundation–sponsored *Basic Development Plan for the Calcutta Metropolitan District, 1966-1986* (Calcutta Metropolitan Planning Organization, 1966). The 1966 basic development plan proposed that Kolkata should have a second center to the north, which is the opposite of this proposal for the south.

In the previous chapter I set out the wider political and institutional context of urban policy for Kolkata, addressing how and why its periurban areas are represented as a blank space. I did this through an analysis of central-level, as well as state-level government urban reforms and development planning for the Kolkata Metropolitan Area, the extended Kolkata Metropolitan Region, and the State of West Bengal. This chapter draws the blank space imaginary closer into the study area by focusing on the institutional and policy framework specifically relevant to an urban local body—Maheshtala Municipality. Like the story of New Calcutta City, I provide an account of how the settled-rural is ignored in the implementation of central and state-level urban policy directives. Before I begin my emplaced account, I must however introduce the site selection criteria that led me to a small study area within this specific municipality.

Sampling Kolkata

The study area was selected by meeting certain criteria, one of which was that it had to be a one-kilometer-square area.[1] I justify the sampling method used to select the study area below, but for now I note that this spatial scale allowed me to get to know the area well, dependent as I was on moving around on foot. This scale was also sufficient to incorporate a range of different settlement logics evident in close proximity, while being small enough to align with what those living in the area would recognize as their locality or *para*. A second criteria that I wanted the study area to fulfil is described in terms of land cover morphology characteristics evident in aerial imagery. I wanted a study area that incorporated an older, extant village with wooded areas, one or more major transport linkages, as well as paddy fields with newer settlements called "colonies" (newcomer housing developments).[2] That is, a mix of rural and urban characteristics in the landscape: notably, everyday features of new urbanization as well as persistent or residual features of being rural. Third, with these land cover morphology characteristics in mind, I then searched for evidence of this in a part of metropolitan Kolkata that had changed from being a *panchayat* (village council) to being under municipal governance since the 1990s (see Figure 2.02).

My selection evaluation of the new municipalities of metropolitan Kolkata followed a process of elimination. The northern new municipalities of Kalyani and Gayeshpur were created as part of the earlier (1960s to 1970s)

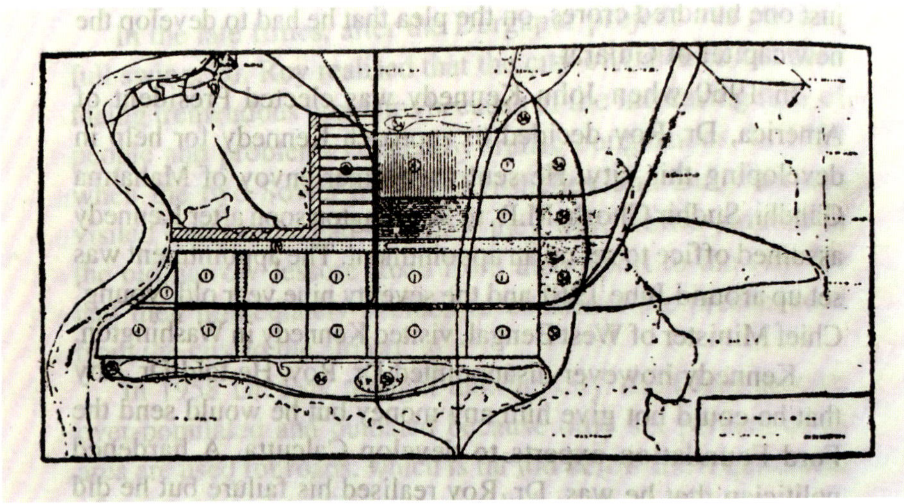

Figure 2.01. Map of New Calcutta City. Located south of Budge Budge, which is seen in the top left-hand corner and on the eastern bank of the Hooghly River.

(Source: Samaren Roy, 2001. New Calcutta City. Scale unreadable. *Witness to History*, p. 102., Manuscript India.)

failed experiment for the "bi-nodal city" mentioned earlier in this chapter. While Madhyamgram, Kalyani and Gayeshpur were considered potentially suitable for this study, they were eliminated, as they are not proximate to the "city"—meaning the Kolkata Municipal Corporation area. Next, the new municipalities in the east of metropolitan Kolkata were studied. They were not considered suitable as they have exceptional development and ecological notoriety. In Rajarhat Gopalpur, urbanization is linked to the international airport at Dum Dum. Bidhan Nagar is anchored by spectacular, and contested, new towns and the East Kolkata Wetlands. They are the worlds largest wastewater fed aquaculture system (EKWMA, 2020) and are characterized by Ramsar-endorsed conservation, and the contestation of those measures.[3]

Figure 2.02. Map of the Kolkata Metropolitan Area. Municipal corporations and municipalities are shown in pink with the name and foundation date noted. Municipalities founded after independence and since the 1990s urban reforms are shown in brown with foundation dates noted in yellow. *Panchayat* (village council areas) are shown in light brown. The founding of a municipality is a politically motivated territorial decision - a "political technology" (Elden, 2010). For instance, on the northeast, the newest municipality of Haringhata is noted. In this case, a panchayat area with many education institutions became both metropolitan and municipal at the same time, while the many other panchayat areas already within the metropolitan area have been retained (or chosen to remain) at the panchayat level.

(Source: author, 2020; Census of India, 2011; Google Earth Pro, 2018; Kolkata Metropolitan Development Authority, 2020.)

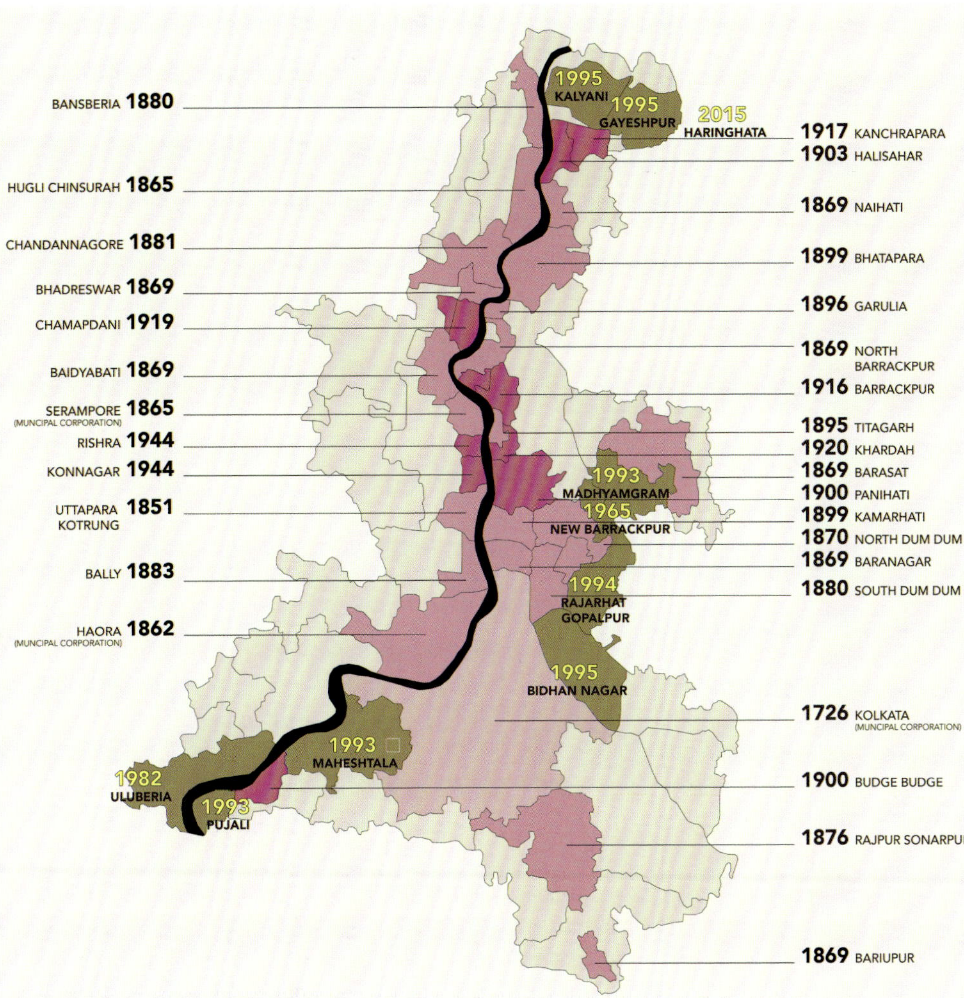
BANSBERIA 1880
HUGLI CHINSURAH 1865
CHANDANNAGORE 1881
BHADRESWAR 1869
CHAMAPDANI 1919
BAIDYABATI 1869
SERAMPORE 1865
(MUNCIPAL CORPORATION)
RISHRA 1944
KONNAGAR 1944
UTTAPARA KOTRUNG 1851
BALLY 1883
HAORA 1862
(MUNCIPAL CORPORATION)
1995 KALYANI
1995 GAYESHPUR
2015 HARINGHATA
1917 KANCHRAPARA
1903 HALISAHAR
1869 NAIHATI
1899 BHATAPARA
1896 GARULIA
1869 NORTH BARRACKPUR
1916 BARRACKPUR
1895 TITAGARH
1920 KHARDAH
1869 BARASAT
1900 PANIHATI
1899 KAMARHATI
1870 NORTH DUM DUM
1869 BARANAGAR
1880 SOUTH DUM DUM
1993 MADHYAMGRAM
1965 NEW BARRACKPUR
1994 RAJARHAT GOPALPUR
1995 BIDHAN NAGAR
1726 KOLKATA
(MUNCIPAL CORPORATION)
1993 MAHESHTALA
1982 ULUBERIA
1993 PUJALI
1900 BUDGE BUDGE
1876 RAJPUR SONARPUR
1869 BARIUPUR

Of the new municipalities in the south, Pujali was not considered suitable as it has maintained a very low population density since the 1990s. Uluberia was considered somewhat suitable, but its pressure and promises for change lie in centrally funded, port-related infrastructure. For instance, it is tightly linked by highway to Howrah, the growing seaport of Haldia farther to the south, and a long-promised bridge across the Bhagirathi-Hooghly River. This left Maheshtala, which is adjacent to the "city," and given its unexceptional, small-scale, incremental character, was considered the most suitable. It was my hope that this proximity to the "city" would generate dynamics that would help me better understand a periurban condition in which becoming a "kind of urban" area is not a vague or distant possibility, but a tangible, proximate, and lived reality for the residents. Furthermore, this area still retained agricultural or paddy land, healthy ponds, and heavily wooded areas, so another puzzle to be solved was to understand why such "village" features persisted within metropolitan Kolkata.

I adopted this areal method of site selection while being aware of critical commentaries on the bird's-eye view of planning, starting with de Certeau's observations in *The Practice of Everyday Life* (1984, p. 93). Within geography, for example, the 1990s seeded a vibrant critical dialogue ranging from the structures of power embedded in the cartographic imagination (Harley, 1989; Wood, 1992), to the implications of the "automated" geographies delivered by a geographical information system (GIS) (Aitken & Michel, 1995; Crampton, 2001; Dobson, 1983, 1993; Lake, 1993; Openshaw, 1991; Pickles, 1993, 1995; Sheppard, 1993, 1995). These debates challenged assumptions about a supposedly inherent (dominant, universalizing) power of cartography and GIS, and conclude that it is the use it is put to that matters. That is, there is an increasing understanding that remotely sensed knowledges are not, in and of themselves, problematic. Indeed, such knowledge can be used in ways that are linked to progressive, critical or revisionist efforts of knowledge and spatial production (see Crampton, 2010). Furthermore, as will be evident, a visual analysis of remote imaging is but the first step in my re-rendering of "blank" periurban conditions. My re-rendering is in the interest of seeing the study area up close, in space and over time.

Although not experiencing high-profile change, as a periurban area, Maheshtala Municipality is changing, nonetheless. Maheshtala had a population of approximately 448,317 in the 2011 census, an area of 44.18 square kilometers, and an average density of 10,147 inhabitants per square kilometer (Census Organization of India, 2011). According to Sahana et al.'s (2018) "urban sprawl matrix" framework used to quantify land cover change during the periods 1990 to 2000 and 2000 to 2015 for periurban, metropolitan Kolkata, Maheshtala had a "very high urban growth rate" of 49.1 percent during 1990 to 2000 and 67.4 percent during 2000 to 2015, a ranking of fifth out of all thirty-eight municipalities measured (2018, p. 1562). Maheshtala Municipality is thus densely inhabited, and land cover conversion is significant within the context of the metropolitan area.[4]

Within Maheshtala Municipality, my study focuses specifically on a one-kilometer-square area sample that incorporates Ward 13 and some territory extending beyond the ward boundary. As noted above, the one-kilometer-square area is large enough to encompass many instances of the land cover morphology characteristics—the tripartite settlement conditions of older, extant villages with wooded areas, densely settled transport linkages, and newer settlements called colonies. Figure 2.03 shows the many areas in Maheshtala Municipality that I might have selected, and speaks to the visual assessment method I used to settle upon the final case study site. Using remote-sensed images, I carried out visual analysis of land cover morphology, triangulating that information with other data on the political and demographic status of the sample areas. Ward 13 has an area of 3.12 square kilometers, and a population of 18,829 persons (Maheshtala Municipality, 2014, p. 84). Of the thirty-five wards in Maheshtala Municipality, Ward 13 is the largest in terms of area, second-largest in terms of population, and the fourth-lowest in terms of population density, at 6,034 persons per square kilometer. Thus, while it is large in area, with high population numbers, it is less densely built-up than the other smaller wards in the municipality. This feature can be attributed, in part, to its location immediately adjacent to an airfield, thus hindering accessibility and limiting vertical development. The inhabitants are predominantly Hindu landowners and the land use is predominantly residential.

Overall, my sampling method was adopted to make visible a part of the city that might otherwise be overlooked by research focused on high-profile or highly visible change, be that unusually rapid and unequal development or stark and unjust ecological crises. As noted in the introduction chapter, ordinary periurban is a condition where there is no singular big conflict; where power, understood topologically and with nonhumans and their diverse agencies in mind, is diffuse. In addition, when the concept of ordinary periurban is thought to include the settled-rural, a linear transition from rural to urban is complicated by evidence of multidirectional change. By this emphasis on diffuse power and multidirectional change, I do not mean to argue for the conservation of the "rustic" rural. Rather, I ask, does the poorly understood, ordinary periurban hold clues for other possible hybrid futures, something different than an urban continuum? The selection of the case study site was anchored in this interest.

Figure 2.03. Map of Maheshtala Municipality showing the one-kilometer-square area study area sampling options.
Bounded area: Maheshtala Municipality
Black lines: Ward boundaries
Squares: possible one-kilometer-square study areas
Yellow symbol: Selected study area within Ward 13

(Source: author 2020; Google Earth Pro, 2018; and drawing on data from the Government of West Bengal 2020.)

Self-Governance?

As noted in chapter 1, while urban local bodies are meant to be empowered in the decentralization initiative of the 74th Constitutional Amendment, they have not always been able to benefit from that new positioning. In part this is about a persisting inability of local-level governments to be autonomous, itself a result of ambiguity in the 74th Constitutional Amendment (Mohanty, 2014, pp. 123–24). Through another lens, the institutional capacity of urban local bodies has been found to be lacking, as they struggle to be accountable to residents and deliver the wide range of services that are their responsibility. Also noted is that the implementation of urban reforms by the central-level government in "mission-mode" has led to an extension or "reach" of central government power into local-level government. For example, and as I show, Maheshtala Municipality's development trajectory and visions are strongly shaped by the opportunities and objectives of central government and state ruling-party policy directives.

Urban local bodies have a long, troubled history in India. Political scientist Gangadhar Jha (2018, p. 56) notes that while urban local bodies existed in India during colonial rule, "they did not find any place in the Constitution of India, much less [given] status of an autonomous and independent entity as a level of self-government at the local level in urban areas."[5] Jha (2018, pp. 66–67) explains that the priority given to reconstruction and modernization after colonial rule meant local self-governance in the initial decades of independent India was given "low priority," and the institutions continued to decline thereafter. Diminished urban local bodies were so pervasive by the early 1990s across India that they acquired a connotation which was identified with everything that is "second grade and inferior" (Jha, 2018, p. 73).

The Constitution of India (1949) had adopted a colonial principle from the Government of India Act (1935) whereby local self-government institutions were made "creatures of the state governments," and so state-level governments created urban local bodies by delegating to them some of their own powers and tax authority (Jha, 2018, p. 59). In independent India, every state government went ahead and implemented their own discretionary rules regarding their urban local bodies: however, they "were not taking the required steps for strengthening the local government institutions" (2018, p. 59). It is in this context that the 74th Constitutional Amendment Act was passed in 1992. It regularized such fragmented practices and decentralized planning and decision-making, in the hope of giving "local communities ... a greater say in devising of local plans and programs for their own development

THE TELEGRAPH TUESDAY 21 DECEMBER 1993

Police on stoneman trail again

BY A STAFF REPORTER

Calcutta, Dec. 20: The body of a middle-aged newspaper hawker, with his head crushed by a huge stone was found in a pool of blood near a Grindlays Bank branch on Netaji Subhas Road early this morning. This has led to speculation that the elusive stoneman is back and the police are on the lookout for the serial killer again.

A huge blood stained stone was found beside the hawker's body, reminiscent of the manner in which a number of pavement dwellers were killed between 1989 and 1990. The victim has been identified as Chandrabhang Singh.

Senior city police officials, including the DC(DD), Mr Goutam Chakraborty, rushed to the spot and carried out preliminary investigations. The police found nothing suspicious except the stone. The stoneman, who remains untraced, had killed 13 persons, most of them pavement dwellers, from June 1989 to February 1990.

In the previous cases, the police discovered some clues, but this time the killer left nothing behind, not even his footprint. Forensic experts are likely to submit their report within 72 hours. The body has been sent for post-mortem.

Chandrabhang was reportedly killed between 3 and 5 am. Forensic experts who visited the spot are likely to match the blood group of the victim with the blood on the stone.

Kurseong bus toll 11

BY A STAFF REPORTER

Calcutta, Dec. 20: The toll in yesterday's bus accident in Kurseong town rose to 11 with two more passengers succumbing to their injuries today.

Hospital sources quoted the driver of the bus as saying the accident occurred due to brake failure. Preliminary investigations revealed that dense fog had *enveloped the area when the accident took place. The bus rammed into a stationary truck before falling into a ditch below the Hill Cart Road.*

RIGHT TO WORK: Kanoria ju picture by Kishore Roychowd

Spent N can be

BY OUR SPECIAL CORRESPONDENT

Calcutta, Dec. 20: The spen nuclear fuel lying at Tarapur ca cause radiation hazards, Dr R Chidambaram, chairman, Atc mic Energy Commission (AEC said here today.

Dr Chidambaram cited the rec ent case of an American nuclea facility where prolonged storag of spent fuel led to radiatio hazards. He was, however, nc perturbed by the delay in signin the deal with the Internationa Atomic Energy Agency (IAEA on reprocessing the spent fuel a Tarapur.

The deal was to be finalised b December 31, but has been pos poned till March 31 because o US opposition to India's reproces sing it. As per the contractua obligations, the US, supplier o the fuel, was supposed to tak back the spent fuel, but it late reneged on this promise. Indi then declared that it would repro cess it on its own under an agree ment with the IAEA.

Asked if the delay was not *matter of concern, Dr Chidamba ram said this was only necessitat ed by formalities and there was nothing to worry about.* However, "indefinite storage is

Figure 2.04. The public announcement for Maheshtala Municipality on December 21st, 1993. It reads, "Calcutta, Dec. 20: A new municipality has been constituted in the Maheshtala area in South 24 Parganas. The new municipality will include 40 moujhas and will be run by 12 commissioners. The state government has also declared the Pujali area of the same district as a 'notified area' and six other moujhas – Kalipur, Ramchadrapur, Raghunathpur, Raijbpur, Achhipur and Rajarampur – have been included in the notified area". It is noteworthy that other "metropolitan" news of the day was the right-to-work activism among jute mill workers; the politics around the power bases of the All-India Youth Congress; and the land reforms of the ruling Communist Party India (Marxist)-led Left Front. The page encapsulates how Maheshtala Municipality was formed in a context of industrial decline and the rise of the so-called "Mamata phenomenon" in West Bengal (Ramaswamy, 2011), Mamata Banerjee being at that time a West Bengal Youth Congress member who later became the Chief Minister of West Bengal.

(Source: *The Telegraph*, 1993. New Municipality, p. 8. Kolkata.)

premises on Sunday, exult in their show of strength. A Telegraph

Somen ready to make up with Mamata

BY A STAFF REPORTER

Calcutta, Dec. 20: After talks with the all-India Youth Congress(I) chief, Mr M.S.Bitta, in Delhi recently, the PCC(I) president, Mr Somen Mitra, has decided to mend fences with the state Youth Congress(I) president, Ms Mamata Banerjee.

Though bitter rivals, both Mr Mitra and Ms Banerjee have agreed in principle to forge a working relationship for the sake of party unity. Ms Banerjee has already stated that she is willing to work with Mr Mitra and the PCC(I) president today remarked that he wanted an "understanding with Mamata from the day I became president.

"My meeting with Mr Bitta will help party unity if we are both sincere," he said adding that problems with Ms Banerjee had continued for over a year-and-a-half because "both sides lacked the initiative to do anything."

Mr Mitra is willing to speak to Ms Banerjee soon, but at the moment is not ready to consider the cases of the seven youth Congressmen thrown out of the party.

The expulsions are a sore point for Ms Banerjee and it is hard to see how any alliance between the two can work if the expulsion issue is not settled. "The question of changing my mind does not arise. only if I find these people to be penitent will I think of taking them back. So far, there has been no sign of that," Mr Mitra said.

Mr Bitta has reportedly assured the PCC(I) president that there will be no problems and did speak of a communication gap which led to the misunderstanding. But any alliance will still be difficult. Mr Mitra, for example, has not been invited to Ms Banerjee's padyatra on December 28.

Collective leadership, a phrase coined by Mr P.R. Das Munshi, is the word in vogue in the Congress.

Left should go it alone: Surjeet

BY OUR SPECIAL CORRESPONDENT

Calcutta, Dec. 20: The CPI(M) had decided to lay greater emphasis on independent mass action instead of relying solely on other democratic and secular parties to fight "the Congress(I)'s anti-people policies."

The CPI(M) general secretary, Mr Harkishen Singh Surjeet, told newsmen at the end of the party central committee meeting that the Janata Dal's failure to unite had created serious problems on the eve of the Assembly polls. "That is why we feel that the Left should make greater efforts to launch a mass struggle on its own," he said.

Asked whether the party was planning to severe ties with the Janata Dal, Mr Surjeet said: "There is no question of changing our policy. It is only a change in the emphasis. Left parties have clear-cut views on price rise and similar issues which other parties lack."

However, the general secretary ruled out an alliance with the Indian People's front (IPF). "We can consider the question of accepting the IPF within the Left front only if it stops attacking our party," he said.

The central committee was hard put to explain the Congress(I)'s gains in the Assembly polls. While describing the election results as "a victory for secularism, national unity and social justice," the party said the results "do not imply an endoresement of Congress(I) policies."

The CPI(M) felt the Congress(I) had made electoral gains in Madhya Pradesh and Himchal Pradesh since there was no other alternative. "This is clear from the results in Uttar Pradesh where an alternative existed and the Congress(I) was routed," Mr Surjeet said.

The central committee, howe[v]er, was glad that the BJP had b[e]en beaten and that people had r[ej]ected its Ayodhya policy. "The [fa]ct that the BJP has failed to wi[n] a majority in all the four state[s] where it had governments is a s[et]back for their communal platf[or]m," it said.

De[sp]ite its unconditional support [to] the SP-BSP government in Ut[tar] Pradesh, the CPI(M) has [illegible] to the casteist po[li]cics of these two parties. While [p]ledging support to Dalits and b[a]ckwards in their struggle for so[ci]al justice, the CPI(M) has also [v]owed to counter "all narrow p[l]atforms which seek to perpetuate casteism for consolidating vote banks."

According to central committee sources, the party is now engaged in a struggle to distribute land to landless peasants in Bihar despite opposition from the Laloo Prasad Yadav goverment.

The central committee also concluded that despite setbacks, the BJP continued to wield "substantial influence in Uttar Pradesh, Madhya Pradesh, Himachal Pradesh and Rajasthan, both in terms of percentage of votes polled and seats won." The party's communal ideology continues to have a wide following.

CPM not to back BJP on Dunkel stir

BY OUR SPECIAL CORRESPONDENT

Calcutta, Dec. 20: The CPI(M) will not support any BJP-sponsored censure motion against the Rao government over the Dunkel draft, but will "take to the streets to build public opinion on the issue."

Briefing newsmen on the outcome of the three-day meeting of the CPI(M) central committee which ended here yesterday, the party's general secretary, Mr H.S. Surjeet, said: "We do not think the BJP is going to oppose the Dunkel agreement since the party has been supporting the Congress(I)'s economic policies. Our party will oppose the agreement both inside and outside Parliament and build up a mass movement against it. But there is no question of supporting any BJP move."

Asked whether the CPI(M) considered the BJP a greater enemy than the Congress(I), Mr Surjeet said: "At the moment, the Congress(I) is a greater enemy as far as the nation is concerned. however, the BJP is a more harmful party as far as national unity is concerned."

Mr Surjeet said the Rao government had ignored Parliament and even the advice of the standing committee attached to the commerce ministry [illegible] examined the Dunkel draft. He said his party would not mind bringing down the government over the issue, but remianed evasive on how this could be done without Opposition unity.

[T]arapur [...]us

brilliant works was that they were yearning for self-expression while the country was under British rule.

Delivering the keynote address Prof. T.W.B. Kibble described the role played by the so-called cosmic strings in the early epochs of the universe. Cosmic strings are the thread-like structures that run across the geometry of spacetime. They are thought to be remnants of the Big Bang origin of the universe and have immense gravity.

Prof. Roger Penrose, Rouse Ball professor of mathematics at Oxford University, in his lecture on "the role of gravity in quantum state reduction" described the possible scenarios of the ultimate fate of the universe.

Prof. J.V. Narlikar of the Inter-university Centre for Astronomy and Astrophysics spoke on the Saha equation in the cosmological context. While admitting that he was not a champion of the Big Bang theory, Prof. Narlikar said he was speaking the language of [illegible] highlight the importance of the Saha ionisation equation.

In his welcome address, Dr Bikash Sinha, director, SINP, highlighted the growing importance of particle physics studies.

Nothing wrong with Salt Lake function: Subhas

BY A STAFF REPORTER

Calcutta, Dec. 20: The state sports minister, Mr Subhas Chakraborty, today said there was nothing wrong with the function held at Salt Lake stadium on December 12 with filmstars and artistes from the Bombay filmdom. He said it was part of the concluding ceremony of the tourism festival in the city.

When pointed out that the song and dance sequence from *Khalnayak* (Choli ke peechee) had kicked up a lot of controversy, Mr Chakraborty said: "Everyone has a right to choose his or her type of culture. Those who like Hilsa may not like oth[er types] of fish and classical music [l]overs may not like light mus[ic]. But while organising the prog[ra]mme I have not broken any ac[ce]pted norm of the society."

Mr Chakraborty, ho[w]ever, said he was not aware [even] before the programme th[a]t the dance would be performe[d] along with the song. He said: "I[f] I had known about the dance ea[r]lier, I would have asked them [n]ot to perform [illegible]

"Ila Arun is associate[d] with the Indian People's T[h]eatre movement for the last 20 years and she has given Raja[s]than folk music a special [s]tatus

New municipality

Calcutta, Dec. 20: A new municipality has been constituted in the Mahestala area in South 24 Parganas. The new municipality will include 40 moujhas and will be run by 12 commissioners.

The state government has also [illegible] and six other moujhas — Kalipur, Ramchadrapur, Raghunathpur, Rajibpur, Achhipur and Rajarampur — have been included in the notified area.

and well-being" (2018, p. 59). Shortly thereafter, the West Bengal Municipal Act, 1993 (2017) was ratified. Maheshtala Municipality was created in this post–74th Amendment context with the aspiration for it to be a responsive, responsible independent planning entity (see Figure 2.04).[6]

The West Bengal Municipal Act, 1993 (2017) formalized a transition from rural to urban in the area that became Maheshtala Municipality. Yet the assumption that the locality is nominally and politically urban is troubled from the start by a local reality of environmentally unhealthy intermixing of rural and urban conditions. This is well illustrated by a transcript taken from a 1995 meeting between the recently formed Maheshtala Municipality and the West Bengal Department of Environment. A Maheshtala representative explained the challenges Maheshtala faced:

> The seven irrigation canals here are stagnant. Mosquitoes and related diseases abound. This is overlooked. The canals are full of hyacinth. We have a population of 3.25 lakhs [325,000], within a 50 sq. km area. Calcutta's solid wastes come into our area, in the Garden reach, Brace Bridge, Metiabruz areas. The cow slaughterhouse has not been improved since the British period. The stagnant wastes from here enter the drainage system, and during the rains this spreads everywhere. There are massive diarrhea problems. There is no solid waste management, and consequently no health infrastructure commensurate to the situation we face. The growth happening nearby, in Budge Budge: about a 100 factories, each with between 50-300 workers (aside from Bata [an established shoe factory]); there is no monitoring of factory wastes for their pollution content. The Calcutta Metropolitan Water and Sanitation Authority's surface drinking water facility only partially covers our area. So, we need to run deep tube wells. Environmental pollution and health hazards in such fringe areas of Calcutta Municipal Corporation need to be improved for better living conditions in our area (Transcript of Meeting 1995. Personal Archives of V. Ramaswamy. Accessed 2018).

Such an extensive list of problems was a source of real concern, for under the West Bengal Municipal Act, the municipality has the duty to fulfil a set of obligatory functions including comprehensive planning, infrastructure provision, conservation, public service functions, and more.[7] The dilemma is that these immense burdens of responsibility, all of which are predefined by conventional accountabilities of "town" planning and "municipal" governance, were improbable in newly founded Maheshtala. Furthermore, they do not strategically support a vital, but dilapidated, local reality.

What agricultural elements and cultivation practices might persist or coexist productively with urban life is not addressed and thus, not safeguarded in the act. While the Municipal Act does mention certain natural features (notably water bodies and trees) and specifies regulations relating to their management, they are conceptualized as serving a predominantly urban landscape. Furthermore, settled-rural features such as paddy fields or related agricultural elements like stock, ponds, and plantations (like those highlighted in my sampling) are actively disconnected from any residual or coexisting rural ecology in the act. For instance, rules specify that waterways cannot be used to wash animals or clothes, and the keeping, feeding, and selling of animals is highly regulated. This is perhaps best exemplified by the fact that most such specifications appear in the sections of the Municipal Act entitled "Public Safety and Nuisances" (2017, p. 193-203) and "Restraint of Infection" (2017, p. 203-207). There is a provision to regulate or prohibit "any practice related to cultivation, or use of any pesticide or manure or irrigation so reported to be injurious" to human health (2017, p. 198). A regulation such as this is inherently hostile to cultivation. For example, under this provision an intentionally flooded paddy field can be reported as a health hazard if it is seen as a breeding ground for mosquitoes or as an unsanitary "receptacle of stagnant water." This regulation reinforces the construction of agrarian land and life as troublesome, and as a hindrance to urban development.

The Government of West Bengal tightly controls the municipality at the ward level. This is because, under the Municipal Act, the state-level government determines the number of wards within a municipality, as well as the composition and function of the ward committee (2017, pp. 17, 36).[8] Wards are a type of locality-level authority, which in periurban areas like Maheshtala, often replace existing rural-council institutions, including *gram panchayat* (village council), *panchayat samiti* (block development council), *zila panishad* (district council) and *mahakuma parishad* (subdistrict council) (2017, p. 27). In Maheshtala, each municipal ward is presided over by an elected ward councilor, who is the chairperson of the ward committee for that ward (2017, p. 37).

Ward committees are placed in a difficult situation, as the chairperson of the Ward 13 committee highlighted in this study points out: "We represent the people and they feel that we have all the power to redress all their problems, not knowing that we have only a limited authority" (Maheshtala Municipality official, interview, K02, 2019). Such limited authority extends to the highest level of Maheshtala, as a state government appointed and unelected Maheshtala official explained to me, "the state government is very cooperative [with the municipality]. They are also the controlling authority. So naturally, they must have the control [of the municipality]" (Maheshtala Municipality official, interview, K01, 2019). That is why he reasoned that without guiding directions from the state government, "a municipality cannot run."

The Government of West Bengal also tightly controls the unelected municipal staff. Unelected municipal staff hires are made political, as they are approved and promoted by the state-level government. The act stipulates that municipal authorities should have an elected board of councilors, a chairman-in-council, and a chairman (2017, p. 20), and while in office, under five-year terms, are expected to carry out the provisions of the act. Elected ward representatives serve under the board of councilors which, in Maheshtala Municipality, has seven members, supported by unelected municipal staff (Maheshtala Municipality, 2014, p. 28). In Maheshtala, 30 percent of the staff positions were vacant in 2016, and accordingly, the Maheshtala Municipal Chairman protested to the state government in a report that the activities of the municipality are thus being "hampered" (West Bengal Legislative Assembly, 2016, p. 3).

In sum, the contradictions surrounding the Municipal Act are intractable. The act regulations not only project an improbable "town planning" authority, but they also ignore and actively disconnect the settled-rural, and do not reflect the particular rationalities of the periurban land market. Plus, the State of West Bengal is so deeply entrenched in the implementation of the act, it leaves the autonomy of an urban local body as limited. In what follows, I show how the narrow autonomy of Maheshtala Municipal elected officials is enmeshed in party politics and overwhelmed by meeting the mandate of the urban reforms directed by the central government.

Party Politics

The story of Maheshtala Municipality cannot be told without recourse to the party-political context. Planner Anirban Pal notes (2008) that decision-making by the municipalities of the Kolkata Metropolitan Area is characterized by "extreme" politicization along party lines. Meaning that while there is stability with long terms in power for a particular party, there are many minority parties in play at any time, and there is strong identification with either this or that party. Furthermore, as elsewhere in India, party politics are shaped by client politics and kin-based loyalties (Wilkinson, 2007).

Briefly, the ruling political party of the Government of West Bengal was the Indian National Congress (1947-1977); it then changed to the Communist

Party India (Marxist), which ruled for two decades (1977-2011). Most recently, the ruling state-level party changed to All India Trinamool Congress (2011-present), while at the central-level of the government of India, the ruling party changed to the Bharatiya Janata Party in 2014. The majority political party in Maheshtala Municipality is the All India Trinamool Congress, and the majority political party for Ward 13 is the Indian National Congress. This means that the elected Ward 13 councilor represents a minority party within the municipality and the state-level of government.

The 2015 ward-level election outcome for the thirty-five wards in Maheshtala Municipality reflects all of these parties as follows: Indian National Congress, eleven wards; Bharatiya Janata Party, nine; All India Trinamool Congress, seven; Communist Party India (Marxist) seven; and All India Forward Bloc, one (Government of West Bengal, 2020). Thus, the residents of Ward 13 support an established but, less influential party at the municipal, district, state, and central levels. This 2015 ward-level election outcome also means that Maheshtala Municipality as a whole supports a regional party at the state level, and this puts the municipality in the midst of a (violent) struggle for power with the central-level ruling party, which wants to claim political power in metropolitan Kolkata and the State of West Bengal. Ward 13 and Maheshtala Municipality must be viewed in this volatile context of alliances and negotiations.

Livelihood and Land Use

The story of Maheshtala Municipality also needs to be told with reference to its livelihood, land use, and spatial patterning context. Like my sampling approach discussed earlier in this chapter, in this section I approach the study area in the interest of seeing this particular "kind of urban" area up close, in space and over time. As I shall show, even though official, statistical, and cartographic accounts downplay the settled-rural livelihoods and the inherited materiality of agrarian infrastructure in Maheshtala, these characteristics are nevertheless described and accounted for.

A 2016 fact-finding report by the West Bengal Legislative Assembly (2016, p. 1) stated that Maheshtala Municipality is of value because of its relation to the Port of Kolkata, its road infrastructure, and the fact that the area "has gradually become a growth center of manufacturing units where tailoring industry holds an important position." This assessment reflects the economic diversity of Maheshtala Municipality as a whole. Like many parts of metropolitan Kolkata, the informal economy plays a critical economic role (Shaw 2016), and the majority of the working population of Maheshtala works outside of the formal sector, including home-based tailoring activities linked to more formalized industrial production.[9] For instance, in 2014, official figures from the Maheshtala Municipality estimated some 27 percent of the municipal population was engaged in work in the informal economy (2014, p. 26), including work as rickshaw or van pullers, mason/construction workers/helpers, carpenters, tailors, leatherworkers, hawkers, grocers, maidservants, and firecracker workers (Maheshtala Municipality, 2007, p. 46). Within the formal sector, the three key industries, in order of importance, were: (1) large-scale shoe, chain, and cable manufacturers; (2) medium-scale brick fields, chemical, and packing box manufacturers; and (3) smaller-scale fabrication, bakeries, and pharmaceutical industries (2007, pp. 45-46). The workforce is localized, with 2007 data indicating that some 80 percent of the workers in these formal industries were from Maheshtala (2007, p. 47).

To only focus on formal and informal workers masks the fact that most of the people in Maheshtala are thought of by the Government of India as not being in work at all. For instance, in 2011, 36 percent of the total population of Maheshtala were classified as "workers", and the remainder 64 percent were classified as "non-workers" (Census Organization of India, 2011, pp. 58–59). Nonworkers are defined by examples such as "an adult woman engaged in household duties but not doing any productive work to augment the family resources"; students; and "persons like beggars, pensioners, etc., who received income without doing any work" (Government of India, 2020). In this study, I acknowledge the work of female householders, as they are central in shaping periurban space through everyday practices. Similarly, there are very few recognized agricultural workers in Maheshtala, but this does not mean that they do not exist. For instance, in 2011, of the 36 percent of the total population of Maheshtala classified as workers, 87 percent were classified as "main" workers and 13 percent were classified as "marginal" workers (2011, pp. 58-59).[10] And of the main worker population, only 0.3 percent were classified as cultivators and a further 0.3 percent as agricultural workers. The remainder main worker population were engaged in household industry (10.8 percent), and "other work" (88.6 percent) (2011, pp. 58-59).[11] Thus, there are actually many more agricultural workers than these statistics indicate.

Maheshtala's land use profile does not reflect the economic statistical emphasis on manufacturing. Most notably, it is heterogeneous, with residential and formerly agrarian uses predominant. The 2014 *Maheshtala Municipality City Development Plan* (2014, pp. 22, 83) estimated that 65 percent of the municipality was residential land use, with 55 percent of that residential area classified as "notified" or "non-notified" slum[12]. Formerly agrarian land uses include both former paddy fields and ponds. The former paddy fields, which are tellingly categorized as "open," implying that they are available for development, comprised 10 percent of the municipality, while wetlands and ponds covered 6 percent of the area. The presence of ponds reflects the widespread use of private water bodies as an extension of the household, for paddy field irrigation and fish farming. Altogether, these residential and formerly agrarian uses cover 81 percent of the municipal area, forming a much larger part than the 8 percent classified as industrial, 5 percent for "mixed," 1 percent for commercial, and 0.5 percent for institutional.

The spatial pattern of settlement in contemporary Maheshtala Municipality reflects this land use profile. With respect to built-up areas, Figure 2.05 reflects the long-lasting role of the Bhagirathi-Hooghly River in the urbanization of metropolitan Kolkata. Densely built-up areas are located along the river levee and less dense built-up areas are located on the lower ground farther from the river. Note that the Ward 13 study area is located within the less dense built-up areas and categorized as "periurban" in this map provided by the Department of Health and Family Welfare, Government of West Bengal. With respect to slum areas, the patterning shown in light purple in Figure 2.05 reveals an even distribution across the municipality with some clustering along major roads and the rail line. It is in the interest of the municipality to classify large areas as slums, as there is much central government funding available for infrastructure improvement works in categorized slum areas. Within the Ward 13 study area, the areas shown as slums correlate with long-term residents' homes. According to the West Bengal Municipal Act, 1993 (2017, p. 2), a *bustee* or slum is "an area containing land occupied by, or for the purposes of, any collection of huts or other structures used or intended to be used for human habitation." A hut is categorized as different from a building, because a "building" is a structure with a more solid roof than, say, corrugated sheet.

With respect to industry, the patterning shown in Figure 2.06 reveals clear concentrations. The traditional brick kiln and heavy industries are located along the river, whereas the medium and light manufacturing units are strung along the main road transport corridor, in a linear extension pattern typical of periurban areas in India (Balakrishnan, 2013; van Duijne & Nijman, 2019). The rail line and road network are also shown in Figure 2.06. The airport, located on the eastern edge of Maheshtala, adjacent to the study area (shown in dark pink), is a secured area owned by the central government Airports Authority of India. It is not a civil airport but rather is used in multiple ways: as a privately owned flying school; for state government officials' regional air travel, particularly the chief minister of West Bengal; and as a driving test

Figure 2.05. Map of Maheshtala Municipality showing areas classified as urban (red) and periurban (pink) and areas classified as slum (purple). The data for these two maps of Maheshtala Municipality, and the later maps in this chapter are from the Department of Health and Family Welfare, Government of West Bengal. They were disaggregated by the author from a layered GeoPDF provided to the author by Maheshtala Municipality. The spatial data in this 2018 map set does not necessarily reflect tabulated data from the 2014 Maheshtala Municipality City Development Plan. I have drawn the Ward 13 study area into each map, shown as a brown square on the right-hand side of the Municipal area.

(Source: author, 2020. Drawing on data from Geoinformatics and Remote Sensing Cell, West Bengal State Council of Science and Technology, Department of Science and Technology, Government of West Bengal. 2018; National Urban Health Mission, Maheshtala Municipality, South 24 Parganas, West Bengal. 1:8,000. Sponsored by the Department of Health and Family Welfare, Government of West Bengal.)

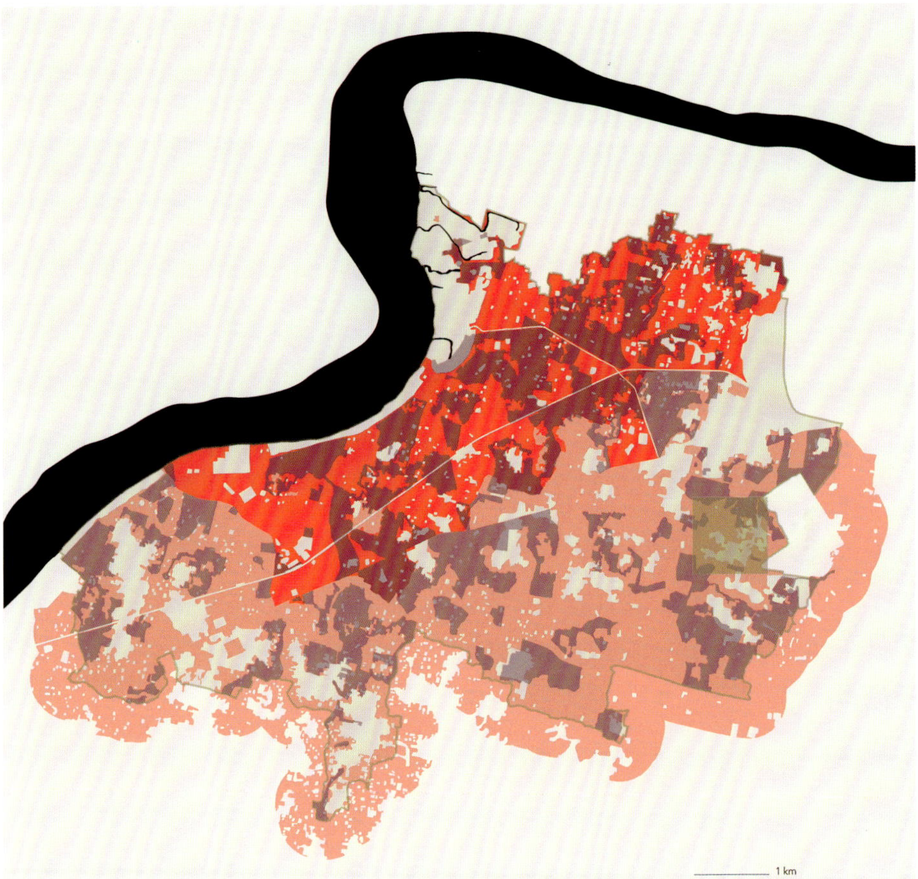
1 km

ground by the many upmarket car dealerships now located along Budge Budge Trunk Road (Airports Authority official, interview, K06, 2019).

With respect to the coexistent agricultural uses, the patterning shown in Figure 2.07 reveals two things that are worth noting. First, Maheshtala Municipality remains threaded with waterways, both natural and human-made: the Bhagirathi-Hooghly River that bounds the northwest of the municipality, and the Monikhali canal system. While in the past the canals have functioned to drain the area, they have been ineffective for some time and a new municipality-wide, underground drainage system is planned. Second, these areas, like most of Gangetic West Bengal, are intermixed paddy land with tree-lined ponds and low-lying marshes. The small amount of so-called crop land/open land, shown in Figure 2.07 (shown in dark green), indicates land where viable crops are still being cultivated. However, many of the marshy swampy areas (shown in light green) are also private cropland but are waterlogged, often because of the ineffective drainage by canals and other development-related issues.

Figure 2.06. Map of Maheshtala Municipality showing rail and road infrastructure; and industrial and commercial land use. Showing brick kilns along the Hooghly River (light brown), industries along Budge-Budge Trunk Road (dark brown) and the airfield (dark pink) located adjacent to the Ward 13 study area. Also showing the Budge Budge-Sealdah railway track with three railway stations, Nangi (west), Akra (center) and Santoshpur (east). This map also shows Budge-Budge Trunk Road (long, straight grey line), which runs east-west and parallel to the railway, and the fine-grained, secondary-road network (shorter, angular grey lines).

(Source: author, 2020. Drawing on data from the Government of West Bengal.)

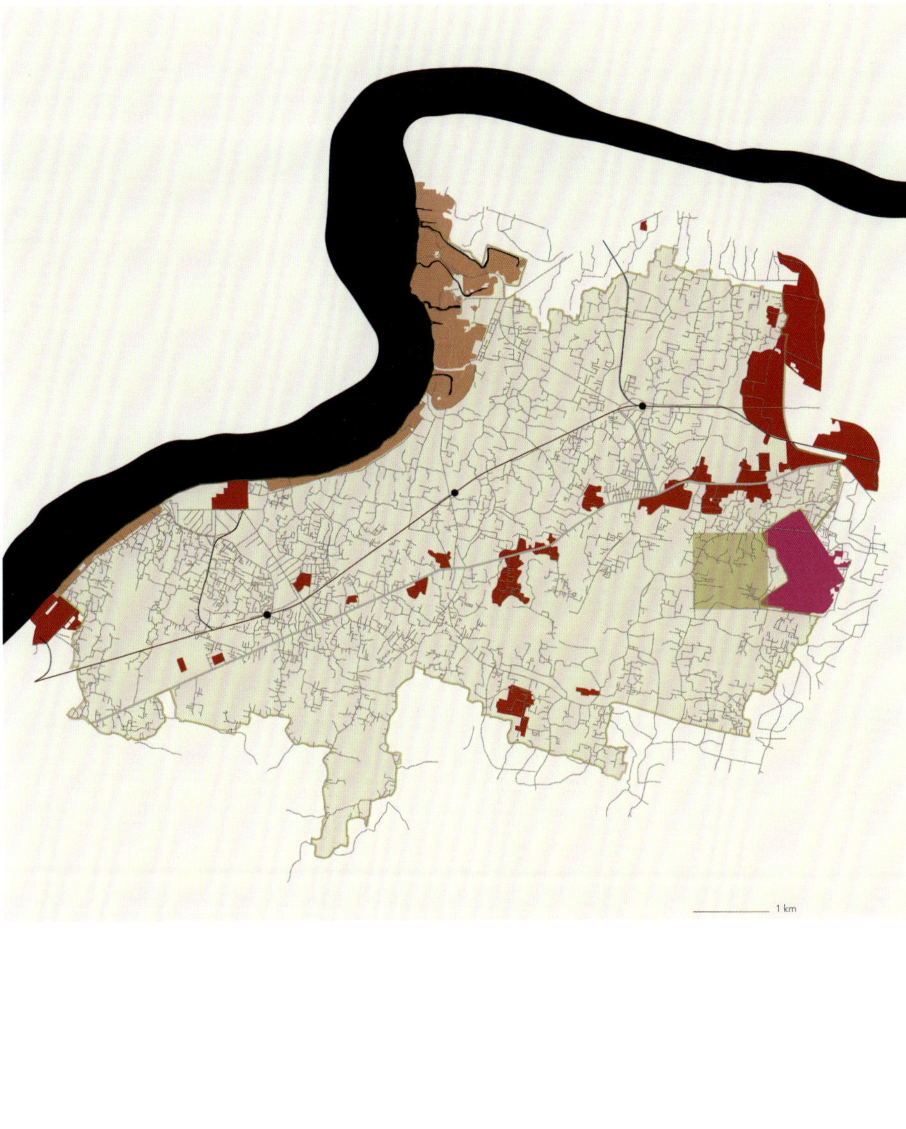
1 km

1 km

The Ward 13 study area is centered on one such marshy area and ineffective canal. A state government–appointed, unelected municipal official contradicted what this state map shows (Maheshtala Municipality official, interview, K01, 2018). He took care to point out to me that the municipality "was agrarian fifty to sixty years ago." When challenged on that claim he responded, "only on the outskirts of Maheshtala Municipality…there was some agrarian [once], but right now there is nothing." Thus, revealing that while the state still sees the municipality as having cultivated land, the municipality doesn't see it this way. They simply see private agrarian land as "open land" or "marshy land" and therefore ready for urban development. It is an example of a teleological imagination of "becoming urban" in which evidently cultivated, agrarian landscapes are either intentionally disregarded in a practice of "unmapping" (A. Roy, 2003) or categorized as "residual," and therefore envisioned as being in the past. What is in the present is a "city in the making," and it is to those envisioning practices that I turn next.

Figure 2.07. Map of Maheshtala Municipality showing the Hooghly River and canals (black lines). The northern canal network is the Monikhali Canal System (which has two parts, Begore Canal and Monikhali Canal). The south to north canal on the eastern edge of the Ward 13 study area is the Begorkhal (Begore Canal) and the east to west flowing canal on the northern edge of the Ward 13 study area is the Monikhali Canal, which then flows west, and connects to the Hooghly River at a tidal gate and pumping station at Akra. Also shown are areas designated as playgrounds and parks (yellow and pink), lakes and ponds (black blobs), marshy swampy areas (light green) and crop land/open space (dark green).

(Source: author, 2020. Drawing on data from the Government of West Bengal.)

A "City in the Making"

As noted above, the West Bengal Municipal Act (1993) bestowed formal authority on urban local bodies to engage in comprehensive urban planning.[13] This includes the obligation to prepare a development plan every five years in consultation with a district planning committee, which must then be approved by the State of West Bengal (2017, p. 182). Even though it was founded in 1993, Maheshtala Municipality does not appear to have engaged in such an exercise until 2007 or, if it did, the plans produced were purely internal documents, not available for public scrutiny. It was only after the Jawaharlal Nehru National Urban Renewal Mission (JnNURM) was launched by the Government of India in 2005 that development planning and visioning in Maheshtala Municipality became more transparent and the plans produced became publicly available. Since 2005 three such plans have been produced by Maheshtala Municipality: the *Draft Development Plan of 2007-2008 to 2011-2012* (Maheshtala Municipality, 2007); the subsequent *Second Generation Draft Development Plan for 2012-2013 to 2016-2017* (Maheshtala Municipality, 2012); and the *City Development Plan 2014-2015 to 2018-19* (Maheshtala Municipality, 2014) (hereafter referred to as the first, second, and third development plans).[14] All three were drafted following the format offered in a planning toolkit provided through the JnNURM (Ministry of Urban Development, 2005, 2012). This was in line with the JnNURM capacity-building initiative within its urban reform directive. In addition to these plans, there is also an overview *Vision Document of Maheshtala Municipality up to 2015-16* (Maheshtala Municipality, 2015). Unlike in other municipalities in India, the Maheshtala Municipality development plans were not created by professional planning consultants but were produced in-house.[15]

By submitting compliant development plans, Maheshtala Municipality was eligible for central-level and state-level government funds. Maheshtala has benefitted both from the sub-missions that comprised the central-level JnNURM, as well as the Atal Mission for Rejuvenation and Urban Transformation or AMRUT, which replaced JnNURM. For instance, infrastructure upgrading in categorized slum areas of Maheshtala Municipality has been funded by the JnNURM Sub-Mission for Basic Services to the Urban Poor.[16] The municipality also benefits from a long-planned, municipality-wide drinking water provision and a soon-to-be-implemented municipality-wide underground stormwater drainage system funded initially under the JnNURM Sub-Mission for Urban Infrastructure and Governance and then under the AMRUT. Both schemes are transmunicipal and so are managed by the Kolkata Metropolitan Development Authority (Maheshtala Municipality, 2014, p. 23).

Central to the JnNURM-defined planning process is a three-part vision statement, defined as "a vivid and idealized description of a desired outcome that inspires, energizes and helps the stakeholders create a future picture of the city with positive changes" (Ministry of Urban Development, 2012, p. 36). Vision statements are intended as medium- to long-term (beyond five years but within fifteen to twenty years) aspirations and are also described as a "dream with deadlines" (2012, p. 36). For example, in Maheshtala Municipality's third development plan, the vision statement stresses "systematic growth" for a "city in the making" (2014, p. 20). The first core value underscoring this growth is the provision of "infrastructural facilities for all." This is consistent with the central government's goals of universal basic service provision. The second core value is "pro-poor" and "pro-women" community development. In my interpretation, this core value is a legacy of the Maheshtala Municipality first development plan, which was produced in part with the UK Department of International Development. The third core value is a commitment to a municipal service culture of transparency, impartiality, and accountability, which is a requirement of the 74th Constitutional Amendment.

The aspirations of the municipality are therefore, as might be expected, shaped by the parameters of thinking promoted through the central government's mission-led initiatives and associated toolkits, including wider values such as those in the United Nations' Sustainable Development Goals. Although the vision statements contain lofty goals, these are operationalized through a range of more technical and practical projects, many of which have an infrastructural, as opposed to social, emphasis. This outcome is consistent with an assessment of all sixty-six JnNURM mission cities by the consultancy Grant Thornton (2011). They found that the city development plans generated through JnNURM read more like "an investment plan for projects in the immediate term" than "a vision document for the city" of the future (2011, p. 13). Grant Thornton specifically noted that there was a "delink" in relation to the specific culture and heritage of cities (2011, p. 39) as seen in the neglect of consideration of agricultural land, cultivation practices, and rural livelihoods in Maheshtala's third development plan.

The vision and values articulated in the development plans are not readily realized on the ground. Reflecting on their early planning efforts in a report, Municipal Chairman Dulal Das alluded without specification to "certain intervening factors", which impacted the budget and meant that many of the projects outlined in the plans not being implemented (Maheshtala

Municipality, 2015, p. 3). These unspecified circumstances mean that the chairman regularly adopts "ad hoc measures" that deviate from the published plans (2015, p. 3). By his own admission, the chairman has been building experience and capacity through a "trial and error method" (2015, p. 3).

Despite the rhetoric of compromising circumstance and diminished capacity, the municipality nonetheless realized a range of infrastructural and community development projects (see Figure 2.08). Maheshtala Municipality managed then to deliver a plan in line with its aspirations, but one that was implemented incompletely using experimental and unpredictable mechanisms. This admission of limitations with respect to the "ideal plan," supports Maheshtala Municipality's ultimate aspiration to engage in the JnNURM-defined visioning mechanisms of rational, modern planning. Their inability to realize "systematic growth" simply confirmed the need to move incrementally towards improving their capacity in municipal management so that plans could be fully realized in the future. The disciplining structure of JnNURM's compliance and support mechanisms, which assumed a seven-year transition period for urban local bodies to get up to speed on new requirements, incentivized such learning processes (Ministry of Urban Development, 2005, pp. 13–14).

Figure 2.08. Completed and planned infrastructure projects Maheshtala Municipality 2014-2016.

(Source: West Bengal Legislative Assembly, 2016. *Fifteenth Legislative Assembly: Twenty eighth report on study visit to Maheshtala Municipality*, p. 13. Government of West Bengal.).

4. Development Schemes executed during the year 2014-15 & plans for 2015-16

Year **Development schemes executed**

2014-15
(i) Road reconstruction
(ii) Water supply net-work expansion
(iii) Street light
(iv) BSUP infrastructure work in slums
(v) on going 200 bedded hospital construction
(vi) Town Library Construction
(vii) Drainage Nikashi
(viii) Procurement of Garbage Disposal Hydraulic Van 4,
(ix) Construction of Hot Mix Plant %f
(x) Boundary wall & vehicle shed in SWM site

Year **Plan for this year**

2015-16
(i) Road reconstruction
(ii) Water supply net-work expansion
(iii) Street light
(iv) B SUP infrastructure work in slums
(v) on going 200 bedded hospital construction
(vi) Town Library Construction
(vii) Drainage Nikashi
(viii) Procurement of Garbage Disposal Hydraulic Van
(ix) Second Scientific Landfill site for SWM
(x) Procurement of Tri-Cycle, Hydraulic Van, Backhoe Loader, Tractor etc. for SWM works.

The techno-managerial skills needed to comply with multistage, funding opportunities offered through mission-modes can create strain at the local level. Urban local bodies like Maheshtala Municipality engage in many funding exercises simultaneously. For instance, in the first phase of Maheshtala Municipality's third development plan, which covers 2014 to 2015 and 2015 to 2016, there were 7 schemes funded by the national Government of India under three different programs; 12 schemes funded by the State of West Bengal under twelve different programs; 6 schemes with mixed funding; and 52 schemes funded by Maheshtala Municipality (2014, pp. 172–77). The total number of schemes for the Maheshtala third development plan was 328 and there were thirty-three different sources of funds, testifying to the dizzying complexity of fiscal arrangements for (modest) municipal development.

Maheshtala Municipality is financially insecure. Only 25 percent of the Maheshtala Municipality third development plan budget is met with municipal funds and the remainder comes from central and state governments.[17] To fix this, the Government of West Bengal wants the municipality to increase its property tax collection from 42.37 percent to at least 90 percent of households and enterprises, (West Bengal Legislative Assembly, 2016, p. 8). This is however a challenge, because with faltering service delivery and a vision that aspires to not much more than a desire to be compliant with urban reforms based on central and state plans rather than local needs, Maheshtala residents are reluctant to pay taxes to their municipality. Another way for a municipality to become more financially autonomous is to become a municipal corporation. In 2014, twenty-two new municipalities were announced by the Government of West Bengal (Press Trust of India, 2014). This announcement included a proposal for four "mega municipal corporations" within metropolitan Kolkata (Times News Network, 2014).[18] One such proposed mega municipal corporation combined Pujali, Budge Budge, Maheshtala, and Amtala Town, with the headquarters in Maheshtala. While this proposal has not been implemented to date, it indicates something of the aspiration of the municipal chairman.

In sum, urban local bodies continue to have a long, troubled history in India. The issues that municipalities typically face now include: perennial fiscal stress; a shortage of adequately qualified and skilled staff; freezes on recruitment; the absence of modernized recruitment rules; antiquated organizational structures not fit for purpose with respect to emerging municipal functions; and a lack of commitment to professional development through training and performance systems (Jha, 2018, pp. 14-15). Under such conditions it is difficult for urban local bodies to be proactive and address the challenges emanating from uneven urbanisation (2018, p. 15). Furthermore, urban local bodies, like municipalities, "are crumbling under the weight of a maze of urban sector programs and missions" launched by both central and state-level governments (2018, p. 15). Maheshtala Municipality fits this description.

Conclusion

This chapter builds upon the previous chapters, which described urban policy at the central and state levels, and explains how Maheshtala Municipality interacts with, and has its urban policy goals shaped by, wider urban policy frameworks. This is expressed in the cartographic representations of the region, city, and municipality. State-level bureaucratic and political expectations play a role in municipal, district-level, and metropolitan-wide negotiations, such that the municipality has not been able to harness power to build its autonomy or finances to better serve its residents. Instead, the municipality's approach to development planning is manifested in a dizzying array of funding sources and schemes. Furthermore, the post 1990s urban reforms have little to say about the inherited materiality of agrarian landscapes and hybrid rural-urban conditions. It is within these piecemeal practices of municipal governance that the periurbanization of Ward 13 proceeds. It is also within these piecemeal practices that my re-rendering of Ward 13 occurs. Starting from chapter 4, I tell the same story, but from the perspective of local knowledge and lived experience read through entangled landscapes and settlement patterns. Before I do this, I must first introduce the graphic elements of my cartographic kit in chapter 3.

Endnotes

1 This spatial sampling method was consistent with the methodology being used in the ETH-Future Cities Lab Urban-Rural Systems group, with which this study is affiliated. The group investigates contemporary patterns, processes, and practices of urban-rural settlement in Monsoon Asia, seeking to understand their dynamics, and proposing knowledge strategies, design scenarios, and action plans for sustainable development pathways (Future Cities Lab, 2020).

2 I learnt about this distinct land-cover patterning as part of previous research that I undertook in Kolkata from 2010 to 2016. I often prepared for my fieldwork by studying the edges of metropolitan Kolkata for hours through the Google Earth Pro history tool. My observation of ubiquity of these tripartite settlement conditions led me to think of them as ordinary.

3 The Ramsar Convention on Wetlands is an intergovernmental treaty that provides the framework for the conservation and wise use of wetlands and their resources. The Convention was adopted in the Iranian city of Ramsar in 1971 and came into force in 1975. Since then, almost 90 percent of UN member states, from all the world's geographic regions, have acceded to become Contracting Parties (Ramsar, 2019).

4 Here I am using population density as an indicator of being built-up. In the study I argue that this measure is limited, and a better method would be to evaluate heterogeneous densities of land cover, and the encouragement of co-habitation and care.. In my analysis of remote-sensed imagery I did land cover analysis visually, using the history tool in Google Earth Pro for Maheshtala Municipality, whereas Sahana et al. (2018) have done this more computationally for metropolitan Kolkata using hybrid land use/land cover classification and GIS.

5 According to Jha (2018, p. 56), the Constitution of India (1949) laid primary emphasis on the organization of village councils or *panchayats* as a unique local self-government institution in rural areas. However, it did not lay down details of form, structure, functions, and finances of such institutions.

6 The Municipal Act (2017, p. 15) requires that a public "proclamation" be made "either by the beating of a drum … or other publicity media." In the case of Maheshtala Municipality, the announcement was through the "metropolitan" section of Kolkata's *Telegraph* newspaper.

7 According to the West Bengal Municipal Act, 1993 (2017, p. 59-62), the other obligatory functions relate to the spheres of public health and sanitation, and administration. Discretionary functions relate to the spheres of public works, education, public health and sanitation, administration, and development.

8 Following Pal (2018, p. 68), after the 74th Constitutional Amendment in 1992, West Bengal was one of the few states that ensured that ward committees were formed in every municipality in 1995. However, he notes that the functioning of ward committees is not uniform in all municipalities within the State of West Bengal, and it can differ from one ward committee to another within the same municipality.

9 Much has been written about the significant environmental costs of the tailoring industry in Maheshtala (see Gupta et al., 2015, 2017). The tailoring industry in Maheshtala is a cluster based in and around Chatta and Kalikapur and is linked to the textile cluster in nearby Metiabruz. Many of the textile workers are Muslim, and so this industry does not have a strong presence in Hindu-dominated Ward 13.

10 "Main" workers are those workers who had worked for a major part of the reference period, i.e., six months or more. "Marginal" workers are those workers who had not worked for a major part of the reference period, i.e., less than six months (Government of India, 2020).

11 They are "other" as they are defined as not doing cultivation, agricultural labor, or household industry labor (Government of India, 2020).

12 Being "non-notified" can be a barrier to legal rights and basic services such as water, sanitation, and security of tenure.

13 In 1997, the West Bengal Municipal Act was amended, giving urban local bodies actual power to plan autonomously, as the earlier act only empowered the state-level government to plan on behalf of municipalities (2017, p. 184).

14 Development planning uses the word "city" even though municipalities such as Maheshtala, which are integrated within a very large city, must create such documents as well. Sometimes Maheshtala refers to itself as a town. In other JnNURM documents, the term "urban local body" is used to refer to municipalities as well as municipal corporations. All municipalities in West Bengal must follow the West Bengal Municipal Act, whereas municipal corporations follow a different act and have more autonomy. To avoid confusion, I refer to Maheshtala Municipality as an urban local body or a municipality to distinguish it from Kolkata Municipal Corporation, which is a municipal corporation and is sometimes more broadly thought of as "the city."

15 Although, the city assessment and slum infrastructure section of the first development plan for Maheshtala Municipality was assisted by the Department for International Development, UK.

16 32.8 percent of the total Maheshtala Municipal area is classified as slum (a category that is not defined) and 13 percent of the total third development plan budget is listed as "mixed funding" from the JnNURM Basic Services to the Urban Poor Mission, and includes the required matching funds from the Government of West Bengal and Maheshtala Municipality (2014, pp. 75, 173).

17 The budget breakdown is as follows: Government of West Bengal schemes 34 percent; Maheshtala Municipality funded schemes 25 percent; Government of India schemes 20 percent; Government of India, Government of West Bengal schemes and municipal funded schemes (to implement JnNURM projects) 13 percent; unallocated 5 percent; Government of India and Government of West Bengal schemes 3 percent (Maheshtala Municipality, 2015, p. 173).

18 According to the plan, four mega municipal corporations were to be formed in North and South 24-Parganas. One corporation was to be created with the municipalities of Rajarhat-Gopalpur, Barasat, Madhyamgram, and New Barrackpore and adjoining areas, with its headquarters in Barasat. Another was to be formed with the municipalities of Baranagar, Kamarhati, Khardah, Panihati, Dum Dum, North and South Dum Dum and adjoining rural areas, with its headquarters at Dum Dum. The third corporation was to be constituted with the municipalities of Titagarh, Barrackpore, North Barrackpore, Bhatpara, Garulia, Naihati, Kanchrapara and Halisahar and adjoining rural areas, with its headquarters at Barrackpore.

3/

VISUAL MATERIALS

Geographer Gillian Rose (2014) defines "visual research methods" as methods which use visual materials of some kind as part of the process of generating evidence in order to explore research questions (also see Rose, 2016). This understanding is built upon earlier modes of theorizing the visual in anthropology. For instance, anthropologist Sarah Pink (2006, p. 4) explored the anthropology of experience and the senses, applied visual anthropology, and new visual and digital media as central to the future of "visual anthropology." In this book, I engage both visual materials generated by myself as well as "found" visual materials, and both of these are central to the dissemination of the results of the research. The visual materials generated by me are introduced in this chapter. They are not understood here as located within the realm of art. As Tolia-Kelley (2012, p. 137) explains, geographers producing (more-than-text) material through research are often best defined within the discipline of "visual culture" rather than as "art"—that which is produced and determined by the practitioner of art—where art is a way of life and a vocation (2012, p. 136). Visual culture, the discipline, offers a dynamic and practically oriented account that "encompasses research forays towards the production of paintings, drawing, installations, exhibitions, performances and/or indeed collaborations with practitioners" (Tolia-Kelley 2012, p. 137).

Visual ethnography is "inevitably collaborative and to varying extents participatory" (Pink 2008, p. 2). This book is built upon local knowledge and lived experience read through the household, entangled landscapes, and settlement patterns. Resident participants' knowledge of their localities is respected in its own right, and thus research subjects enact agency as active co-researchers. I also consider my assistants as co-researchers who acted as interpreters, translators, and guides, gatekeepers, and confidants.[1] Very often in research involving translation, the voices of assistants are oddly silenced even though they can be "more central to research than [is] often disclosed" (Leck, 2014, p. 66). Overall, visual research methods are more-than-representational (Lorimer, 2005): they not only undertake "enquiries based on looking, seeing, analyzing and writing text," but also enquiries that consider "the (geo)politics of embodied, material encounter and engagement" (Rose & Tolia-Kelly, 2012, p. 3).

The central visual research method in this study is based in the tradition of critical cartography in geography and social science. Crampton and Krygier (2006, p. 13) state that the purpose of critique is to understand, and to suggest alternatives to, the "categories of knowledge" that we use, because such categories (i.e., assumptions and familiar notions) shape knowledge "even as they enable it." Critique does not seek to escape from categories, but rather shows how categories come to be, and what other possibilities there are. In the case of this study, critical cartography is drawn on to understand the politics of knowledge surrounding periurbanization, and to augment the way it has been framed to date, thus expanding the ways in which it might be understood and engaged with in the future. One direction this critique has taken is the emergence of "critical mapping practices" which explore how maps are political and how mapping can be a political act (Crampton, 2010, p. 17; also see Thompson, 2008).

In India, as pointed out by anthropologist Chitra Venkataramani (2015, p. 7), there exist not only critical cartography practices that focus on "how people draw maps," but also "how people are drawn into maps and the mapping process." By "draw in" she means not just how people are drawn in as populations, but also "how they intervene within a process of drawing—even that conducted by another entity such as the state—in order to control the possibilities of how they come to be drawn, named, or categorized" (2015, p.7). Such engagement with the mapping act points toward a subsequent approach for research in cartography, that of "object-oriented cartography" and the "gentle politics" of maps (Rossetto, 2019, p. 8). In what follows I move back and forth in approaches; from the ontological power of maps (practice-oriented) to their continuous state of becoming (object-oriented).

What I observe in this study is the arc of state-led mapping practices in Kolkata, and I position my visual research methods amidst trends at the time of writing. I reflect upon what Hull (2012) terms the "government of paper" by looking closely at the nonhuman agencies of paper and digital maps, including the original maps that I have created in this study. The critical cartography terms relevant to this study are "rendering" how categories of knowledge came to be and "re-rendering" other possibilities. That is, I analyze how the area had been rendered in secondary data (chapters 1, 2, and 5) and I re-render it (chapters 4, 5, and 6) using my field-based data along with visualizations of the study area. These visualizations are maps, illustrative photographs, and transects, which show information by way of symbols, boundaries, and invented shading. In what follows, I introduce each of my graphic conventions.

Cropping and Symbols

In chapters 1, 2, and 5, the collected representations of the study area illustrate how it has been rendered by the state. In order to clearly explain this point and make comparisons, I have reformatted and annotated many of the original maps. In all cases the policy-planning and colonial maps are reformatted so that north is facing the top of the page. Many of the maps have been cropped, that is, only fragments of some maps are shown. Cropping is used to highlight Gangetic West Bengal, Maheshtala Municipality, or the Ward 13 study area in maps that cover much larger areas. In addition, the fragments of maps have been carefully cropped so that they can be shown as comparable in scale with other maps when placed side-by-side or one after the other. This affords a reading across maps from different dates and mapping conventions.

In addition, to further enhance reading across maps, many of the cropped maps have been altered with the addition of symbols, lines, and numbers. I have added the boundary of Maheshtala Municipality, the one-kilometer-square of the Ward 13 study area, and in some cases, the New Monikhali Canal system is shown as a line. Letters are added to indicate where something described in words is located on the map. The addition of shapes and lines also affords another type of reading: the additions orient the viewer who may be unfamiliar with metropolitan Kolkata or Gangetic West Bengal, and link the maps together. The shapes and lines allow inter-referencing so that the Ward 13 study area is positioned within the municipality, which is positioned within Gangetic West Bengal. While topographical scale is not central to the theoretical underpinning of the study,[2] the positional "nesting" of locality, ward, municipality, district, delta, and Monsoon Asia is nevertheless a way for a reader to quickly and repeatedly locate the study area, both on a map and in this book, which regularly moves between images and words.

In chapters 4, 5, and 6, I employ conversation mapping, drawing on in-depth, and on occasion, repeated, informal interviews with a nonrepresentative sample of consenting households. I also draw on some rudimentary geographic information systems (GIS) data sourced from Maheshtala Municipality (see Figure 3.01). The informal interviews are introduced in detail in chapter 4. In each conversation map, all stories relevant to a situated entanglement (like waterlogging or land conversion) were geolocated with a letter symbol and linked to "quotes" from interview transcripts, thus revealing patterns of clustering or distribution. The maps that were created from this data form the main reference base for my re-rendering. For privacy reasons, I have not retained my detailed symbol notations in the conversation maps shown in chapters 4 and 6. Rather, I have created one symbol that shows each interview location, and this is repeated in many of my conversation maps (see large "+" symbols in Figure 3.01.), reminding the reader that the topic of the map, and the data in the body of the text is partial, and was sourced from accounts of land and livelihood entanglements of participant households.

Boundaries

Another re-rendering method I use comes from a critique of both landscape ecology and land use categorizations, most recently reported on through the forma and language of the atlas. This is a method I am familiar with in my training as a landscape architect and urban designer, where I have with others reported on the utility of this method in a recently published atlas (see Marshall et al., 2020). As anthropologists Lorraine Daston and Peter Galison (2007, p. 3) note, atlases are "systematic compilations of working objects." Those working objects of science can be "atlas images, type specimens, or laboratory processes—any manageable, communal representative of the sector of nature under investigation." Standardized working objects are essential, they say, "for unrefined natural objects are too quirkily particular to cooperate in generalizations and comparisons." In this instance, the working objects of analysis are heterogeneous land cover "patches," meaning spatially continuous and internally similar types of mixes of land cover. Unsurprisingly, the patch mapping method has been described as a type of "biological drawing."[3]

According to Daston and Galison, atlases are the "dictionaries of the sciences of the eye" (2007, p.4). The atlas trains the eye to pick out certain kinds of objects as "exemplary" and to regard them in a certain way. When atlases present images derived from new instruments, everyone addressed by the atlas begins to learn to "see" anew. A new way of seeing urban form is one of the aims of the science and design of our "patch" cover analysis and rendering method. Heterogeneous patch analysis re-renders architecture and "urban landscape"[4]: it shows "unseen" ecological objects to be looked at and makes a case for their worth. Seeing and discerning those patches is based on a "trained judgement" (2007, p. 309) using remote-sensed and

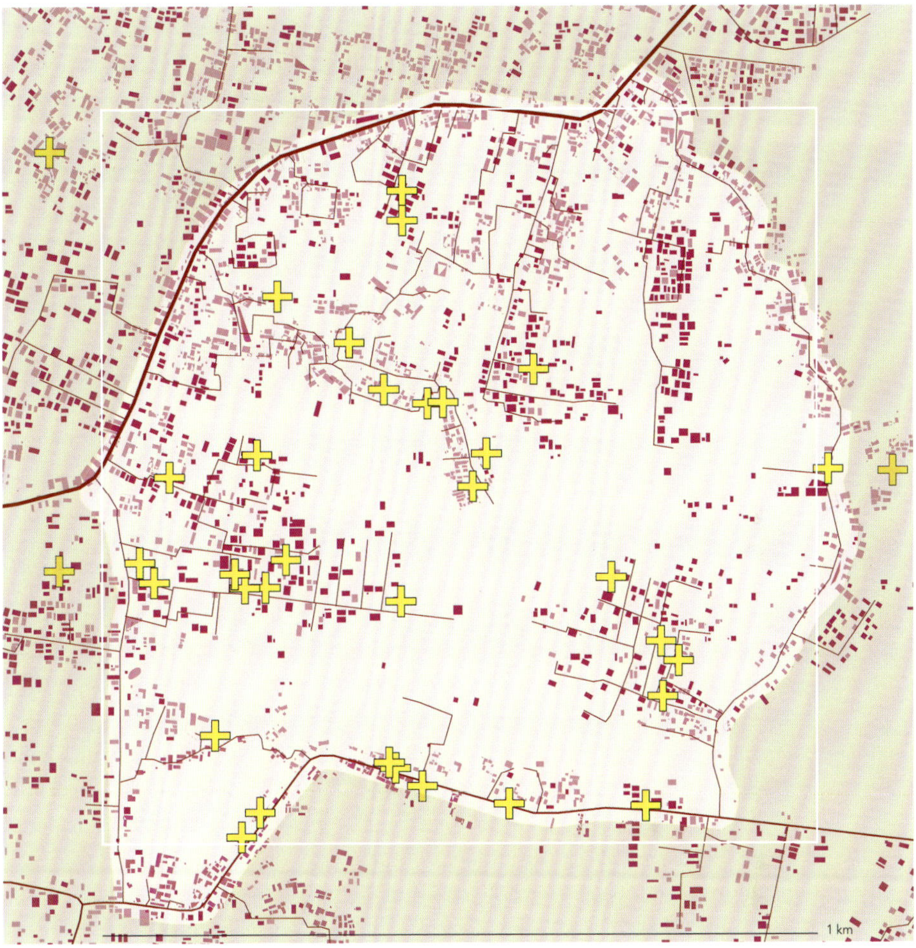

Figure 3.01. Study area data layers:
Light pink rectangles: older buildings (2004 data)
Dark pink rectangles: newer buildings (2018 data)
Thick red lines: local, main roads (with cars and trucks)
Thin red lines: pathway roads (with some or no cars)
Yellow symbols: participant households (approximate location)
White line: one kilometer-square study area

(Source: author, 2022; Google Earth Pro, 2018; and unassembled and unpublished GIS files provided by Maheshtala Municipality, 2019.)

ground-truthing methods. It was this method of observing patches that was tan early step I took in seeing periurban Kolkata differently. Specifically, land cover mapping and analysis captures visually the mixity and patterning of the study area land cover. To this I add other re-rendering methods, with the intention of filling out what that "objective view" occludes.

Briefly, the technique classifies patches that differ from one another based on the mixture and relative abundance of five elements: buildings, woody vegetation, herbaceous vegetation, paved surfaces, and bare soil. These five elements can vary independently of one another in different situations. This means that adjacent patches may differ in the amount of cover of any number of the five elements. A new patch is drawn whenever the relative cover of any one of the five elements changes from one abundance category to another (Marshall, 2020, p. 8).[5] Overall, the technique builds upon figure/ground and typo-morphological classifications from architecture and urban design, which carefully examine how historical transformations of urban form and public space are constituted of mixes of use within building blocks and changes in building and landscape uses over time (McGrath, 2013; Shane, 2005). These established approaches bring explanatory power to the relationship between built and open space, whereas the urban ecology analysis technique of patch mapping used in this study add vegetation and soil into the narrative (Marshall et al., 2020, p. 3). The project of designing with heterogenous, land cover patch dynamics been discussed as central to "ecological urban design" (McGrath et al., 2019) and as key for integrating ecology and the "architecture of the city"(McGrath, 2018). With respect to this study, the technique of mixed land cover–based patch mapping offers a way of revealing the periurban form of the study area that is otherwise rendered invisible in official maps based on land use.[6]

Clarification

It is important to note that the five-element, land cover–based technique of patch mapping used in this study is often confused with another method in which a cartographic spatial imaginary of the "patch" dominates. The other more-established technique—the patch/corridor/matrix formulation—is derived from island biogeography theory (see MacArthur & Wilson, 1967) and it has been advanced as "landscape ecology" (Forman, 1995, 2008; Forman & Godron, 1986; Sukopp, 2002). Landscape ecology aims to inform environmental planning, as do other methods for "human ecology mapping" (McLain et al., 2013).[7] Both efforts, the five-element, land cover–based technique and the patch/corridor/matrix formulation re-render territory through what Pickles (2004, p. 146) describes as different types of “abstraction.” As such they not only produce different territories in the representations, but also seed certain modes of engagement with territory, resources, and species. Importantly for this study, the patch/corridor/matrix formulation carries a predetermined assumption about what constitutes an ecologically valuable landscape, whereas the five-element, land cover–based technique does not depend on such suppositions.

For instance, the patch/corridor/matrix formulation deduces ecological processes from the pattern of a landscape and argues that “flows of any interest occur [only] along corridors” (Marshall et al. 2020, p. 3). That is, the patch/corridor/matrix view of landscape recognizes three kinds of sites: patches that act as habitats for a target organism; corridors that enhance dispersal among habitat patches; and a matrix of land inhospitable for the species, which therefore does not serve as habitat.[8] In contrast, in the five-element, land cover–based technique of patch mapping, every element (buildings, woody vegetation, herbaceous vegetation, paved surfaces, and bare soil) is “on the map.” There is no pregiven assumption that any particular element or patch pattern is more ecologically or socially relevant than another. As such, the technique of five-element land cover-based patch mapping applies equally well to “wild,” “spontaneous,” semi-built-up and built environments; for the separation between “natural” and urban environments is not used. In my map, the study area is represented as a “heterogenous phenomenon and a shifting mosaic” of land cover types, in which distinct elements are understood as modified “by design or by happenstance, and which respond to legacy and intention” (2020, p. 21). Importantly, built and biotic heterogeneity (spatial patterning) is understood as both an outcome and a driver of periurban change. The five-element, land cover–based technique thus aligns with an approach that acknowledges the entanglement of humans, nonhumans, and their diverse agencies (as noted in the introduction).

Tracing

Figures 3.02 and 3.03 show enhanced remote-sensed, satellite imagery of the one-kilometer-square study area for 2004 and 2018[9] . The tracing highlights the periurban form of the study area and its immediate context as patches of varying mixes of land cover elements. The land cover mapping shows no “blank spaces” for everything is filled with identifiable conditions, enabling a spatial description of the elements that cover these conditions. When compared over time, this land cover re-rendering indicates something of the change of elements that comprise the settlement of the case study area between 2004 and 2018. The intention of re-rendering the one-kilometer-squate study area in this way is to create a different representation of Ward 13 in relation

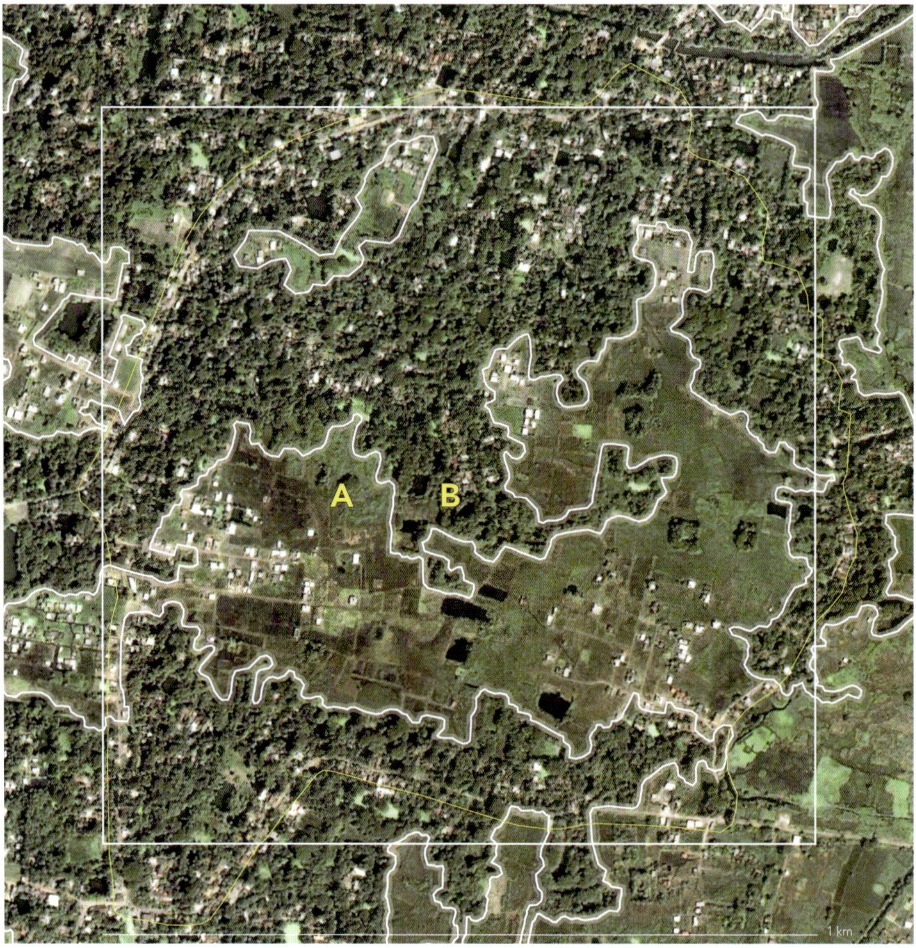

Figure 3.02. Enhanced, remote sensed image from 2004 of the Ward 13 study area (white square) showing "patches" of distinct, land cover mixes. "Patches" (bounded by white lines) are based on the mixture and relative abundance of five elements - buildings, woody vegetation, herbaceous vegetation, paved surfaces, and bare soil - that can vary independently of one another in different situations.

A. Predominantly "jungly" paddy fields

B. Tree-lined ponds, plantations and gardens with scattered buildings

(Source: author and Google Earth Pro, 2020).

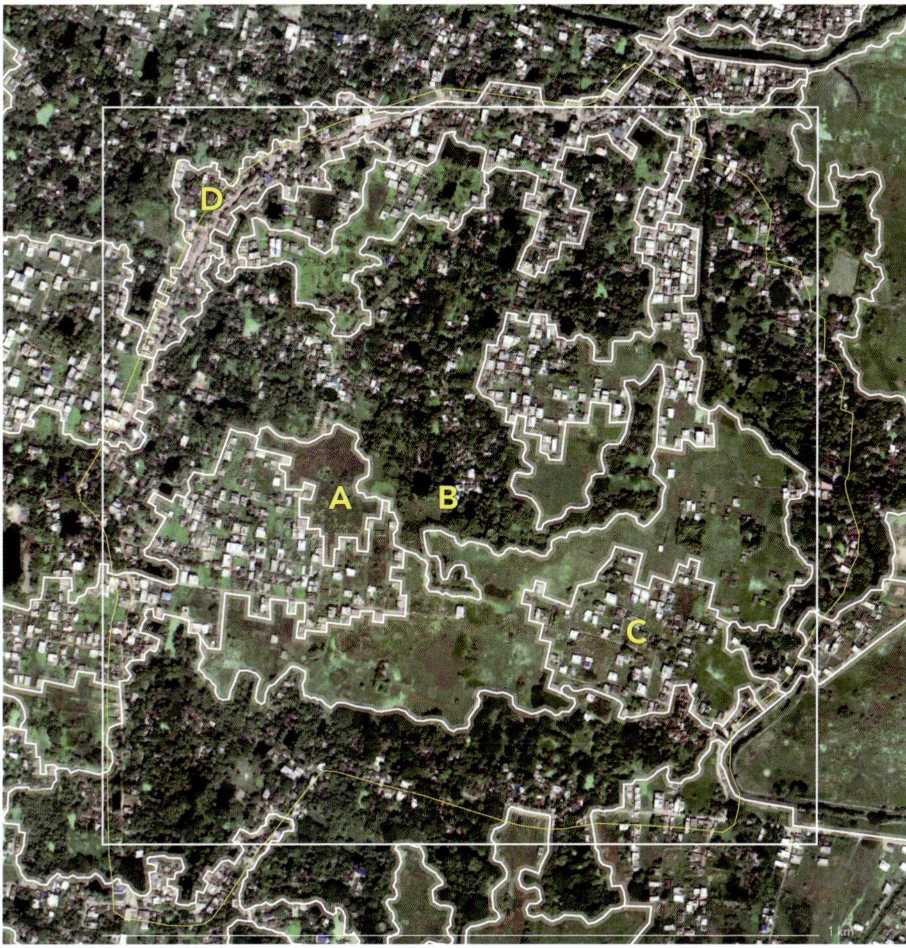

Figure 3.03. Enhanced, remote sensed image from 2018 of the Ward 13 study area (white square) showing "patches" of distinct, land cover mixes. "Patches" (bounded by white lines) are based on the mixture and relative abundance of five elements - buildings, woody vegetation, herbaceous vegetation, paved surfaces, and bare soil - that can vary independently of one another in different situations.

A. Predominantly "jungly" paddy fields

B. Tree-lined ponds, plantations, and gardens with scattered buildings

C. Predominantly densely built-up buildings with some "jungly" paddy fields

D. Densely built-up buildings also with tree-lined ponds, plantations, and gardens

(Source: author and Google Earth Pro, 2020).

to other ideological maps, including land use maps. That is, this re-rendering reminds us that specifying the area as predominantly either residential or vacant is based on assumptions and masks important temporal dimensions. For example, areas that are classified as merely residential or vacant in a 2012 development planning map from the report entitled *City Development Plan Maheshtala Municipality 2014-15 to 2018-19* (see Figure 4.01 in chapter 4), are shown in Figure 3.03 to include a variable mix of land cover conditions, from predominantly paddy fields (A), to scattered buildings also with tree-lined ponds, plantations, and gardens (B), then to densely built-up colony buildings with some fields (C), and to densely built-up but with complex landscape elements such as tree-lined ponds, plantations and gardens (D). All these urban elements—buildings, vegetation, and surface materials—may influence ecological processes differently.

A comparison between the temporal samples depicted in the enhanced remote-sensed satellite imagery pair shows that there has been change over time. Certain types of land cover patches have increased in size or number, while others have decreased. For example, the areas that are densely built-up but with complex landscape elements (D) represent a typical local socio-ecology of dense buildings with treed ponds, plantations, and gardens. Along with areas with scattered buildings interspersed with fields (C), both of these settlement patterns have increased in area cover over time. This reflects the growth of settlement along local main roads as well as the transformation of former paddy fields to plotted, residential colonies. Mirroring this tendency, areas with scattered buildings interspersed with tree-lined ponds, plantations, and gardens (B), and areas predominantly with paddy fields (A) have reduced in area. Such agrarian settlement forms (the arrangement of linked wooded, settled villages and rice paddy fields) are repeated across Gangetic West Bengal and have been shaped over time, and it is this long story of settlement that I introduce in chapter 5.

Beyond "Sprawl"

It is important to note that the project of drawing boundaries from aerial imagery is not new in the context of periurban West Bengal. As we may recall from chapter 2, the challenge of the *Perspective Plan for Calcutta: 2011* was to conceptualize the settlement and development of Kolkata beyond the city itself, a task which required ambitious thinking and planning. One aspect of realizing and communicating this ambition was the ability of the 2011 perspective plan to draw upon new capacities of geo-visualization, including maps derived from remote-sensed imagery by the Space Application Centre in Ahmedabad.[10] Three analytical mapping projects were created specifically for the purpose of the 2011 perspective plan, and they depict the territory of Kolkata and its surrounds as a continuous field of diverse land uses. The maps were created at the scale of the Inner Metropolitan Region, which includes the Kolkata Metropolitan Area, using data from 1998 remote-sensed imagery. The Space Application Centre undertook the mapping projects with a specially formulated, and replicable, methodology intended to give planners in Kolkata "maximum benefit" by providing "timely, accurate and repetitive" data (Pathan et al., 1991, p. 105). That is, there is an assumption by the Space Application Centre that such maps would inform ongoing development planning decisions in an iterative process. As will become clear, the promise of this variegated land use visualization battled against another kind of spatial conceptualization of extended Kolkata, one that aimed to shape a so-called balanced urban continuum. In what follows, I briefly describe each mapping project.

The first mapping project was the *Urban Sprawl Study of Calcutta and Its Environs*, which used a combination of remote-sensed imagery and topographical maps. The 1991 urban sprawl study map shown in Figure 3.04 "depicts details on the physical growth of the city and the direction of growth" from 1922 to 1990 (Pathan, 1991, p. 13). The authors of the map study reported that metropolitan Kolkata had grown at a rate of ten square kilometers per year since the 1960s, and thus warned that "the entire [Kolkata Metropolitan Area] will be filled up by built-up land in another 30 to 40 years" (Pathan, 1991, p. 16). The second mapping study, shown in Figure 3.05, entitled *Urban Land Use Studies of Calcutta and Its Environs*, was the first land use survey of Kolkata undertaken using satellite imagery (earlier surveys using aerial photographs were done in the periods from 1961 to 1964 and 1976 to 1977) (Pathan, 1991, p. 17). In the 1991 urban land use study, a special classification system was devised to match the Gangetic West Bengal context, and thirty-one detailed urban land use maps were prepared at a scale of 1:25,000 (Pathan, 1991, p. 18). Figure 3.05 depicts a composite map from the Space Application Centre land use set at 1:100,000 scale that was published in the 2011 perspective plan. The category of vacant land is used interchangeably with the category of "wastelands" by the Space Application Centre, and is described as "lands which are capable or have the potential for the development of vegetative cover and are not being used due to different constraints of varying degrees." Sandy land is defined as "sand accumulations occurring in coastal plains, river flood plains or inland areas." Fallow land is "basically an agricultural land but devoid of any crop

Figure 3.04. A map outcome of the Urban Sprawl Study of Calcutta and its Environs at 1:100,000 scale using multi-date Landsat MSS, TM, SPOT and IRS LISS data in conjunction with survey of India topographical maps. The spatial resolution of the SPOT data is 20m. Also shown, as an overlay, is the Ward 13 study area (yellow symbol). The bounded area is the Calcutta / Kolkata Metropolitan Development Area, which is also called the Calcutta Metropolitan District in Perspective Plan 2011. The darkest tone in the center of the map represents the extent of built-up area of Kolkata in 1922, the next increment of tone is the extent in 1960, then 1976, and then 1990. The white tone, areas with no hatching at all, are described as agricultural land. This map shows that the early trend of the growth of built-up land of Kolkata was linear, following the banks of the Hooghly River, particularly toward the north. Later, the trend shifted to "ribbon development" along main roads, particularly to the north, south-west (the site of this study), north-east, and south-east (Pathan, 1991, p. 15). In 1991, there is little growth toward the east as this area encompassed the waste-recycling region of East Kolkata Area. In 2002 this eastern area was later designated as the East Kolkata Wetlands, a protected area where development is supposedly prohibited.

(Source: Pathan, et al., 1991. *Urban Land Use Studies of Calcutta Metropolitan Development Authority area using Remote Sensing techniques.* Fig. 3. 1:100,000. Ahmedabad, Space Application Centre, and Calcutta Metropolitan Development Authority.)

LEGEND
SCALE
LEGEND
HABITATION WITH PLANTATIONS
RIVER / STREAMS
ROADS
RAILWAY
CMDA BOUNDARY

Figure 3.05. Land use/land cover map from the Urban Land Use Studies of Calcutta and its Environs study, published in the report entitled *A Perspective Plan for Calcutta: 2011*. Also shown, as an overlay, is the Ward 13 study area (yellow symbol). The map shows types of land use; Orange (built-up land), yellow/ unhatched yellow (settlement with orchards), green/ unhatched green (fallow), dark green (agriculture), brown (orchard), white (vacant/sandy), blue (waterbodies). The map image is blurred because a vigorous ceiling fan made pages flutter and my iPhone did not focus properly. Nevertheless, seen in this map is the built-up area of Kolkata surrounded by "settlement with orchards" that are then interdigitated with a variety of land uses. The case study area can also be seen as predominantly covered in "settlement with orchards", which is defined by the Space Application Centre as "habitation with plantations" such as coconut, areca nut, citrus, banana, cashew, casuarina, eucalyptus, and other orchards/nurseries (Pathan, 1991, p. 69).

(Source: Government of West Bengal., 1990. *A Perspective Plan for Calcutta: 2011*. Map 3.11, 1:100,000. Kolkata, State Planning Board, Development & Planning Department, Government of West Bengal.)

Built Up
Settlement with Orchard
Fallow
Agriculture
Orchard
Vacant / Sandy
Land Use / Land Cover Map as Obtained from Visual Interpretation of Satellite Imagery for I.M.R.
Note :
Data used Multispectral Spot Data FCC Path 233 (1.2.3) Row
Dated - 29.01.88
Map No. 3.11
5 0 10 Km
Perspective Plan For Calcutta 2011

at the time of the collection of remotely sensed data." Lastly, agriculture is "broadly defined as the land used primarily for production of food and fiber and includes cropped areas, fallow lands, and plantation or orchard areas" (Pathan, 1991, p. 69).

The third mapping study created by the Space Application Centre is a recoding of the above 1991 urban land use study and is entitled *Suitability Zones* (see Figure 3.06). It is a type of suitability analysis that "assessed the fitness of the different land characteristics (soils, physiography, slope, land use, etc.) for urban development" (Pathan, 1991, p. 28). It is worth noting that the consultant, Space Application Centre image makers, had assumed that their work would support the implementation of a "green belt" that would "save" the best agricultural land on the periphery. They assumed that by representing the expansion of the boundary of the city—as seen in the sprawl map—the areas beyond the boundary would then accommodate "green" agricultural land (Pathan, 1991, p. 1, 2). The authors of the 2011 perspective plan however, understood the suitability analysis study in a different way. Even though the suitability map shows a patterning of a continuous field, the planners focused on the white-colored vacant/sandy lands of the land use map as sites for tabula rasa, greenfield development for projected population density. For they noted, "In these maps the vacant/sandy areas in large chunks could be traced for creating new towns"; and suggested that "in the event of non-availability of vacant/sandy land [then] fallow land may also be brought under future development areas, thus making the least possible threat to the high productive agricultural land" or encountering the added expense of filling in wetter land (Government of West Bengal, 1990, p. 91).

Figure 3.06. Suitability zone map from the Urban Land Use Studies of Calcutta and its Environs study, published in the report entitled *A Perspective Plan for Calcutta: 2011.* Also shown, as an overlay, is the Ward 13 study area (yellow symbol). In this map most of the areas shown as vacant/sandy lands in Figure 3.05 are re-categorized as "good for development" (shown in green). The study area is in a zone marked as predominantly "good for limited development" (shown in dark pink). The map image is in focus however, it appears blurry because of an error in aligning the different plates of color in the offset printing process.

(Source: Government of West Bengal, 1990. *A Perspective Plan for Calcutta: 2011.* Map 3.12, 1:100,000. Kolkata, State Planning Board, Development & Planning Department, Government of West Bengal.)

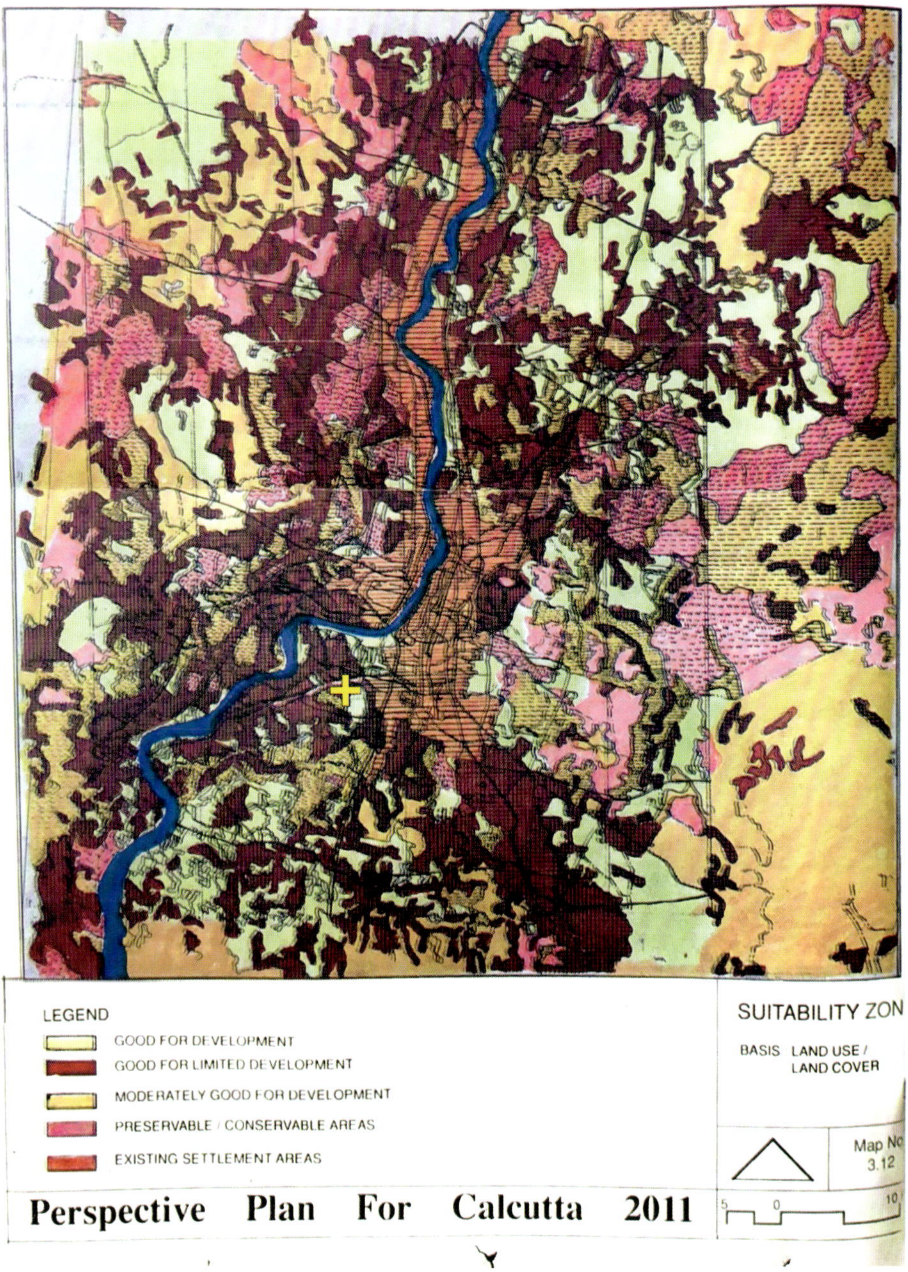
LEGEND
GOOD FOR DEVELOPMENT
GOOD FOR LIMITED DEVELOPMENT
MODERATELY GOOD FOR DEVELOPMENT
PRESERVABLE / CONSERVABLE AREAS
EXISTING SETTLEMENT AREAS
SUITABILITY ZON
BASIS: LAND USE / LAND COVER
Map No
3.12
Perspective Plan For Calcutta 2011
5
0
10

The urban land use and suitability zone maps can be read another way. I do not see the future "green belt," as seen by the data scientists, or the "chunks" of potential, urban real estate property, as seen by the planners. Rather, learning from my land cover maps from the previous section, I see temporal patterns. The suitability zone map shows a continuous field of color, and the patterning of the color fields points to the possibilities of more fully understanding how the settled-rural "uniquely accepts" (Cairns, 2018) urbanization, which itself has varying temporal intensities of population density that may or may not be predicted. The fully colored maps allow me to imagine a space where in more-autonomous municipalities might be thought of as actively shaping just, ordinary periurban form. While I do not necessarily agree with the classification values created by the land use map-makers, the map itself points toward a possible temporal-spatial image—a hybrid patterning that changes over time—one that is different than say the ominous, darkly rendered "figure" of the urban sprawl map.

Invented Shading

Typically, the areas located within land cover and land use boundaries on a map are rendered with aerial imagery or unbroken fields of color mixed with hatches. In this study I have chosen a different graphic technique, what I consider as "invented shading." Within cartography, my interpretation of invented shading sits somewhere in between a land use hatch and terrain representations. Before I begin my introduction to the technique I must extend my discussion on the 1991 sprawl study of Kolkata through the lens of density.

As noted in chapter 1, the 1991 sprawl study assisted the 2011 perspective plan authors in constructing the problem of the Calcutta Metropolitan District as "full," and the task of the plan was to discern which parts of Calcutta Metropolitan Region could absorb "over-spilled or surplus population" (1990, p. 91). Problems of extreme congestion and sprawl are also problems of density which is defined in the plan as "an index to measure the degree of concentration of population in a given land area and therefore indicate the intensity of pressure on land" (1990, p. 99). It is "expected to throw light on whether or not within any area land is underutilized or over utilized on a comparative basis" (1990, p. 99). At the time of writing the 2011 perspective plan, the demographic projection for the Calcutta Metropolitan District was an additional eight million people by 2011, and the planners' goal was to figure out where to put them.[11]

Geographer Colin McFarlane (2015, p. 630) argues that "density is a political problem" and has no necessary pregiven geography. He notes that the history of urbanism is, in significant part, a history of a "maelstrom of politicized densities: [with] overcrowding, illness, pollution, congestion as the familiar villains of the piece; [and] planning, regulation, infrastructure, services, housing, decongestion incentives, and public space so often cast as the remedies." In the case of the 2011 plan, the solution to a population density problem was communicated as a cartographic puzzle of siting multiple dots connected by lines of movement. Such an urban model meant that everything else was "off the map." However, as McFarlane (2016, p. 630) points out, density cannot be conceived of or acted upon in and of itself, because it is always in a relation to other issues, spaces, and actors. That is, density emerges not just as a topographical, linear, or numerical problem, but as a topological problem connecting multiple concerns and spaces in ways that have consequences for other spaces, some planned and some unplanned (2016, p. 631). There are thus, "multiple spatialities of density," including relational (translocal, human and nonhuman, and connection between physical and digital densities), volumetric (from vertical multistory densities to dense underground networks), as well as experiential, and perceptual dimensions (McFarlane, 2016, p. 632). My visual materials aim to account for these other spatialities, particularly those that come from participants' accounts of the settled-rural. Building on this intention, my invented shading is comprised of three graphic steps.

First, learning from design research traditions in visual description from architecture and landscape architecture, I sought to represent the "facts of everyday life through its visible ordinariness" (Pousin, 2003; Venturi et al., 1972). As Pousin notes, there are functions of visual description: the "creation of data and, hence, the construction of 'objectivity'; the diffusion of information and knowledge; and the creation of tools for design" (2003, p. 167). I selected illustrative photographs from my fieldwork archive, pulling out those that most clearly represent the characteristics of my found land cover patches. Second, I then translated the characteristics into data, by tracing and interpreting the visual information within the photograph (see Figure 3.07). Third, I assign the data into the patch boundaries and I use these graphic elements in my maps in chapters 4, 5, and 6.

Like a hatch, my invented shading is a simplification and a reduction. However, unlike a hatch, the intention is not to standardize but to practice mapping in a way that is open-ended and flexible. My "working objects" are created using basic design skills and software. I describe my drawing process here so that others might borrow and enlarge it. In addition, unlike

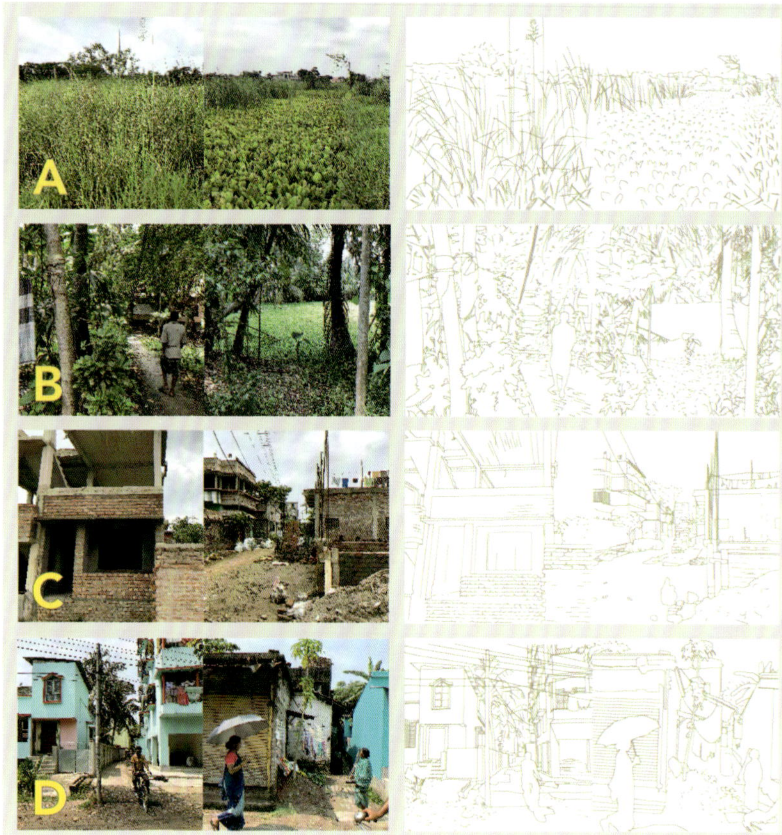

Figure 3.07. Tracing of selected illustrative photographs from my fieldwork archive, pulling out those that most clearly represent ordinary characteristics of periurban phenomena.
A. Predominantly "jungly" paddy fields
B. Tree-lined ponds, plantations, and gardens with scattered buildings
C. Predominantly densely built-up buildings with some "jungly" paddy fields
D. Densely built-up buildings also with tree-lined ponds, plantations, and gardens

(Source: author, 2020).

the rendering of "relief," my goal is not to express terrain "scientifically" (see Imhof, 1982). I create a hatch pattern that expresses the illusion of volume and depth in another way. Similar to traditions in Kantha embroidery, which is an art form in Bengal (Ghosh, 2020), my use of repetition in the hatch pattern suggests the "range of encounters" surrounding households over time (2020, pp. 93-94). Furthermore, the shaded patch map is inter-referenced with the final re-rendering technique, that of the transect.

Transect

Along with my research assistants, I regularly walked Ward 13 to casually observe, systematically audit the area and its built landscape, and to conduct interviews. This walking practice also included three intentional journeys for the purposes of methodical photographic documentation of the study area (see Figure 3.08). The intentional journeys, or three half-kilometer transects, serve two purposes. First, I extend the satellite-sensed register of land cover that emphasizes a continuous surface in a temporal snapshot of a shifting mosaic. In my approach, continuous surfaces are also assumed to have volume and depth in various ways—to be the spatialized surface evidence of deeper systems, and the product of processes over time.[12] Thus, like my invented shading technique, the transects further communicate the types of settlement patterns, land use logics, and landscape "densities" of the study area. For instance, the transect allows me to point out volumetric elements like "jungle," ponds, and gardens, which are often masked by remotely sensed tree canopies, as well as waterlogged, low-lying fields, which have a subtle but important vertical dimension. The transect also allows me to use my body as a sensing device to capture the heterogeneous volumetric densities of people, vehicles, sounds, smells, air, and light.

Second, I seek to address the political aspects of vertical and perspective representations of periurban Kolkata. In writing about the concept of "suburb" in Calcutta/Kolkata since the late 1800s, architecture historian Swati Chattopadhyay (2009, p. 10) observes three phases. The first two phases, which began after 1945, arrived with the advent of "township visions" (2009, p. 13). In these two phases, she points out that separation of the elite from ordinary spaces was "neither the primary objective, nor the outcome." In the current phase of "selling suburbia," the elite seek to isolate themselves from the non-elite. Perspectival visualizations of master-planned real-estate developments in the second phase are carefully chosen to avoid appearing like the "Bengal countryside" (2009, p. 16). If occasional reference is made

C
A
B
1 km

to the Bengal countryside, she says, it is always in a gesture of "superseding its 'deficiencies,'" even though, as historian William Glover (2012) shows, village community is central to planned township visions in India. That is, town planning schemes often recuperate key features of an "older imagined village milieu," promising to "nurture 'inherited tendencies and habits' in first-generation urban migrants, rather than produce wholly new modes of urban subjectivity" (2012, p. 108). In these instances, periurban landscapes and societies are either rendered invisible or commodified.

Furthermore, as Chattopadhyay observes (2009, p. 16), the visualizations that sell suburbia are almost all borrowed, being copied from fairly generic images of "Western-style suburban and park landscapes." Such carefully selected, "generic" imagery differs from the ethos of earlier thought about designed settlements in India. This ethos advocated climate sensitive buildings and midrise, high-density urban form that invokes the formal vocabulary of "Indian vernacular architecture in a modern idiom," she says (2009, p. 16).[13] In relation to this book, the visual documentation of the transect aims to open up this impasse by highlighting periurban areas as coproduced by entangled urban and agrarian transformations. I highlight my case study area: (A) where it "appears like the Bengal countryside"; which is threaded with (B) "colony" developments where most newcomers reside; and (C) the local main road, where all residents mix. I render all three transects equally and discuss them as interacting.

Figure 3.08. Map showing "patched" invented shading, participant residents (yellow symbols) and three, half kilometer transect walks.
A. Half kilometer transect walk in wooded, settled area with buildings, tree-lined ponds, plantations, and bagans (gardens).
B. Half kilometer transect walk encompassing a "colony" and former paddy fields.
C. Half kilometer transect walk encompassing the local, main road.
In Chapters 4, 5, and 6 elements of this map and Figure 3.01 are recombined to describe distinct characteristics.

(Source: author and Google Earth Pro, 2020).

Importantly for this study, the three transects are not indexed to a gradient, as is often the case in the technique: that is, they express variations in space rather than variations of an ideal such as a continuum from rural to urban (see Duany & Talen, 2002). Each transect is a journey comprised of many small images. Using my iPhone camera I took up to ten photos for each increment: I captured the ground I stood on, then the horizon, and then tilted vertically up to the sky. If a person or car crossed my screen, I accepted them as part of the scene.[14] By moving my body with my camera I systematically and selectively documented my intentional walk. This method can be thought of as a type of vertical tilt scan, as divergent but not dissimilar from the scan of the satellite sensor (see Marshall, 2014) or a movie camera (see McGrath & Gardner, 2007). Later, in studying the visual data, and unlike the scan of the satellite sensor, I was reminded of the sensory aspects of the ward, which I enfold into my description of each transect below. In addition, I express these sensory qualities through the repetition of images, as expanded details of treed canopy, building, or sky that are layered behind the horizontal array of tilt-scans.

The first transect is of a wooded, settled area (see A in Figure 3.07 and Figure 3.08). It incorporates many long-term residents' households, which are comprised of buildings, tree-lined ponds, gardens of useful plants (referred to locally as a *bagan* or, in agroforestry scholarship, as a "homegarden"),[15] and groves of economically valuable trees (referred to locally as a "plantation" and in forestry terms as "social forestry").[16] These types of "wooded" spaces are characterized by buildings dispersed in a variety of scattered and clustered arrangements, usually very shady and interspersed with water bodies and narrow pathway roads.[17] In this section, I point out these landscape conditions as distinct in order to explain my terms, whereas in reality the boundaries between buildings and bagans, and bagans and plantations, and plantations and tree-lined ponds is indistinct. I have also shown these landscape characteristics as distinct in the invented shading section above in this chapter. These landscape characteristics are typical of other wooded, settled areas in Ward 13 and beyond.

The top visual sequence in Figure 3.09 incorporates a grouping of households surrounded by dilapidated, untended ponds including a field of water hyacinth (A). These ponds are atypical in relation to the traditional setup, as the trees on the pond bunds have been removed due to water-related "drowning." As is typical, useful and decorative plants are evident, including banana, coconut palms, and a climbing hibiscus (B). Painted symbols representing political parties are evident on buildings and boundary walls (C). Also captured in this visual transect is a clubhouse, here a small building with a blue door is evident with several men chatting outside (D). The painted symbols and the clubhouse express the everyday presence of party politics deep in the locality.

In the second row, the images document the more usual house garden condition, which is well tended, tree-lined ponds, seen in the near distance as a bright green, watery surface (E). The buildings in such wooded, settled areas tend to be hybrids of more traditional features, including tiled roofs and a courtyard space, along with the newer features of added rooms, walls, and outbuildings, usually built in brick or concrete (F). These settled conditions with plantations and bagans are cut across by a residual rivulet or creek, the landscape quality of which is documented visually in the third row of images (G). The rivulet supports dense water plants and is lined with trees and other useful plants. The rivulet is intermixed with other uses, including domestic shrines and laundry, as well as the pathways that cross it (H). The pathways are built up and effectively transform this creek into a string of informally zoned areas (or ponds), which overflow and join together to drain the area in the rainy season. In the bottom row, the transect journeys off the paved pathway road and documents the more unusual feature of a private plantation with a fallow bagan (surrounded by an old bamboo fence) (I). Paddy fields and "colony" plots can be seen in the far distance (J).

The second transect (see Figure 3.10) seeks to express the quality and character of emerging settlements or colonies within areas of former paddy fields. The transect incorporates a new road constructed for access into the colony. In the top row of the illustrated transect, the intersection between the colony road and the wider, local road can be seen (A). Colony development does not always stand spatially apart from older development and this is captured here with the transect passing a homestead of a long-term resident family. Their property includes a large and well-tended, tree-lined pond (B) and a bagan embedded within a plantation (C). The remainder of the transect then follows the unpaved colony road until it terminates. Former paddy fields can be seen as areas overrun with tall grasses and water plants (D). In between the grassy areas are newly constructed, single and multistory buildings (E), buildings that are under construction and plots that are marked with small boundary walls (F). The colony has few mature trees or house gardens, and no ponds.

The third row of visual documentation of the colony transect shows roads leading toward more colony plots in the middle distance (G, H, I). An extended area of jungly, waterlogged, formerly cultivated paddy field is documented in the bottom row (J). The transect terminates at the most remote house in the colony, which is surrounded by a field of water hyacinth.

Figure 3.09. Visual documentation of the half kilometer, transect walk encompassing a wooded, settled area with buildings, tree-lined ponds, plantations, and bagans.
A. Untended pond
B. Decorative and useful plants
C. Signage
D. Clubhouse
E. Tended pond
F. Households with plantations and bagans
G. Rivulet
H. Large plantation
I. Wooded-settled boundary (in distance)

(Source: author, 2020.)

F

I
J

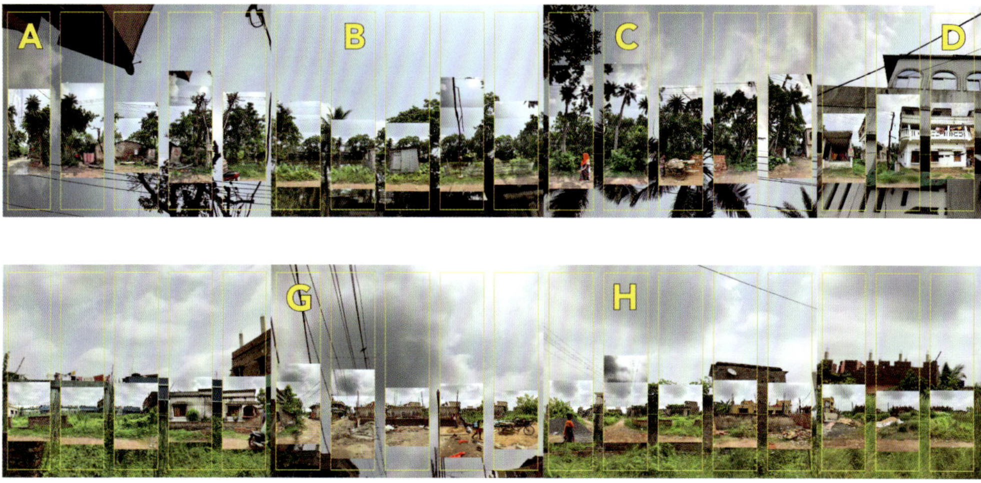

Figure 3.10. Visual documentation of the half kilometer transect walk encompassing a "colony" and former paddy fields.

A. Local, main road
B. Tended pond
C. Plantation
D. Former paddy fields
E. Colony buildings
F. Boundary wall around a plot
G. Secondary colony road
H. Secondary colony road
I. Secondary colony road
J. "Jungly" former paddy fields
K. Wooded, settled area (in distance)

(Source: author, 2020.)

E
F

J
K

Figure 3.11. Visual documentation of the half kilometer transect walk encompassing the local, main road.
A. Multi-story apartment building
B. Walled bungalow also termed, bagan-bari (farmhouse)
C. Long, tall wall with locked gate
D. Tea shop
E. Plantation
F. Carpentry shop
G. Construction company
H. "Sweets" shop

(Source: author, 2020.)

D
E

H

In the far distance, the wooded, settled area shown in Figure 3.09 can also be seen (K).[18]

The third transect encompassing the local main road (see Figure 3.11) is typical of many periurban areas; such roads are ribbons of urbanized development, lined with a mix of residential buildings and storefront enterprises, interspersed with often walled-in, tree-lined ponds, plantations, and bagans. They often back onto either residual rural or field conditions, or hybrid field/colony conditions. In this transect, for example, multistory apartment buildings are visible (A), evidence of the higher land value along such local main roads. Evidence of a mix of old and new land uses can be seen in a well-tended, walled bungalow (*bagan-bari* or farmhouse) (B) adjacent to an unusually large plot of land with a high, painted wall with a large, formal gate (C).

In the second row, a grouping of modest enterprises and wooded elements is evident, including a tea shop (D) adjacent to a plantation (E). A similar grouping is repeated farther along in the transect. In the third row of the visual documentation, a modest carpentry shop is evident (F), as well as a bright blue building, branded as a construction company (G). Such enterprises, linked with the construction aspect of periurbanization, are typical of local main roads and serve the colony developments in the locality.

In the bottom row of the visual documentation, a modest "sweets shop" with a red awning is captured (H). This is a local landmark and serves as a stop-off point and transit hub for "autos" (three-wheeled, motorized rickshaws). In the mornings and evenings this local main road is busy with people shopping and commuting, congested with mobile street vendors, noisy with many car horns, with assorted vehicles, and covered with associated dust. The road serves not only the locality, it is also a local route to a nearby clothing manufacturing area called Chatta Bazar, and the secondary road to a high-rise, residential enclave development called Greenfield City. On weekdays and weekends this road is thus additionally used both by trucks loaded with blue jeans and upmarket, private cars.

While the visual documentation of the transects is intended to communicate the differences between three types of landscapes in the case study area, the assembled visual register also acts as a reminder of my nonvisual impressions, made through slowly walking and documenting each transect. That is, I recall how all three landscapes are lived in everyday life through residents' mobility. The wooded settlements and newer colony areas are quiet, compared to the local, main road. Daily, these household areas are quickly emptied of their (mainly male) commuter-worker residents who journey to Budge Budge Trunk Road by bicycle, or on foot along the local main road. Most of the wooded settlements, and even some of the newer colonies, are only accessible by paths that are only possible for foot, bicycle, or at most, motorbike traffic. During the day, household areas in both the wooded settlements and newer colony areas are mainly the preserve of stay-at-home women (see Figure 3.12). They care for small children and elderly family members, shop, cook and clean, and do paid home-based work of various kinds.

Cooking for a family is a time-consuming occupation, for Bengali "taste" has been documented as romanticizing a " 'tradition' of plenty, pure and home-cooked food" (Ray, 2009, p. 61). A typical meal consists of a combination of dishes including salad, rice and/or chapati, dhal, a vegetable dish, a fish dish, and a meat dish, if desired. The routines, sounds, and aromas of Ward 13 during the day are a testament to this labor: the local morning market trip, cooking and serving, washing pots and clothes, cooking and serving, nap, bathing, a change of clothes from housedress to sari, chatting and strolling, early evening market, cooking and serving, and to sleep.[19] As well as looking after children, putting them to bed, dressing them, getting them off to school, etc. Thus, most women also journey to the local main road and back home, routinely.

Conclusion

In this chapter, I have introduced the visual materials and graphic elements that organize my cartographic practice for re-rendering the study area. In my mapping kit I use cropping, symbols, boundaries, and invented shading as well as transects and illustrative photographs. Visual ethnography uses audiovisual media and methods as "a medium through which knowledge is produced" (Pink, 2006, p. 16) "throughout its processes of research, analysis and representation" and usually entails understanding "sets of materials in relation to each other" (Pink, 2008, p. 2). Thus, while the visual materials introduced in this chapter are thought of as a set or kit, it is not assumed that they create a whole. Together they form a scaffold for researching with people, words, and images to express the variety of "kinds of urban" that exist at present or might exist in future.

Both critical cartography and visual methods afford an understanding of incremental periurbanization. My re-rendering of the one-kilometer-square study area through the lenses of my household conversations seeks to animate incremental and diffuse characteristics in a multifaceted way. This is difficult to represent and narrate. Pink (2004, p. 9) expressed this thought too. While "situating visual research," she says, we "should not stop writing."

But perhaps, she says, "some problems we face when we write linear texts with words as our only tool can be resolved by thinking of ethnographic knowledge and its representations as not solely verbal but also visual and not simply linear but multilinear." Chapters 4, 5, and 6 can thus be read in this spirit. They are written as sequential but they can also be thought of as side by side, like heterogenous neighbors. After all, households often transform alone, some along one trajectory of change, while the others work hard to stay the same; some become dilapidated, and others move on.

Figure 3.12. Image of stay-at-home women. They are wearing "housedresses" or work-clothes and talking together in a pathway road. The small ramp in the front step of the house is for a bicycle, which is stored inside the dwelling.

(Source: author, 2018.)

Endnotes

1 My fieldwork co-researchers are Dipanwita Manna and Swastika Bhattacharya, who both graduated from the Department of Geography, University of Calcutta. The fieldwork recordings were transcribed by Mandalika Sanyal.

2 The study focuses on topological notions of power and scale as described in the Introduction.

3 This term was used by an examiner in my PhD defense.

4 The idea of urban landscape is based on "an aesthetic attitude as well as on an aloofness toward the city, and this is very different from the notion of urban landscape as constituted by the presence of nature in the town" (Pousin, 2003, p. 163).

5 A minimum patch size is also defined. The tracing of the imagery was carried out by the author using the graphic software Adobe Illustrator and by using a simplified version of a more comprehensive method that employs GIS (see Marshall et al., 2020). I only marked a boundary where the mix of abundance shifted from a predominance of one or more land cover to another predominance of one or more land cover. The simplified version employed in this study demonstrates that a relatively fast and low-skilled method of drawing patches can create valuable data. Another way to map patches, not explored here, is a highly skilled and comprehensive quantitative study using GIS and higher resolution, proprietary imagery (see Zhou et al., 2014).

6 The technique of patch mapping discussed here arose from the following question: "What are the links between the amount and distribution of various elements of urban form and ecological and social processes?" (Marshall et al., 2020, p. 2). To address this question, depictions of urban form based on land use were seen as inadequate and a different conception was required (see Cadenasso et al., 2007).

7 "Human ecology mapping" methods for ecosystem-based management and planning, and for scientists designing socioecological research include tenure and resource use, local ecological knowledge, and sense of place (McLain et al., 2013, p. 651).

8 In some cases, that deduction may be correct, while in other cases it may be incorrect, so that the deduction demands empirical testing (Marshall et al., 2020, p. 3).

9 Google Earth is a computer program that renders a 3D representation of Earth based primarily on satellite imagery. Sourced from a variety of satellite companies, these images are combined into a mosaic of images taken over many days, months, and years. The collected imagery is then displayed as one blended image, which is what is seen on Google Earth. While Google Earth automatically displays

current imagery, it is also possible to save high-resolution images of historical imagery. The two images shown here were downloaded from Google Earth Pro for 2004 and 2018 as they were, relatively, the clearest images selected from many imperfect others.

10 Studies were done for Kolkata, Mumbai, and Ahmedabad.

11 For instance, the plan estimates that the Calcutta Metropolitan District can "absorb" not more than two million people because Calcutta and Howrah are said to be "already saturated" (1990, p. 92). Thus, it is reasoned there will be an "overspill" of six million people to be settled in "areas outside Calcutta Metropolitan District and preferably within the Inner Metropolitan Region" (1990, p. 93). In addition to the proposed development of new settlements outside the Calcutta Metropolitan District, the *2011 Plan* proposed a set of "density zones" to signal the intention to limit settlement within the Calcutta Metropolitan District.

12 In urban ecology scholarship, volume has been thought of in relation to patch boundaries and fluxes among and within patches (Cadenasso, Pickett, & Jones, 2003; Cadenasso, Pickett, Weathers, et al., 2003; Pickett & Rogers, 1997).

13 Chattopadhyay (2009, p. 16) points out that the architectural ethos of the 1970s and 1980s, represented by the work of Charles Correa, Lawrie Baker, Balkrishna Doshi, Raj Rewal and others, was to a large degree a reaction against the midcentury International Style, and championed innovative solutions in terms of materials and building *parti* (an organizing thought or decision behind an architect's design).

14 Some images of residents have been edited or blurred for privacy reasons.

15 Homegardens have been defined by Chakravarty (2017) as a practice of deliberate mixing of field crops, herbs, and shrubs with trees and livestock within the compound of a house. They create a "forest-like, multi-story canopy" on "land marginal to field production" and with "labor marginal to major household economic activities" (Chakravarty et al., 2017, p. 517).

16 Plantations are further discussed later, when I examine local logging practices.

17 To avoid listing buildings, tree-lined ponds, plantations, and bagans too often, I also group all of these elements together as a "wooded, settled area" or as an area with long-term residents' households and bagans.

18 Although there are no streetlights in these images, they were installed shortly after the transect was documented.

19 All three transects were walked on the same day, and during the afternoon naptime. This is why many shops are closed and there are fewer people in the photographs than at other times of the day.

4/

FROM THE HOUSEHOLD

In the previous chapters, I have focused on the graphic entities and spatial imaginations of planning for periurbanization in municipal Maheshtala, metropolitan Kolkata, and the extended Kolkata region. A range of cartographic languages were encountered, giving expression to various settlement propositions; and resulting in a fragmented set of competing, spatial imaginations backed up by piecemeal practices of municipal governance. Throughout the presentation of those official maps I marked out the one-kilometer-square study area within Ward 13, the specific focus of my detailed case study of situated periurbanization. In many of the maps, especially those representing nodes of settlement or major transport networks, the study area is merely a blank spot: neither a settlement node nor part of the planned-for integrated, urban mobility system. The study area is not only on the edge of Kolkata but off the informational maps intended to represent the extended metropolitan area, now and in the future. More troubling are indexical representations that bridge urban and rural, but contain no spatial strategies whatsoever. In other maps that show continuous coverage conditions, certain aspects of the study area's character are represented, although often in un-nuanced fields of color representing land use or population density.

Going closer, at the ward level there is, unsurprisingly, a formal cartographic accounting of the area's land use attributes, as I shall show. What is revealed is that the agrarian character of periurban areas is almost entirely missing in the predominantly urban imagination of these plans, preoccupied as they are with finding space (often former agricultural land) for "overspill" urban population or yet-to-be-realized, infrastructure-led urban development. In this and the following three chapters, the intent is to push past the representational blind spots of this envisioning, in order to document and give alternative visual and spatial expression to the particular characteristics that comprises the case study area within Ward 13 of Maheshtala Municipality. Central to this is the (inherited and emergent) materiality of certain agrarian characteristics, namely drainage, what is practiced as village "property," and an emplaced land market. My alternative rendering seeks to reterritorialize the landscape and point toward the kinds of futures that drawings make possible. In my stories and maps, I animate the temporalities of interlinked, agrarian and urban change. As I shall show, not only is a hybrid and nonteleological "kind of urban" emerging in periurban Kolkata but the amicable politics of change within this ordinary "kind of becoming" is at stake. The futures that my drawings make possible speak to these findings.

"Vacant" Land?

The Ward 13 map in Maheshtala Municipality's third development plan is densely detailed (see Figure 4.01).[1] In that map, Ward 13 is shown to have a large part of its area taken up by residential land use (A). This land use also features many scattered "water bodies," "slum regions," as well as a road and pathway network. Located to the north is an industrial area and below that is a small commercial strip. The depiction of the ward also clearly marks its many "community facilities," which are mainly *mandirs* (Hindu temples). There are no "dedicated open spaces" in the ward although there are two, almost impossible to discern, "public and semi-public areas," located in the middle of the ward and on its southern boundary. The remainder of the map is represented as white space, so-called "vacant land" (B), which is privately owned land either in use as fallow paddy field or former paddy field now sold and plotted for colony development. Basically, in the categorical imagination of this official map, vacant means an area that lacks urban infrastructure and so is available for future urban development. This representational convention is consistent with other official maps provided by the municipality (shown in chapter 3), where the same land is classified as being without purposeful use, as "marshy/swampy" or "open space."

When these same spaces are viewed through other representational tools, another story is told. In what follows, I re-render the residential and vacant areas of the municipal map of Ward 13 by drawing on in-depth, and on occasion, repeated, informal interviews with a nonrepresentative sample of consenting households. Such household accounts were solicited in order to

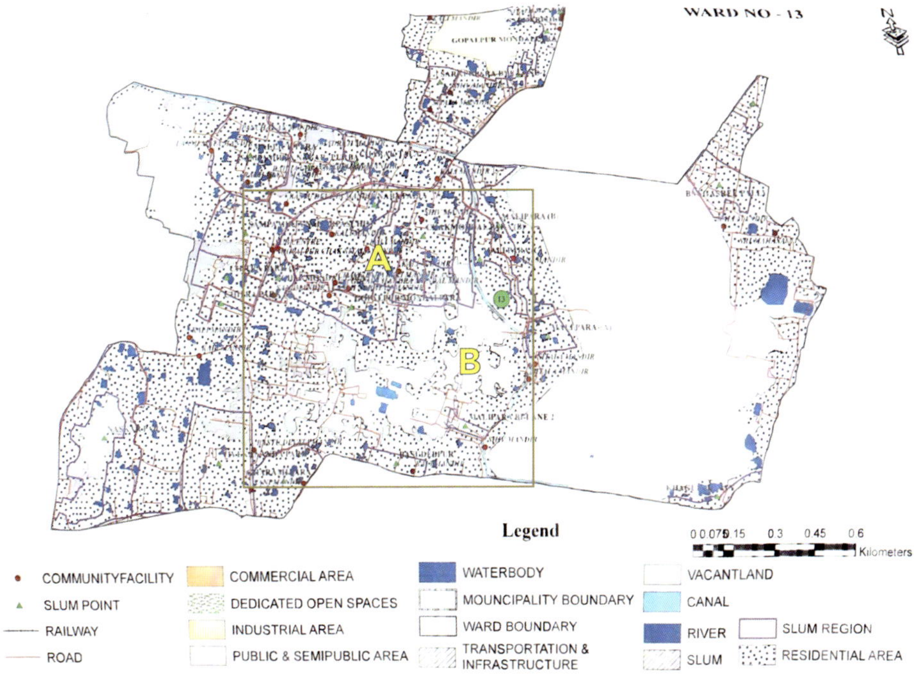

Figure 4.01. Official map and legend showing land use for Ward 13, Maheshtala Municipality. Also shown, as an overlay, is the Ward 13 study area (brown square).
A. Residential land use
B. "Vacant" land use

(Source: Maheshtala Municipality, 2012. *Draft Development Plan: 2012-2017, Second Generation*, Ward No. 13.

generate an understanding of land and life in the tradition of environmental history. McNiell (2003, p. 42) defines environmental history as that which "pleads for recognition that nature not only exists, but changes." Moreover, it changes "both of its own accord and on account of human actions, and in so doing changes the context in which human history unfolds" (2003, p. 42). When such land and life histories are built from the recollections of those living today, they necessarily cover a relatively short temporal frame—the frame of direct living or indirect, handed-down memory. Batterbury (1999, p. 171) argues that this temporal frame is particularly useful for "identifying those forces driving contemporary environmental transformation and land degradation." Moreover, land and life accounts such as this can allow voices that are underrepresented in official records and processes to have a say (Berg, 1995, p. 171; see also Fairhead & Leach, 1996). Certainly, the residents of Ward 13 I spoke with had never had their lives, thoughts, or their land experiences recorded or represented before.[2]

What was learnt from these interviews was diagrammed and mapped. The conversations not only open ed up a discussion of what constitutes a resident but they also disaggregated the residential and vacant categories shown in the official Ward 13 land use map. Both categories are relevant to this study. Foremost, I include nonhumans and their diverse agencies as part of what constitutes the element of resident. Second, not all human residents are the same, as it is meaningful to speak of long-term residents and newcomer residents. Figure 4.02 expresses this distinction between human residents visually and it is useful to pause around the graphic elements of this diagram. In what follows, I describe the diagram and what this visual documentation of household conversations communicates.

First, the diagram shows comparative long duration of generational occupancy (A), which extends from 1850 to 2020, and mid-duration residency, which emphasizes from 1990 to 2020 (B), with time indicated on the horizontal axis. The temporal reach of the horizontal axis extends sufficiently across time to capture how thirty-seven households spoke about their time in the locality. The white-toned area on the left highlights the time period before the establishment of Maheshtala Municipality (C) and the time period after the formation of the municipality is represented in a light brown tone (D). Each bar on the vertical axis represents a household who participated in the study. These are organized with the longest-term residents at the top of the diagram and the newest newcomer residents located at the bottom. Household stories do not only extend across time, but indicate different phases of occupation and action, coded by color into the household bar. The threshold between long-term and newcomer residents can be seen as the temporal space in-between the group of residents who arrived before the 1960s and those who began arriving after the mid-1990s .

In a broad view, what the timeline shows is that the families of long-term residents who participated in the study had been moving into the area since the 1850s, and that most were originally engaged in paddy cultivation. These long-term residents owned paddy fields (represented by the bright green lines) and built mud houses (represented by brown lines) at first, but most also subsequently built concrete houses (marked by a change from a brown to a red bar). Most long-term residents also related stories of how they had either sold their paddy land (marked by a green bar terminating) or stopped cultivation on it (marked by a change from a bright green to light green bar). Most newcomers (arriving since the mid-1990s) had built concrete houses (red bar) from the start, and most often on plotted land (marked by a change from a light green to a red bar). Several newcomers had subsequently bought more plotted land (marked by a new light green bar above a red bar). The ward also has tenants (dark red bars), and of those tenants we spoke to, all were newcomer residents.

A goal of this diagram is to capture and communicate something of the nonteleological nature and pace of change in the case study area. That is, to show that there are multiple temporalities of interlinked agrarian and urban change in space and time. Each bar tells a story of rural to post-rural, periurban change, each with nuanced differences reflecting, for instance, the variety of ways households are shifting livelihoods out of agriculture or in other instances, the ways newcomers are moving into the ward. In some cases, long-term residents did not own the land but were sharecroppers who cultivated others' land and retained a share of the crops produced. Similarly, some long-term residents did not upgrade their homes with concrete rebuilding, preferring to, or needing to, remain living in mud houses. Some sold their paddy land to developers, others continue to own paddy land even when they do not cultivate it. The newcomer resident stories are similarly diverse. Some bought already surveyed and plotted land that was formerly paddy and built immediately. But some bought land but did not build a house until many years later, making them landowners, but with no intention of cultivating their land. Finally, some long-term and newcomer residents have built concrete houses and then bought even more land in the locality with a view to plotting it out to sell for colony housing. The long-term residents doing this tended to leave the land undeveloped and fallow, but one newcomer resident cultivated his speculatively purchased plot as a temporary "hobby" garden (shown later in Figure 6.13).

Another way to see further into the nuance of the land use category of residential is to compare long-term and newcomer households, based on

Figure 4.02. Linear timeline showing how long the residents interviewed in this study had lived in Ward 13. The timeline is also a representation of changes in housing material and paddy field or fallow/plotted field use and ownership over time. Newcomer tenants residing in concrete houses are also differentiated. There are approximately 875 households in the one-kilometer-square Ward 13 study area. I engaged in repeated conversations with 18 long-term resident households and 18 newcomer resident households, a total of 36 households. The sample is not representative of all residents across the Ward. As geographer Nora Fagerholm (2014, p. 161) notes, participatory research by its very nature "cannot involve all people with an interest in an area". The participation of a household group was determined by an intention to conduct semi-structured and object-led interviews with a range of ages, occupations, and gender. The goal was not a comprehensive account reflecting the Ward's whole population as a statistical sample might. Rather, I sought participants across the study area who were willing and able to engage repeatedly and deeply with the research. I have, then, in-depth, but necessarily partial, accounts of life and land in Ward 13.

(Source: author, 2020.)

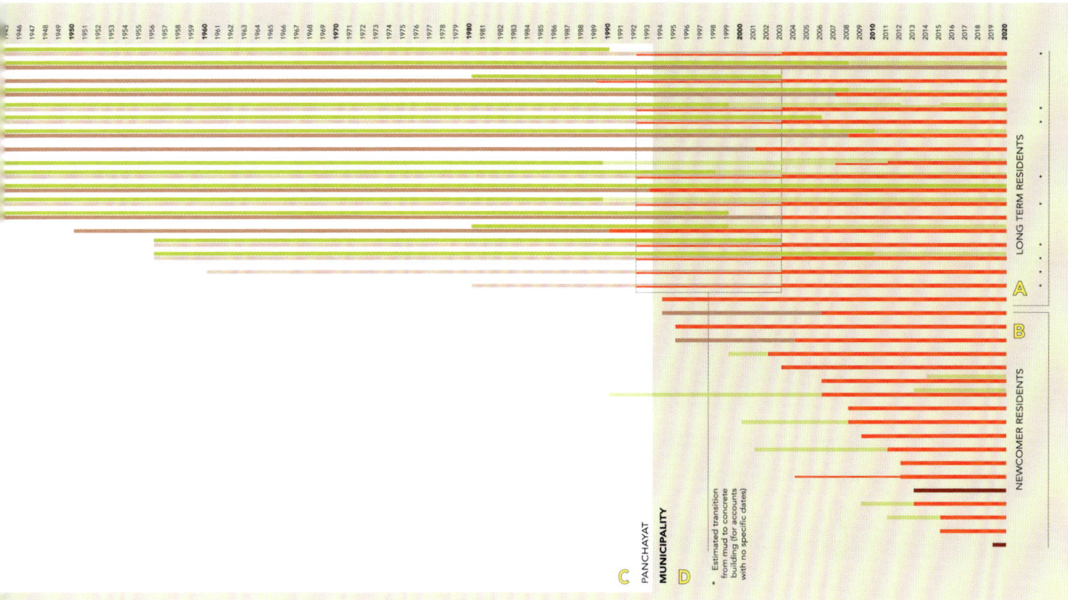
LONG TERM RESIDENTS
NEWCOMER RESIDENTS
A
B
C
PANCHAYAT
MUNICIPALITY
D
• Estimated transition from mud to concrete building (for accounts with no specific dates)

the household interviews conducted. The "ancestors" (a local term that refers to the male family line) of long-term residents were usually either tenant farmers or sharecroppers, or some combination, although most often they reported that their household also included a waged salary earner. In other words, the long-term ancestors of contemporary long-term residents were typically mixed income (agrarian and wage income), even prior to the cessation of paddy cultivation. In contrast, the newcomer household interviewed did not have agrarian ancestry, but prior to moving to Ward 13, had lived in government quarters or in rented tenancies in towns or cities. Thus, unlike long-term resident households, for the newcomers interviewed, residing in a self-owned house on self-owned land was a first-time experience.

The divergent household histories are also reflected in the amount of land these respective household groups own. For instance, long-term resident households retain between five *kotha* (0.8 acre or 335 square meters) to four *bighas* (1.3 acre or 5,351 square meters) of land, whereas newcomer households typically occupy a much smaller "plotted" lot, at an average of around two kotha (0.3 acre or 134 square meters). This variation is because the majority of long-term residents own the land on which their houses are built, with some additional land such as garden land (with or without a pond) and or paddy land. This additional land is sometimes contiguous with house land, but more often it is a separate parcel of land located nearby. While some newcomer resident households have a courtyard garden, boundary garden, garden land, or a separate plot of speculatively owned "vacant" land, most only have land with a building that covers almost the entire property. Importantly, long-term residents who have more land are not necessarily more prosperous than their newcomer counterparts. The household incomes of long-term residents are rarely mixed agriculture and wage incomes: incomes from agricultural production are a rarity, with most incomes coming from a mix of sources, some quite precarious, including pensions, tutoring, food stalls, driving, daily wage work, and salaried work. In contrast, newcomers generally have higher and more stable incomes, the majority sourced either from pensions (for the retiree) or salary work.

Another difference is household size. Long-term households are larger, with many multigenerational households. The largest such household interviewed comprised some twenty-two persons. Newcomer households typically follow a smaller nuclear family structure, the largest interviewed being only seven persons. So, although long-term household income may at times be greater than that of newcomer households, this income often needs to stretch further. Lastly, the differences between long-term and newcomer households also has a distinct spatial patterning. All of the long-term residents interviewed, except one, live in "village" areas with gardens, plantations, and ponds. Most newcomer residents live in former paddy areas that are being converted into colonies.

In what follows, I extended my household conversations. I tell household stories that are read through periurban settlement patterns, norms, and institutions. The stories are not only thought of in a linear way—as describing one incremental change after the other—but they are also thought of as equal, and side-by-side, as related temporalities of periurban change that are coproduced or "becoming with" the other. By pausing around this multidimensional geography, I resist reproducing a dominant teleology of rural to urban transition. Rather, I bring into view the conditions of living with, and in, a faltering and incremental condition of rural-urban transformation. As noted in the introduction, the ordinary area being investigated is a condition where there is no singular big conflict, where power, understood topologically and with nonhumans and their diverse agencies in mind, is diffuse. My interest is in representing the variety of relevant socio-spatial-ecological expressions of slow and incremental change. I begin by looking at stories about the drainage works and the related, paddy field cultivation practices.

Water Ecologies

Ward 13 and its surrounding area are crisscrossed by an interconnected network of canals, now called the New Manikhali Canal System (Figure 4.03). That system flows toward the Bhagirathi-Hooghly River with an outlet near Akra Dutta Bagan of Ward 7, Maheshtala Municipality. Two parts of that canal network cross the study area—the *Begorekhal* or Begore Canal (A), which flows from south to north, and a second east-west running canal called the Manikhali (B). These interconnected canals are managed by the Irrigation and Waterways Department, Government of West Bengal, although the entire New Manikhali Canal System is a recent renovation by the Kolkata Environment Improvement Trust of a drainage canal that was originally built by the British in the early 1900s as part of the 1891-1906 Suburban Sewerage Scheme, undertaken for the southward extension of Kolkata (Dasgupta, 2004, p. 16) (see Figure 4.04). While Ward 13 was not part of the suburban expansion of the 1900s, the Manikhali Canal System reduced waterlogging in the study area, making it more suitable for agriculture.

Figure 4.03. Map showing the Manikhali Canal System as it crosses the study area. The irregular shaped black dots are ponds, and the white square is the study area. All resident respondents are shown (yellow symbols). The map also shows areas with dense colony buildings (yellow shapes) and "overgrown" paddy (invented shading). The canal system is comprised of:

A. Begore Canal

B. Monikhali

C. The old bed of the Begore Canal.

D. The canals and ponds are overlaid on a tracing of a web of tidal creeks or "rivulets" from a 1785 map. A residual rivulet can be seen as a "string of ponds" that are longer in shape than the others in the map.

The spatial patterning shows how transboundary flooding is an issue for newcomer households near the Begore Canal, and localized flooding is an issue for almost all households near old creeks and rivulets.

(Source: author, 2022; unassembled and unpublished GIS files provided by Maheshtala Municipality, 2020; Mark Wood, 1785. *A survey of the country on the eastern bank of the Hughly, from Calcutta to the Fortifications at Budge budge, including Fort William and the Post at Manicolly Point, and shewing the extent and situation of the different courses, embankments, tanks, or broken ground, likewise representing the sands and soundings of the river at low water in spring tides, from January to May, from the year 1780 till 1784.* 1 inch = 2 miles. Calcutta, Mark Wood, Capt. Of Engineers.)

B
A
D
1 km

Figure 4.04. Rotated map showing the planned "garden suburbs" of Calcutta according to the 1911 Calcutta Improvement Act. Also shown, as an overlay, is the current Maheshtala Municipality (brown shape) the Ward 13 study area (white square) and the Manikhali Canal System (black lines). The planned areas on the southwest of Calcutta are shown in a diagonal green and pink hatch, and are defined as Working Class Suburbs of Single Family Contiguous Dwellings. While the Ward 13 area was not part of the suburban expansion of the 1900s, the Manikhali Canal System was built to support such expansion in Calcutta. For, the canal drained wet land and functioned as a sewage outlet for the planned garden suburb.

(Source: E. P. Richards, 1913, *Destination of Areas Map, City of Calcutta*. Jennings & Bewley. Scale 1:21,120. Harvard Map Collection Pusey Library, Massachusetts.)

The water ecology history, as told by residents, can be conceptualized through three distinct phases of water management: first, the work that happened prior to 2007; second, the Begore Canal renovation of 2007 and what that generated; and third, the 2013 New Monikhali Canal System renovation, the effects of which are ongoing. The first phase is narrated through a creek, which predates the colonial Monikhali Canal System, and for this reason is thought of as a residual "rivulet" (local term) (D in Figure 4.03). Up to the 1990s the rivulet was hydraulically connected to the Bhagirathi-Hooghly River via the Monikhali Canal System and was said to "ebb and flow" with the tide (Resident, interview, L03, 2018). As one elderly resident recalled, the rivulet was important for agriculture as "the high tide would bring in fresh water from the river and also deposit soil, while the low tide would drain out the waste water" (Resident, interview, L10, 2018). In the 1990s a sluice gate was built at the Bhagirathi-Hooghly River, which stopped the tidal flushing action of the rivulet and the Monikhali Canal System.

In this first phase of water ecology engineering prior to 2007, the rivulet in the study area had also been subject to more incremental hydraulic changes. Before the formation of Maheshtala Municipality in 1993, local residents often encroached upon the creek by building small weirs or filling in the creek edge to extend their land (see Figure 4.05). The weirs allowed those living alongside the creek to appropriate it, first into a productive pond and then, later, to sometimes fill in the pond to create land to accommodate an extension to the house or to make space for storage. As one long-term resident explained, "people have segmented [the creek system] and converted [it] into individual ponds ... even roads have been built [over them] in some areas" (Resident, interview, L12, 2018). Another resident explained that "bit by bit this [creek] has been encroached upon by everybody, including me" (Resident, interview, L03, 2018). Although such encroachment was and remains "illegal," residents living alongside the creek emphasized that they "paid nothing" for this right. As the resident explained: "[w]e are mostly permanent residents and didn't have to pay any extortion money" (Resident, interview, L03, 2018), suggesting that there is an understanding of the waterway as part of a commonly held, if not commonly managed, infrastructure.

Such statements about encroachment indicate that residents themselves played their part in the appropriation and degradation of the tidal creek in their ward. Yet residents are now concerned about, and openly reflect on, the negative state of the creek. As one resident admitted, blocking the creek flow has "created a problem [as] the water level doesn't go down during the monsoon," also explaining that now "water has to be pumped out" (Resident, interview, L03, 2018). Another long-term resident described the tidal creek

Figure 4.05. The "rivulet" or tidal creek covered in water plants on the left, as viewed through the tree-lined creek bank. The foreground space used for drying clothes and coconut, and for growing a small medicinal garden was created by filling in an edge of the tidal creek.

(Source: author, 2018.)

as now being in "bad shape," further lamenting that the ponds created by residents from the creek are "not being tended" and "are getting encroached by shrubs and grass" (Resident, interview, L04, 2018). Before 1993, the *panchayat* (village council) was expected to "maintain" the waterways of the locality, including excavating clogged side channels and removing weeds. They would collect payments for this work, although residents recalled that funds often went directly to panchayat *pradhans* (village leaders) who, instead of fixing drainage problems went on to "enrich themselves" (Resident, interview L05, 2019). From the point of view of the participant residents, the tidal creek is now a poorly regulated, abandoned infrastructure. Such degradation of creeks and canals has been noted elsewhere in Kolkata (see Bose, 2008; Mukherjee, 2015).

In 1993, with the formation of the municipality, the water ecology again changed. Residents interviewed reported that by 1996, the parts of the Monikhali Canal System that cross the study area had become unreliable, resulting in excessive seasonal waterlogging of land adjacent to the canals and poor drainage of the land around the creek.[3] Such seasonal waterlogging was not just an inconvenience. This made reliable, productive farming difficult. As I shall explore later, waterlogging was named by residents as a major contributing factor in farmers' decisions to sell their paddy land, especially if it was in low-lying areas. Excessive seasonal waterlogging meant that "water would remain stagnant for three to four days at a stretch" and paddy plants would "start rotting" (Resident, interview, L04, 2018). The cultivation of paddy declined precipitously between 1996 and 2007. Although some residents persisted, a drainage renovation in 2007 which was undertaken for the Behala airfield made the problem worse. By 2015, cultivation, including subsistence vegetable farming, was discontinued among all but one household participating in this research.

The second phase in the recent history of water ecology in the study area relates to the renovation of the Begore Canal, starting in 2007. According to one resident, the Begore Canal "was not in existence" prior to 1993 (Resident, interview, L11, 2018). From the point of view of a resident this may well have felt true: the canal did exist, but was located far away, near the eastern boundary of a nearby airport.[4] The 2007 work on the Begore Canal involved a range of engineering interventions: it was straightened, its depth and width were increased, and its banks stabilized. But most dramatically, it was realigned from running along the distant eastern edge of the airport to running through the study area (C in Figure 4.03). This renovation and realignment brought Begore to Ward 13, but not for the benefit of the residents. These works were intended to improve drainage of the adjacent Behala Airfield, which the central-level Airports Authority of India had proposed become a "modern facility for regional flights" (Behala Flying Club, 2007).[5] Those aspirations have never been realized, even though the canal renovations were carried out.[6] The effects on the residents were significant. The construction phase alone meant that there was more waterlogging, as material dredged from the canal renovation works was piled up on the banks and left there for two years. This newly created embankment blocked surface water flow into the Begore Canal, and the backed-up water stagnated in adjacent paddy fields and colonies. Households reported that the renovation of the relocated canal meant even more waterlogging and "floods every year" (Resident, interview, L08, 2018).

The third moment of water ecology change was the "New" Monikhali Canal System renovation, started in 2002 and reported to have been completed in 2013 (Express News Service, 2009), although works are still continuing at the time of writing (see Figures 4.06 and 4.07). This renovation project is being undertaken by the state-level Kolkata Environment Improvement Investment Program, funded by the Asian Development Bank. The main focus of the so-far completed works was dredging the Monikhali Canal, including the parts that pass through Ward 13. The "New" Monikhali Canal System renovation has also included the building of a pump house on the Bhagirathi-Hooghly River, which improved canal discharge during the increased water flow of the monsoon season or when there are high tides.

As with the Begore Canal renovation, the New Monikhali Canal System renovations are not being carried out to improve agrarian livelihoods of long-term residents or even to stabilize new colony development for newcomer residents in Ward 13. The New Monikhali Canal System renovation is actually part of a multistage project to serve upstream residents in the Kolkata Municipal Corporation area (Kolkata Municipal Corporation, 2018). For the project includes three pumping stations that mitigate problematic seasonal waterlogging of densely settled localities in upstream Behala.[7] As noted above in this section, the Monikhali Canal System was built by the British to serve the then-suburban expansion of Kolkata, and thus it has long been thought of as infrastructure that serves the "Corporation."

The experience of the water engineering works is mixed. Initially, the renovations were viewed positively by locals, who thought "the system of dredging was good" (Resident, interview, L04, 2018). As one resident reflected, after the renovation, the Monikhali Canal started to "pull the water away" meaning their farm lands "don't face the waterlogging anymore" (Resident, interview, L08, 2018). But other residents report that ever since the three pumping stations have become operational, they feel there is less capacity for water to drain away through the canal system. This observation

Figure 4.06. The Begore Canal in Ward 13. Behala Airfield is on the right, behind the houses. Clumps of floating, water hyacinth can be seen on both sides of the canal and a stabilized, concrete embankment can be seen in the middle-distance. The water appears black as it is sewage laden.

(Source: author, 2018.)

Figure 4.07. The Monikhali Canal in Ward 13. As with the Begore Canal, the water appears black at is it sewage laden. The Monikhali Canal is older than the wider and shallower Begore Canal, and it is thus concrete lined, along with long-established vegetation and settlements. The lack of water hyacinth and plastic suggests that the Canal has recently been cleaned by the Municipality as part of their yearly maintenance obligation.

(Source: author, 2018.)

rings true for residents who live in especially low-lying areas adjacent to the canal system, as they are experiencing direct negative effects. This is because the New Monikhali Canal System is now overflowing. Most troubling is that the overflow is mixed with wastewater from a new, "Corporation" sewage treatment facility near Jhinjira Bazar, which is located on the Maheshtala-Kolkata Municipal Corporation border.

The participant residents have thus seen an increase in the volume of water coming from upstream and a decrease in the quality of that water. It has created transboundary flooding and pollution in the study area. A resident explained the temporal aspects of the unhygienic overflow: "Normally the water in the low lands dries out by December. This year, water hasn't drained till March" (Resident, interview, N07, 2018). It is not surprising that in Ward 13, residents and ward officials alike refer to the "perennial problem" of the New Monikhali Canal System, and how so-called renovations contribute to, rather than solve, a "perpetual waterlogging problem" (Resident, interviews, L02, L07, L06, K02, 2018).

The lowlands of the study area were the first fields to suffer from excessive waterlogging, both as a result of the Begore Canal realignment and the aftereffects of the major New Monikhali Canal System renovations. It is not surprising that these were the first lands in the study area to be sold as colony plots. Ironically, the newcomers who bought this land also bought the ecological problem of waterlogging. These lowland colonies now struggle with problems of excess water. The lived experience of unhygienic transboundary overflow is difficult for the affected residents. A newcomer resident, who is fifty-five and retired, told us "we get submerged in knee-deep water" (Resident, interview, N04, 2018). She explained, "we have to wade through water eight to ten days at a stretch" and "for half an hour before we can access any transport." This particular newcomer had her house designed in anticipation of waterlogging, having the building put on a higher plinth level, yet "water [still] inundates houses with lower plinths and water enters the houses." Another newcomer resident reflected on the waterlogging on the road near her house, which stays for two to three months (Resident, interview, N02, 2018). Her solution is to "stay away [with relatives who live nearby in Ward 13] during the period our floors remain flooded." This particular resident has a clear sense of the transboundary water system she is in: "all water from Behala and Parnashree are accumulating here. They have benefited and we are the sufferers."

The hydrological interventions discussed above range from localized adjustments to a residual creek, to state and central government-led changes to a transboundary canal system. Each of these interventions were undertaken to solve a geographically specific water problem. None of the problems—the expansion of household buildings, the renovation of an airfield and the efficient drainage of one especially problematic waterlogged locality—appear to have been conceptualized by the intervening authority as part of an interconnected and shared water infrastructure. The ward councilor referred to the uncoordinated attempts to address the drainage works in Ward 13 as creating a "chaotic situation" (Municipal Official, interview, K02, 2018).[8] In the next section I focus on how long-term and newcomer residents have tried to adjust to these chaotic water ecologies, setting this within the larger, related landscape transformation of the decline of paddy cultivation.

Fields to Plots

In the once rice-growing areas of Ward 13, and in similar periurban areas beyond, former farmers earn a relatively marginal living. As in many rice-growing areas in Asia, generational shifts have resulted in fragmented plots with the gains of farming having to be distributed across ever-increasing numbers of family members—what Geertz (1969) famously and controversially described as "agricultural involution." Although a number of the households interviewed experienced this kind of economic "thinning," this classic story of agricultural impoverishment sheds little light on the complexity of household and environment restructuring that has happened in the study area over recent decades. There are a range of reasons why long-term residents stopped cultivating paddy: some of these "push" factors relate

Figure 4.08. Map showing the location of long-term households that continue to own cultivable land, apart from their "house land". About half of the participant long-term residents own cultivable land. The lone, long-term resident household with land under active cultivation (pink symbol) is shown in relation to long-term resident respondents who own land separate from their immediate household plots, but no longer cultivate it (black symbol). All other resident respondents are shown (yellow symbols). The dark red shaded areas show the most densely build up areas, which are along the local main road. Mouzas (light brown lines) are a pre-municipal revenue collection unit and act here as a stand-in to show land unit size and patterning. It can be seen that many paddy land/colony area's mouzas appear larger than those in wooded settled areas.

(Source: author, 2022; unassembled and unpublished GIS files provided by Maheshtala Municipality, 2018; Google Earth Pro; 2018)

1 km

to the changing condition of land as a consequence of waterlogging; others relate to the lack of economic options, forcing the sale of land for livelihood.

All paddy landowners who were interviewed engaged in cultivation of their land at one time or another, with the best agricultural land continuing to be harvested up to three times a year. Those residents who retain their paddy describe it variously as "cultivable" to "lying fallow" to "not cultivable." Figures 4.08 and 4.09 locate the lone remaining farmer-family with a cultivated field in relation to the nine households who own "fallow" paddy land separate from their immediate household plots. The map cannot communicate how this transformation from fields to plots is highly political, with strong economic drivers, as explained by long-term residents in our conversations.

The experience of one long-term resident who owned low-lying paddy fields is illustrative of the motivations for shifting away from agriculture (Resident, interview, L09, 2018). His family have lived in the study area for "around a hundred years," but they stopped "tilling the land" between thirty and thirty-five years ago (1983 to 1988). His was "one crop [of rice] land," which is typical when the land is low-lying and susceptible to flooding. This farmer would switch wet paddy cultivation for vegetables (eggplant or ridge gourd) in the drier months of "summer."[9] Prior to the family selling the land, finding labor to farm was getting harder. Various members of his family had started to seek and find more prosperous work in Kolkata, as had many in the casual farm labor workforce. This meant that there were not enough "hands to till the land" (among the family or hired workers), nor enough experienced family members to "supervise" farming activities.

Another long-term resident also referred to the issue of shortages of farm laborers to work the land as a result of laborers taking up better-paid jobs in nearby factories and ports (Resident, interview, L06, 2018). She explained that most hired farmworkers before the 1990s "were people from the surrounding area" hired to work on a daily basis, especially during the peak harvest period. These workers were paid about 120 rupees a day (or 80 rupees if they took part of the harvest as wages). Pay in other sectors has increased and often this higher pay is for less arduous work. She reflected that "now labor is very scarce," and wages are 400 to 500 rupees per day. This restructuring of local labor forced farmers to "do all work ourselves," especially if there was not a family member to turn to for help. Farming thus became less and less viable. As another long-term resident, whose family has lived in the area for seventy years, put it, he stopped farming twenty years ago (1998) simply because "we do not get time" (Resident, interview, L14, 2018).

Others repeated the refrain about the "risky proposition" of sustaining paddy production when household participation in work was diversifying and

Figure 4.09. Being shown the lone residual commercial farm in the Ward 13 study area. Rather than rice, the family now cultivates vegetables for sale at the nearby Jinjira Bazar, which is an important wholesale market for vegetable distribution in Kolkata.

(Source: author, 2020.)

farm wages had to compete against better-paying jobs (Resident, interview, L16, 2018). For example, an elderly resident explained that ultimately "the cost of production" was such that it was "cheaper to buy than to produce," concluding "that's why cultivation has stopped and lands have been sold off for housing" (Resident, interview, L07, 2018). Another resident, whose family still owns paddy land, concluded that "no one is interested in farming anymore," noting that "all young people" prefer to pursue studies rather than engage in farming or "look for a job for earning money" (Resident, interview, L12, 2018). She added that changes in local consumption have consolidated this trend. "People earlier," she recounted, were entirely dependent on farm products because "essential food" was not readily available from the market. Now that residents can get fresh food items from the market and "it is no longer a vital necessity to [be] farming, which needs so much effort." This kind of reasoning is consistent with a more widely experienced "agricultural stagnation" and greater fluidity in occupational choices linked to a so-called "break in caste rigidities" in villages across India since the 1980s (Gupta, 2005, p. 19).

The accounts given above suggest that the ecological drivers that reduced the quality of farm land intersected with changes in the labor market leading to decisions to sell land. Other residents had different and more contentious experiences which suggest compromised agency in a political process of speculative change. One elderly, long-term resident told how he sold some of his paddy land "about twenty to twenty-two years back" (1996-1998) because he "had not choice" (Resident, interview, L10, 2018). He said there was a "cartel" which bought up land all around one of his paddy fields making accessibility difficult and forcing him to sell his land at 30,000 to 35,000 rupees, "out of fear." He continued with the story of his land being urbanized by a land mafia, who "created a road of eight to ten feet wide" and then "sold the rest … after dividing it [into] plots at five to six *lakhs a* kotha [600,000 per 70 square meter]." So, he reflected (using the third person to speak about his own plight as a more general condition), "the poor man who has sold the land neither gets adequate money nor has an alternative." Accordingly, "his living condition becomes far worse … a farmer is converted to van driver and ekes out a difficult living." Indeed, many of the former farmer respondents in Ward 13 worked as "auto" drivers and struggled to cover the expenses of their household: this problematic livelihood transition has been reported elsewhere in periurban Kolkata (See, Mallik, 2016; A. Roy, 2014).

The above example suggests there is a point when the initial plotting of a colony starts to have a determining effect on the farmland around it. For example, in another case this was manifested as the problem of how to guarantee access to land in a context of rising land prices (Resident, interview, L04, 2018). Like many others in Ward 13, this family owned paddy land that was not directly accessed by a public road. "We have to reach it by travelling over someone else's land," the son reported. The adjacent land belonged to members of the extended family and while they used to allow access for farming, they recently no longer wanted to "leave any land" for a laneway, on the grounds that the "land is so expensive." To "give" access to another landholder, even if they were family, would need costly recompense. Given stories like this of his own family, the son observed, "So, why will someone do farming? ... Instead, if the land is sold and the money is kept in the bank, we will get a monthly interest of two thousand five hundred rupees."

As colony development proceeded in the study area, other negative environmental externalities affected the farming potential of land. For some, waterlogging is a highly localized outcome of colony construction. In one instance, a road constructed for a colony blocked overland water flows to the New Monikhali Canal System, creating extensive local waterlogging. In the same instance, there is overflow from the colonies that includes wastewater, especially common in newly built colonies with no septic tanks (see Figure 4.10). As one respondent reflected, this type of waterlogging "creates a stagnant pool of putrefied water" (Resident, interview, L10, 2018). It can extend beyond nearby paddy and into the settlement of long-time residents, "drowning" tree-lined pond bunds and killing plantations and *bagans* (gardens) (as will be discussed in chapter 6).

Another underlying and important reason for discontinuing farming and proceeding to sell agricultural land is related to a sudden increase in land tax or rent *(khajna)* on agricultural land *(sali)*. These increases happened in the years immediately after the formation of the Municipality, although not all such charges were simply municipal. According to the West Bengal Municipal Act, all municipalities have the power to levy property taxes on lands and buildings (1993, p. 79). In Maheshtala, the property tax on "homestead" land *(bastu)* is paid to Maheshtala Municipality and this rate increased.[10] But there were also increases in the land tax or khajna payment on sali land paid to the state-level Block Land and Land Reforms Officer (BLLRO). The increase in khajna imposed the most significant burden on the long-term residents over the 1990s as most of their land was sali. That is, many long-term residents have not "mutated" from rural to urban land use (converted their land from sali to bastu), and so they do not pay property tax.[11] One long-term resident remembered how the khajna increase was a "sudden jump," going up from two to twenty-two rupees per kotha and the topic was a major "talking point" at the time (Resident, interview, L05, 2018).

Figure 4.10. Being shown a wastewater "stream" that flows across, and stagnates in, former paddy fields in the Ward 13 study area. The resident would like to restart cultivation, but only if this this issue is resolved.

(Source: author, 2020.)

While the residents were displeased with the increase, they did not resist. "Against whom will one protest?" he said, pointing to confusion about who to turn to after the panchayat was disbanded. He continued, "What could people do? One had to adjust according to the circumstances," noting that "for survival" people then took to different modes of livelihood. Today the khajna rate is said to be sixty-five rupees per kotha: and residents who have held onto their waterlogged agricultural land feel that it is not only "useless" but a financial "burden" (Resident, interview, L04, 2018). Once again, there a sense of resignation to the situation reasoning that "sooner or later we will have to sell it off as there is nothing else we can do about it."

These household stories show the multivariate and incremental forces that mean that farming simply no longer makes sense—be that in terms of family obligation, access, economics, environment, even politics. Once farming stops or is no longer viable, the step to selling all or part of one's agricultural land is a short one, even when done reluctantly. In some cases, farmers were so reluctant to sell land they would hang on to it, leaving the fields temporally fallow, as they or members of the household earned money in other ways. For a number of these farmers, the aspiration to return to farming depends on their hope that waterlogging can be managed or might disappear as a problem. After all, in the last two decades, waterlogging in the study area has come and gone according to various known and unknown factors, as I have shown.

Scholars studying the farmers in urbanizing contexts elsewhere in India have noted a range of adaptive behaviors (see Marshall et al., 2009). One direction is for farming to retract from a commercial output to smaller, more marginal subsistence agriculture, supplementing the household income with other work (Narain, 2009). Alternatively, others may modify their commercial production toward, say, "best-quality" vegetables destined for now-nearby city markets, often introducing problematic levels of fertilizer and agrochemicals used to sustain production (Hussain and Hanisch, 2014; Patel et al., 2019). While subsistence agriculture is evident in the study area, it is limited, and the "best-quality" vegetable cultivation was present only in one instance of the household respondents. In other parts of India, this kind of agricultural restructuring has given rise to various kinds of advocacy work to support the retention of agriculture in periurban areas, often under the flag of food and nutritional security initiatives (see, Marshall and Randhawa, 2017). No such initiatives were evident in Maheshtala, and for the most part former farmers felt discarded by the state. As one elderly resident put it, the locality had been "wasted" (Resident, interview, L07, 2019).

Conclusion

While paddy land in the one-kilometer-square study area is not directly or forcibly appropriated by either the state or the market, the neglect of land management issues by relevant state agents and their need to increase taxes to fund urban projects (both routine and more spectacular), as well as the entrepreneurialism of small developers leads to appropriation and transformation of agricultural land. Notably, the failure of the residents, the municipal authority, and the Irrigation and Waterways Department to manage the canal network as a system, as well as the other factors presented in this chapter, has meant that waterlogging has emerged as the most visible and visceral actor in weakening and even inverting the communicative meaning and economic value of paddy land ownership. This leads to the outcome of an agricultural-based locality becoming bankrupt, exactly at the moment that its monetary worth as real estate increases. In Ward 13, owning paddy land no longer signals prosperity or security in the way it used to. Instead, owning paddy land has become a signal of pending probable unsettlement, an asset that households either plan to "let go" of, or are merely "holding on" to for now. In the next chapter, I look at the multifaceted increments of nonhuman change that unfold in parallel with the unsettling of paddy land cultivation practices.

Endnotes

1 The extensive "vacant" space on the eastern part of the map is the Behala Airfield.

2 I am aware that my interviews generated data that is limited to what participants were comfortable telling and showing me and my co-researchers. I am also aware that there is a majority of female participants, as they were most often at home during the day when research was being conducted.

3 If the canal-creek system was not dredged regularly (by the panchayat) its capacity to hold and transfer water is continuously reduced, as silt continues to be deposited every year.

4 I assume that the realignment of the Begore Canal in 1993 also contributed to the excessive waterlogging issue although not much was said about this.

5 The Behala Airfield is closely tied with the colonial history of the locality. The airfield was created in 1960/61 with the assistance of Biren Roy, Chairman of South Suburban Municipality (1932-1948), who was an active pilot and founder of the Bengal Flying (Training) Club (B. Roy, 1982, p. 51). Biren Roy was one of the "Roys of Behala," the former *zamindar* (landlord) of the region (1982, p. 221). Residents of Ward 13 confirm that the Roy family was the zamindar for the ward, and more, including Maheshtala. This suggests that the Behala Airfield land and Ward 13 was part of the Roy family estate prior to land reform in 1977.

6 While the runway was paved and extended at this time, the transformation of the facility into a regional, commercial airport is on hold (Airport Official, interview, K06, 2019). The Behala Airfield is managed by the Airports Authority of India or AAI, which is a statutory body working under the Ministry of Civil Aviation, Government of India.

7 Behala has a persistent and long-publicized problem of "choked canals" and related dengue fever cases (K. Bandyopadhyay and Ray, 2018; Express News Service, 2009; S. Ray, 2018; Yengkhom and Ray, 2019).

8 According to available information, the problem of drainage under Maheshtala Municipality has now been taken up by the state-level Kolkata Metropolitan Development Authority. A municipal-wide drainage master plan has been prepared and is said to be implemented soon (Maheshtala Official, interview, K01, 2019).

9 "One crop land," meaning just one paddy harvest a year. Higher land in Ward 13 is "three crop land."

10 Prior to the formation of the municipality, residents paid *khajna* (land tax) to the *panchayat* (village council), and before that, it was paid to the *zamindar* (landlord) through a *gomasta* (landlord's agent).

11 There are exceptions, as one long-term resident reported that their land was "mutated" without their knowing in 1993, and they only found out when they received a property tax bill from the municipality. This is not unusual. For instance, in the Kolkata Municipal Corporation area there is a proposal to "automatically" convert all sali land within the corporation's jurisdiction, reasoning that "[i]t is impossible to keep agriculture land in Calcutta" (TT Bureau, 2019).

5/

CULTIVATION PRACTICES

After paddy fields are no longer tended and cultivation ceases they do not disappear: other plants grow in them, regardless. Paddy fields become covered in hyacinth, tall *hogla* (cattail), and other spontaneous plants that thrive in waterlogged land in Gangetic West Bengal. The timeline at the start of chapter 4 showed the simultaneous decline of cultivated paddy fields, the increase in plotted land, and the construction of newcomer residents' households. In what follows, I look at the very different perspectives that long-term and newcomer residents have of land that has fallen out of cultivation. The perspectives remind us that these fields, while "fallow" in a productive sense, are not "vacant." They have a vegetative density and are home to many plants and animals, making them known but unforeseen agents in the case study area. The changes that paddy fields, as well as plantations and *bagans* (gardens) undergo once cultivation stops are not a romanticized decline of an ideal agrarian past, nor simply the return of a so-called wild nature. Rather, this transformation is reflective of the often mundane agencies of vegetative spaces, and the social construction of power and its changing relations within processes of rural-urban change in periurban Kolkata. To fall out of cultivation in Gangetic West Bengal cannot be understood without an historic account on how the land "fell into" cultivation. In this chapter, I do this by drawing primarily on what is rendered in old maps and link this to other relevant sources about Gangetic West Bengal.

Jungle

An important idiom in the periurban transformation of agrarian land in Gangetic West Bengal is that of the multiple meanings and connotations of the term "jungle." Jungle is the term used by both long-term and newcomer residents to describe untended, waterlogged paddy fields covered in tall grasses, as well as untended tree-lined ponds, plantations, and bagans. When no longer tended, all these once-cultivated landscapes are described as having "gone to jungle."

Environmental historian David Arnold (2015, p. 47) enlarges a postcolonial understanding of the Indian environment between the 1860s and 1930s by examining the "shared idiom" of the idea of jungle, and does so specifically in relation to rural Bengal and urban Kolkata. The source of the term jungle is *jangala*, which is of Sanskrit and north Indian vernacular origin.[1] Through a comparison of two different narrative visions—the 1937 Bengali novel entitled *Aranyak* (of the forest) (B. Bandyopadhyay, 2017) (see Figure 5.01) and colonial sanitary texts—Arnold (2015, p. 47) observes how environmental idioms and attitudes "flit, often unconsciously between one textual form and another." Starting with nineteenth-century European travel writing in India, he observes how Europeans tended to present a negative view of the rural jungle as "dark, dangerous, and unproductive, the haunt of wild beasts and bandits" (2015, p. 43; see Ball, 1880), whereas the Bengali character in *Aranyak* revels in the "beauty and variety" of the rural jungle, but can never entirely free himself from the colonial travel-writing genre or from "the desire to plant English seeds in an Indian jungle" (2015, p. 41, 47). Arnold then points to the "modern colonial sanitarians" in Calcutta and shows how they used the "appearance of jungle in the city" to capture the established negativity associated with rural jungles (2015, p. 43). This is because the Indian monsoon along with a tropical climate and vegetation was seen by the colonial engineers as impeding sanitary progress, for it implied "swamp, luxuriant vegetation, high temperature, great humidity, and active decay of organic matter, vegetable and animal" (2015, p. 44).

In the study area, the term jungle similarly "flits" between the subjective constructions of old and new residents. However, rather than a dialectic of forest and city, "jungle" in Ward 13 refers to a transformation of the agrarian landscape in and out of cultivation (see Figure 5.02). Others have observed the emergence and reemergence of jungle in Gangetic West Bengal. Geographers Sulka and Jyotirmoy Sen (1989) documented changes in agrarian settlement patterns and the related emergence of jungle as an outcome of shifting river channels and population increase (pre-1850), subsequent population decrease (1850-1945), and then the huge population increase in the wake of the partition of India and Pakistan (1946-1985).[2] Partition involved three phases of both immigration of Hindus from then East Pakistan and emigration of Muslim populations in the reverse direction (1989, p. 136). In each moment

Figure 5.01. Cover jacket of the first edition of the book entitled *Aranyak* (of the forest) by Bibhutibhushan Bandyopadhyay (1976). The back cover reads "The Gods of the Forest had not forgiven me for my heinous deed … and they never will. I had heard that confession somewhat diminishes the load of sin from the shoulders of the sinner. If not, at least speaking from my guilt shall unburden my heart of the rock solid grief I bear. This narrative is my act of penance. And with this I start my tale." The cover art, painted by Ashu Bandopadhya, represents a dense, dark, barrier of trees. The ominous vertical textures of this "forest" are contrasted with bright dots, possibly representing abundant flowers or fruit, and the eyes of creatures.

(Source. Bandyopadhyay, B., 1976. *Aranyak*. Mitra and Ghosh.)

Figure 5.02. Map showing "jungly" former paddy land (areas with invented shading) in relation to older buildings (seen in 2004 data; light brown rectangles) and newer buildings (seen in 2018 data; dark pink rectangles), as well as areas that are no longer cultivated, not settled, and thus "overgrown" (yellow-shaded areas). Areas with water hyacinth (mat-forming floating plant) are wetter than areas with *hogla* (a type of tall grass), which is a vegetal patterning informed by local topography and cultivation infrastructures but constantly adjusting through various actions in colony settlement. Long-term resident respondents (yellow symbol) and newcomer resident respondents (black symbol) are also shown.

(Source: author, 2020.)

of depopulation, jungle emerges. Briefly, in times when there is "more land than cultivators," land fit for cultivation often remained untilled and "tended to be covered with jungle" (1989, p. 143). Similarly, when a village site became "jungly and therefore unfit for habitation," the residents chose a new site (1989, p. 146). In the wake of partition, the "agricultural population settled in the village" and those who followed a different profession settled in sites along railways and roads (1989, p. 145). Other displaced people, "driven by despair" forcibly occupied "large masses of land which remained in jungly, waterlogged areas" (1989, p. 145).

The use of the term "jungle" in the study area has its own contemporary values and voices shaping it, however, these older and wider colonial and post-colonial currents echo through the local discursive terrain. For example, the appearance of periurban jungle today is not a "lapse of respectability," as Arnold reported of colonial perspectives (2015, p. 44). Nevertheless, there are pragmatic judgments of its worthiness that still align it with a wild West Bengal.

Jungle is manifested in the study area as an outcome of two contradictory tendencies. On the one hand, it signals the cessation of cultivation, but on the other, it signals that a claim of ownership to that land remains (even while it is being acted on more through speculation than cultivation). In other words, the presence of jungly land is not simply a sign of abandonment. For instance, an elderly long-term resident, using both past and present tense, told us "this is farmland" (Resident, interview, L15, 2018), gesturing to the area where a colony is being built. "From here up to Behala [two kilometers away] was all farmland at one time," he explained. When asked if there was jungle earlier, he replied, "No, none at all," meaning it was all well tended. Describing the same farmland condition today, another long-term resident observed that "the land is full of shrubs and weeds" and has "turned into a jungle" (Resident, interview, L18, 2018). In other words, some former farmers see overgrown nonfarmed land not as jungle but simply as farmland temporarily covered by something else. Their land is "lying fallow" (Resident, interview, L07, 2018) or "idle," even though "full of undergrowth" (Resident, interview, L03, 2018). Often the overgrown state of farmland is a signal of an intent to return to farming, when the time is right: "myself and other owners intend to restart cultivation, after clearing the weeds" (Resident, interview, L10, 2018), a time routinely linked to a future when "the water is drained out." Then, "whatever you grow, you will get a fantastic crop" (Resident, interview, L04, 2018).

Newcomers see jungly land differently, and for many it has always been a feature of the locality. Most newcomers, for example, do not share the experience of one early newcomer who settled into the locality in the late 1990s and recalls that most of the non-colony land around his new home was under cultivation. The experience of his nineteen-year-old daughter is more typical—she does not recall a time where there was not overgrown "empty space all around" and "the area was a jungle" (Resident, interview, N05, 2018). Another young newcomer resident had only "heard" that there were farmlands but confessed she had "never seen it" as it was "very long back" (Resident, interview, N03, 2018). While some newcomers saw only jungle, others were relieved to report that it was now in decline. For instance, a newcomer resident, who arrived in the late 2000s reported that with the arrival of newcomers and house construction activity, "it has become much less now" (Resident, interview, N10, 2018).

The presence or absence of jungle intersects with judgments about its desirability as a landscape element. Some newcomer residents relate to the jungly land in positive ways. They enjoy the breeze and ambience of the jungly fields, and see jungle as evidence of being in a rural setting. For instance, an elderly resident who arrived in the early 2010s reported, "I feel that safety of the place and peaceful surroundings are the two things most cherished by me" and they "give me the greatest satisfaction" (Resident, interview, N12, 2018). Others forage in the jungle, harvesting the holga for thatch, or they create clearings for soccer fields and cricket pitches during the summer. Some residents even have an ecological understanding of the jungle, seeing it as a positive landscape feature because of its ability to "absorb" waterlogging (Resident, interview, N06, 2018). But others find the jungle oppressive and unsafe, sometimes specifically citing the presence of snakes and insect pests (Resident, interview, N10, 2018), and complaining that the municipality does nothing about it. In one colony, a resident and her neighbors were tired of waiting for the ward committee to clear it, and so they cut back the jungle that encroaches on the pathway road to their homes (Resident, interview, N09, 2018) (see Figure 5.03). Lastly, when newcomers arrive and remove the jungle, it does not mean that new colonies are devoid of plants altogether. Many newcomer residents tend domestic plants and trees around their homes within the land that they own.

Overall, jungle is a provocative if temporary landscape condition, prompting a variety of responses. It emerges and reemerges in relation to changes in drainage, cultivation, and colony settlement. The various attitudes and practices that emerge in relation to the presence of jungle range from seeing it as temporary, as a foraging or ecological resource, or as a signal that land is in (neglectful) private hands. Jungle is also an ecological

Figure 5.03. A "jungly," waterlogged, formerly cultivated paddy field surrounding, and within, a colony in the Ward 13 study area. Some of the holga in this image are lying horizontal as the residents have worked to cut and clear them.

(Source: author, 2020.)

condition that is relational to other infrastructures (like canals) and densities (like waterlogging). Together, drainage, fields, and jungle are thus both an outcome and a nonhuman agent of ordinary, periurban change in Gangetic West Bengal. This is because perennial waterlogging and impenetrable, grassy areas are expensive to remedy, and thus do work to repel rapid, small-scale, periurban and infrastructure-led change. Such forceful, obdurate agrarian settlement forms are repeated across Gangetic West Bengal and have been shaped over time, and it is to this long story of settlement that I turn next.

Settling Gangetic West Bengal

The case study area's incremental change happens in the present but is necessarily shaped by the history of settlement in the region, including some foundational infrastructural legacies and settlement practices. One such legacy relates to colonial practices of the interrelated logics of managing waterways so that they could reach existing, cultivated land, and at the same time, assisting in the management of flooding. Such landscape transformations were part of a wider colonial project of "improving" what was considered "wasteland" into land that could be productively used for the cultivation of rice and other crops. Another legacy relates to the patterns of rural settlement. Most characteristic here is the intermixing of rice cultivation fields with relatively well-treed settlements, still evident today. Many of these legacies can be read in the colonial maps of the area which, as geographer Matthew Edney (2009) argues, did so much more than simply map space. They also expressed colonial aspirations and legitimated colonial transformations of land and resources.

Ward 13 and its surrounding area are crisscrossed by an interconnected network of colonial drainage canals, now called the New Manikhali Canal, as discussed in chapter 4. These canals were built over an older system of navigable tidal creeks and *bils* (marshlands), part of a vast "maze" of waterways that in 1914 was lauded as one of the "most important systems of river canals in the world" (O'Malley, 1914, p. 158). A 1780 Survey of India map of Calcutta and surrounds (see Figure 5.04), reproduced in Rennell's *Bengal Atlas* (1783), captures the watery world of the locale which is today's contemporary Maheshtala Municipality. The 1780 map clearly shows the dominance of the Bhagirathi-Hooghly River (A), which is tidal and was central to the colonial settlement of Calcutta,[3] and beyond. It also shows shorter tributary creeks as well as the more extensive navigable tidal creeks.

This includes the Surman's Nulla (later renamed Tolly's Nulla), which was an important inland waterway connector (B). It is part of what locals call the *Adi Ganga*, an early channel of the Ganges River. The significance of water transport at this time is verified by the way settlements are strung along the navigable waterways, built on the relatively higher ground of natural levees. The map also indicates a tidal wetland located east of Calcutta labelled Salt Lake (C), which flows eastward toward the Bay of Bengal. Finally, there are large areas of the map labelled as "morass" (D) meaning low-lying, freshwater marsh areas, including Fresh Lake, typical of the lower delta plain of the Ganga-Brahmaputra-Meghna Delta.

The intersection between water, land, and colonial aspiration is further articulated in a 1910 Survey of India map (see Figure 5.05), which shows the Gangetic West Bengal portion of the much larger "Delta of the Ganges." The study area is surrounded by Company Lands (A), referring to the lands expropriated by the British East India Company and controlled for agrarian use, suggesting that the "morass" lands were being transformed into productive use. Central to such transformation was the British introduction of the Permanent Settlement System in 1793, which created a class of *zamindars*—recognized land owners with rights to collect rents from peasants working the land on behalf of the colonial state (Iqbal, 2010, p. 6). In the map, there is also evidence of the British governance structures, with the administrative districts of Hooghly, Gur, and Jessore demarcated. The map indicates that the *Sunderbund* (Sundarban) mangrove (B), marked by the small trees, is not so evident in the study area, although accounts record much more extensive and earlier clearing of mangrove across the lower delta plain (see Eaton, 1993). The coverage of the tidal creeks is evident as a fine scale waterway network that connects far inland across the extensive, braided delta (C). These tidal creeks were originally quite shallow and often silted but "could be negotiated by *saltees* (dug-outs) drawing about 8 or 9 inches of water when laden" (H. Bandyopadhyay, 1990, p. 44). By the late 1800s, such craft were common on the waterways, conveying rice, fruits, and vegetables to British exporting houses in Calcutta (Bandyopadhyay, 1990, p. 44). Again, this map indicates that the effort to reach existing cultivated land and transform cleared but uncultivated land from "morass" was ongoing, with many areas still marked (by soft horizontal lines) as marshy (D). As Bhattacharya (2018, p. 5) notes in relation to nearby Calcutta, its settlement depended on drying "the mobile landscape of soaking ecologies" to create stable property (also see D'Souza, 2006).

As these colonial maps testify, the modern history of the study area's political ecology was structured around the management and negotiation

Figure 5.04. Re-oriented part of a 1780 map entitled The Hoogly River from Nuddeah to the sea, showing the Hooghly River not long after land ownership had passed from local landowners to the East India Company in 1757. The map is rotated to show the study area in the same orientation as the other maps in this chapter. The study area (yellow symbol) can be seen as part of the river levee extent between Ballia (Behala) and Budge Budge. The creeks near the study area can be seen to flow westward.

A. Bhagirathi-Hooghly River
B. Surman's Nulla (later re-named as Tolly's Nulla)
C. Salt Lake
D. "Morass" meaning low-lying, freshwater marsh areas, including Fresh Lake, typical of the lower delta plain of the Ganga-Brahmaputra-Meghna Delta.

(Source: Survey of India, 1910, The Hoogly River from Nuddeah to the sea, with Balasore Road and Plans of the Attack of Oudanulla. Published August 25, 1780. Rennell's *Bengal Atlas* 1783, No. XIX. Calcutta, Survey of India. National Library of India, Kolkata.)

A
B
C
D
Morasses
Morass
Called the Fresh Lake
Buoys
Hoogly Point
Buffalo Point
Diamond Point
Otogunge
New Harbour
Mud Point
Tingorcally River
Roopnaran River
Mizen

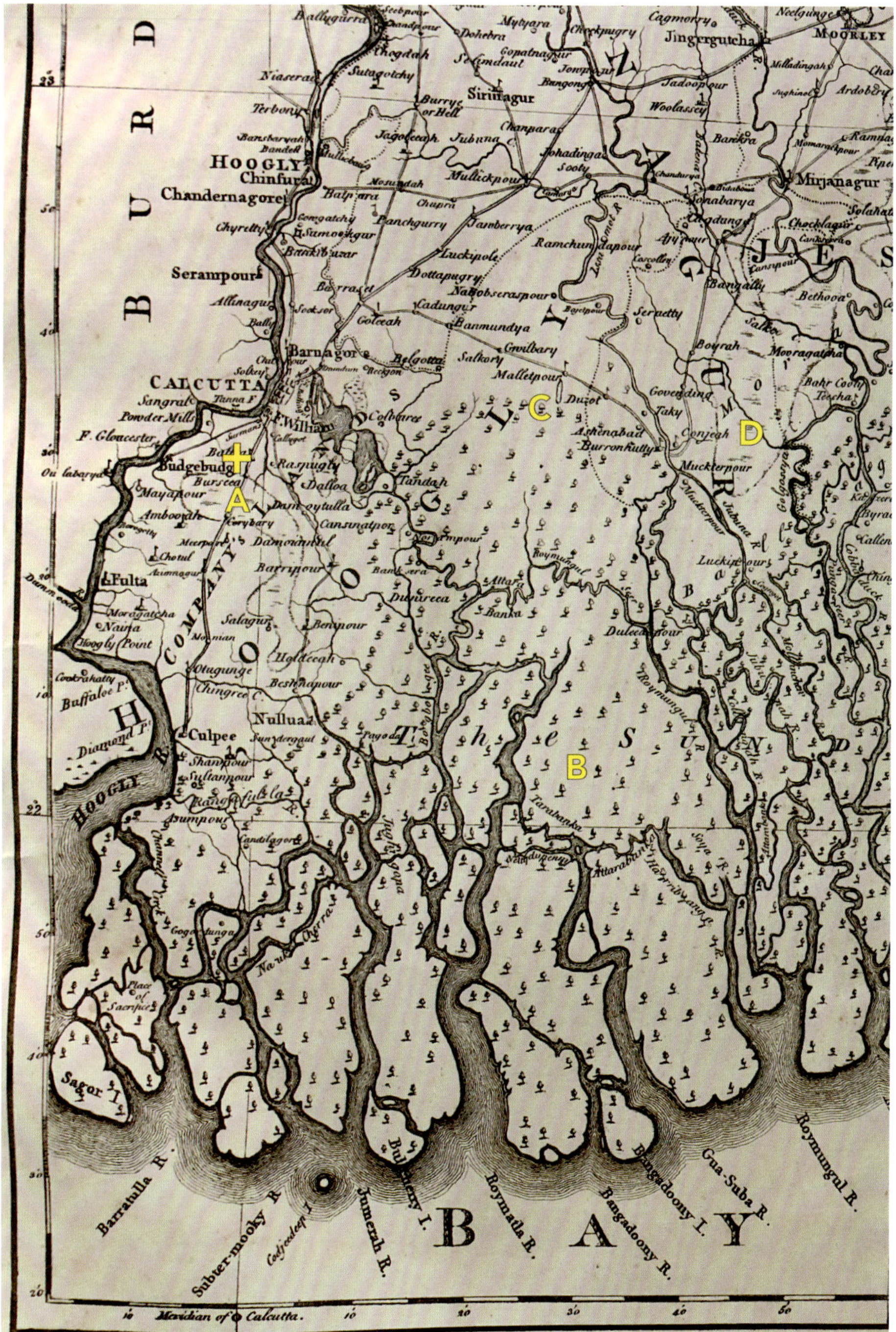
HOOGLY
Chinfura
Chandernagore
Serampour
CALCUTTA
F. William
Barnagor
Budgebudge
Fulta
Culpee
Nulluaa
Sagor I.
Mirjanagur
Jingergutcha
MOORLEY
B U R D
COMPANY
HOOGLY R.
A
B
C
D
B A Y
Barratulla R.
Subter-mooky R.
Jumerah R.
Roymatla R.
Bangadoony R.
Bangadoony I.
Gua-Suba R.
Roymungul R.
Meridian of Calcutta.

of water. Of course, these maps, as colonial artefacts, erase the precolonial fluid ecologies and economies of the Ganga-Brahmaputra-Meghna Delta. But in fact, colonial-era use of the waterways for transport was continuous with precolonial uses. The historian Richard Eaton (1993) describes the early settlement of the delta as one of moving "frontiers." The sacred geography of the Ganges River (today's Bhagirathi-Hooghly River) was a powerful conduit that brought Brahaman settlers from the north from the sixth and fifth centuries B.C. (1993, p. 5). From the thirteenth century on, sporadic efforts were made to clear the mangrove and marshlands of the delta, initially by the Bengal Sultanate (1204-1575), then by the Mughal Empire (1575-1765) (1993, p. xxiv). Eaton (1993, p. 310) notes that the settlement of the delta was composed of several interwoven processes:

> [T]he eastward movement and settlement of colonizers from points west [that is, from the long-settled Ganga/Bhagirathi-Hooghly River], the incorporation of frontier tribal peoples into the expanding agrarian civilization, and the natural population growth that accompanied the diffusion or the intensification of wet rice agriculture and the production of surplus food grains.

Geographer Kalyan Rudra's (2018, p. 2) account of the dynamics of the Ganga in West Bengal verifies that the colonial Government of Bengal worked hard to understand the hydrology of the delta. From the late eighteenth century until the first half of the twentieth century, much

Figure 5.05. Part of a 1910 map of the "Delta of the Ganges," with this fragment showing the western Ganga-Brahmaputra-Meghna Delta. The study area (yellow symbol) is marked on the western part of the map, southwest from Calcutta and of east of the Bhagirathi-Hooghly River.
A. "Morass" near the study area
B. Sunderbund (Sundarban) mangrove
C. Extent of tidal creeks
D. Another "morass"

(Source: Survey of India, 1910, The Delta of the Ganges; with the adjacent countries on the east: Comprehending the southern inland navigation. Inscribed to Francis Russel esq. by his affect. Friend J. Rennell. Published December 1, 1778. Rennell's *Bengal Atlas* 1783, No. I. Calcutta, Survey of India. National Library of India, Kolkata.)

scientific inquiry was conducted, and many scholarly reports issued. There were two key agendas. The first was to understand ways of improving navigation so as to find the best possible channels for sailing. The second was flood management, to be achieved primarily by embanking the rivers and waterways. Another solution was canal construction. For example, a 1936 map of the District 24 Parganas, showing the "rivers, khals, jheels & jungles" (see Figure 5.06) shows the Charial (or Churial) Canal (A). This canal was excavated in 1887 precisely to drain thirty-seven square miles (O'Malley, 1914, p. 120). In 1906, the Manikhali Canal System was proposed and when built, drained sixteen square miles (O'Malley, 1914, p. 126), including the study area. The map also shows revenue districts (thin black dotted lines) the primary *khals* or canals (blue-green lines) and embankments (thick black lines) around Calcutta, and remaining areas of mangrove or "jungles" (bright green).

Figure 5.06. Part of a 1936 map of the District of 24 Parganas showing the "rivers, khals [canals], jheels [lakes] & jungles". Framed here is the area showing Maheshtala as a revenue-district and thus, as a territory that produces income for the colonial Government of Bengal. The Churial canal is marked A. Also shown, as an overlay, is the Ward 13 study area (yellow symbol).

(Source: Government of Bengal, 1936, Map of Dt. 24 Parganas: showing the rivers, khals, jheels & jungles. *Final Report on the Survey and Settlement Operations in the District of 24-Parganas: for the period 1924-1933*. Scale 1 inch = 4 Miles, No. 5. Calcutta, Government of Bengal. National Library of India, Kolkata.)

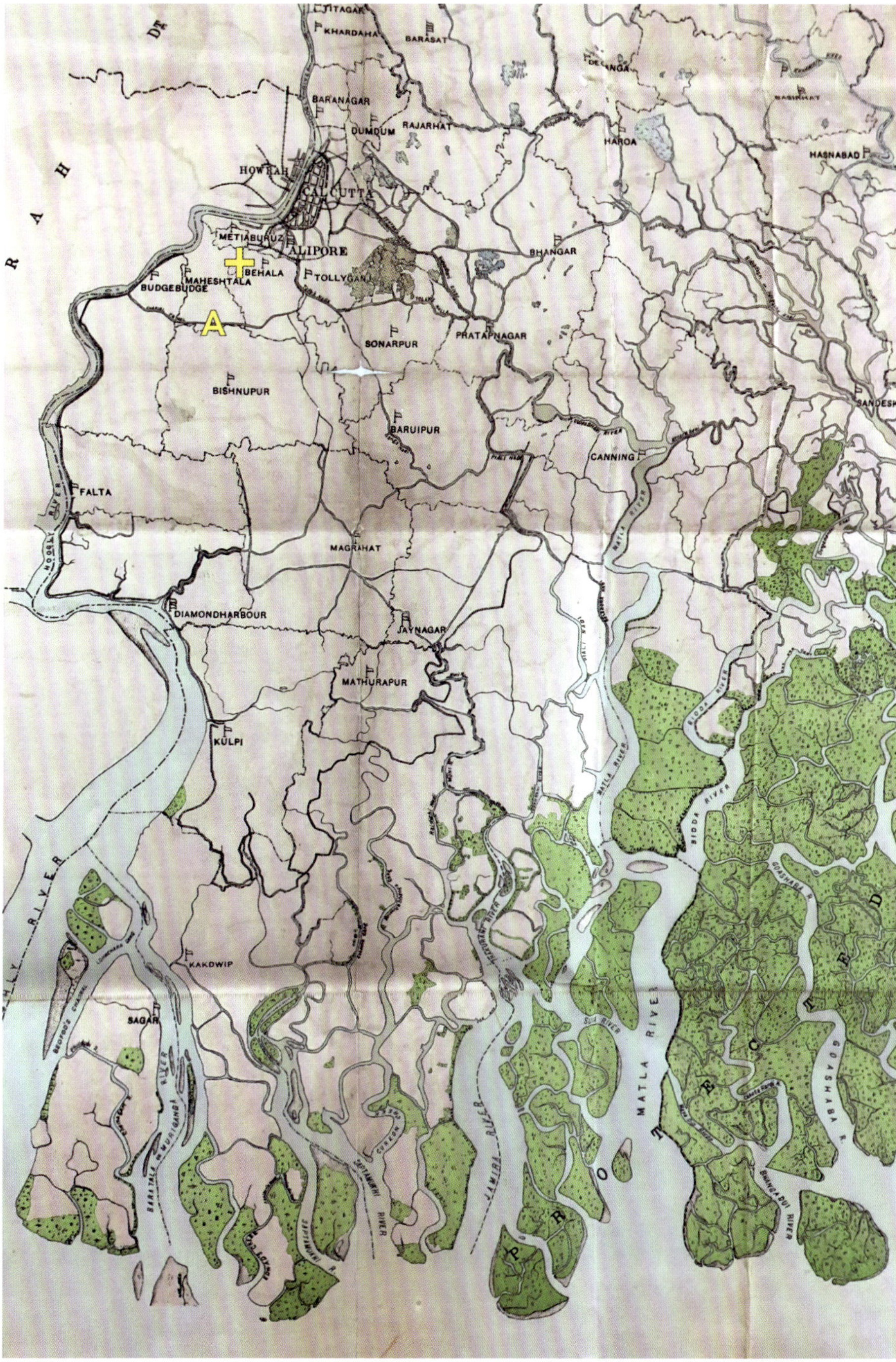
TITAGAR
KHARDAHA
BARASAT
DEGANGA
BASIRHAT
BARANAGAR
DUMDUM
RAJARHAT
HAROA
HASNABAD
HOWRAH
CALCUTTA
METIABURUZ
ALIPORE
BEHALA
TOLLYGANJ
BHANGAR
MAHESHTALA
BUDGEBUDGE
A
SONARPUR
PRATAPNAGAR
BISHNUPUR
BARUIPUR
CANNING
FALTA
MAGRAHAT
DIAMONDHARBOUR
JAYNAGAR
MATHURAPUR
KULPI
KAKDWIP
SAGAR
MATLA RIVER
BIDDA RIVER
GOASHABA R.
P R O T E C T E D

While the colonial goal was to control flooding, Rudra (2018, p. 2) notes that this goal was not aligned with the needs of local farmers, whose practices accommodated and depended on seasonal flooding and its ecological role of dispersing sediment and enriching the fertility of their rain-fed agricultural fields. As historian Rohan D'Souza suggests (2015, pp. 138-39), villages, and their production contexts in the delta were strategically suited with regard to drainage: however, it was a "fragile or tenuous" relationship. Quoting the *Bengal Drainage Committee Report* of 1907, he explains that "[t]he drainage of all villages … in Lower Bengal is effected by the water first running into the nearest paddy-fields lying in the direction of their slope, thence it collects in the beels [marshes] from which it rushes through khals [creeks] into larger streams, which again communicate with navigable rivers" (D'Souza, 2015, p. 138). Water, in effect, he says, was kept "circulating" between different types of depressions and basins and finally left unhindered to a flowing stream or river.

Figure 5.07. Map showing the channel of the Adi Ganga or old channel of Ganga. The Bhagirathi-Hooghly River is the western branch of the Ganges River and as river channels in a braided delta tend to switch course, this is one of countless examples of this process. The map also shows administrative districts (black dotted lines) and the primary navigable waterways (including Tolly's Nulla noted above), as well as the emergent railway network (black lines). Shown, as an overlay, is the Sealdah-Budge Budge rail line marked A and the Ward 13 study area (yellow symbol). This map reflects a hinge point in the transportation mode between the waterways network and the railways (H. Bandyopadhyay, 1990; Banerjee, 2018; Mukherjee, 2020). The emerging railway network of the Eastern Bengal Railway Company had devastating ecological effects. For instance, the Sealdah-Budge Budge rail line (A) that runs east-west through the present Maheshtala Municipal area, compartmentalizes the area lying south of the line, stopping free drainage of creeks that naturally flow northwest toward the river and creating a waterlogging problem, including in the study area.

(Source: Government of Bengal, 1936, Plan showing the course of the Adi Ganga. *Final Report on the Survey and Settlement Operations in the District of 24-Parganas: for the period 1924-1933*. No. 4. Calcutta, Government of Bengal. National Library of India, Kolkata.)

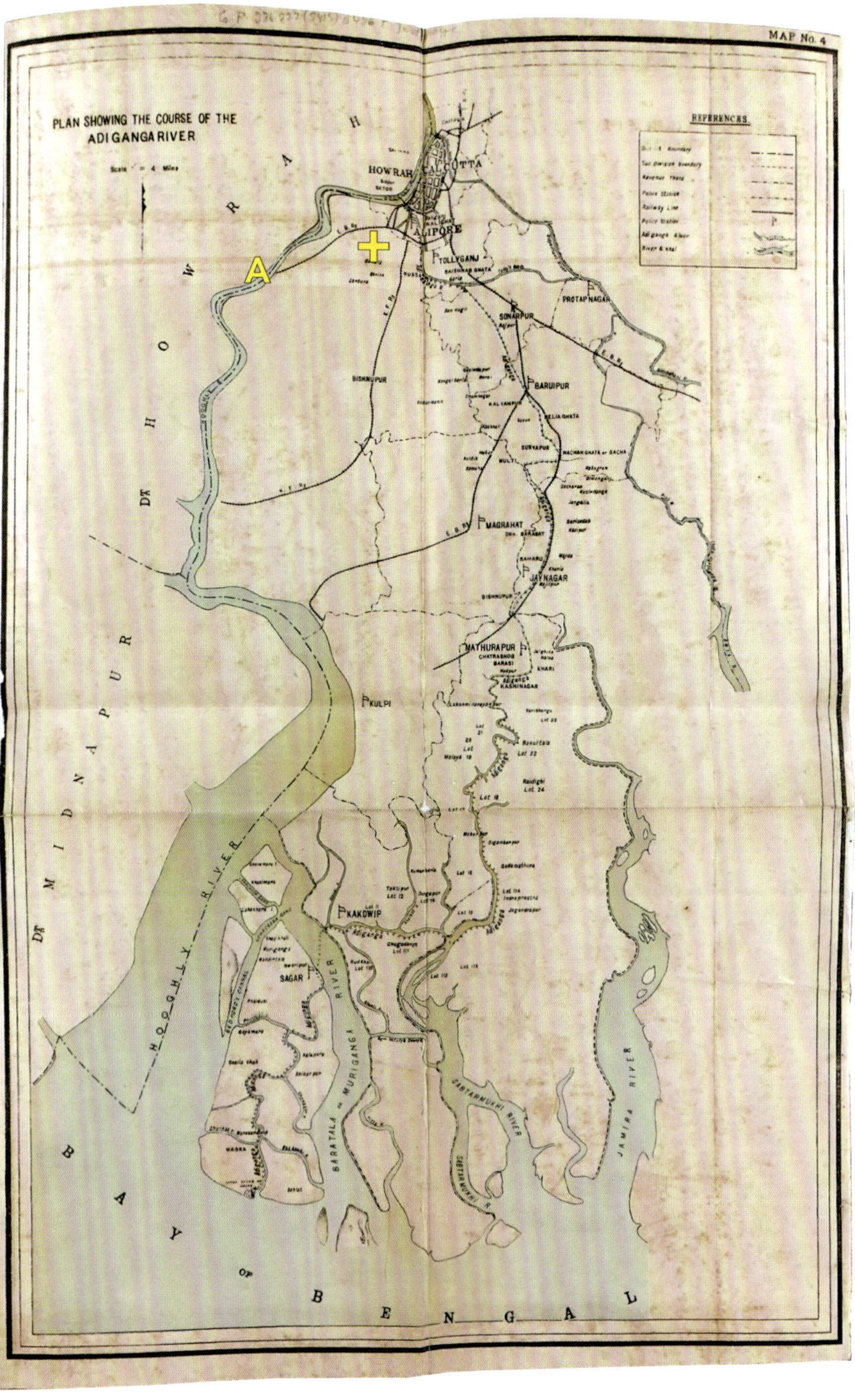
MAP No. 4
PLAN SHOWING THE COURSE OF THE
ADIGANGA RIVER
REFERENCES.
HOWRAH
CALCUTTA
ALIPORE
TOLLYGANJ
A
SONARPUR
PROTAPNAGAR
BARUIPUR
BISHNUPUR
KALYANPUR
SURYAPUR
MULTI
MAGRAHAT
JAYNAGAR
MATHURAPUR
KASHINAGAR
KULPI
KAKDWIP
SAGAR
HOOGHLY RIVER
SARATALA or MURIGANGA RIVER
SAPTAMUKHI RIVER
JAMIRA RIVER
D T H O W R A H
D T M I D N A P U R
B A Y OF B E N G A L

There is further evidence that colonial perspectives on land management were working against and not with the landscape of the delta. For example, the arrival of railways came with the construction of railway embankments. As historian Iftekhar Iqbal (2010) explains, the railways altered the "water regime" across the delta. The embankments divided the delta into "innumerable compartments," the result being a "total disruption of the free-flowing water systems and loss of the concomitant benefits of the spread of silt and salubrious flushing of the landscape" (2010, p. 15). One district gazetteer in the early twentieth century (O'Malley 1914, p. 109), for example, reported on severe waterlogging resulting from what he described as the "great basin shut in" between the Diamond Harbor Railway and the Hooghly embankments. Canal systems that had originally been constructed for transport or to drain a "morass," increasingly had to also serve as drainage devices to alleviate this human-made circumstance of waterlogging in these carelessly created basins (see Figure 5.07). One such "drainage works" canal, the Manikhali Canal System, passes through the study area.

The railways were not the only negative impact on the water ecology of the area during the colonial period. It was during this time that there was also a "biological invasion" of the area's waterways and wetlands by the introduced water hyacinth. Railway infrastructure and introduced species "brought havoc to agrarian production processes," argues Iqbal (2010, p. 15), and contributed to reduced agricultural production output and increases in water-related diseases, setting the conditions for the Bengal Famine of 1943. Given troubled local water histories such as this, it is perhaps not surprising that the *Masterplan for the Water Supply, Sewage and Drainage of Calcutta Metropolitan District 1966-2001* noted that many of the lateral waterways ("ditches," creeks, and canals) that feed into the Manikhali Canal System were deemed "relatively ineffective" (Calcutta Metropolitan Planning Organization, 1966, p. 63). The main drainage canals, for example, were reported to have a carrying capacity that was "greatly reduced by silt deposits" and to be "poorly maintained."

In 1983, when the jurisdiction of the Kolkata Municipal Corporation was extended spatially, it took on responsibility for managing the Manikhali Basin, the Manikhali Canal and its branch channels—what is collectively called the Manikhali Canal System.[4] Together with Tolly's Nullah and the Churial Canal, the Manikhali Canal now serves the drainage requirements of roughly sixty-six square kilometers (twenty-five square miles) covering the Kolkata Municipal Area and adjoining municipalities, including Maheshtala. Although adjustments are sporadically made to the drainage infrastructure, those interventions are often limited and have not solved the specific waterlogging issues faced by residents in the study area. As I showed in chapter 4, often any dis/benefits Ward 13 residents receive from these water infrastructure renovations are incidental. Furthermore, improvements to the canal have not necessarily been coordinated as, or even conceptualized as being about, an interconnected water system. This has meant that, hydrologically speaking, Ward 13 residents have faced many challenges and changing fortunes in response to hydrological adjustments. Such incremental changes are also entangled with cultivation, and it is to this history that I turn next.

Cultivated and Uncultivated Land

The opening up of Bengal's waterways to colonial settlement was entwined with efforts to further transform the delta into something recognizably productive. Figure 5.08 shows the extent and density of rural and urban population in undivided Bengal, based on 1941 Census data. As Chatterjee explains of his map (1949, p. 38), the distribution of dots (each dot representing one thousand rural population) shows that at that time most of the people, as elsewhere in India, lived in villages. A 1936 survey report of the colonial survey and settlement operations in the district of 24 Parganas (Lahiri, 1936, pp. 29, 31, 34, 155–156) provides specific data about the cultivation of Maheshtala *thana* (a revenue district). In what follows, I delve into this data about the villages of Maheshtala.

In 1936, 87 percent of Maheshtala thana was "culturable" (meaning cultivatable) and 67 percent of that cultivatable area was measured as being actively "cultivated." That is, of the total area of 17,210 square miles of Maheshtala thana, 11,014 square miles was cultivatable "village." Of the village or total cultivatable area, two thirds were sown and one-third was considered "uncultivated" or as potentially productive, but as yet uncultivated land. Looking first at the two-thirds sown area of Maheshtala thana; 76% of that area was rice, 15% fruit and vegetables, and 8% was under pulses and other food. What this points to is that most of the land is dedicated to rice cultivation - indeed, across the whole 24 Parganas, rice accounted for 94 of the crops grown at that time. A distant second to rice, was the cultivation of jute at 5 percent. The scale of this enterprise for export can be seen in Figure 5.09, which shows the extent and density of land under rice and jute. Second, the remaining one-third of cultivatable or uncultivated lands within the villages of Maheshtala thana are described as a combination of house sites and ponds, as well as land that is considered

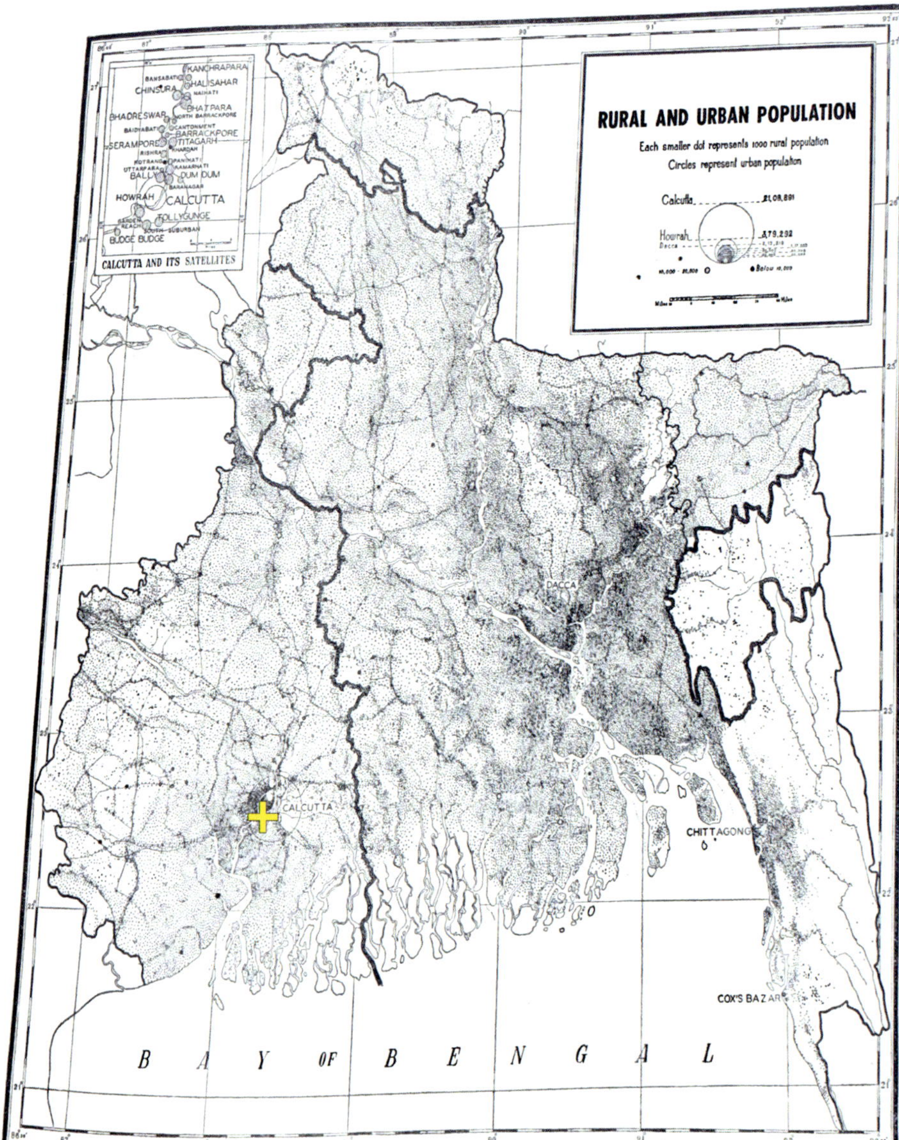
RURAL AND URBAN POPULATION
Each smaller dot represents 1000 rural population
Circles represent urban population
Calcutta 21,08,891
Hourah 379,292
Dacca
CALCUTTA AND ITS SATELLITES
KANCHRAPARA
BANSABATI
HALISAHAR
CHINSURA
NAIHATI
BHATPARA
BHADRESWAR
NORTH BARRACKPORE
BAIDYABATI
CANTONMENT
BARRACKPORE
SERAMPORE
TITAGARH
RISHRA
KHARDAH
PANIHATI
UTTARPARA
KAMARHATI
BALLY
DUM DUM
BARANAGAR
HOWRAH
CALCUTTA
TOLLYGUNGE
GARDEN REACH
SOUTH SUBURBAN
BUDGE BUDGE
DACCA
CALCUTTA
CHITTAGONG
COX'S BAZAR
BAY OF BENGAL

more proximately cultivatable, including "old fallow," woodland "groves" that are not fruit-bearing, and "culturable jungle." This indicates the wide extent of a colonial prism seeing the whole agrarian landscape as potentially cultivatable. It brings some agrarian elements like fields into sharp focus while other elements are made present but out of focus, like house sites, or off the map, like uncultivatable plants.

It is important to point out that the cultivation of rice for export did not mean that the villagers were prosperous. As the 1936 survey report details, "a good number of people of the district live a life below the average comfort" (Lahiri, 1936, p. 79). It is beyond the scope of this book to explain in detail the burden of the Permanent Settlement. As Iqbal (2010) has noted, the practical goals of the Permanent Settlement were to increase tax revenue as well as to establish a Western-style land market in which there could be investment. It imposed a complex tenure system and institutional arrangement on agrarian production, and had ideological dimensions designed to create a yeoman class of farmers alongside rich landowners. Farmers, it was assumed, would be loyal to landlords, and landlords to the British. In contrast to its goals, the system contributed to the stagnation of the rural economy and society in the colonial period (Iqbal, 2010 p. 6).[5] One reason often given for stagnation of the rural economy is that the system fit poorly to land with small plot sizes. For instance, in Maheshtala thana, the average land size for *raiyats* (a person acquiring a right to hold land directly from the government mainly for the purpose of cultivating it) is 0.92 acres, and for *under-raiyats* (a person holding land by cultivating it) it was 0.38 acres (Lahiri, 1936, p. 79). In 1936,

Figure 5.08. Map of the "Ganges Delta" or Ganga-Brahmaputra-Meghna Delta showing extent and density of rural and urban population in undivided Bengal based on 1941 Census data. Also shown, as an overlay, is the Ward 13 study area (yellow symbol).

(Source: Chatterjee, S.P., 1949. *Bengal in Maps: Land under rice.* No. 50. Calcutta, Orient Longmans Ltd.)

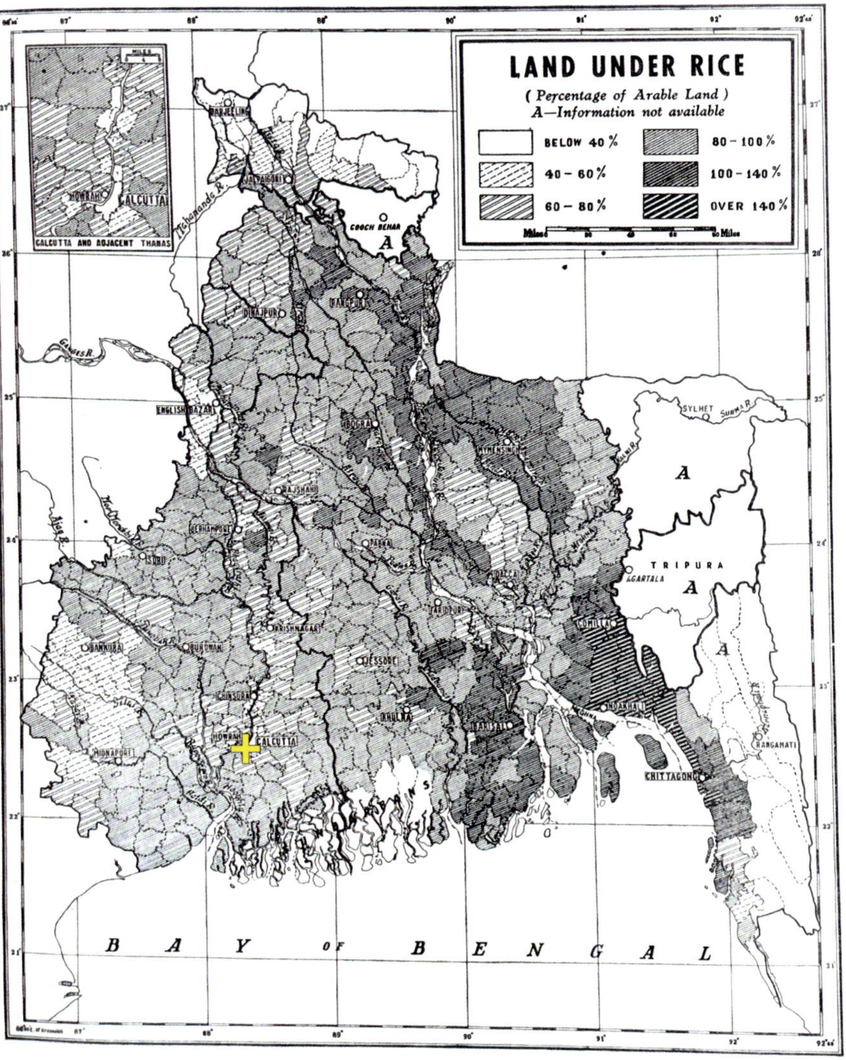

Figure 5.09. Two maps from the book *Bengal in Maps: Land under rice.* Left: Map of Bengal showing extent and density of rice cultivation in 1949. As Chatterjee explains (1949, p. 66), the high percentages indicate that rice was by far the most important crop and where the percentage is over 100% it means that more than one crop of rice is raised annually from the same plot of land. The study area of Maheshtala thana (a measurement unit) is shown to have 80-100% of its arable land under rice cultivation. Right: Map of Bengal showing relationship between

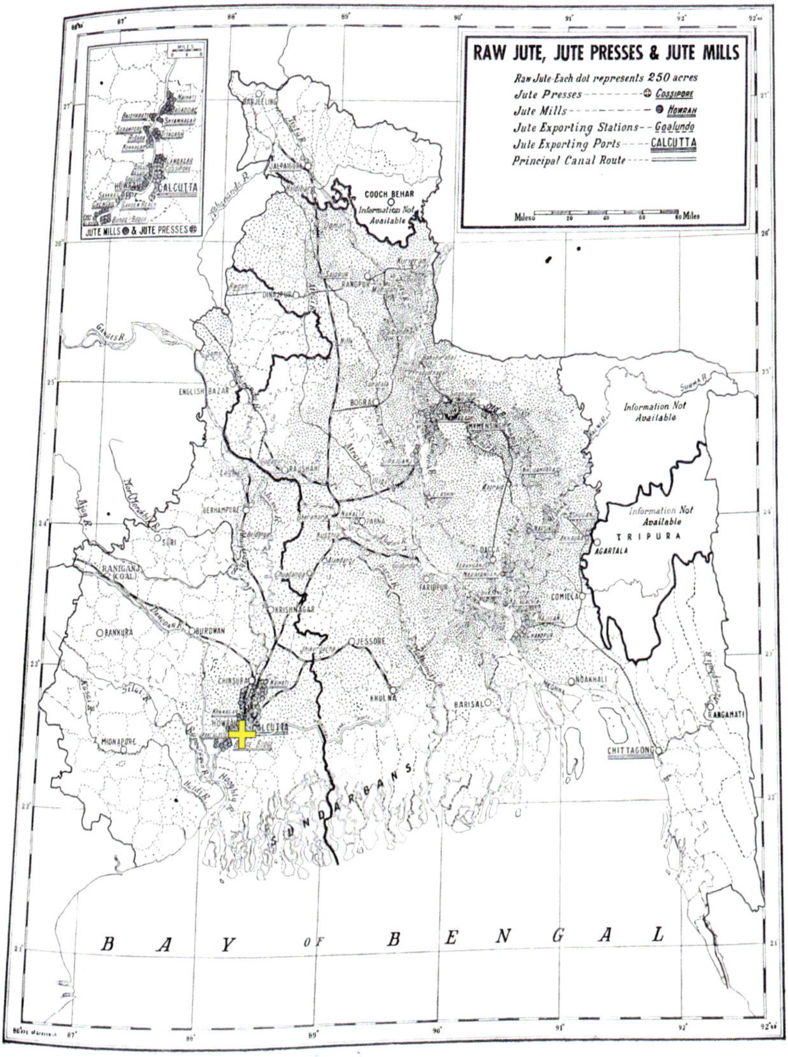

raw jute, grown predominantly in East Bengal, and the jute industry centered in Calcutta, including the study area of Maheshtala. The movement of raw jute to Calcutta occurred via both waterway and railroad, described above in this chapter. Also shown, as an overlay, is the Ward 13 study area (yellow symbol). (1949, p. 76).

(Source: Chatterjee, S.P., 1949, *Bengal in Maps: Land under rice*. No. 50 and 55. Calcutta, Orient Longmans Ltd.)

there were 10,601 landholding raiyats and 2,975 landholding under-raiyats in Maheshtala thana (1936, p. 79).

The colonial state's teleological emphasis on establishing productive land was enacted upon existing and co-created practices of settlement and cultivation in Gangetic West Bengal. According to historian Vinita Damoradan (2015, p. 92), many rural inhabitants were disturbed by the interventions of the East India Company and their revenue and agricultural regimes which increased taxation, encouraged settlement, and attempted to restrict "raids, hunting, and nomadism" (also see Rangarajan & Sivaramakrishnan, 2012). This earlier or wild Gangetic West Bengal can be glimpsed through colonial accounts. For example, in 1901 the botanist David Prain (1901) described the lower delta plain of Gangetic West Bengal as comprising two botanical districts. The southern portion of the delta nearest to the sea is the tidal Sundarbans mangrove and is "an intricate system of sea-creeks and half-formed islands, densely clothed with a tidal forest," which "separates itself spontaneously" from the northern region (1901, p. 15). The alluvial rice plain to the north is "where the river banks are higher, where tanks can be dug that will retain fresh-water, and where only the larger streams are much affected by the tides" (1901, pp. 15-16). The study area lies within the thick boundary of these two botanical districts.

While it is unclear when the mangrove or "jungle" that once covered the study area was cleared, what is known is that it was not an easy task.[6] Again, colonial accounts of the time offer some insight. An 1874 account by J. Westland, the magistrate and "collector" of Jessore, a district directly to the west of the study area, reflected on the "arduous undertaking" of clearing the mangrove of the delta. He described how "the trees intertwine with each other to such an extent that each supports and upholds the other" and "some of the trees are of an immense size … spreading and sending down new stems till it covers perhaps an acre of ground" (1874, p. 177). There was also "a low and almost impenetrable brushwood which cover[ed] the whole surface" and "no small danger from wild beasts" (1874, p. 177). Getting the mangrove under control was not only an arduous, but also an insistent task, for "[u]nless the greatest care is taken of the land so cleared, it will spring back into jungle and become as bad as ever," Westland bemoaned (1874, p. 178). The area of the lower delta plain, of which the study area is a part, was burdened with what Westland described as an "evil fertility of the soil." He warns that the mangrove takes at least "three eradications to expel" and must be cultivated for ten to twelve years before it lost any tendency to "at once cover itself" (1874, p. 178).

Trees were not the only obstacle for colonists. Speaking of nearby Khulna in 1908, the then Bengal District Gazetteer, L. S. S. O'Malley (1908), described the struggles to create cultivatable land in his district. Clearance, according to his accounts, always included "embanking" the land "to keep salt water out:" only then could "tanks [be] dug and huts constructed" (1908, p. 194). Another 1901 colonial account by Prain (1901), further describes how the practice of digging and embanking silty clay to separate salt and fresh water shaped both settlement patterns and vegetation distribution. This was a vernacular practice, not a colonial practice. He says the mounds and embankments "thrown up here and there" were often thickly covered with species characteristic of "Bengal village shrubberies" when they were not "occupied" by houses or by roadways (1901, p.17). Similarly, he reflected, the banks of streams were often covered in "a narrow hedge," while seasonal riverbeds and ponds were covered with "water-plants," thus transforming "the whole country [into] a semi-aquatic rice-plain" (1901, p. 18).

Writing in the mid-twentieth century, but building upon an earlier account (see Jack, 1927 [1916]), the geographer Oskar Spate (2017 [1954]) described the settlement patterns. He says while settlements are not clustered in (nucleated) villages, they are seen as a "dense stipple of separate homesteads" that were never far from another dwelling and thus, "hardly isolated." These homes were built on "mud plinths" usually 15 to 20 feet (4.6 to 6 meters) above "the general level," with the "necessary earth ... obtained from excavated [water] tanks." When there were rains, the continuous settlement pattern was transformed into a landscape "dotted with scores of thousands of tiny islets," each household "an island on its little earthen plinth" (2017 [1954], p. 580 and p. 198).

Spate (2017 [1954], p. 580) also gives us a further picture of an intertwined environment of mud, tidal water, vegetation, and settlement. Reiterating Prain (1901), he describes the vegetation character of the area as a "varied bush and tree culture." The water tanks he notes are "abundant" and support localized horticulture with banks "carrying vegetables, tobacco, mango and other fruit trees, as well as the indispensable bamboo and coconut palms." Mud from the excavated tanks, and vegetative materials from the tank bund and home gardens were also used to construct buildings that had a desirable "airiness," with "gabled ... high-pitched" roofs made of *palmyra* (toddy palm) thatching, nipa leaves or corrugated iron, "where available and within the means of the householder." House walls were made from various natural materials, including split bamboo, reed, jute-stalk matting or mud, and "more rarely" of wood and "very rarely... (except in towns)" of brick. Floors, although of mud, were "scrupulously clean."

Figure 5.10. A detailed 1785 colonial survey map of the southern periphery of Calcutta. Also shown, as an overlay, is the Ward 13 study area (white square).

A. Patterning of paddy fields and tidal creeks

B. Swampy land or "morass"

C. Linear and clustered settlements with treed-lined ponds, home gardens, and plantations

D. Behala area mango plantation

E. Mangrove-lined creek

(Source: Mark Wood, 1785. *A survey of the country on the eastern bank of the Hughly, from Calcutta to the Fortifications at Budgebudge, including Fort William and the Post at Manicolly Point, and shewing the extent and situation of the different courses, embankments, tanks, or broken ground, likewise representing the sands and soundings of the river at low water in spring tides, from January to May, from the year 1780 till 1784*. 1 inch = 2 miles. Calcutta, Mark Wood, Capt. Of Engineers. The British Library, London.)

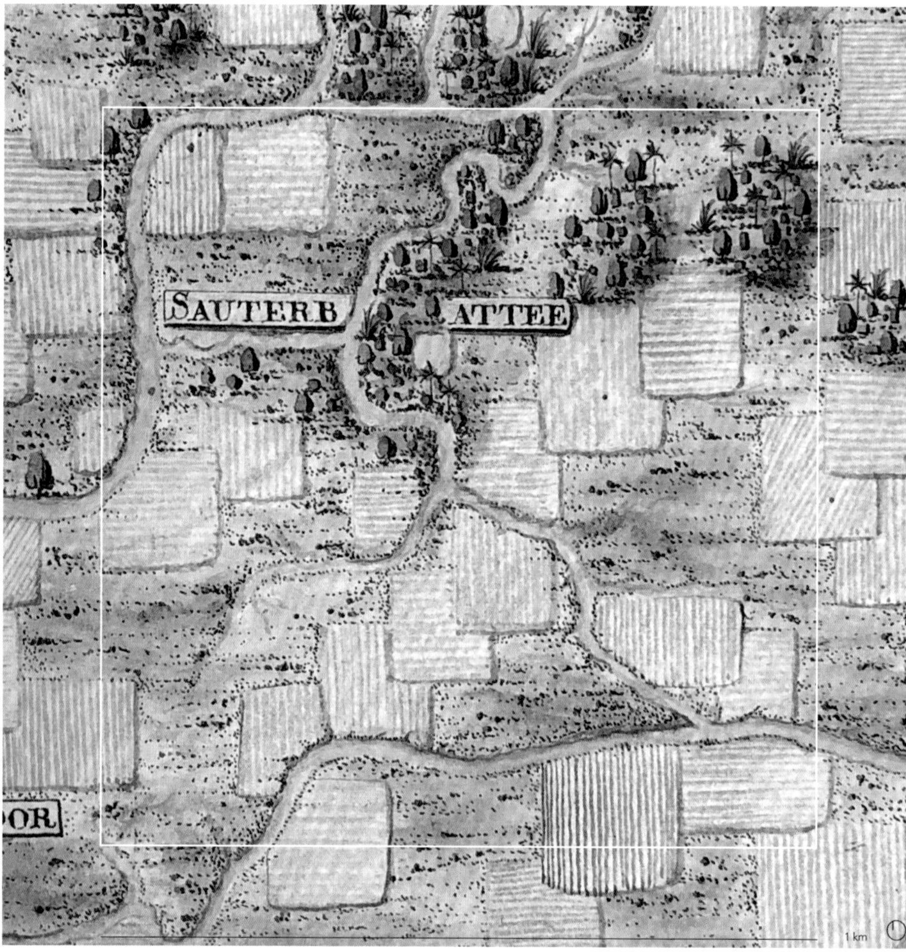

Figure 5.11. Map showing close up of the 1785 colonial survey map colonial survey map by Wood. Ward 13 study area (white square). The village name Sauterbattee is shown, however the correct name of Gopalpoor (Gopalpur) is written above (see Figure 5.10), which is how the study area is known today. Using invented shading, the map shows small rivulets with huts, temples, trees and pond/tank symbols along the embankments.

(Source: Mark Wood, 1785, Calcutta. The British Library, London.)

Although describing Bengal in 1910,[7] the settlement pattern and landscape formation that Spate documents appears very consistent with the earlier historical depictions including cartographic records at appropriate scales, such as shown in this rare 1 inch: 2 miles 1780 map (see Figures 5.10 and 5.11). Here are beautifully rendered clusters of homesteads, with treed tank bunds or tree-lined ponds amongst paddy fields. Figure 5.10 can be seen to be comprised of a patterning of paddy fields (A), and swampy land (B), and linear and clustered settlements with tree-lined ponds, home gardens, and plantations (C). In the Behala area (D), the tree-lined pond settlement appears denser, as this area was known as having a mango plantation (Resident, personal communication, K05, 2018). On the Howrah side of the Bhagirathi-Hooghly River (E), the dense treed area along a creek shown with few ponds or buildings suggests a mangrove thicket.

Writing around the same time as Spate, an account by the botanist-surveyor A. P. Benthal (1946, pp. 16–24), gives us further insight into the settled tree-lined pond and paddy field landscape of the study area. Benthal's survey was done in pursuit of writing a definitive account of the "trees of Calcutta and its neighborhood," a quest that took him on foot, like "a stranger approaching," through an expanse of paddy fields to a "typical Bengal village." Notably, and not unlike the impression left by a remote-sensed image today, he remarked that villages were barely discernible as clusters of buildings and could easily be mistaken "from a little distance to be no more than a wood or a grove of trees" or "forest on the horizon." Upon entering such vegetation clusters, the observer could be "surprised … to find how great a number of huts, and houses, and tanks, and small enclosed plots of vegetables, were concealed among the dense foliage around and above them." Benthal records a wide variety of plants in the treed village, most of which were grown by the villagers and "must of necessity" serve a "useful purpose" by yielding "edible fruits, or building material, or something else of value." Such villages, he observed, were scattered a mile or more apart across what was a "wide expanse of open paddy fields." The only other trees and shrubs to be found in this rice "expanse" were those "scattered here and there … forming hedges round plots of vegetables, irregular lines along the paths and tracks that connect neighboring villages, [or] clumps marking the position of swamps or patches of ground that for some reason are not used for cultivation." An 1861 map of Calcutta with a detailed legend (Figure 5.12) shows the settled "environs" patterning through symbols of buildings, tanks, and various cultivated trees and gardens. Furthermore, an 1853 map (Figure 5.13) shows this wooded settlement pattern as characteristic of the periphery of nineteenth-century Calcutta.

In sum, the colonial accounts of Gangetic West Bengal represent contradictory currents. There are the aspirational accounts that seek to chart the availability of territory and ground for colonial enclosure and productivity, and wrestle with the technical challenges of colonial expropriation. There are other accounts that revel in the dense mixes of use and settlement, aestheticizing and exoticizing it in various ways. And there are the later colonial accounts, like that of the development geographer Spate, which carry traces of a salvage paradigm (Clifford, 1989). The diversity of these historic representations reflects the living diversity of the area into the present. The on-the-ground periurban reality of Maheshtala Municipality and the one-kilometer-square case study area carries many of the features accounted for.

Figure 5.12. Part of a 1861 map of Calcutta showing the "City and Environs." This part shows the map legend (inset) and the junction of Diamond Harbor Road at Behala (adjacent to the study area, toward the east). The invented shading for paddy cultivation is rendered as a fish-scale hatch and everything else shown in this map detail is labelled in the legend as "Environs of Calcutta covered with huts and trees." The environs invented shading is further categorized into types of trees: mango, tamarind, *palmyra* (toddy palm), coconut, date, betelnut, bamboo grove and *jhow* (jhau or tamarisk tree) trees. Also shown are motifs for temples, mosques, tanks and unmetalled roads.

(Source: Survey of India, 1861, *The city and environs of Calcutta, including the Government Estate of Punchunnogram, with Allipoor, Khiderpoor, Garden-Reach, Seebpoor, Howrah and Sulkea*. Scale 6 inch = 1 mile, No. 5. Surveyor General's Office, Calcutta. National Library of India, Kolkata.)

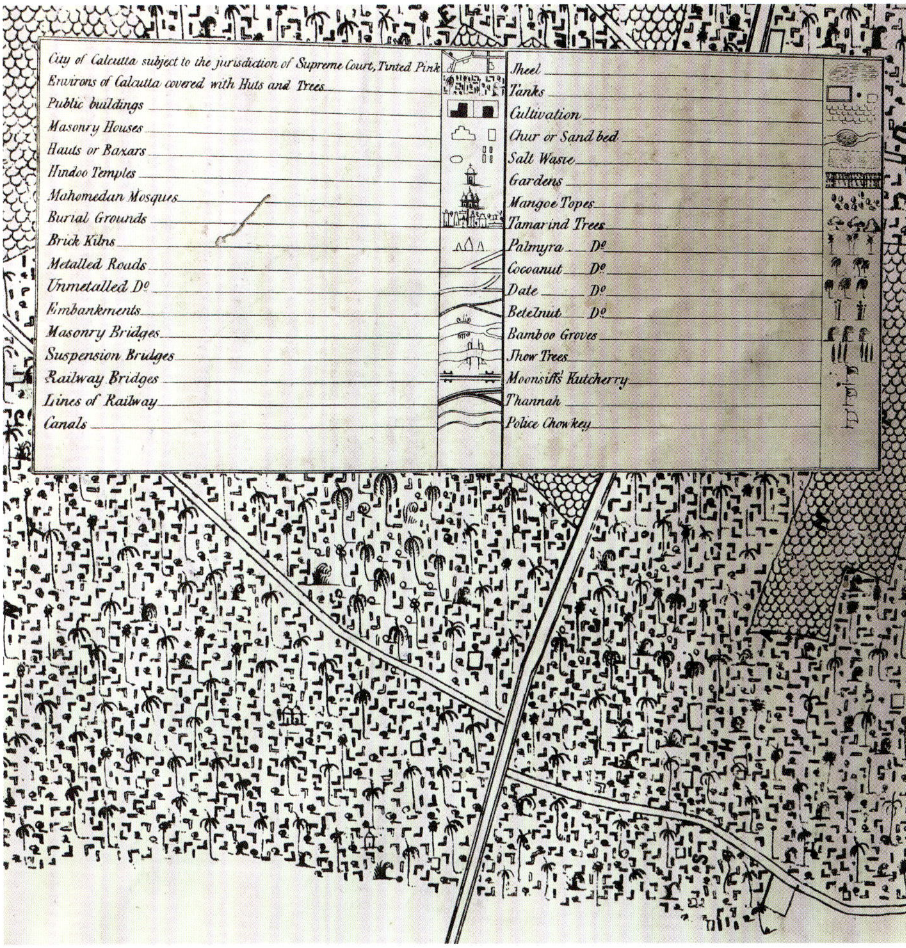
City of Calcutta subject to the jurisdiction of Supreme Court, Tinted Pink
Environs of Calcutta covered with Huts and Trees
Public buildings
Masonry Houses
Hauts or Bazars
Hindoo Temples
Mahomedan Mosques
Burial Grounds
Brick Kilns
Metalled Roads
Unmetalled Do
Embankments
Masonry Bridges
Suspension Bridges
Railway Bridges
Lines of Railway
Canals
Jheel
Tanks
Cultivation
Chur or Sand bed
Salt Waste
Gardens
Mangoe Topes
Tamarind Trees
Palmyra Do
Cocoanut Do
Date Do
Betelnut Do
Bamboo Groves
Jhow Trees
Moonsiffs' Kutcherry
Thannah
Police Chowkey

MAP OF THE COUNTRY 10 MILES ROUND CALCUTTA
RIVER HOOGLY
SALT WATER LAKE
Copied in the Survr Genls Office from the Original Compilation
Scale 1 Br. Mile = 1 Inch
83

Conclusion

In this chapter I continued my re-rendering of incremental transformations in the study area in Ward 13, Maheshtala Municipality. In my account of jungle, I reiterated the way in which residents live alongside of the consequences of wider periurban changes, marked by the coming and going of vegetative profusion and different attitudes to its presence. Just as waterlogging is powerfully agential, so too is jungle, although this slow entangling of drainage, jungly field, and colony is rarely discussed as such, or represented as the "Bengal countryside." In order to situate these conditions, I then turned to historical accounts of the forms of agrarian settlement in Gangetic West Bengal. In space and across time, I historicized colonial drainage and transportation works. I also described the study area in more depth through the long-term, interlinked fluid and agrarian ecologies of Gangetic West Bengal. To do this I engaged with colonial Government of Bengal and geographic atlas maps and accounts of the 1700s to 1900s, which revealed characteristics of both the settlement patterns at that time and the situatedness of the map-makers and authors.

On the one hand, I introduced how the study area is tightly tied to a string of faltering drainage works. On the other hand, I indicated that the desire to comprehensively map agrarian societies as productive land has nevertheless left some things off the map, or at best, only indistinctly present. Such faltering works and missing practices and spaces nevertheless have agency amidst periurban transformations. In the next chapters I re-render the study area even further, providing situated accounts of how ordinary entanglements with plants and property are given presence by residents. I will not only continue to discuss characteristics of the settled-rural as important, but I will also show how emergent imbroglios have agency.

Figure 5.13. 1853 map of the "Country 10 miles round Calcutta" showing wooded, settled areas in light brown with symbols of trees and red hutments. Also shown, as an overlay, is the Ward 13 study area (yellow symbol).

(Source: Abdoos Sobhan, 1853. *Map of the Country 10 miles round Calcutta*. I inch = 1 mile, Copied in the Surveyor Generals Office from the Original Compilation. https://zenodo.org/record/3596441#.XzxcV5MzZTY.)

Endnotes

1 Arnold argues that jangala had become naturalized in English and other European languages before Kipling's *Jungle Book* of 1894. Furthermore, he suggests that Kipling's book was perhaps a source for Upton Sinclair's 1906 novel *The Jungle*, about the Chicago slaughterhouses in which the oppressed and exploited poor struggle to survive (2015, p. 43).

2 The case study area in the book includes the West Bengal districts of Murshidabad, Nadia, and North 24 Parganas (Sen, 1989, p. 1).

3 Calcutta's name was changed to Kolkata in 2001. In this section, I use Calcutta to talk about the pre-2001 city and Kolkata to refer to the current city.

4 The jurisdictional complexity of the Manikhali Canal System is not easy to untangle. My understanding is that the short sections of the canal system that pass through land owned by the Calcutta Port Trust are the responsibility of the Trust, while all other parts of the canal are the responsibility of the state-level Irrigation and Waterways Department. However, as the canal basin is covered by both the state-level Kolkata Municipal Corporation area (upstream) and local-level Maheshtala Municipality (downstream), and discharges into the Bhagirathi-Hooghly River (covered by central-level *Ganga Action Plan*), much coordination is required to fund and carry out any improvement in the drainage works.

5 As Iqbal argues, the outcome of scholarly inquiry into the Permanent Settlement is the field of peasant and subaltern studies (2010, p. 10).

6 While Rennell's 1783 map (shown above in Figure 5.05) locates the boundary of the mangrove south of the study area, mangrove-lined creeks and inlets nearer the study area are possibly shown in a 1785 map (see Figure 5.10).

7 Spate bases his summary on Jack's 1906 to 1910 account (1927, p. 7) about the district of Faridpur, which is in today's Bangladesh.

6/

LIVED PROPERTY

In this chapter I continue the process of re-rendering the one-kilometer-square case study area. I do this through the social institution of property and its associated infrastructures. I focus on an element known as *bagans* (gardens). In the next chapter, I focus on the colony land market including its middlemen, buyers, and associations, as well as the associated infrastructures provided by the municipality. A colony is essentially a small cluster of newly built housing, serviced by an access road. According to a ward councilor, Ward 13 has around thirty such colonies (Maheshtala official, interview, K02, 2018). These fully social institutional and infrastructural assemblages are formed in a land ecology where animals and plants also shape space for themselves and, as a side effect, for residents too, often in undesirable ways. As I will show, the two lived property stories, one of the village and one of the colony-linked land market, are necessarily embedded in the situated, urban political ecology of drainage, fields, and jungle.

Rather than a term like "homegarden," I use the Bengali word bagan to encompass the many elements that may comprise the wooded areas around houses in the study area. I use this term because it is how such spaces are referred to locally. A bagan typically includes one or more of these elements: tree-lined ponds, tree plantations, and vegetable gardens, as well as religious, medicinal, aromatic, or other plants cultivated in the ground or in pots located around the houses or on a balcony or a rooftop (see Figures 6.01, 6.02, 6.03).

In Ward 13, residents' everyday experiences of living settled in, or newly settling into, a slowly changing periurban area depends in large part on their authority over land, its associated environmental resources or infrastructural provision, as well as certain dimensions of local social knowledge ("social capital"). Technical property rights are, then, only one part of this attained authority to settle. Settling or staying settled depends on a more nuanced, definition of property or proprietorial rights. Nearly all residents— long-term or newcomer—are landowners rather than tenants. A definition of

Figure 6.01. A long-term resident's healthy, fish stocked, *bagan* (garden) pond including a plantation on the pond bund. "Jungly", waterlogged land and colony buildings can be seen in the near distance. For many Hindu, caring for the banks of a pond is a religious practice, as such space can be understood as an embodiment of the divine.

(Source: author, 2018.)

Figure 6.02. A long-term resident's bagan with a bamboo gate and a fence that surrounds fruit trees and other edible plants. A pond and houses can be seen in the near distance.

(Source: author, 2018.)

Figure 6.03. Being shown an extensive, extended family owned bagan with three ponds, vegetable and medicinal garden, and plantation.

(Source: author, 2018.)

property that reifies static and formalized structures of rights between "persons, things or relations" (Hann, 1998) is usefully extended in a context such as this, where authority over a range of extended needs—infrastructural and ecological—can be precarious. Anthropologists Veronica Strang and Mark Busse (2011, p. 4) offer one way of approaching this extended notion of property. They think through property as the "wider processes of interaction between people, and between people and the physical environments that they inhabit." They highlight the notions and acts of owning and appropriating that precede, underwrite, and inform formal property relations and they place special emphasis on the modes of communication through which people assert and contest rights over property—be that land they own, a crop they have grown, or trees or ponds they care for (2011, p. 6). I engage this "processual" approach to property in order to learn how local governance and residents' norms and institutions interact through public infrastructure, land ecologies, and private land practices.

There is a specific need to think of property in process terms in the Indian context, as has been documented by other scholars. Anthropologists Geert De Neve and Henrike Donner (2015, p. 257), for example, chart what they refer to as the "social life of property" in Indian cities, and bring into focus the way in which emergent real estate markets are "organized, understood and appropriated in different contexts and by different actors." They argue that property is a set of negotiations framed by particular knowledges and requiring "perpetual work," ranging from everyday practices of making a home, tending kin relations, and mobilizing social capital, through to (in) formal brokerage and political mediation, and on to legal pursuits and collective mobilization (2015, p. 260). Scholarship in the vein includes studies of property-related "paperwork" (Tarlo, 2000), "class and kin work" (De Neve, 2015; Donner, 2015) as well as land market "link work" (Cook, 2015). These studies similarly emphasize that even while neoliberal market values now shape real estate transactions, this has not lessened the role of wider social relations, which "transform … the way property surfaces" (De Neve and Donner, 2015, p. 261).

I consider this elaboration of property to include ecological dimensions, as manifest in local knowledges of, and engagements with, cultivated and spontaneous plant ecologies. As such, the property transformations charted in this chapter seek to extend revisions of what property is, and to do so within the situating urban political ecologies of ordinary periurban change. The lens used in what follows seeks to lay bare the social life of ecological property. This is evident in many ways: as the inherited responsibilities for a state-managed canal; or a jungly paddy field; the norms around use of and access to residential bagans that comprise the wooded, settled parts of the case study area; or the fabrication of a localized land market for new colony housing.

Rules and Norms

In chapter 5, I provided an historical environmental account of the agrarian settlements of Gangetic West Bengal. I showed how the wooded settled areas within the study area are consistent with historical accounts of villages in the region. In what follows I explain that rules and norms persist with respect to cultivation of bagans. Like Robbins's study of *Lawn People* (2007, p. 99) in the United States, I see bagans (with their tree-lined ponds, vegetable gardens, and tree plantations) as a "collective ecological project." In the case of suburban lawn people, shared values regarding how a garden should look and be tended generated collective anxiety amongst residents about tending their lawns. In Ward 13 village settlements, residents also share a sense of how the inherited bagan landscape should be managed. However, compared to the lawn people there is a far more pragmatic and flexible stance in relation to how the collective ecological project of bagans should appear and be managed. For instance, there are those who worry that "nothing is being done in it" (Resident, interview, L07, 2018), while others are unconcerned because "they grow by themselves" (Resident, interview, L18, 2018), or they "don't expect anything [from their pond-garden]" (Resident, interview, L01, 2018). Others manage to keep tending their bagan, ranging from those who "do just a small amount of gardening" (Resident, interview, L03, 2018), to those who have transformed what was likely once a paddy plot or subsistence patch for the household into "my hobby" (Resident, interview, L13, 2018) (see Figure 6.04, 6.05, and 6.06).

There are localized but varied norms about sharing the many plants that grow in a particular household's bagan. One elderly long-term resident (Resident, interview, L07, 2018) articulated his adage that guides him with respect to who owns the produce from his plants and pond: "the owner only enjoys the fruits of nature's offerings," meaning only the owner can enjoy the harvest from the plant.. His rigid understanding is not shared by all. Another long-term resident (Resident, interview, L03, 2018) explained that if fruits, flowers, dry leaves, and twigs from someone else's trees fall, then anyone can use them. Such sharing is possible, he explained, because there already exist "good relations among neighbors"; his locality, after all, he elaborated "still looks village-like." Another long-term resident (Resident, interview,

Figure 6.04. Map showing the location of the only long-term resident respondent with an actively cultivated "hobby garden" (pink symbol). More typically, long-term resident households own bagans with "plants that grow by themselves" (black symbol). Wooded settled land covers are also highlighted (yellow-bounded areas).

(Source: author, 2022; Google Earth Pro, 2018; and unassembled and unpublished GIS files provided by Maheshtala Municipality, 2019.)

Figure 6.05. A long-term resident's bagan described as a "hobby garden" with many flowering plants and a lawn in the foreground. Plantation trees can be seen in the near distance.

(Source: author, 2018.)

Figure 6.06. A long-term resident's more economically productive bagan comprised of an actively cultivated plantation, seen as trees planted on the perimeter of the plot of land. A recently felled tree and a rudimentary, enclosed vegetable garden can be seen in the foreground.

(Source: author, 2019.)

L08, 2018), explains that such sharing is allowable, but that she always asks for permission: "We tell them [the owner of the property] … and] once we tell them, we then use it." When the "fruits of nature" are located on land or waterways that are public or on private land or water, but the owner is not known or locally present, then other rules apply. Some residents catch fish from *nullas* (common drains) near their houses (Resident, interview, L18, 2018), especially "during the rains." Such catches are small in quantity and only used for the household, not for sale.

Newcomers in the colony settlements bring their own understandings of who has rights over the produce of bagans in the locality. "Produce" means not only fruit but leaves and flowers, twigs, and branches. For example, one newcomer resident was cautious when asked about sharing plants, explaining that an "owner of a tree will not allow anyone to use it or its fruits," but that trees whose ownership is not known are "available to everyone" (Resident, interview, N13, 2018). Newcomers do not always have a clear sense of who owns what land and the norms and rules that surround the use of plants and ponds, especially because owned land may also be run down and jungly. Long-term residents who were interviewed articulated judgments about newcomers and their lack of knowledge about informal conventions about access to locally grown plants. One long-term resident said newcomers did "not bother about ownership" and just went "plucking … taking away the coconuts, the branches for brooms—betel nuts are taken when they fall" (Resident, interview, L03, 2018). He accused others of "chopping away trees … without even informing" anyone. In the mind of this long-term resident, this activity was deliberate and planned. He felt that his pond-garden was vulnerable to "outsiders," but if he confronted them, they would then "start creating problem[s]." He was acutely aware of the change in his locality, noting that "earlier this [problem] was not there" as "we had only a few people residing here." The neighborhood, he lamented, was "no longer the same."

This testimony speaks to unauthorized foraging by "unruly" newcomers who do not abide by informal norms around plant use. But these norms are evolving: long-term residents' general attitudes towards the use of local resources have changed. For instance, although trees and shrubs for firewood and fuel are "all around," most residents in the study area now elect to use gas for cooking, meaning there is now "no need" for anyone to collect firewood (Resident, interview, L10, 2018). Furthermore, both long-term and newcomer residents simply do not have the time to tend large, tree-lined ponds and vegetable gardens, nor glean from their surplus, as they now engage in paid work. Similarly, piped drinking water has meant that pond-owners no longer feel it necessary to carefully manage the water quality in their ponds.

Finally, the older "village-like" localities in the area are becoming polluted. Waterlogging by sewage-laden runoff from colonies has resulted in the "drowning" of once stand-alone, tree-lined ponds and vegetable gardens. In addition, private plantation trees planted in bagans are dying, or are being felled but not replaced. In what follows I look at these two issues in more detail.

Drowning

While there is no official data about the number of tree-lined ponds in the case study area, there are 77 large ponds located in Ward 13, as mapped in the third development plan (Maheshtala Municipality, 2012).[1] In addition, many smaller tree-lined ponds were identified by walking the study area and cross-tabulating with remote-sensed imagery. For instance, among the long-term residents interviewed, most (n=11) owned tree-lined ponds. Extrapolating from this, if two thirds of the total number of households in the study area are estimated to be long-term residents, then there are some 355 tree-lined ponds in the area, a much larger number than indicated in the third development plan. Much like the concrete-lined tanks that exist in other parts of metropolitan Kolkata and West Bengal, tree-lined ponds can be seen as a as a composite "pondscape" resource (Cornea et al., 2016; also see Ray, 2015). These ponds are certainly ecological entities, but they are also embedded within complex relationships of power. For one thing, they are a source of food and water amenity, and so can "mitigate" social disadvantage. They have also been found to be embedded in the concerns and politics of local institutions such as neighborhood clubs and political parties (Cornea et al., 2016, p. 396), suggesting their importance as a multifaceted resource across Gangetic West Bengal. The ponds of Ward 13 are all privately owned and the wider social role they play necessarily relates to practices of sharing amongst extended family members and trusted neighbors.

In the past, tree-lined ponds were a key everyday resource and a number of the older practices persist today. For instance, one resident recalls how "in earlier days" her household relied on the fish from the pond for "daily meals." Her father would buy fish from the market only "once a month" and it would be "only sea fish" that would be bought (Resident, interview, L15, 2018). This same household did what many long-term families do: they extended their home at the expense of the garden pond. This happened in stages. For example, in 1982 they replaced their old mud house with a new house. In 1992 one room was added by filling in part of the pond. Then, in 2003, another room was added, again encroaching on the pond area. While the pond remains, is it smaller and it is no longer cultivated. In another household, the daughter recollected how "long back" almost everyone in the village would "come and bathe in [their] pond" (Resident, interview, L15, 2018). Today nobody comes as everyone has their "own water taps." "In fact," she explained, "we also don't use the pond to bathe or anything ... we have also taken water connections at home." In this house, as with many others, "the pond is pretty much unused." Nevertheless, the tree-lined pondscape remains actively cleaned and stocked with fishlings (fry) by an elderly family member and provides the occasional fish for household meals (see Figure 6.07).

In the past, long-term residents were known to lease their tree-lined ponds for raising fish, often gaining some benefit from a well-stocked pond. For instance, one long-term resident (Resident, interview, L06, 2018) recounted how they used to lease their pond out on a five-year lease for a one-off payment of 25,000 rupees. Every time the lessee harvested from the pond; he was obliged offer fish to the family. In this instance, leasing the pond did not mean the household lost the amenity of the pond in their bagan, nor complete loss of access to the fish stock. However, the resident remarked, the lessee only cultivated one type of fish whereas the diversity of fish had been greater earlier. Prior to 1990, when the rivulet was tidal, he said fish would swim into ponds from the river via the canal, especially during the rains when the many local ponds flooded and became linked with adjacent neighbors' ponds. During the rains pond-owners would protect their fish stock by netting parts of their ponds to "prevent the stock from fleeing." Today, this householder has resumed management of his own pond but he misses the array of fish that were once present including "different types of carp," such as *rui* (grass carp), *mirgel* (silver carp), and other species of *bata* (small fish). This same householder also grows *patabahar* (croton) around the edge of his tree-lined pond, as the plant functions as "barrier fencing" and, he says, also "beautifies" the surrounding area. This suggests that an actively productive pondscape also has an aesthetic register.

Ponds in Ward 13 change in other ways. This same resident reported that many ponds are actually "getting larger and shallower" (Resident, interview, L06, 2018). Changes in size and depth like this have multiple causes, but a key reason is the deterioration of the tree-lined bunds and the subsequent siltation of the ponds. This deterioration starts with the loss of trees on the bund for, as he explained, "[t]he trunk of trees [roots] sunk deep on the side (*ara*) retains the banks." Without this vegetation stabilization, soil from the bund starts to "wash down" into the ponds. He proudly reflected that "our aras are intact." The loss of trees on bunds is partly a consequence of excessive waterlogging, which effectively drowns the tree roots. As noted in

Figure 6.07. A former commons or shared pond that is now only cultivated by the owner for fish rearing.

(Source: author, 2019.)

the previous chapter, such waterlogging is a result of neglect of the creek and canal system, by both state entities and residents. Waterlogging is also often the result of the plotting of land by colony development, which can block the overland flow of water. Today, densities of waterlogging have negative effects on tree-lined ponds, submerging the roots of the trees planted to stabilize the pond bunds, leaving them vulnerable to erosion. When aras deteriorate, adjacent ponds link up, and when not tended, linked ponds become stagnant and algae blooms occur (see Figure 6.08).

One ponded bagan was especially affected by polluted water coming from an adjacent colony (Resident, interview, L10, 2018) (refer back to Figure 6.03). Unlike the other, more modest, colonies in the study area, the newcomers in this instance built large multifamily homes without septic tanks (as sewage infrastructure had been promised by the promoter, but not yet delivered). The long-term resident pond-owner reflected on how they used to live in "very pleasant and quiet surroundings." The trees they had planted cooled the environment and a "soothing wind used to blow all the time," while their "whole house looked like fruit garden." His household comprises three families, a father and mother, their two sons, and their families. Their bagan contains three tree-lined ponds; one is a shared pond for the family, and two are the property of two brothers, respectively. The bagan also has a clearing for vegetable growing and for medicinal plants, as well as many plantation trees.

One of the brothers explained their experience of waterlogging. "Accumulated water," as he called it, happens during "the rains" because the water is no longer "getting drained naturally." The daughter-in-law added that they were then surrounded by "a stagnant pool of putrefied water." As we walked around this bagan, the son was able to point out the changes: "Look at that tree there and this tree here ... both trees are ... dying out ... [they] shrink and ultimately die. Every year some tree or other is dying like that." He concluded the tour by noting how the "greenery is gradually getting obliterated." This is not technically true, as the bagan is still very "green," but what he meant is that productive plants are dying out, and because waterlogging makes tending the land virtually impossible ("we can't even reach our garden then"), they are being replaced by unproductive, spontaneous plants. His bagan is "now full of wild growth," he mourns. The narrative of this bagan expresses the change in composition and patterning of the "wooded" part of the study area more broadly. The overall tree cover has not only changed in composition, but it is also less dense.

Certain trees are more vulnerable to waterlogging than others. Fruit-bearing trees like *asphal*, *jamrul* (rose apple), mango, and jackfruit are most vulnerable, whereas, where present, larger plantation trees may survive.

Figure 6.08. A deteriorated pond with an eroded *ara* (pond bund). The submerged ara is visible as a ring of trees in the left foreground and in the middle of the image. The extended pond surface is covered in an algae bloom, which can lead to eutrophication (a condition whereby oxygen is prevented from getting into the water, making it harmful for fish and other aquatic life forms). The deterioration of the pond is also evident in that there are no large old plantation trees present. Of the young trees that are visible, many appear to be dying, which can be seen in the unusually open canopy, yellowing leaves and many bare branches.

(Source: author, 2019.)

For example, in this bagan a tamarind tree was "still surviving" and a wild variety of jamrul (used mostly as firewood rather than for its small fruit) was holding on. We were shown empty areas where once had stood *kadamba* (kadam), *shishu* (north Indian rosewood), jackfruit, and guava that had "withered away." Flowering plants, grown for both aesthetic and religious use, suffer in his bagan. For example, a china rose was "surprisingly in flower," but other "precious flower" plants in the garden like the *sthal poddo* (hibiscus) and *karabi* (oleander) had died off and now "nothing survives." Bagans also contain plantations. A bamboo patch that was once regularly harvested is now "lying just like this as they are no longer tended." The coconut trees were also "lying diseased as they are not looked after either." However, trees planted for timber such as *mahogani* (mahogany) and *shirish* (albizia) are less affected by waterlogging. For instance, in this garden we were proudly shown healthy young saplings said to be too young to cut, but which will yield "useable wood" when mature in some twenty-five to thirty years' time.

This particular household was troubled by the current state of their bagan. They wanted their old garden back, with even more "vegetable and fruit-bearing trees." They had yet-to-be-realized plans to "raise" the level of the land by "dumping soil," which they hoped would free their land from waterlogging. Readying for this, the family had "cleaned [a] portion of land of undergrowth." Restoring the bagan is costly, and the expenditure competed with other household needs, most notably the family's aspiration to extend their house to accommodate an increasing family size. Households such as this generally invest not in the garden, but in maintenance of the house or its extension as needed. Bagan restoration and maintenance are lower priorities. The slow degradation of the bagan becomes an intractable predicament for such families, and one that is intensified by a process of waterlogging which they are increasingly unable to control through their own actions.

In the case of this household, the waterlogging they wrestled against was intensified by the combined action of the local promoter who had plotted the nearby colony and consolidated the access road, as well as the cumulative effects of each buyer-builder who constructed houses and built no effective operational solution to their domestic waste needs. Instead, they just let wastewater run off at a distance from the house along a rudimentary drain. These other actors periurbanization have little or no voluntary obligation with respect to the effects of their actions on the surrounding landscape. They enter colony development and residency with considerable aspiration but limited means, and little regulatory oversight. They are not under any legal planning obligation to build in a way that reduces the impact of their actions on the surrounding environment and the associated livelihoods or amenity of existing residents. This is even though solutions to these localized ecological problems can be very simple, low-tech, and low cost. For example, in the case of this household, merely redigging a functional drainage channel to the Monikhali Canal would help to alleviate the problem, as the pond-owner household explained. But there are no trusted mechanisms for ensuring such action. This family, for example, did not see a solution coming from the municipality, and were resigned to the fact that a ward councilor was known to be a "beneficiary" of the colony promoter.

The aspiration of this family to restore their bagan was unusual. Most households no longer tried. For instance, another pond-owner household, (Resident, interview, L03, 2018) reported that his two pond-gardens are "still there" but they are "lying idle." Such "idle" gardens succumb quickly to spontaneous undergrowth which can turn previously cultivated lands "into jungle compared to earlier times." Jungly land is owned but ends up being unusable. With this household, for example, the pond and its fish resources were lost to the family: "The ladies and the children would catch fish from the ponds at this time of the year … [but] … no one will dare go there now." The water quality has also been degraded in this family's pond, and there was "no question of drinking from the pond." In the study area, few households nowadays rely on pond water for drinking, as there has been municipally supplied piped drinking water since 1983. But families report thinking, as this family does, that the water from their pond had been "healthier." Ironically, the arrival of piped water was one more component in changing the structure of responsibility with respect to the ponds. When not used for drinking water, they were less cared for, even becoming repositories for "dumping" of hard waste. This same family who was nostalgic for the now-lost healthy water of the old pond, admitted they had used the pond for dumping plastic and other materials, and that now "everything has got spoilt."

Cutting

Many long-term residents recall that the locality was previously more wooded. An extended family with ten members have lived in their home for seventy years (around the time of the partition of India and Pakistan) and were tenant farmers (Resident, interview, L14, 2018). The son, recalling what his forefathers had told him about the village area, reported it was "wooded completely" with "not a single house." Their home, which was "a *kutcha* [makeshift] house made of mud," and that of a nearby "doctor's house" were the only residential buildings in the immediate neighborhood. Looking around, the son pointed at the mix of old and new homes: "The people you can see here [now] have come from the other parts." The son noted especially how the presence of "huge trees" had changed over time. Such trees were planted by residents to supply hard timber for building and fabrication or for sale. The convention of cultivating a small plantation or single hardwood tree is fading: "People do not give the tree [time] to grow [for] timber." Instead, "they just slash it down beforehand [before it matures]." The overall effect in the ward is that vegetation is now "smaller and thinner," he says. The aunt in this household confirmed that the removal of large trees began twenty-five to thirty years ago (1988-1993) at a time when "there was an ample amount of space between two houses."

The experience of other households gives us further insight into the qualities of these changes in vegetation. One resident also recalls that "earlier" the tree cover in the area was such that "even sun's ray wouldn't peep through," and "the whole area would be completely shaded because of these trees" (Resident, interview, L03, 2018). Explaining the change by way of example, he pointed and said: "You see that house over there? There was a banyan tree, a *shirish* tree [albizia] and a tamarind tree over there." Of his own land he explained, "my area used to be dark as well," including banyan trees and a shirish tree whose "girth was huge." While the residents may lament the loss of a familiar and large tree, the choice to remove it by the owner is also respected. For instance, too much shade is seen as problematic in domestic gardens and for pisciculture. Direct sun is needed for the drying of clothes, and a shady pond "hampers fish cultivation" (Resident, interview, L01, 2018). Also, managing some trees for the benefit of the household may no longer make economic sense. For example, in earlier times most gardens would have coconut trees for home use. But harvesting the tall coconut often depended on hiring a specialist person to climb the trees. Things have changed: "It wasn't this expensive before" one resident recounted. "Right now even to climb a coconut tree you cannot find a person," whereas "you could find people easily before." Finally, in this cyclone-prone area, trees can be damaged, and this can cause burdens and benefits beyond just the loss of the tree. One resident (Resident, interview, L06, 2018) recalled how in Cyclone Aila (2009) his "roof sheets were thrown … distant away, trees … uprooted, fruits … torn away." He explained that he was responsible for clearing all the fallen trees and tree branches. As explained by another resident, if a tree is uprooted in a storm, the landowner is "entrusted" to cut and clear it, and to take the wood away (Resident, interview, L12, 2018).

There are a number of long-term residents who still manage plantations of trees, grown for their economic value (refer back to Figure 6.06). These trees are cultivated with the intention of being cut when mature or when the income is needed by the family; for example, if there is economic need or a special event, like a marriage, to be paid for. One long-term resident owns three plantations: palm, bamboo, and mahogani (Resident, interview, L05, 2018). He says, the mahogani plantation was created "twenty years back" and "has very good valuation," because it is "top quality" (see Figure 6.09). The family also use the wood for making the "premium wooden furniture" that is given to a bride at the time of marriage. Another resident who still grows trees for income, has planted a shirish tree, which is said to be good for making furniture: "bed, dressing table, and *almirah* [cabinet]" (Resident interview, L19, 2018). His family has been engaged in plantation cultivation for "generations … two hundred years." His plot has just eight trees, which are cut after ten to twelve years. At any one time the trees are of varying ages, and he can harvest from the plantation every five to six years. Another long-term resident (Resident, interview, L07, 2018) explained how various trees (*shal* [sal], *shagun* [teak], *tal* [palmyra-palm], and mango) are also used for making wooden doors and window frames in the local construction industry. Typically, a small-time grower sells a tree to the local sawmill and the sawmill in turn sells the wood to a local carpenter. There is some evidence that local entrepreneurs are keying into this economic opportunity, running small businesses that approach landowners to sell their trees to them directly (see Figure 6.10).

Overall, managing a plantation for the supply of wood for furniture or for buildings is now relatively uncommon and seen as a practice from a past time. A local carpenter corroborated this account (Entrepreneur, interview, K07, 2018), reporting that shal, shagun, and *gamar* [white teak] are no longer available locally. The five local sawmills now source their wood primarily from Malaysia. The number of trees suitable for using in cabinetry has "drastically reduced" and "only a few replantings have been done." Some residents are still planting trees of higher value, like shirish and mahogani, but currently most saplings are "small" and many now die before reaching maturity because of waterlogging. This local carpenter laments that there is only "awareness to some extent" of the economic and amenity value of a treed landscape, but some residents are now "cutting less … and planting more": however, he admits there are other forces that lead to landowners deciding not to plant. First, there is less demand for wooden furniture, which is expensive relative to alternatives, such as stainless steel. Everyone wants "modern furniture now," he explains. A Ward 13 sawmill owner also described

Figure 6.09. A long-term resident's plantation on a tree-lined pond bund. The foreground tree and other wide-girth trees in the middle view are a *mahogani* (mahogany) plantation. Jungly former paddy fields and a colony can be seen in the far distance.

(Source: author, 2019.)

Figure 6.10. A Ward 13 sawmill yard with stored logs. Smaller logs are seen in the foreground and larger, more recently felled, local logs are seen stored behind. These logs are not considered valuable for re-sale and are stored until the owner pays for their milling. The mill—a shed where mostly imported logs are cut—is not visible.

(Source: author, 2018.)

a downturn in demand for the milling of local timber (Key Player, interview, K08, 2018). This miller mills about fifty trees a month altogether, but only a minor proportion are sourced from the Maheshtala area because this local wood is now "all low-grade." Overall, his business had "suffered badly" in recent times, despite the steady rate of colony home building. This is because there is "no demand" from furniture makers as the "solid wood market is negligible."

The tree cultivation practices within private bagans, as evidenced in the study area, are a subset of what the West Bengal Forest Department categorizes as "social forestry," meaning "forestry outside of the [official] forest area," also sometimes called "non-forest greenery" (West Bengal Forest Department Officer, interview, K03, 2019).[2] Under the West Bengal Trees (Protection and Conservation in Non-Forest Areas) Act, 2006, residents of metropolitan Kolkata are technically required to obtain a permit before cutting their privately owned trees. This provision is intended to preserve some of the "green" character of metropolitan Kolkata, and the rule applies to all urban local bodies across West Bengal. However, as the West Bengal Forest Department officer in charge of Ward 13 explained, this regulation is rarely observed. As a relatively new regulatory provision, many residents are unaware of it. Furthermore, compliance cannot easily be monitored as most existing trees have not been incorporated into a state-based audit framework (West Bengal Forest Department Officer, interview, K04, 2019). Also, the regulation only applies to certain species of trees that are known to be of economic value by the Forest Department, such as mahogani. Other plants in wooded settled areas are not so protected, even though they may contribute to landscape quality and local periurban household economies. For instance, medicinal and aromatic plants and the everyday knowledge and practices associated with them are known to play an important role in primary health care in Maheshtala (Chaudhuri et al., 2019).[3]

Creatures

When asked to reflect upon the negative side of periurban change, residents offered accounts of the "menace" of snakes and "infestations" of mosquitos (both terms are used locally). In this section, I situate each of these problematic creatures as lived ecologies in this particular "kind of urban" condition, for these animals and insects are also adjusting to periurban changes. They too "negotiate and learn to inhabit complex, dynamic environments, apprehending them according to their own knowledges, speeds and rhythms, with or against the grain of urban design" (Barua and Sinha, 2019, p. 1161; see Philo and Wilbert, 2000). I begin by reflecting upon this statement in relation to the long-settled rural of West Bengal.

Anthropologist Annu Jalais (2010) has reported upon the *pir* cult in deltaic Bengal, noting that there is historical evidence of "symbiotic relations" (2010, p. 153) between *pirs* and tigers.[4] *Pirs* are Sufi holy men, or charismatic persons popularly identified as such, and they have been associated with mangrove forest clearing and land reclamation in Bengal since the sixteenth century (Eaton, 1993, p. 207).[5] Their story is reflected in a "persisting relationship" in West Bengal between Islam and the mangrove forest (Jalais, 2010, p. 153). The "return to the forest" is a recurring feature of these pirs and the stories about them tell how, even after receiving large tracts of cultivable land or initially lording over them, "they always redistributed them and went back to live in the forest as recluses" (Jalais, 2010, p. 153). The stories also recount how, through ascetic power, a reclusive pir took the form of a tiger called *Dakshin Rai* (king of the south). What emerges is that these Sufi men are mentioned in "two different contexts" (2010, p. 155). The first sphere portrays them the "patron saints of Bengal villages where their memory is sung and respectfully marked by graves and shrines" and the second depicts them as "*fakirs* [holy men who possess supernatural or miraculous powers] controlling the forest" (Jalais 2010, p. 155). "Down" island[6] residents in turn, believe that they share with tigers a "unique geography, a shared history, a set of common laws – and, crucially, 'interactive experiences'" (Jalais, 2010, p. 203). For instance, the hybrid Hindu-Muslim story of Bonbibi (written in the 1800s) continues to be evoked by tiger-charmers (themselves woodcutters or persons performing on behalf of woodcutters and bee collectors) as they enter the Sundarban mangrove (2010, p. 203). Likewise, Dakshin Rai persists in being celebrated in the "mainland" of Ward 13 (see Figure 6.11) and the story of Bonbibi has since been written again for an English-speaking audience and visualised by artist Salman Toor (Ghosh, 2021).

I what follows I shift from tigers to snakes, before turning to the lived ecologies of mosquitoes. The participant residents consider snakes a menace when they are visible in everyday life, and especially when those visible snakes are poisonous (see Figure 6.12). The most problematic or menacing scenario is when a poisonous snake like a cobra enters a household and bites a resident. The least menacing, but nonetheless troubling, scenario is a sighting of a snake, say, crossing the road at night, particularly if the road is poorly lit, or not lit at all. The frequency and location of these types of encounters have changed over time. For instance, many of the long-term residents often encountered poisonous snakes earlier but say the "menace is decreasing with

years" (Resident, interview, L03, 2018). One resident, who was bitten as a teenager, recalled that it was not unusual to "find a cobra below a prepared bed." Another long-term resident (Resident, interview, L06, 2018) noted that both the variety and the number of snakes has declined "substantially" as "earlier, different species cobras and all types of snakes were to be found."

The observation that encounters with poisonous snakes in the home has decreased does not mean the menace has gone. A newcomer resident told us how snakes are a "common occurrence" (Resident, interview, N01, 2019). She reflected: "We often find snakes in our rooms." Although some were poisonous, they were not considered problematic as "they leave on their own." Similarly, another newcomer resident reflected on the "intrusion of snakes in our house," noting "[t]hey have just left" and "there [has] not been any snakebite." This categorization of snake encounters as being expected, remarkable, but not dangerous, was typical (Resident, interview, N14, 2019). In understanding the acceptance of the snake in everyday life, it is relevant to note that snakes are associated with the Manasa cult, a snake goddess venerated locally. This gives an added dimension to an encounter with a snake—a subtle shuttling between repulsion and reverence. According to historian Wendy Doniger (2015, p. 3), the human relation to snakes in the Manasa cult is "hedged in ambivalence." Snakes are invoked to come, bringing water and fertility, but also to encouraged leave without harming the worshipper, a framing consistent with the accounts of everyday encounters in the study area. Aligned with this, most residents would never

Figure 6.11. In the eighteenth century, a line on a map was drawn by the surveyor Lieutenant Hodges and Sundarbans' Commissioner, William Dampier. The line was an instrument for separating the management of forest and field as distinct zones for revenue extraction and governance. They defined and surveyed "the line of forest" and formally affirmed "Princep's line [an earlier surveyor]" in 1832-33 (O'Malley 1908, p. 46). Titled the Dampier-Hodges line, it was the "authoritative limits of the then Sundarbans forest" (1908, p. 46) and it is now held in place by Sundarbans Reserve Forest governance. Nevertheless, local practices that relate to the long settled "forest of tigers" (Jalais, 2010) persist "above" the Dampier-Hodges line in South 24 Parganas. This is evidenced in the above image, one of many *Dakshin Rai* deity in Ward 13, Maheshtala.

(Source: author 2020.)

consider harming a snake, allowing them always to leave their houses on their own. One nonlocal newcomer thought and acted differently, living in an overly jungly part of a colony she admitted, "we have killed a number of them" (Resident, interview, N09, 2019).

Indeed, many residents associated an increase or decrease in encounters with snakes with changes in the absence or presence of jungly conditions. For instance, a newcomer resident living near jungly land complained that "snakes abound in this jungle" and can be seen "all the time" (Resident, interview, N02, 2019). Other colony residents were happy to report that because their local "jungle has been cleared" there was no longer a "snake scare" and they could now live with "no fear" (Resident, interview, N05, 2019). Others expressed a more nuanced understanding of the relationship between jungle and snakes. An elderly newcomer resident explained that although her colony was becoming increasingly settled by newcomers, the jungle around her somewhat remote house was "still infested." She knows that snakes are "cautious to appear in front of human eyes," but the snakes near her house "dare to come out in the open more often." This hints at the fact that periurbanization might mean changes in patterns and behaviors of "animals themselves" (Wolch, 2002, p. 735).

Another creature that is entangled with the case study area is the mosquito. As Nanding (2014, p. 202), who has studied dengue-endemic communities, states: "people, pathogens, vectors, and their shared surroundings are always in the process of becoming, together" because "environments do not just cause health problems; rather humans and non-humans incorporate one another's actions." Earlier, when ponds were used daily, when the canals were tidal, and paddy was inundated with slowly flowing water, residents were able to control mosquito breeding. "We would not even need a mosquito net for sleeping," a long-term resident recalled (Resident, interview, L02, 2019). Today there is said to be a major mosquito problem across with serious health consequences. As a long-term resident pointed out, gesturing to the mosquitoes in his courtyard, "even now you can see them [in the afternoon], but it will be very severe after sundown" (Resident, interview, L01, 2018). While the municipality does spray pesticide, they come "just once" a year, which is "ineffective," she says (Resident, interview, L01, 2018). For this resident, the mosquito infestation became even more troublesome after the municipality renovated their pathway road without maintaining the previously functioning side-drain, thereby creating stagnant water adjacent to every household along that pathway road. In other instances, the mosquito infestation is attributed to a nearby *khatal* (cowshed) and, more commonly, to the problem of waterlogging associated with colony development.

Figure 6.12. A snake crossing a pathway "shortcut" between a wooded settled area and a playing field.

(Source: author, 2018.)

For newcomer residents, who live in the low-lying, waterlogged colony areas, the mosquito infestation is "severe" (Resident, interview, N18, 2018) and a "perennial problem" (Resident, interview, N04, 2018). Indeed, in 2019, Maheshtala and nearby Behala were considered the "worst hit" areas in metropolitan Kolkata for dengue cases (Yengkhom and Ray, 2019).

All told, for residents to freely move around their homes and surrounds during the day and in the evening, they need to negotiate two creatures seen as pests, the presence of which has altered because of transformations in the built environment, and perspective. While there are no encounters with tigers in the study area, encounters with snakes persist, and mosquitoes, and the disease they deliver, remain endemic. Cohabiting with these other species alters where residents move and when they move, and how they manage their interior spaces. Residents no longer traverse former paddy land at all, nor do they sit or sleep outside in the evenings as before. The rearrangement of everyday life in relation to previously agrarian spaces and in intimate household spaces points out the importance of what geographer Jennifer Wolch (2002, p. 729) says is an understanding of how "animals are [also] critical to the making of places and landscapes."

Figure 6.13. A retired, newcomer resident's bagan with a bamboo gate and poster/donation box showing the Hindu goddess Kali (who is noted to be the ultimate expression of nature, both destructive and benevolent). The garden occupies his, as-yet undeveloped, housing plot in colony/former paddy land. The garden is described by the owner as a "hobby garden" for the cultivation of household vegetables and flowers for *puja* (worship ritual). Overgrown paddy fields can be seen behind the far garden fence.

(Source: author, 2018.)

Conclusion

The "perpetual work" that over the decades has sustained bagans is declining. This decline is a result of various factors including residents' actions, poorly developed colonies, changing taste, and limited, if evolving, environmental governance frameworks. The planting and maintaining of bagans was once sustained by necessity: tree-lined ponds provided drinking water and fish; slow-growing plantation trees were cultivated for income or used for fabrication of furniture; domestic gardens were cultivated for household use; firewood was collected for fuel; and shade and breezes would cool the household. Nevertheless, the cultivation of bagans holds on in a transformed state. Many residents, including newcomers (see Figure 6.13), continue to cultivate vegetables and fruit trees for their own consumption, plants with medicinal and aromatic benefit, plants associated with *puja* (worship), and trees for shade.

What also persists are the norms that surround the use of plants and ponds, even though there are rule-breakers like newcomers and promoters aided by local officials. The interpersonal work to continually reproduce ordinary norms around private bagans is hard. Sustained attention and polite chitchat are required to maintain an amicable locality where resident-defined norms are valued as meaningful in social, economic, and ecological ways. This hard work to withstand change is not valued by the municipality, nor are the bagan spaces created seen as "residential" or even "environment." For instance, bagan practices are not discussed in any of the municipal development plans. The wooded environment of the municipality is thought to only consist of street trees and tree planting in parkland that is owned by the municipality, and there are only a few official parks. This is remarkable given that readily available satellite imagery of periurban Maheshtala is visibly wooded and "green" (refer back to Figure 3.03).

With incremental periurban transformation, it is reasonable for long-term residents to view the potential of both their paddy and household lands as enduring. As was discussed in chapter 5, the transformation of paddy into jungle does not mark an abandonment of ownership, merely a change in approaches to how owned land is managed. Ownership persists in fallow land, barely tended land, even inaccessible drowned lands and ponds. Importantly, while residents may be resigned to such changes, and are often agents of these changes themselves, they also live with the injustic that many of the changes to their land are the result of the actions of indifferent others. Residents whose productive land has suffered from the negative externalities of excessive waterlogging or poorly regulated colony development do not feel able to take recourse through an appeal to the local government entities, for they are little trusted or underequipped to exercise basic regulatory frameworks. The legislative frameworks and urban policies provided by the State of West Bengal, or the national Government of India offer little safeguard. In this sense, the apparently neglected and uncared for appearance of the land held by long-term Ward 13 residents means their formal property rights are largely invisible and weakly protected. One recourse is to see colony development positively. While long-term residents work hard to withstand incremental ecological transformations of their land and their socioeconomic foundations, many also embrace colony development, for it brings with it some opportunites. Long-term residents shape how colony property settles in their locality—for their own benefit—and it is to this practice that I now turn.

Endnotes

1 Shown in Figure 6.04. The West Bengal Inland Fisheries Act, 1984, says that no person shall convert a water body measuring 5 kotha (0.035 hectares or 350 square meters including the embankment) or more without approval. I suggest that this is a reason why the many smaller ponds that are below this threshold are not shown on this official map.

2 A second way that urban tree cover is governed, or considered government property and is made political, is a digital register. Urban forest cover has been measured from satellite imagery since 1993 (Sudhakar and Raha, 1993), and is reflected in annual reporting and as newsworthy. A 2020 report on forest cover change showed that "non-forest greenery" in the Kolkata Metropolitan area has decreased, while "Bengal's forest cover" has increased, creating concern amongst the residents of Kolkata (Niyogi and Mukherjee, 2020). Cyclone Amphan (2020) reduced this cover even further (see Chowdhury and Bhattacharyya, 2020).

3 Chaudhuri et al.'s (2019, p. 91) study found that residents use diverse plant parts and various modes for preparing and administering herbal formulations to ameliorate a broad spectrum of common ailments. Such ailments include problems of the gastrointestinal tract and its related organs—the liver and pancreas; problems of the cardiovascular system, respiratory tract, and urinary tract; dental, eye and ear problems; skin problems and injuries; as well as animal bites, which are still common.

4 Jalais also reflects upon the pir cult more broadly, noting that it was both a challenge and opportunity for the earlier Brahman settlers who respected the Ganga Cult (2010, p. 156). She wonders if somewhere along the way, "the tiger became a Hindu symbol – or was it because it was already a Hindu symbol that gave weight to all these narratives about pirs controlling tigers?" (2010, p. 156).

5 There were two modes of settlement. First, instead of first receiving the patronage of a higher authority, some pirs "went directly into uncultivated regions, organized the local population for clearing the jungles and, only later, after having established themselves as local men of influence, entered into relations with the Mughal authorities", say Eaton (1987, p. 90). The second mode of settlement was led by "the Mughal government's ever-increasing revenue demand" in the late seventeenth and early eighteenth centuries (1987, 87). In this second mode, pirs functioned within a complex chain of tenure with those who had obtained a grant of a plot of land, or "ta'alluq, bestowed either directly by Mughal authorities in Dhaka or Murshidabad, or by lesser chieftains closer to the fields of reclamation" (1987, 88). Notably, Eaton highlights "the activities of European trading companies, especially the Dutch and the English" in this process of land speculation at this time, as "immense quantities of silver came into local circulation" providing the capital the means by which credit could be advanced (1987, 87).

6 The "down" islands are the tidal lands that were cleared and settled in the mid-nineteenth century. "Mainland" are the lands that were cleared much earlier, before the thirteenth century, and are the location of my study area.

7/

"BASIC" INFRASTRUCTURE

While it is the obligation of the municipality to provide public works and town planning as described in chapter 2, there is also a mandate to provide "universal basic services" like paved and well-lit roads, proper drainage and drinking water, and sewage and waste management services. In Ward 13 there is inequality in local delivery of such services. Long-term residents generally enjoy access to services, while newcomer residents in colonies have to wait, with many adopting makeshift, privately provided solutions in the interim. These local solutions shape the urban political ecology of colony development. In this chapter I look at the infrastructures that surround colony settlement. Central to this story is the role of middlemen, many of whom are long-term residents themselves.

Infrastructure

As noted in chapter 1, funding for infrastructure has been central to national Government of India urban reform initiatives since the 1990s. One of the first tranches of funding from the national urban infrastructure initiatives was apportioned at the state level for large, impressive public-private funded projects. One example of such a showy project is the recently completed elevated highway along Budge Budge Trunk Road, located on the northern boundary of Ward 13 (see Figure 7.01). The highway is a kind of extended flyover, and is one of many built in metropolitan Kolkata with the intention of alleviating congestion and improving metropolitan mobility. Unlike other flyovers in Kolkata, the Budge Budge elevated Trunk Road is a tollway directly servicing a 106-hectare (262-acre) planned township called Calcutta Riverside,

Figure 7.01. Budge Budge Trunk Road on the northern boundary of Ward 13 (at Sarkarpool), with flyover pillars under construction in the middle of the road. Residents can be seen waiting for the bus. A bicycle-parking shop and newly constructed sidewalk and drain (underneath the sidewalk) can be seen in the dusty foreground.

(Source: author, 2018.)

which gives built expression to the idea of "elite capture" (Mahadevia, 2011). The Ward 13 councilors view this flyover as being of little benefit to the "common man" of the ward (Maheshtala Official, interview, K02, 2018). Few Ward 13 residents own cars and most mainly use the bus route that services the older congested road that lies below, and which remains "worse than hell" (IST, 2019).

The big infrastructure works are now occurring in parallel with incremental, municipal-level infrastructure improvements being undertaken in the study area. Later projects to emerge from the tranches of funding from the national urban infrastructure initiatives are more relevant to the participant residents. These projects include an upgrading of the drinking water supply in southern metropolitan Kolkata, including Maheshtala. There is also an upcoming Maheshtala Municipality–owned "scientific" landfill and a transmunicipal drainage and sewage system planned (funded by the Asian Development Bank).[1] These costly projects are very late in arriving in periurban Maheshtala, given that the urban reforms began almost fifteen years ago. Furthermore, when these construction works do commence, they are painfully slow to reach completion. Nevertheless, the Ward 13 councilors say they will "tolerate this inconvenience" for these less showy projects, because these "basic" infrastructure improvements are much needed (Maheshtala Official, interview, K02, 2018). In what follows, I examine the case of ward-level drinking water infrastructure, which is being provided equitably, before I turn to local road infrastructure, which is not.

The residents have had piped drinking water for some time, even before the founding of Maheshtala Municipality, although it is only since around 2016 that they have been able to enjoy reliable, and reasonably good-quality drinking water. Prior to the founding of the municipality, drinking water was mainly sourced from a centrally located, hand-driven tube well, supplemented by pond water. Water supply was hard work in that period, as much physical effort was required to "collect it in earthen vessels by turn" (Resident, interview, L06, 2018). After the hand-driven tube well became defective, the residents protested and demanded pipe water. This was provided by the Kolkata Municipal Corporation from a source located nearby at Garden Reach. After the founding of the municipality, and as the population increased, the quantity of Garden Reach water each household received "reduced drastically" (Resident, interview, L04, 2018). To fix this problem, the municipality tapped a local bore in 2016. The new bore water increased the supply but was of lesser quality, and it was around then that water in Ward 13 "started creating a health problem all round" (Resident, interview, L04, 2018). Residents responded to the problem of the "infected" water supply by buying bottled water if they could afford it. Today, while an adequate quantity of water is delivered reliably by pipe, the quality of water is variable. Five resident respondents reported that drinking water supply is "okay" and eight said it was "dirty." This reveals that drinking water quality may vary within a locality and that judgments of drinking water quality are subjective. A new, bigger pipeline is under construction and will bring enough good-quality water from Garden Reach for the whole municipality (Ray, 2019). Water provision in Kolkata is free on delivery, as the state ruling party has a popular policy of "not laying water tax on common people" (Mondal, 2020). However, it seems that the new pipeline may be moved towards a public-private delivery model and, as a ward councilor noted, "whether water will be available to us free or we have to buy it hasn't been decided as yet" (Maheshtala Official, interview, K02, 2018).

In Maheshtala, funding for local roads, including pathway roads, comes from a variety of sources. Certain national-level government funding for infrastructure is apportioned at the municipal level (Maheshtala Municipality, 2014, pp. 188–89). This includes funding for "*bustee* improvement" (provision of basic services for slum areas) under the Ministry of Housing and Urban Poverty Alleviation "Slum free India" program, or the Rajiv Awas Yojana Mission (before 2015, bustee improvement was funded under the JnNURM, Basic Services for the Urban Poor program).[2] There is also funding for "intra-municipal infrastructure" provided under a scheme entitled the Backward Regions Grant Fund, which is managed by the Ministry of Panchayati Raj.[3] The "backward regions" funding was created to "bridge critical gaps" in local infrastructure that are not being adequately met through other funding means (Government of India, 2007, p. 4). Thus, Maheshtala Municipality qualifies for both village or (rural poor) and municipal (urban poor) improvement funding from the national level. These funds both come with requirements that the projects meet Sustainable Development Goals.[4] As such, and unlike the faltering and slow transmunicipal infrastructure works, the infrastructural projects advanced through these schemes have been making a positive, but unequal, impact in the study area.

One example of this is the case of roads. Residents in the case study area report that their previously unsealed, or poorly sealed, pathway roads and local main roads have been progressively improved, starting from around 1998 for brick-paved pathway roads and from 2013 for concrete-sealed pathway roads and bitumen-sealed local roads (see Figure 7.02). Prior to these improvements, residents reported that getting around the ward was "extremely difficult" (Resident, interview, L18, 2018). Not only were the roads "absolutely muddy," but there was also no street lighting (Resident, interview,

Figure 7.02. A resident with a bicycle on a newly sealed pathway road alongside the study area rivulet.

(Source: author, 2018.)

Lo3, 2018). One resident recalled that during the rainy season commuters had to "carry their bicycles on their shoulders" to get to Budge Budge Trunk Road, at least a kilometer away (Resident, interview, No3, 2018).

Changes in electricity infrastructure have also occured. Electricity arrived in Ward 13 in 1998, with street lighting incrementally installed since then. Combined, the improved roads and street lighting have afforded better connectivity to job opportunities in nearby industrial centers. Road improvements have come with changes in transport. While residents continue to commute by bus or by bicycle, it is more typical for a household to own at least one motorcycle, and for some households, a car. The use of ride-hailing apps such as Uber and Ola are widespread. Importantly for the residents who live in the southern part of the study area, "autos can now ply" from Budge Budge Trunk Road "throughout the year, irrespective of the time of the year" (Resident, interview, No6, N18, 2018).

It is the duty of the municipality to "make reasonable and adequate provision for the construction, maintenance, alteration, and improvement of public streets" (Government of West Bengal, 2017, p. 58). In practice, the delivery of such services to newer colony areas is spotty, inadequate, and may even be intentionally delayed. In Ward 13 colonies, house owners construct their own septic tanks, while electricity and drinking water connections are obtainable from the municipality at a fee. The building of a good quality access road is meant to be done by the colony developer (or "promoter" in local parlance); however, they often fail to do so. The width of the access road is determined more by what the promoter can afford, and the land can physically accommodate, than through compliance with any infrastructure regulation. According to a ward councilor, "poorly constructed" and "ill-planned" roads are a problem as they soon "start crumbling" (see Figure

Figure 7.03. An under-construction, promoter-built, colony road leading into a former paddy field/future colony. This area is in a Ward adjacent to Ward 13. Colonies are arranged on former paddy land in a grid-like road layout. Given that such paddy land is low-lying, road construction is tricky. While a simple "rubble" road can be thought of as pragmatic, as it can absorb monsoon water and afford surface water flow, its uneven surface makes everyday life difficult. On the other hand, a properly constructed, but poorly engineered road (without culverts), can be problematic, as it can aggravate local waterlogging and neighborly tensions, by forcing monsoon water (also sewage and plastic waste) to pool in areas where it is not wanted.

(Source: author, 2018.)

7.03). In effect, the infrastructure provision requirement placed on the promoter means the municipal-level government has "no role to play," yet the roads often end up becoming "a big headache for the municipality to maintain" (Maheshtala Official, interview, K02, 2018).

Although promoters know they must construct roads to ensure their colony developments are accessible, often they adjust the road size to achieve the right price point for the customers they are targeting. They must also build roads within their budgets to ensure profit margins. Land value alters according to the width of the road, with plots with wider and better access roads obtaining higher prices. For instance, a twenty-foot-wide "road frontage" is considered appealing for buyers with financial means, whereas a six-foot-wide "road frontage" is attractive to low-income buyers (see Figures 7.04 and 7.05). While some colonies in Ward 13 have twenty-foot-wide roads, most have pathway roads that are barely wide enough for motorcycles, bicycles, and pedestrians to pass by each other. Here it is important to remember how economically unexceptional the case study area is—the promoters are small-scale, and while the colony house builders have a stable income, overall, they are low-income, "lower-middle-class households" (Ranganathan, 2011). In short, the small-scale local promoters of colonies in Ward 13 are targeting households of relatively modest income.

The ward councilor bemoaned the fact that these small promoters with limited finances target lower-price buyers, even though the ward is growing steadily and relatively peacefully. This is because the lower price point model of development pushes costs related to poor colony access road construction onto the municipality. Although the West Bengal Municipal Act (Government of West Bengal, 2017, p. 132) requires that a new residential development leave space between the access road and a house to accommodate the construction of a roadside drain, this is rarely observed or monitored in the small colonies. As the ward councilor explained, the provision of a future proper drainage scheme requires about two feet on both sides of a road, but that easement is rarely set aside, making the future provision of drainage challenging and costly.

Many small colony developments are appearing simultaneously, driven by small-scale speculative promoter activity. Ward councilors, however, reason that they can ignore newcomers' needs for basic services on the grounds that the "demand" is insufficient. Colony-building activity is certainly fragmented spatially and under-regulated, which creates a range of infrastructure provision challenges. As a ward councilor put it: "[if] there is increased demand ... the municipality has to act," but in the context of "small-scale speculative development" with "sparse population" (as is the case

Figure 7.04. A 20-foot-wide "rubble" road with a large, multi-family colony building, a van, electricity, and street lighting.

(Source: author, 2018.)

Figure 7.05. A 6-foot-wide "rubble" road and modest colony buildings within "jungly," former paddy fields.

(Source: author, 2018.)

with all of the colonies in the study area) the "obligation to provide amenities is not so [urgent]" (Maheshtala Official, interview, K02, 2018). This disregard is further justified on the grounds that there is insufficient property tax income from these emergent colony settlements, which may only have three to five households on an access or pathway road. This means that while water is more equitably supplied than roads, there is a some disparity in access to services in the ward, with long-term residents largely receiving services, but newcomer colony householders going without.

Disregard by municipal officials does not mean that colonies are neglected completely, for newcomer residents are important to both the local economy and the potential tax base of the municipality. As noted in chapter 5, property tax is paid to the municipality, and land tax (on agricultural land) is paid to the State of West Bengal. It is therefore in the interest of the municipality to support the conversion of agricultural land to residential land, and to have many contented, taxpaying, newcomer residents. Newcomer residents who come in search of an affordable locality are not blind to the realities of the municipality and of colony development trickeries. They know they must wait, as they have chosen to live in a situation where an impoverished municipality is trying to lay the costs of basic infrastructure onto promoters who do not deliver. In short, the municipality is taking a wait-and-see stance so they can raise the funds for such infrastructure at a later date.[5] In the meantime, there are many promises and ties formed within this barely trusted but mutually binding situation.

As I show later in this chapter, the residents self-organize to make up for shortfalls in basic services. But before I describe the newcomer residents' associations, I must first explain how newcomer residents come to arrive at a colony and purchase a plot of land being sold by a farmer-turned-promoter. Central to this process is a social infrastructure of "middlemen" or promoters and brokers, which in Ward 13, tend to be long-term residents.

Middlemen

After farmers decide to sell their land, it enters a complex local market of land suppliers, land developers, and middlemen—a localized land market. Anthropologist Ian Cook (2015, p. 292) argues that in Indian contexts where property is being "disembedded" (Hann, 1998) from longer-term structures, such as family-based farm tenures, and transitioning to shorter-term transactions, "link work" is very important. Indeed, Cook argues that links are a form of property, and that the establishment of link-work is essential to transformations commodifying land and housing (2015, p. 312). Such link work is populated by middlemen. Learning from Kolkata, interdisciplinary scholar Nikita Sud (2014, pp. 593–94) focuses specifically on link-work, arguing that "men in the middle," or middlemen, are part of the "vast world of shadows and informality that underpins land." Sud (2014, p. 594) says that middlemen can be understood as a highly organized field of "go-betweens, mediators and negotiators."[6] In this section, I look at those who Sud would term "land brokers" and "local brokers," but I call just "promoters" and "brokers," as this is how these roles are referred to in the case study area.

Promoters are those who aggregate smaller plots into larger areas, and they are the biggest players in the brokerage chain. They literally create plots of land viable for commercial use by aggregating several smaller landholdings. There are many scales of aggregator work in Indian cities. In the study area, such promoters are small-scale players, and they develop periurban colonies largely for local and regional buyers. This is in sharp contrast to, say, the large-scale promoters working in Special Economic Zones or assembling large plots of land for gated, high-rise developments targeted at nonresident Indian buyers. For instance, some former farmers have become small-scale promoters. They start by selling their own extended families' lands as subdivided plots to buyers, or they work with other former farmers and neighbors to form a promoter group that aggregates more neighbors' lands. In other instances, a politically well-connected resident might aggregate land from disparate owners over time. For example, a medium-sized colony within the study area has a total area of 14 *bighas* (1.9 hectares), which was aggregated from a number of different transactions with local farmers. It was then surveyed into 140 plots, with each plot sized at an average of 2 *kotha* (0.13 hectares) (Resident, interview, N07, 2018).

For promoters to plot their colonies, they need to have both a supply of land and buyers for that land. Long-term residents, too, require someone to broker between them and promoters when they sell their (often jungly) former paddy fields. This linking work is done by middlemen called brokers who are the next level below promoters in the brokerage chain. As Sud (2014, p. 61) explains, brokers are paid on a deal-by-deal basis and act as the "anchors," as they transact with both buyers and sellers. In the study area, the brokers are local, and this means they share social relations with sellers. For farmers wanting to sell, the broker is an essential link into a land market because "[a] person who sells knows no buyer" (Resident, interview, L05, 2019). The broker also translates the process and guarantees trust: as one elderly former farmer put it, "we do not know the customers" (Resident, interview, L04, 2019). Brokers also link "outside" buyers to promoters who have plotted colonies. The work of a broker is more than just matching; they also offer administrative services linked to the sale. In other words, the broker is involved in the land transaction "from the time the land is negotiated, which involves legal searching, existing document presentation and its updating [e.g., conversion of land use]" to getting the land "mutated," meaning a transfer of title (Resident, interview, L04, 2018). After the land sale, brokers can also assist (for a fee) with getting house plans approved. Altogether, act as "rule-makers who personalize, localize and actively shape the land economy" (Sud, 2014, p. 593).

Being local is essential to the work of brokers for, as one broker explained, "outsiders will have scant knowledge about local setup" in the area including the "facts about landholdings and other intricacies" (Resident, interview, L04, 2019). One such broker has been providing services in the area for at least twelve years (Resident, interview, L04, 2019). The broker is from a long-term farmer family (in the area since the early 1900s), although more recently the family livelihood is from mixed incomes. Like his retired father, he works full-time for a company in Khidirpur, the nearby docklands area of Kolkata Port. He noticed that there were port workers coming from "outside" who had families and so wanted housing, could afford to buy, yet did not know how to find the right land. And so, the broker decided to do "deals in real estate" part-time. He does not have a team working with him, and his supply of "outsider" clients to link to the land for sale in Ward 13 is maintained by creatively using an informal team of "mutual acquaintances" at the port. For instance, "a petty shopkeeper" in his network might hear that one of his customers has a land "requirement" and might be a suitable buyer. He would then notify the broker "knowing that I deal in real estate." For this work, the shopkeeper would get monetary "settlement": "that's how we operate … the shopkeeper works as a contact person and would get his cut."

Although the stated purpose of a broker is to facilitate "parts of a chain linking two end points, or points leading to the two ends" in a land transaction, they can also obstruct and create outcomes that benefit one side over another (Sud, 2014, p. 594). Brokers cannot just bring any "outsider" into the local land market. As the broker noted: "our work is dependent on people's belief [i.e., trust] … the faith they repose in us creates our foundation." Establishing and maintaining a reputation means finding reliable buyers, people who have reliable incomes and the likelihood of obtaining credit financing. As such, everyone in the informal network must be attuned to spotting the right kind of buyers not simply by discerning a need for land, but the ability to pay for that land as well as fund the building of a house on it. Furthermore, as Cook (2015, p. 313) notes, part of the skill of brokerage is to identify what particular constellation of characteristics are desirable and undesirable (for particular groups of people) in the locality at any one moment. Cook also points out that these acts of mediation take place within, and thus are part of, an "unfolding, dynamic citywide mediation" of wider changes, including, say, the nationwide growth of Hindu nationalism. The broker then must be "dynamically skilled" in both "old class" symbols as well as "more malleable markers."

The largely informal marketing pitches in the study area are modest and often depend on the reputation of the locality as a "peaceful area where there is no political or social unrest" (Resident, interview, N01, 2019). That said, there is some evidence that the pace of development and the pitch of promoters is changing. The ward councilor reflected that since 2013, established local promoters with newly accumulated means had started to "change tactics." This has included trying to "engage renowned land developers" and "dress up the property" to make Ward 13 "more attractive to rich people," including those who might be from "outside" West Bengal (Maheshtala Official, interview, K02, 2019). In 2013, land in Maheshtala became more valuable as a result of funding under JnNURM being approved at the national level for the construction of the elevated highway along Budge Budge Trunk Road (Niyogi, 2018). Since this time, Maheshtala is increasingly pitched in marketing jargon as a healthy and green alternative to the congested core of Kolkata. This is evident in the more flashy and aspirant online marketing and branding of nearby lifestyle developments, like Greenfield City, Eden City, and Calcutta Riverside. Reputable local brokers exercise much care with these nearby larger-scale projects, especially those led by outside developers. For example, the local broker had been given the opportunity to earn lucrative fees brokering deals for an outsider-developer's project and had his "papers … all ready" but was "apprehensive": "to tell you the truth, there are a lot of rules and regulations which make you feel that everything is not aboveboard." (Resident, interview, L04, 2019). For him, preserving his family's "reputation in the area" was more important than the money. All in all, the broker was not achieving significant financial success in his brokerage enterprise, and he preferred to focus on gaining promotion in his salaried position at the port.

The local embeddedness of brokers, and their reliance on being seen as trustworthy in order to remain competitive, shapes how they operate. For instance, one elderly householder described her broker as "a very good man" (Resident, interview N12, 2019) because he had assisted in managing the construction of her house while her husband was sick. Another broker, who had directly developed and sold his own family's paddy land and was thus also a promoter, talked with pride about how the newcomers in the colony he developed thought of him: "Those who have bought these houses consider me as a part of their family as they get all the help from me … whether it is assisting in procurement of blood for a sick person or cremation of a poor man, I am there to help" (Resident, interview, L09, 2019).

There are also brokers who take advantage of the land transactions. One member of a long-term resident family reflected on the nefarious activities of brokers in the troublesome colony near his household (Resident, interview, L05, 2019). He recalled how a "cabal" of four or five brokers, "heavy boozers," had laid claim to all the transactions associated with the colony, pushing prices up to "skim off their share." If a seller tried to bypass the brokers and deal directly with a buyer, the brokers would approach the sellers asking for money and hint at "all sorts of mischief." They could assert their "muscle power," he reported, by "veiled threats" and mention of their "protective role" in "any adverse situation" that might arise. Other residents verified that undesirable brokers had laid claim to the colony and operated out of a local clubhouse (Resident, interview, N08, 2019). These brokers could offer potential buyers valuable information about "availability and prices," but they also operated like actual gatekeepers of the colony. From the clubhouse perch, they "keep a watch on people" and "target … anyone seeking to know the availability of land." By all accounts the wait [for clients] for these brokers is worth it, for "if they can strike a deal for even a single plot, their day is done for months" (Resident, interview, N05, 2019). These local brokers and their precarious transactions are a scaled-down echo of "land-losers' co-operatives" (Mallik, 2016, p. 42) and the later, well-documented "racket" of the "syndicate raj," known to make claims for a financial cut on large-scale developments ranging from high-rise buildings to highway construction projects in West Bengal (see Nath, 2017).[7]

In sum, brokers continually work to insert themselves into land and housing transactions. In so doing they are part of the topology of power associated with property relations in the study area. Brokers have varying styles and reputations: there are well-respected individuals who respect the amicability of the locality at one extreme, and at the other, there are teams of local men who exert coercive authority, sometimes legitimated by their close political connections.

Buyers

Property values in Ward 13 are increasing. By one account, land that was bought at the end of 2010 for twenty thousand rupees (0.2 lakh) a kotha is now valued at 2.5 lakhs a kotha, "an increase of more than ten times in nine and a half years" (Resident, interview, L06, 2019). This same resident predicted that "in the next five years it will go up to five and a half lakhs a kotha." This kind of price means that the usual buyers for land in Ward 13 are "regional," from West Bengal or neighboring states. Most of these "new migrants," as the ward councilor refers to them, seek approval for construction of new houses being built on "lowlands"—the newly forming colonies on former paddy fields (Maheshtala Official, interview, K02, 2018). Newcomer buyers are often referred to as either Bengalis or "non-Bengalis" and the ward councilor estimated that 20 percent are Bengalis and 80 percent are non-Bengalis, "from Bihar followed by those from Orissa." This means that colony development is bringing previously absent ethnic diversity to the study area.

Ethnic diversity is often evident in the different Hindu practices of those who are Bengali and those who are non-Bengali. According to the ward councilor, "there is no conflict in co-existence … no animosity between communities … complete harmony" (Maheshtala Official, interview, K02, 2018). She elaborated that during Chat Puja, which is observed by the Biharis, "there is equal participation from Bengalis." Similarly, during the Jagannath Puja held by Oriyas, "we are invited and there is huge participation from the Bengalis." Similarly, "during the social functions held by the Bengalis, like marriages, non-Bengalis are invited in large numbers." These more official views of a municipal official were for the most part also what newcomer residents reported. Both Bengali and non-Bengali newcomers talked positively about Ward 13 and how they felt welcome, reporting on "good relation[s] with neighbors" and living "in peaceful co-existence" with "community feelings" (Resident, interview, N06, N15, 2019). As one newcomer resident who rents a house from a local landlord noted, "people greet us whenever they meet us in the road" (Resident, interview, N19, 2019).

Long-term residents shared a variety of reactions to newcomers, from ambivalence to concern. One former farmer reflected that it was hard to interact with newcomers because they were not in the "same space." (Resident, interview, L04, 2018). This is a fact because the colonies are built as cul-de-sacs. Despite these spatially separate access routes, there are only three main roads in and out of Ward 13, and these are where the shops and vendors congregate. These amenities and main roads are shared by all, meaning that long-term residents and newcomers do brush up against each other. Nevertheless, one self-identified "middle-class" long-term resident reflected on how she does not feel comfortable with the newcomers: "Their culture does not gel with ours," she said (Resident, interview, L12, 2019). Likewise, a former farmer felt threatened by the newcomers who he perceived to now "outnumber the local population," to be "economically stronger," and have "greater influence and say on matters of public interest" (Resident, interview, L10, 2019). Others enjoyed the prosperity that newcomers bring as "they have all paid money, registered their property … it is good" (Resident, interview, L06, 2019). Concluding, "there is no trouble anywhere."

After navigating possibly nefarious brokers and tricky promoters, newcomers then work hard to settle peacefully. Some newcomers do build influence as they settle, whereas others are taken advantage of. With respect to basic infrastructure such as roads, drinking water, and waste collection, long-term residents are, for the most part, better provided for than newcomers, as noted earlier in this chapter. In contrast, newcomers often lack access to basic services when they first arrive and must enter into various transactions to secure these services. Even with respect to acquisition of construction materials and services they may often be disadvantaged, as one long-term resident noted:

> If I have to build or extend my building, I don't need to go to a broker as I am a local man. But people coming from outside will have to engage a broker. I can get construction material at the rated price, but an outsider will be charged much more. Besides, an outsider will also be shortchanged on quantities and will never receive the quantities he paid for. I have full sympathy for those sufferers (Local interview L05, 2019).

This suggests that long-term residents are aware of the manipulation of newcomers but do nothing, and in this way claim some authority over them.

In sum, the buyers, who have been accepted by the brokers as suitable for the locality, generally settle in amicably. There is conflict, but it takes the form of many ordinary, small, and diffuse instances of uneven power. In the absence of agricultural livelihood and jobs that match their skills, some of the younger generation of long-term residents have leveraged their knowledge of the locality and taken up careers as middlemen. While they make claims on newcomer residents, this does not mean that newcomers are passive in these mostly amicable instances of uneven power.

In the next section I look at how newcomer residents make claims on the municipality, and how the provision of basic services infrastructure is entangled with this process.

Associations

As in other parts of metropolitan Kolkata, the newcomer residents in the study area form committees to address gaps between services promised or provided by the developer, and those promised or provided by the municipality. A ward committee is set up by the municipality, and is comprised of elected councilors, whereas a colony committee is set up by the colony residents, and they self-elect office bearers. According to the ward councilor, such colony committees are groups of newcomer residents in a locality who "join hands together and mobilize their resources with the intention of doing some good" (Ward Official, interview, K02, 2019). Of the thirty colonies in Ward 13, half have formed committees, some founded as early as 1990. Colony committees are quite large: for example, in one instance a committee was said to be comprised of thirty households. Colony committees do not have a dedicated space and the members usually gather in one of the houses in the colony for their meetings. As "unofficial bodies" they are not eligible for external funding but they often "arrange money" (in the words of the local ward councilor) within their membership to pay for collective goods. This is not technically illegal, and it is not policed.

It is important to differentiate colony committees from clubs, another type of association present in the ward (see Figure 7.06). Unlike committees, club members are typically long-term residents and the two types of entities do not usually interact. This is also because they have different goals and are set up differently. Clubs have a clubhouse, are meant to be registered and pay an annual fee to the municipality, and as they receive "government grants" they are meant to declare their expenses to the municipality in order to have their registration renewed. According to the ward councilor, financially successful clubs are political entities, because "[i]t is only the clubs which are recommended by the ruling party [that] get the grants" (Ward Official, interview K02, 2019). There are twenty clubs in Ward 13. While some are registered, most of them do not have their registration renewed, and so are technically illegal. Also, while each club's official remit is "social" and nonpolitical, they may still "exercise power and wield public authority" (Cornea, 2020, p. 313; also see Lund, 2006). Most clubs in the ward support a local temple and arrange for community *pujas* (acts of worship) (see Figure 7.07). While the ward councilor acknowledged the presence of clubs in Ward 13, she made it clear to us that she thought they were "not playing any constructive or major social role" (Ward Official, interview K02, 2019), suggesting that the community's puja is secondary to other practices of the club's public authority.

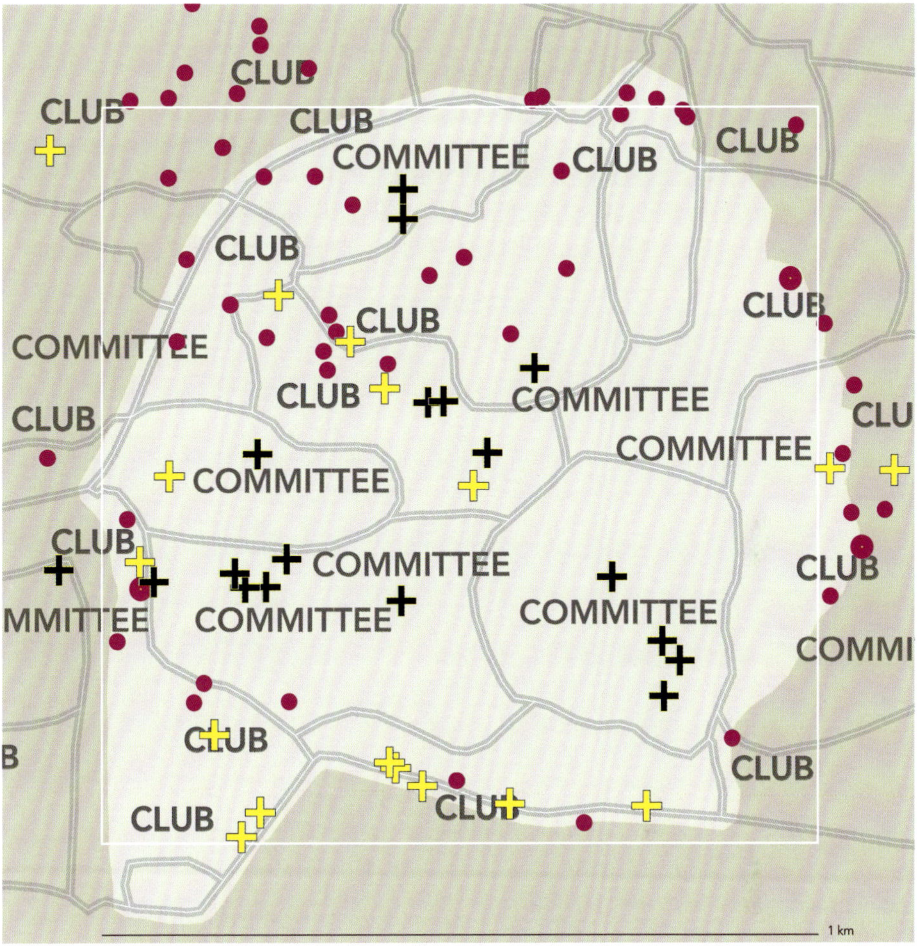

Figure 7.06. Map showing geolocated *mandirs* (Hindu temple) (pink dots) and estimated locations of clubs, and committees. The grey boundaries are the official localities in Ward 13. Long-term resident respondents (yellow symbol) and newcomer resident respondents (black symbol) are also shown. Being an older institution than committees, clubs are generally located in wooded, settled areas and are comprised of long-term residents. Whereas committees, being a newcomer form of association, are generally located in colonies.

(Source: author, 2020; unassembled and unpublished GIS files provided by Maheshtala Municipality, 2020; printed locality map provided by Maheshtala Municipality, 2018.)

Figure 7.07. A local *mandir* (Hindu temple) located on the local main road. The mandir is the bright pink painted structure, seen on the left hand of the image. A partly installed bamboo canopy draped with a yet-to-be unfolded plastic shade cloth covers the road. This temporary infrastructure is one of many regular investments made in preparation for a community *puja* (act of worship).

(Source: author, 2019.)

Colony committees often set up local charges on their newcomer resident members: some committees levy a one-time fee when a buyer comes into the colony; others have itemized levies. Such levies are part of an informal economy to provide public goods. The ward councilors "often [do] not even come to know" about such levies, but if or when they do, they "neither interfere nor dictate them" (Ward Official, interview K02, 2019), meaning they do not participate in the setting of prices. Membership expectations and levies are all part of an informal set of "unwritten rules," although colonies often codify such rules and may even publicize them on a sign posted at the entrance to the colony—signaling to both brokers and prospective buyers (see Figure 7.08). Typically, the initial focus of a committee is road development, and specifically, the sealing of the preliminary access road plotted out by the promoter. A focus on road improvement creates direct benefits for the residents in terms of access and property values, but also attracts more buyers to the colony, increasing the colony's size and its contribution to the taxes of the municipality, and thus increasing the likelihood that the municipality will address other needs. Once the road is in place, committees often turn their attention to the provision of street lighting and road drainage.

Gopalpur Nagar Unnayan Samiti (a pseudonym for a colony committee, and hereafter GNUS) is an illustrative example of the role of committees in bridging the gaps between the municipality's wait-and-see stance and the basic starter services provided by small-scale, local promoters. The GNUS has forty to fifty members, with four to five office bearers, including president, treasurer, and secretary (Resident, interview, N01, 2019). As the resident member explained, membership is not optional: "Whoever comes to the locality becomes a member of the committee." All new members must contribute to a committee fund, and the committee extracts additional

Figure 7.08. A sign posted at the junction of the local main road and a colony access road in the study area. The sign names the colony committee at the top (masked by the author for privacy reasons) and the Ward 13 Committee members' names at the bottom. While the Ward 13 Committee members reported that they were not asked if their names could be included, they did not object after the sign was installed. The sign specifies the levy for the promoter, buyer and seller as well as the levy for the delivery of construction materials by the buyer. The levy type is also specified as either a "donation" in rupees or in terms of truckloads (lorries) of rubble for building and maintaining the unsealed colony access road (a "lorry [of] rabbis" [or rubbish]).

(Source: author, 2019.)

Development Charge
100 Foot to 300 Foot Sand & 1000 to 3000 Bricks Rs. 100.00
300 Foot to 500 Foot Sand / 3000 to 5000 Bricks Rs. 200.00
Rabbis to Silver Sand - Rs. 100.00
New Plot Holder are Donate 5 Lorry Rabbis & Rs. 50 per month from January 2016
New Area Boundary are Donate 2 Lorry Rabbis
Noted by: 10 Wheeler or Damper Car are not allowed
Plot seller & Buyer are donate 5 Lorry both party
Contact with committee member
1. Swapan Dutta
2. Ram Nayan Yadav
3. Ajay Kumar Pandey
4. Tulsi Mondal
5. Noren Mondal
6. Madhai Kanji

funds through levies. For example, GNUS fixes a levy on the delivery of construction materials, which means that most land buyers are paying into the committee funds as soon as they start building on their land. The construction levy is justified on the grounds that heavy lorries carrying building materials damage the simple unsealed roads. To restore the damaged road, the committee secretary uses the pooled levies to purchase "four to five truckloads of rubbish" (brick and concrete rubble) to make the road "somewhat usable again" (Resident, interview, N01, 2019).

GNUS also influences who buys land in the locality. Gopalpur Nagar posts its membership and levy expectations on a sign at the entrance to the colony. This signals to brokers and direct buyers that if a prospective buyer does not have savings or a stable income, they should think about buying elsewhere. Thus, the levy sign indicates that the newcomers of Gopalpur Nagar are not "holding hands" with all newcomers, instead they want to ensure they keep out low-income buyers. Even within the colony, internal distinctions are made, and the newest of newcomers' concerns are not always equitably provided for. This can often happen if a newcomer's arrival means that a new plot "further in" (away from the access road) is developed. Such plot development requires an extension to the existing unsealed road network. As there is no direct benefit to those already in the settlement, they often refuse to use committee funds for this work. One such newcomer to Gopalpur Nagar moved in seven years ago yet was still waiting for the committee to "do their work." Frustrated, she decided that she and her immediate neighbors needed to "do it ourselves" (Resident, interview, N09, 2019). So, in addition to paying the committee's levies, she pooled resources with three neighbors to raise two thousand rupees to buy in a lorry of rubble and raise the level of their approach road. In such cases, the ward rarely steps in, although they often give assurances that they will. At the end of another road, a resident showed us a wall that he and three of his neighbors pooled funds to build in order to make a barrier against an adjacent sewage-laden, waterlogged area (Resident, interview, N05, 2019). Buyers on short side lanes thus face similar difficulties extracting funds from the committee in Gopalpur Nagar.

While there is unevenness in the disbursement of committee resources, favoring the oldest newcomers' access needs foremost, the role of the committee can also be understood as providing a positive benefit for all members in other ways. As geographer Malini Ranganathan (2014, p. 590) argues, a "willingness to pay" for basic services infrastructure rather than demanding that the promoter or the municipality provide them, is a "means to bargain for greater symbolic recognition, respectability and material benefits from the state." Paying is a situated means by which localized and narrow property-related interests are advanced. Colony-built infrastructure, like roads, are not accounted for in the municipal development plans, which simply focus on the length of municipal-owned sealed and unsealed roads. The ward councilors' wait-and-see stance implies that while colony roads are not part of the municipal-owned road accounting, they will be included later. At the same time, the municipality believes they are meeting their responsibilities to newcomer colony residents adequately. In the view of the ward councilor, the "major funding" for colony settlement comes from the municipality, and the committees provide finance for "the peripheral requirements" (Ward Official, interview K02, 2019). Thus, "willingness to pay" has become regularized.

In time, as the newcomer colonies' access to infrastructure is equalized with that of long-term residents, colony committees may disband. As Lund (2006, p. 701) notes, some attempts to exercise legitimate public authority sometimes "run out of steam," while others will prosper in the constellation of "structural pressure, active ingenuity and sheer chance." For instance, one resident, when asked if a committee was present in her colony, was vague, saying, "I heard there was a committee, but I am told that it has disbanded now" (Resident, interview, N12, 2019). Yet in a neighboring colony, the original committee had assumed greater authority, overseeing the pooling of resources to build a temple, and managing a community Durga Puja "where the whole locality takes part" (Resident, interview, N06, 2019). In this case, the committee is shifting toward the kind of authority and activity typical of long-established clubs. In another instance, the founding newcomer residents built a dedicated and registered clubhouse from the very beginning of their colony's settlement. Soon after the establishment of the clubhouse, local youths "muscled in" on the club committee and replaced them (Resident, interview, N07, 219). The new club committee continues to collect membership fees and levies from the colony as well as benefitting from "government grants," amongst other economic and political activities.[8] The founding newcomer residents are extremely displeased with this nefarious takeover and now feel that the club is running the area down. While some residents of the colony have actually moved out, one young female householder explained that she cannot: "If we had money, we would have left this place" (Resident, interview, N02, 219). Thus, not all colonies are the same, and even neighboring colonies can be distinct from each other in terms of power exerted by their clubs and committees.

In sum, middlemen and associations help shape the "social life of property" within the study area, just as the other imbroglios, like waterlogging, jungle, and gardens do. These agents of land and settlement fit within both old and new forms of legitimate order. Middlemen do important work opening land markets and securing buyers that "fit" the ward. Associations emerge and are possibly sustained by the fact that they are making up for shortfalls in basic services infrastructure from an often overstretched and impoverished municipality. As established forms of property shift into something different and unfamiliar, a loose general trust and amicability is formed between the residents and the ward. At the same time, there are a variety of instances of breaches of trust between promoters and ward councilors that take advantage of the residents, and between residents and their associations, and most probably other forms of loss of trust. But all these instances of uneven power work in concert with the wider process of periurban change. No single instance of local power, no single association or even the council can mobilize the whole ward in organized political action against either the logic of periurbanization or the quality of development and environment.

Conclusion

I have sought to deepen understanding of the slow and incremental urban political ecological logics of periurban change. Starting in chapters 4 and 5, I first looked at the relation between drainage and jungle; then in chapter 6, I looked at the practices surrounding bagans; finishing with infrastructures in chapter 7. While all four instances—drainage and jungle, bagans and infrastructure—have been presented as separate lenses, by thinking across space and time and through the medium of landscape and property, they have also been shown to be multifaceted. It is important to note that the obduracy of the contemporary settled-rurality of the study area is not simply about its form. It is also about deeply embedded senses of inherited responsibility with respect to management of property. Furthermore, while the inherited responsibility of the settled-rural is respected, emergent entanglements also have agency. For instance, rules and norms are being invented about colony road construction and its maintenance, how to live with "infestations" of creatures, and what are acceptable or unacceptable compromises in the face of aggressive colony promoters and unwanted waterlogging.

According to archaeologist Ian Hodder, "entanglement sequences" can lead to "untying as much as to stability" (2012, p. 205). This study can thus be thought of as informing needed practices of untying and stability for the benefit of periurban residents, broadly defined. The lived property of the study area is characterized by continual adjustment to policy, new neighbors, and livelihoods, as well as changing nonhuman forces and creatures. I have visualized how ordinary periurban change amidst obdurate and emerging material landscapes is multidimensional. To attempt to evade these complexities by only picturing a known urban future—which in metropolitan Kolkata is not much more than an image of what is already occurring in the centers of cities and towns in West Bengal—misses the possibility that the variety of emplaced "kinds of urban" emerging on the periphery of metropolitan Kolkata and across Gangetic West Bengal might hold clues for thinking through and valuing more types of urban, rural, ecological, and just futures.

Endnotes

1 The municipality has no sewage management and so most newcomer house owners construct septic tanks "on their own land and for their own benefit," as the Ward 13 councilor explained (Maheshtala Official, interview, K02, 2018). She says newcomer residents "are aware that with a small plot of land … they won't be able to live in a hygienic environment if they do not provide a proper septic tank." Other colony residents, as noted earlier in this chapter, chose to live in an unhygienic environment, trusting that a promised sewage management service will arrive soon.

2 As noted in an earlier chapter, Maheshtala Municipality and Ward 13 classify extensive areas as *bustees* (slum), seemingly as a pragmatic way to source much-needed funding for basic services across the municipality.

3 Other sources of funding for intramunicipal infrastructure are fixed grants and planned allocations from the State of West Bengal. Funding for street lighting also comes from a local-level "entertainment tax" (Maheshtala Municipality, 2014, p. 188).

4 For instance, the term "backward" has recently been revised to "aspirational" and enfolded into the central-level government mission entitled the Transformation of Aspirational Districts, led by NITI Aayog (Government of India, 2020).

5 According to the West Bengal Municipal Act, 1993, a municipality can declare a private street as a public street if it has been "in existence for not less than twenty years and used by the people of the locality as a thoroughfare" (Government of West Bengal, 2017, p. 131).

6 As summarized by Cook (2015, p. 295), Sud suggests the following taxonomy of middlemen: land aggregators (who aggregate smaller plots into larger areas, the biggest players in the brokerage chain), land brokers (similar to aggregators, but working on a smaller scale), local brokers (the "anchors" dealing with other buyers and sellers, paid on a deal-by-deal basis), musclemen (who literally push through a deal), consultants (employed by the aggregator/buyer to offer advice on legal, regulatory or other state matters), party representatives (useful politicians who can help get matters cleared), government representatives (those in designated roles that concern land), and touts ("officious hangers-on" who sit outside offices to which they claim to have privileged access).

7 “Syndicate is a group of unemployed youths, allegedly backed by the ruling party, operating mainly in those areas in Bengal witnessing a realty boom. These youths use muscle power and political connections and force contractors and real estate developers to buy inferior building materials from them at a premium … The syndicate problem allegedly started in 1995, when the Left Front government began acquiring land for the Rajarhat Township near Salt Lake, Kolkata … To please the angry farmers, former Urban Development Minister Gautam Deb started a cooperative of unemployed youths who would supply construction material to real-estate companies. Since then the ‘syndicate raj’ started flourishing across Bengal and has now become a ‘headache’ for the Government of West Bengal [because the state is trying to create a healthy atmosphere for investors]” (Nath, 2017).

8 The usurped clubhouse has many economic and political functions (Resident, interview, N07, 2019). It is used as a business—a storehouse of furniture/tenting that is rented out for events, such as weddings; it is government office—once a year an officer sets up a desk so residents can pay their property taxes. It is a bar, teahouse, and broker’s lounge; it is a mobility hub control center—club leaders have some power to limit and provide public transport options. Furthermore, according to one resident, the nearby crossroad supports a drug market, which is somehow enabled by the presence of the clubhouse.

8/

ORDINARY PERIURBAN

In this chapter I step back from the case study area and reflect upon the findings within the wider frame of periurban studies. Interestingly, there are three approaches to thinking about periurban conditions, which I term *edges*, *extension*, and *beyond cities*. In what follows, I briefly review these approaches and draw out what this book aims to uniquely bring to geographies of periurbanization and scholarship on urban edge conditions. As noted earlier in the introductory chapter, I am committed to an ordinary-cities approach with a belief that it helps build a more inclusive and diverse urban theory. As Robinson (2002, p. 549) argues, certain cities and urban processes have been privileged in urban theory building, while others have fallen "off the map," not registering on intellectual maps that chart urban processes, such as the rise and fall of "global and world cities." Kolkata, for example, is "off the map" not only because of its geographical location in South Asia but also because consideration of its "city-ness" is often prison-housed in a priori concepts like "third world" or "megacity."

Ordinary-cities scholarship is dedicated to a comparative urbanism approach, which seeks to broaden the mix of cities and circumstances from which generalizations about urbanism and urbanization are formed. Robinson (2002, p. 549) emphasizes that theoretical reflections must "extend beyond those that come from the West and … [are] based upon Western-dominated forms of globalization." How comparison is put to use has become a live debate in urban studies, focusing specifically on what the "third part" or outcome of comparativism is (Jacobs, 2012). Jan Nijman (2007, p. 1) defines comparative urbanism as a field of inquiry that aims to develop knowledge, understanding, and generalization at a level between "what is true of all cities" and "what is true of one city at a given point in time." While each and every place is different or even unique in some ways, Nijman reminds us that some places can be very similar in certain respects (2007, p. 1), and it is in this sense that every case study matters with respect to "all cities."

There is a specific tradition of periurban scholarship that conforms to this theorizing by shuttling between the particular and the general, and this study builds upon that. Most notably, the geographer Terence McGee (1991, 1989) argued that there was a special type of urban edge condition particular to the rice-growing areas of Asia. He dubbed these zones of economic interaction *desakota* (Indonesian for "village" and "city"). Desakota is a settlement type that is neither strictly urban nor completely rural in character, but a mixture of both. It does not fit established notions of city growth or edge conditions based on the experience of urbanization as occurring in Western Europe and North America (McGee, 1991, p. 5). Through the conditions of desakota, McGee was able to (re)theorize ideas of city growth, or "urban transition" more generally. His adoption of the hybridized Bahasa Indonesian term desakota was intentional: "the reliance solely on the language and concepts of Western social science can lead to a form of knowledge imperialism" (1991, p. 24). His intention was to explicitly facilitate an Asian urban condition to "speak back" (Spivak, 1988), and place into question, the assumptions in existing explanations of the logics of urban edge conditions generally. More recently, the architect Stephen Cairns (2018, p. 117) locates desakota as an example of an urban-rural hybrid, and argues that such conditions should be viewed as having "their own intrinsic worth" precisely because they are neither fully urban nor fully rural. Desakota was thus an early, and highly pertinent, example of Robinson's (2016, p. 187) vision of comparison as a method of theory building.

As early as 1997, Jones and Visaria (1997) observed that the boundaries between rural and urban areas were getting so blurred that it affected the very definition of a term like periurban (Adell, 1999). Some two decades on, Ravetz et al. (2013, p. 13) declared periurbanization to be "the dominant urban form and spatial planning challenge of the twenty-first century." Both statements are true, highlighting that it remains necessary to understand the particularities of the hard-to-define contact zone between rural surrounds and cities. There have been various ways of conceptualizing periurbanization in existing scholarship. For example, there are those studies that focus more on periurbanism as an edge condition (similar to the work on suburbanization) as opposed to those whose curiosity is driven by seeing such areas as components of an extended urbanization (city-region, extended metropolitan regions, etc.), or approaches arguing that thinking about these areas in terms of proximity to a city is missing the point (periurban interface). The periurban interface scholars argue that an understanding of the institutional contexts, socio-spatial transformations and periurban dynamics is more relevant than approaches that only see periurban areas as existing in relation to the city (Iaquinta & Drescher, 2000). In what follows, this movement between edge-extension and beyond proximity to cities conceptualizations is evident.

Edge and Extension

Early periurban scholarship was characterized by approaches that looked at physical characteristics. That is, the extent to which a territorially defined edge had various rural or urban features, be that in morphological, demographic, or functional terms. According to planner Germán Adell (1999, p. 5) the term urban fringe was used for the first time by geographers describing periurban conditions in the United States (see Smith, 1937). During the 1940s and 1950s, urban fringe was then widely adopted under the meaning of "an area where suburban growth was taking place and where urban and rural uses of the land were mixed, forming together a transition zone between city and countryside" (Adell, 1999, p. 5). Various terms were then proposed in rapid succession (see Thomas, 1974); for instance, Pryor (1968, pp. 203–204) points to attempts to clarify differences between fringe and suburb (Kurtz & Eicher, 1958), as well as fringe, suburb, pseudo-suburb, satellite, and pseudo-satellite (Wissink, 1962). Pryor also points out the various differentiations made within an urban fringe, such as the urban fringe and the rural-urban fringe (Andrews, 1942); the limited fringe and the extended fringe (McKain & Burnight, 1953); the suburban fringe zone and the outlying adjacent zone (Reinemann, 1960); and the inner and outer fringe areas (Duncan & Reiss, 1956). Rather than seeking spatial definitions such as these, later conceptions of periurbanism focus on the characteristics of urbanization as an extended condition. It is to these definitions that I turn next.

Following Adell (1999, p. 6), a shift in focus toward the characteristics of urbanization as an extended condition comes from the fact that since the 1960s, cities in Western Europe and North America had been less and less frequently seen as discrete local places, and the urban experience had become, in a sense, universal. That is, the transfer of basic urban functions from a central city, first to suburbs, and then to the still larger decentralized "urban field" having largely been achieved, the urban-rural dichotomy could not be maintained against the emergence of a mobile middle classes that created highly dispersed patterns of activities, developing not in a place, but in a region (Adell, 1999, p. 6; see Gottmann, 1961). In other words, there was a shift from monocentric cities to multicentered urban areas, including the emergence of so-called "edge cities" (Garreau, 1991). In this context, during the 1980s and 1990s, a new lexicon emerged with terms for the urban experience of North America that expressed a phenomenon where not only flows of people, but of capital, labor, commodities, and information leave the central urban core for a "restless and place-less periphery" (Adell, 1999, p. 4; Soja, 1992). In Western Europe, as Adell argues (1999, p. 6-7), the debate on the new spaces in the extensions of cities gave rise to a set of new concepts: in Italy, *citta diffusa*/diffuse city (Indovina, 1990; Vigano, 1999); in France, *métapolis* (Ascher, 1995), *ville archipel*/archipelago city (Veltz, 1996; Viard, 1994); or in Spain, the idea of a *ciudad dispersa*/dispersed city (Monclús, 1998); and in Germany, the *Zwischenstadt*/city-in-between (Sieverts, 1997). The concept of horizontal metropolis now brings this diverse scholarship together under a common research project (Cavalieri & Vigano, 2019; Vigano et al., 2018).

On the other hand, learning from the Global South, periurban scholarship became increasingly informed by French literature on African cities, as well as Latin American and Asian research. The planner John Browder (1995) summarizes four key themes that resonate through this periurban literature up to the mid-1990s. These themes demonstrate that in scholarship about cities in the Global South, the periurban condition was seen as different from the periurban condition in the Global North. The first common theme in the Southern periurban literature underscores the importance of periurban agriculture and rural linkages to periurban areas (Browder et al., 1995, pp. 312–13). A second common theme is the importance of the "informal" or "gray" economy in periurban areas, reflected in the proliferation of petty commodity production, multiple jobholding, construction of rental units, self-built housing, and participation in informal lending associations. A third common theme is the tenuous nature of property ownership in periurban areas, and the fourth theme concerns the demographic processes responsible for periurban development. This last theme ranges from organized land invasion to planned expansion of the edge subsuming existing rural villages, including the speculative subdivision of farmland near the city, and the resettlement of former inhabitants of "eradicated downtown slums" into public housing projects, or even temporary (daily, seasonal, or circular) migration (Browder et al., 1995, p. 313).

Development policies from the 1950s to the 1980s tried to grapple with such conditions of "underdevelopment" in the edges of cities of the Global South, and these bring with them a set of novel theories about periurban areas. For instance, growth pole theory is based on the belief that governments in the Global South could induce regional economic growth and welfare by investing heavily in capital-intensive industries in large urban centers or regional capitals (Adell, 1999, p. 9). Growth-pole-oriented policies had no rural development component and unsurprisingly, had few positive effects on surrounding rural regions; the beneficiaries were essentially already-privileged groups and large urban centers (Douglass, 1998; Hardoy & Satterthwaite, 1986). Another theory, which is more rural-oriented, is in favor of the development of many medium-sized cities (Rondinelli, 1983) and builds on an agropolitan approach proposed by Friedmann and Douglass (1975), as well as central place theory (Christaller, 1966). Rondinelli's approach is essentially concerned with the implementation of rural development through "manipulation of the urban settlement hierarchy" (Adell, 1999, p. 14). Periurban conditions in this instance are thus seen within interactions both between rural areas and small cities, and also interactions between smaller and larger cities (1999, p. 14). As I have shown, such ideal settlement hierarchy policies were in use in Gangetic West Bengal, even though there was no clear evidence from research that "there is such a thing as a balanced pattern of urbanization" (Unwin, 1989). That is, the Government of West Bengal was (and maybe still is) captivated by the future projected in these theories.

In the mid-1990s, periurban literature reflected new observations about urban expansion in the Global North and in the Global South. There was a dispersal process of both population and employment from the center of cities to the periphery, with the largest metropolitan areas converging, and this outward movement was strongly determined by land markets (Ingram, 1998). McGee and Greenberg (1992, p. 24) note that urbanization in Southeast Asia revealed three characteristics of urban expansion that were uniquely different than the Global North. First, the distinction between rural and urban activities was breaking down much faster than was the case in the Global North. Second, the considerable advances in transportation technology—particularly relatively cheap intermediate technology such as two-stroke motorbikes—greatly facilitated the circulation of commodities, people, and capital in such regions, and accordingly, large mega-urban regions were emerging. Third, rapid industrial and economic growth in Southeast Asia was primarily focused on the mega-urban regions, leading to an increasing concentration of economic activity in these areas. Thus, they argue for a conception of "region-based urbanization," as opposed to "city-based urbanization" (1992, p. 25). In addition, McGee and Greenberg (1992, p. 25) reported that Southeast Asia governments were busy redefining urban boundaries (something that I have shown for Kolkata) and they conceptualize the elements of such boundary-work. The first element is entitled the city core, the second element is the metropolitan area, and the third element is the extended metropolitan area, which refers to "the areas of urban settlement which are emerging in corridors, and which radiate outwards from the metropolitan area." The term desakota is also used to refer to this last zone of urbanization where nonagricultural activity was observed as increasingly mixed with agriculture.

McGee proposed three desakota types (1991, p. 12): first, regions that have experienced a rapid transformation of the spatial economy in terms of rural-to-urban shift in population. Second, regions that have experienced rapid change in their economic features in the past thirty years; and third, regions characterized by changes that occur because of high population growth and slower economic growth. McGee (1991, p. 16) identified the "extended Calcutta Metropolitan Region" as fitting the model of Type II desakota (see also Douglass, 1986). Other regions that are Type II desakota include Nanjing-Shanghai-Hangzhou, the Central Plains of Thailand, the Taipei-Kaohsiung corridor, and Jabotabek in Java (1991, p. 8). Type II desakota is characterized by a socio-spatial economic transition in which, over varying periods of time, productivity gains in agriculture and industry, and secular shifts from agricultural to nonagricultural activities are focused particularly on the urban cores and adjacent regions (1991, p. 8). However, McGee's concept of desakota is more than just an extended location near (or in-between) an expanding "urban core." Importantly, it is a concept about a continuum "from the most urban spatial unit to the most non-urban" or from less to more agricultural economic activities (1991, p. 20). The power of McGee's region-based concept of continuum is that "both regions gain": the rural areas through increased earnings and larger markets, and the urban areas through savings on housing cost and less congestion in the built-up areas (Shaw, 2005, p. 129). This important conceptual shift away from a definition of periurban as proximate to a city, is discussed further in the next section.

Beyond Proximity to Cities

In addition to a focus on region, McGee highlights the importance of linkages (internal and external) and this points toward a more thorough reconsideration of many of the edge-extension and core-periphery arguments presented above. For instance, McGee situates desakota both spatially, as an emerging zone of economic interaction (1991, p. 14), and as a condition shaped by a variety of socio-spatial transitions. He states that the "central processes" that shape desakota regions are the "dynamic linkages between agriculture and non-agriculture, and investment seeking to utilize cheap labor and land within a distinctive agroecological setting" (1991, pp. 17-18). Others have similarly turned to finer distinctions: for instance, sociologists Iaquinta and Drescher (2000) argue that "proximity to the city" is not essential to the definition of periurban. The fact that much periurban "place" is proximate to the city is substantively important and instrumental to a comprehensive understanding of periurban, they say, but it is incidental to an "elemental" understanding of periurban (2000, p. 5). In what follows, I look at the breadth of conceptual approaches to periurbanization that have emerged since the late 1990s.

In the late 1990s, an influential linkages approach was put forward (Douglass, 1998; Lynch, 2005; Tacoli, 1998). Planner Cecilia Tacoli's (2011, p. 111) central argument is that ongoing economic, social, and demographic transformations in most parts of Africa and Asia are best understood as processes based on a "complementary relationship" between rural and urban development, and a "blurring of the rural-urban divide," rather than as relatively clear-cut transitions. Such an approach highlights flows—that is, movements of goods, people and ideas—that can take place in "either direction," and reminds us that rural and urban dwellers "exploit urban-rural differentials" as a conscious tactic (Lynch, 2005, p. 31; see also Rigg et al., 2016). Central to the linkages approach is the view that rural-urban linkages are best supported by policies grounded in a careful understanding of the local context.

In another approach, the geographer David Simon (2008, 2004) uniquely brought together a set of concepts that are often in use today, and grouped together under the term "periurban interface" (also see A. Allen, 2003; McGregor et al., 2005). Rather than look at rural and urban as being distinct, Simon uses the concept of an "approximate continuum" between the poles of rural and urban (see McGee, 1991). His interest lies in studying how periurban areas are differentiated within this continuum and argues that this differentiation can be understood in relation to a gradient of urban influences, and with outcomes that are "non-linear and nonuniform" (Simon, 2004, p. 235). For instance, he says a periurban zone may change over quite short periods of time in both width (a measurement of area) and in the steepness of what he call its "rural-urban gradient," with each change "depending on the nature of pressures within [and] towards it" (2004, p. 239). This observation about the multifaceted periurban interface is shared by Iaquinta and Drescher (2000, p. 4), who also see rural-urban as a continuum. They argue that it is important to recognize that the spectrum of change from rural to urban is "discontinuous, lumpy, and multidimensional," and that it arises from underlying social processes (2000, p. 4). The ungainly concept of a "lumpy, rural-urban continuum" concept has since been noted as a successful challenge to conventional distinctions between the urban and the rural (A. Allen, 2014, p. 522). In addition, the premise that processes of periurbanization exhibit distinct dynamics in different settings has been further explored, and this is evident in the next two examples.

The first case engages a systems-based approach. The project entitled Peri-Urban Land Use Relationships, or PLUREL, used a conceptual model to study periurbanization across the territory of the European Union from 2007 to 2011 (Nilsson et al., 2013). As explained by planner Joel Ravetz (2013, p. 27), this model was informed by transition and complexity theory, which includes both ecological thinking on complex adaptive systems and ideas of the "fractal city" (see P. Allen et al., 1986; Batty & Longley, 1994), composed of "endless levels of self-organizing complexity." Using the analytical tool of scenario-modelling of possible urban futures, the PLUREL model afforded an inquiry into the dynamics of periurbanization based on a spatial typology of "rural-urban regions" (Zasada et al., 2013). What this means is that (induced and autonomous) periurban differentiations were modelled as types of nonlinear "urban-driven transitions" (see Rauws & de Roo, 2011).

The second case engages urban political ecology, which is central to this book. The Toronto-based research project entitled "Global Suburbanisms: Governance, Land and Infrastructure in the 21st Century" ran from 2010 to 2019. The related papers assembled in the special issue of *Urban Geography* journal by planner Fulong Wu and political scientist Roger Keil (2020) look through the lens of "sub/urban theory" to enrich what they term a "post-suburban comparative research" field (also see Charmes & Keil, 2015; Phelps & Wu, 2011). A postsuburbia view, they explain, is a theoretical proposition that assumes a plurality of dynamics as a starting point (2020, p. 3), and building on an ordinary-cities approach, learns from "peripheral areas in fast-growing Asian metropolitan regions" (2020, p. 1). The plural dynamics are defined as residential, industrial, infrastructural, and financial, as well as broadly urban and rural dynamics (Wu & Keil, 2020, p. 3). In their study, suburbanization is interchangeable with periurbanization, by which they mean "the combination of non-central population and economic growth with urban spatial expansion" (see Ekers et al., 2015). Thus, postsuburban scholarship is both grounded within periurbanization scholarship and engages comparison as a method of theory building. Overall, a postsuburban positionality implies an historical-materialist approach, and as Keil (2017, p. 59) clarifies, it argues for the centrality of suburban form and society within what Lefebvre (2003) called the "urban revolution." While my research overlaps with many of these starting points, there is one difference, as was discussed in the introduction—my study does not draw on a historical-materialist approach as an a priori theory. It is the entanglement of nonhumans and their diverse agencies with society and space that is at the core of this book.

A major challenge to periurban scholarship in general is the work on planetary urbanism (Brenner, 2014; Brenner & Schmid, 2011), which is an extension and linkage argument taken to the extreme. Brenner (2014, p. 16) argues that planetary (or "extended urbanization"), rather than the city, is the imperative topic for analysis because capitalism is generating a "world-encompassing" urbanization, which is, in turn, "world-making." What the planetary urbanism concept does is replace the rural-urban continuum concept with a notion of the "urbanization of everything" (A. Roy, 2016, p. 813), and as destiny (Ruddick et al., 2017, p. 392). Periurbanism is thus seen as simply another instance of a discontinuous, lumpy, and multidimensional, planetary urbanism, and this indeed, is how the postsuburban approach mentioned above is sited. However, as Adell (1999, p. 37) notes, the validity of the periurban concept must be judged in terms of the context of its use and the function it is expected to perform. Adell says the periurban concept is a useful descriptive and analytical tool, as it takes particular conditions into account while aiming at specific operational functions.

Architect Stephen Cairns (2018) offers a critical engagement with the periurban concept in relation to both planetary urbanism and what he terms "intensive urbanism," where the city is regarded as the defining end point and causal engine of urbanization. In both cases, Cairns observes a "silence and silencing of the rural" as an outcome (2018, p. 119). At best, he says, "the rural is portrayed as a mere backdrop" for the more spectacular processes of urbanization. In response, he (2018, p. 120) suggests that densely settled-rural areas in South East Asia are not just a mere surrounds to the city; rather they exhibit a special type of agency and a viable alternative to the persistent city-centrism of urban studies. That is, he points out, in densely settled-rural areas in Southeast Asia, urban effects and opportunities are "uniquely *absorbed*" by the preexisting rural settlement condition and thus, "have characteristics and substance that weigh upon the terms of reference for both urban theory and practice" (2018, p. 120). The following scholarship offers some clues to how this might be approached.

There is a growing interest in the post-rural. In a special issue of the journal *Cities* on the politics of periurbanization in Asia, planner Michael Leaf (2016, p. 131) situates the periurban within a singular, "global urban transition." He says the core concern of the politics of the periurban in Asia is with "the nature of urbanism and urban life into the future." Thus, as with most of the accounts of periurbanization, there is an acknowledgment that "becoming urban" is a significant event. However, it is not destiny, because it is negotiated, he says. That is, there are many particular kinds of urban futures being negotiated. According to Leaf (2016, p 131-32), periurbanization politics are shaped by planning, local authorities, the market, and what Leaf calls the "non-capitalist market economy," about which we know the least. Important for this book is his inclusion of the rural and the noncapitalist market economy, which are both imbricated in the state. For instance, Leaf states, "periurban is as much post-rural as it is pre-urban, if not more so" (2016, p. 131). This brings with it the implication (as with other "post-instances"), that "certain elements and aspects of the rural past persist and perhaps are re-articulated in new ways in the post-rural periurban." The empirical chapters in this book attest to this observation.

Second, in his commentary on this same special issue of the journal *Cities*, the geographer John Friedmann (2016) looks for "comparative studies of the periurban." Noteworthy, in his view, is the considerable diversity of approaches and interests that are revealed in all the essays, "approaches and interests that cannot be shaped into a single elegant theory or even squeezed into a single theoretical framework of the periurban" (2016, p. 165). What he observes is "history in the making," as densely populated rural areas in Asian countries are becoming radically reshaped. That is, he observes that the theory is not there yet, for it will only emerge through more comparative work on the understanding of periurbanization and urban edge conditions.

The varied pathways of scholarship on periurbanization thus bring into view the necessity for pausing around how it is theorized. While the early scholarship on edges generated many novel categorizations of conditions that were considered distinct in relation to the norm of the concentrated city of the North, the later scholarship on extension explored the fringes or periphery not as an edge of a city but as places, and once again much novel categorization was created. A second thread in the scholarship on extension learned from cities of the Global South and brought with it ideas for state-led territorial development. In particular, the scholarship on Southeast Asia influenced later periurban theorizations to let go of the city as an anchor altogether, and to favor approaches that focus on urban-rural linkages or the situated differentiation of periurbanization processes globally. The conceptual shift from spatial to process-based approaches is significant, and something that is in practice in Gangetic West Bengal, where a mix of spatial (vision plans) and process-based (indicators) approaches has been discussed.

Thus, there is much at stake in these distinctive approaches and perspectives, for their assumptions shape and confirm practical planning and development frameworks. Importantly for this book, the most recent approaches do not discard the periurban as a useful descriptive and analytical tool, but rather bring a deeper interrogation of the transformative politics of the periurban and the agency of nonhumans nature. They point out that it is essential to understand the legacies of the settled-rural, including the negotiations of "becoming (what sort of) urban?" This book uniquely brings these two dimensions into dialog through a focus on ordinary settlements' everyday entanglements, diffuse power, and slow, incremental change. These are characteristics which are often missed, understated, or compartmentalized by other approaches. As noted in the introduction, this study aims to not only open the binary and teleological assumptions linked to categories such as rural and urban, but also to interrogate those that separate society and nature, and human and nonhuman agency.

From India

A close look at periurban scholarship from India reveals that it mirrors the movement between the three approaches to thinking about periurban conditions, which I have termed *edges*, *extension*, and *beyond cities*. In what follows, I trace this movement not only to note the contribution of the scholarship over time, but to reflect how local concerns speak back to assumptions about periurbanization from elsewhere. First, echoing the edge-extension tradition discussed above, early periurban scholarship in India focused on the measurement and classification of the edge of the city. For instance, Brush (1968, 1977) studied the spatial patterns of population distribution as a continuum from urban to rural, and in the case of Kolkata, this was measured up to thirty miles from the "historical core." In another instance, an edited volume by Yadav (1987) includes Indian case studies from Kanpur and Lucknow that reflect a concern with conditions of "underdevelopment" on city extensions. As with the exploration of various terms for describing the edge of cities from the 1940s onward, the Indian case studies interpreted a neologism—*umland* (van Cleef, 1941)—which is a variation on the concept of hinterland or environs from German and French vocabularies. The umland, is (re)defined in the Indian context by Dixit (1987) as a "tributary area immediately around the city and functionally, economically, socio-culturally and politically integrated with it." Thus, periurban scholarship in India at this time was concerned with fitting into so-called universal, European spatial measures.

As noted in the previous section, growth-pole theory in Asia and desakota in Southeast Asia impacted dominant periurban concepts from the Global North by shifting the focus towards urban-rural territories, or urbanization as an extended condition. However, the concerns on the ground in India at the time were focused more locally, and only on the troubled periphery of very large cities. For instance, in the early 2000s there was much focus on land-use conflict in periurban Delhi (Bentick, 1996, 2000; Kumar, 1998; Kundu et al., 2002). At this same time, as noted by urban demographer Veronique Dupont (2007, p. 92), there was a bifurcation in periurban interpretive frameworks. While some studies look at processes that are linked to the urban core, other studies, such as Dupont's, reflect the periurban interface framework. Dupont (2007, p. 92) explains that the periurban scholarship related to the urban core in India was narrowly focused on one modality, its troubled excess. These studies focus on "a preponderance of underprivileged settlers (migration to the cities by the rural poor and the resettlement of slum dwellers from the city after the demolition of their homes), a lack of infrastructure, urban services and amenities, the presence of polluting and heavy industries evacuated from urban centers, and a degraded environment."

Yet, metropolitan peripheries in India are in fact "complex structures resulting from a mix of planned operations and unplanned, uncontrolled processes and the flouting of regulations," and they cover a "wide range of modalities" (Dupont, 2007, p. 93). Accordingly, Dupont finds it more relevant to look beyond the prism of "degenerated peripheralization" (see Kundu et al., 2002), and instead her scholarship turns to a global city-regions framework (see Scott, 2001) and the urban fragmentation thesis—or "splintering urbanism" thesis (Graham & Marvin, 2001). Others have since made similar observations about the splintered, characteristics of the periphery of Indian cities. Scholars have analyzed the uneven impact of new town planning and special purpose enclaves (Kennedy, 2007; Kennedy & Sood, 2016; Shaw, 2004), city-region rescaling in general (Phadke, 2013; Shaw, 2018), and the practical experience of living amidst such newly emerging spatial differentiation (Cowan, 2015; Goldstein, 2016; Srivastava, 2015). In Kolkata, scholarship about a periurban interface is similarly focused on characteristics of unevenness and fragmentation. There is scholarship on a "bypass" approach to urbanization (Bhattacharyya & Sanyal, 2011), city-region rescaling and conflict (A. Roy, 2011b; Shatkin, 2016), and related displacements (Bose, 2015; A. Roy, 2003), as well as the effects of increasing spatial differentiation on periurban governance (I. Roy, 2006; Shaw, 2005).

Another phenomenon that has shaped periurban scholarship from India is the response to the rigid classification of cities by the Indian state. Scholars have challenged the relevance of dichotomous—urban or rural population—categories, noting that they are (intentionally?) out-of-date (Bhagat, 2002, 2005; Dupont, 2004), and this is a topic that continues to be studied (see Vidyarthi, 2017). One retort are studies that build on an urban-rural linkages approach to addressing the concerns facing urbanizing small towns and villages in India. Iaquinta and Drescher (2000) created a "conceptual periurban typology" of five periurban types, which emphasize the phenomenon of "places of social compression and dynamic social change." Places of social compression are defined as areas of "intensification" where "the density of social forms, types and meanings increases, fomenting conflict and social evolution" (2000, p. 2). Also building on a linkages approach, and including the framework of thinking beyond cities altogether, Singh and Narain (2013, 2020) argue that periurbanization in India occurs anywhere that rural and urban economic activities, institutions, and practices coexist (2020, p. 3). In contrast to Dupont and others, who lament the absence of relevant governance structures for periurban India, Singh and Narain (2020, p. 7) argue that the relevant issue is not the "governance lacuna" (see Aijaz, 2019; World Bank, 2013) in periurban spaces, but a need to better understand the "plurality" of mechanisms through which decisions are made and resources are allocated. Accordingly, they argue that periurban India is best theorized as "a space combining both rural and urban features, changing flows of goods, services and resources between rural areas and urban centers" (2020, p. 7).

While the present study similarly looks beyond the city or any urban-rural dichotomy for a definition of periurban, it does not adopt an interface approach with its emphasis on stark conflict, or a linkages approach with its emphasis on flows. Rather, I approach periurbanization through urban political ecology, which is to focus scholarly attention on the expansive, ecological, and political nature of urbanization. Learning from my study area, I take account of how nonhuman nature is represented and ordered, as well as domesticated, dilapidated, and enlivened by documents and socio-spatial processes. Others too consider nature in society conceptualizations when they research Indian periurbanization, and it is this work that I turn to as I conclude this chapter.

Since the late 2010s, periurban scholarship from India includes the settled-rural and the agency of nonhuman nature as constitutive of periurban conditions. First, there is scholarship that looks at periurban areas through the lens of everyday ecological knowledge, which in India focuses on natural resource use and livelihood changes (Banu & Fazal, 2017; Goswami & Nautiyal, 2020; Sreeja et al., 2017), and urban agriculture. For instance, Priya et al. (2017) look to the transformative politics of periurban agricultural knowledge in relation to what they call "local environmentalism." Such research is situated in response to the urban issue that sociologist Amita Baviskar (2004) has highlighted as "bourgeois environmentalism," whereby elite notions of environment are privileged by the Indian state. In Kolkata, much scholarship about everyday ecological knowledge is focused on the important role of the wastewater-fed fisheries of the East Kolkata Wetlands, a system that is argued as central to the "urban ecology" of metropolitan Kolkata (Mukherjee, 2015a, 2015b, 2020). Also in Kolkata, planner Ratoola Kundu (2016) looks at place-making practices by residents of neighboring "urban villages" and gated communities in Rajarhat New Town. Kundu examines the routine activities that go into the material and social construction of place, as well as how place influences social interactions, livelihoods, and aspirations. Both instances are sited on what I have framed as exceptional landscapes of Kolkata, whereas this study is focused on ordinary periurbanization in Gangetic West Bengal.

Another approach that considers nature in society conceptualizations is emerging scholarship that looks at "frontiers" in India. In the special issue of Economic and Political Weekly on "frontier urbanism," anthropologist Subhra Gururani and political scientist Rajarshi Dasgupta (2018) mirror the distinctiveness of the settled-rural, as argued by Cairns (2018). They adopt an expansive definition of agrarian, covering diverse livelihoods including fishing and pastoralism, and highlight the centrality of land and caste. Important for this study, Gururani and Dasgupta engage their "agrarian-urban frontier" (2018) or "agrarian urbanism" (2019) thematic through a vitalist-inflected, neo-Marxian framework and an explicitly agrarian prism. They argue that the agrarian-urban frontier is a type of interstitial agency (see Tsing, 2005), or space of productive confusion (2018, p. 41),[1] and that the "agrarian and the urban are materially and symbolically coproduced" (also see Rathi, 2021; A. Roy, 2011a). And accordingly, they paint the Indian periurban condition as a "volatile and active landscape, caught in a vortex of change, a place full of potential but also of perils" (Gururani and Dasgupta, 2018, p. 42).

In thinking through the terms *rural* and *urban*, *periurban linkages*, *periurban interface*, and more recently *agrarian urbanism*, periurban scholarship from India has reflected both wider debates and concerns on the ground. Such emplaced, periurban theorizations anticipate future scholarship, given that much of the recent interest in periurban India has been "off the map" of places that urban studies scholars turn to for theory-building. In my understanding, there is a broad arc in the scholarship of a gradual transfer from spatial to process- and agrarian-based definitions. That is, while earlier work was too focused on conceptualizing unusual edges, recent work is created in reaction to this. I agree with such innovative responses.

The chapter has provided an analysis of the scholarship on periurbanization, emphasizing work that critically engages with both agrarian and periurban socio-spatial transformations. In this book, I avoid defining the periurban simply in relation to city expansion or by relying on simplistic urban-rural dichotomies. I do not, however, discard the periurban by focusing on flows or linkages, as many now do. Clearly, urban-rural linkages are central to deconstructing urban-rural dichotomies. Rather, I think of the periurban as a "kind of urban" condition that is emplaced and located in settlement, in land use, in urban political ecologies, in topological power. By inserting this condition into debates about what constitutes an urban future, the study offers an intervention into norms about where and how urban theory emerges. My intention is to shift the lens of scholarly attention from the "almost urban" and toward the variety of "kinds of urban." To do this work, my approach builds upon, and aims to advance, urban political ecology.

Endnotes

1 Earlier work in India that used the term "frontiers" looked at periurbanization through the spatial lenses of road development in rural areas (Brook et al., 2003), greenfield development in urban peripheries (Kennedy & Sood, 2016), and in Kolkata, the different meanings that land takes on in the context of the East Kolkata Wetlands (Sangameswaran, 2018).

CONCLUSION

Renderings of periurban areas are often positioned in a developmentalist framework, which assumes a pre-existing rural is in transition towards something that inevitably becomes urban. In India, this teleological approach is rarely questioned by the state or even by residents themselves. However, scholarship about periurbanism has interrogated the notion of a linear, rural to urban transition, finding it too simple and offering more complex interpretations. For in a developmentalist framework, not only are residual rural land uses and livelihoods missed out on, but the characteristics of hybrid, urban-rural mixing (McGee, 1991) are missed out on too. As I have noted, these mixed conditions have been looked at as edge or extensions, and as occurring not always in proximity to cities. In this study, I chose to look at hybrid, urban-rural mixing at the edge metropolitan Kolkata. Despite much emphasis on rapid urban change in Asia, periurban south-west Kolkata is changing incrementally—in fits and starts, or in a piecemeal fashion, resulting in different formations along the way. The lived experience of the so-called "transition" from a rural to a post-rural condition encompasses a range of simultaneous transformations. Such unhurried change includes dense, intergenerational interactions between people, institutions, and nature. I have paused in this slow geography and have taken a close look at the thirty years from 1990 until 2020.

Mixity Disentangled

The study approaches ordinary periurbanization as an emplaced, incremental condition that includes humans, nonhumans, and their diverse agencies. In order to disentangle this mixing, I created three loose lenses, which were informed by the process of making and analyzing visualizations of residents' accounts of the one-kilometer-square study area (see Figure 9.01). In what follows, the findings of each lens are summarized.

Figure 9.01. All study area data layers: Light pink rectangles: older buildings (2004 data). Dark pink rectangles: newer buildings (2018 data). Thick red lines: local, main roads (with cars and trucks). Thin red lines: pathway roads (with some or no cars). Yellow symbols: participant households (approximate location). White square: one kilometer-square study area. Yellow areas: Land cover patches with invented shading (local main road built up areas; wooded-settled areas; colonies; "jungly" former paddy land). White lines; para boundaries.

(Source: author, 2022; Google Earth Pro, 2018; and unassembled and unpublished GIS files provided by Maheshtala Municipality, 2019.)

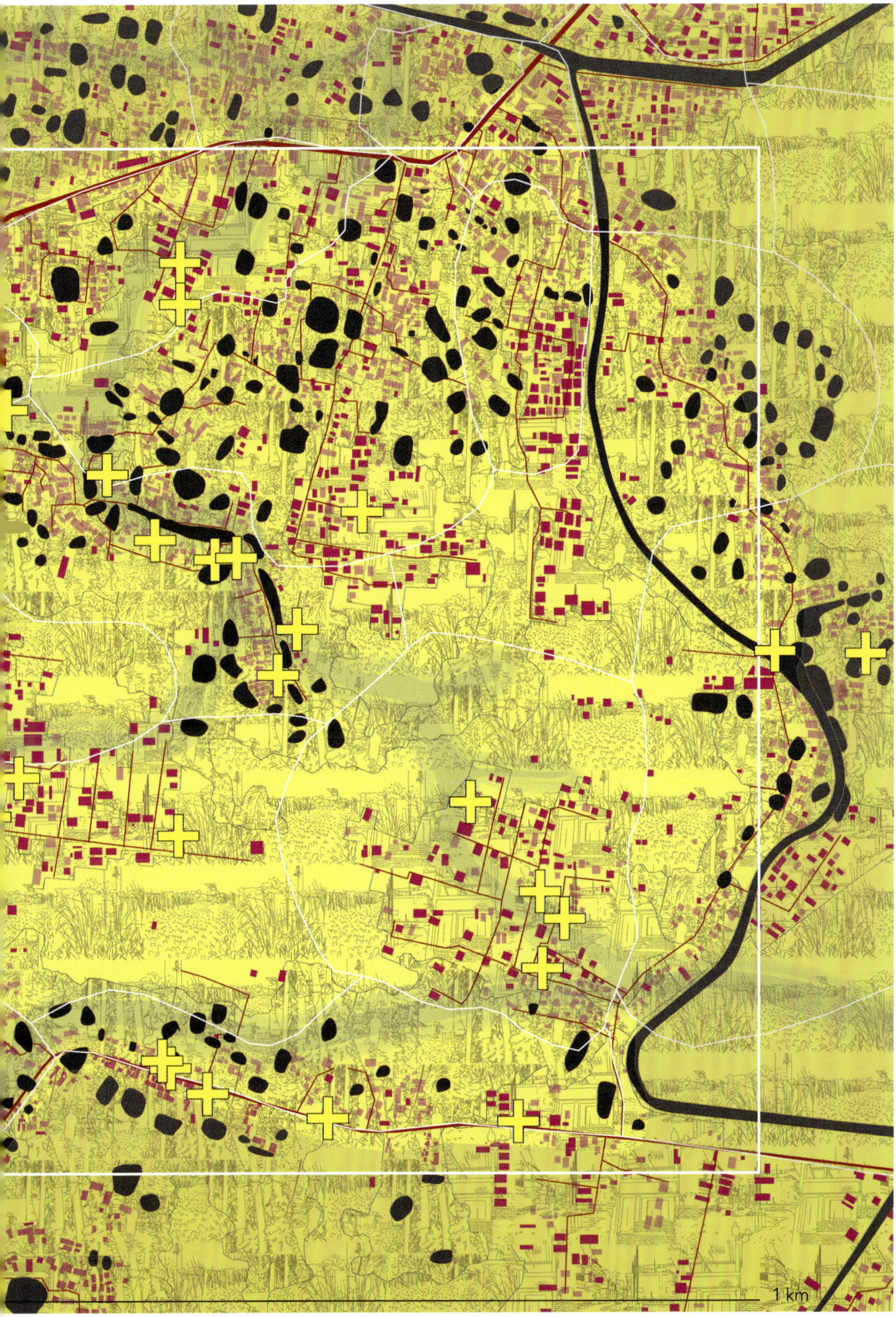
1 km

First, a teleological account of drainage and fields might assume that as rain- and river-fed irrigated fields are transformed into colonies of newcomer housing, farmers will then switch to urban livelihoods, and relatedly, the irrigated fields' water will then be channeled into a modern, underground storm-water system. However, in actual practice, these transformations trouble each other. I provided an account of how ongoing renovations of the canal network disrupted predictable irrigation methods, thus contributing to the end of cultivation in the study area. The cessation of cultivation has several follow-on consequences, including the sale of productive agricultural land, the increase of "jungle," and localized waterlogging with increasingly polluted water, itself an outcome of further renovations of the canal network. These wet and vegetative densities alter the socio-spatial qualities of the study area. Impoverished long-term residents and prosperous newcomer residents equally find themselves living surrounded by seasonal "putrefied water" and are at a loss to know what they can do, especially as the weak municipality and indifferent State of West Bengal are slow to act, if they act at all. Furthermore, the waterlogging, along with changes in household participation in paid labor, lead to the residual productive agricultural land and *bagans* (gardens) becoming neglected. The conventional approach would be that the male farmers tend the fields and gardens, and the women manage the household; however, given that the men now work in service jobs, the fields and gardens are no longer actively cultivated. Untended thickets of vegetation are increasing, creating an unwelcome sense of enclosure along with "infestations" of snakes and mosquitoes.

Second, a teleological account of the periurbanization of village property might assume that former-farmer households become more prosperous with increased income from urban jobs and the sale and development of valuable and sought-after periurban land. However, this is not the case. Former-farmer households not only own "house-land" and fields, but they also own "garden-land" which often includes a pond and many productive or useful plants. Elderly, former-farmers have few skills that transfer into a prosperous urban income, and so they take low-paying, physically demanding day jobs, such as auto-drivers. As they have less time to cultivate their fields and bagans, which may be newly waterlogged and ruined by polluted overflow water, the natural resources from bagans that might supplement a low-income household's means of living are less and less available. The "village-like" characteristics of tree-lined ponds and plantations, and multifamily households residing in courtyard buildings, is seen to undergo slow disrepair. Houses are not repaired, valuable plantation trees are cut down and not replaced, ponds become unused and untended, pond-bunds become eroded, pond-based waterlogging spreads, and useful trees are thus "drowned." Interestingly, amidst accounts of such spaces as "ruined" or "wasted," there is a view that such dilapidated conditions are a temporary situation. Accordingly, rules and norms about the sharing of plants and ponds persist. For instance, untended bagans are often talked about as "growing by themselves," and the soil continues to be thought of as fertile, even though it may be covered in jungle or polluted water. Similarly, the slow geography of dilapidation is thought of as being simply a condition of the increasing presence of "idle" or "fallow" land. Managing land as dilapidated is often seen as an acceptable holding state. Those former farmers who have the means to retain their various properties of field, house-land, and garden-land, manage them in an intentionally neglected state until an opportunity arises or another useful or pragmatic future for it can be thought of. In other words, there seems to be a pull-back or stasis that is a result of periurbanization itself.

Third, a teleological account of the rise of a periurban land market might assume farmers are displaced, followed by colony development for elite newcomers amidst state violence—a logic of change well documented in the scholarship on contemporary Indian urbanization. While such accounts are not unheard of in metropolitan Kolkata and Gangetic West Bengal, the study area does not afford such a crisp account of urbanization on-the-move or such a large differential of power. While some local brokers are nefarious, many of the accounts of middlemen practices revealed that land conversion and settlement of newcomers is mostly an amicable process. My findings reveal that the rise of a periurban land market does not empower any one group over another. Both long-term and newcomer residents benefit and are exploited more or less equally. For instance, long-term residents' waterlogging issues are ignored by the municipality, which prefers to see residents' paddy fields converted to residential uses as colony developments, and to collect property taxes from newcomer residents. Furthermore, as evidenced in my review of the municipal development plans, the controlling, central and state-level governments do not provide the municipality any conceptual or pragmatic foundations for governing a hybrid, urban-rural future. Nevertheless, long-term residents are not abandoned by the municipality. They are taken care of and often privileged or given priority treatment in the apportioning of basic infrastructure improvements, such as roads. In contrast, newcomer residents are expected to self-organize and provide such services for themselves. In turn, newcomer residents form associations and leverage their own good-will towards the area in anticipation of future promised infrastructure improvements, like modern drainage and sewage systems.

In sum, my findings reveal that both long-term and newcomer residents participating in the study area aspire to "become urban," and they live in a reality that is on a slow and fragmented pathway to that urban future. However, the wait for this urban future is so long that the option of "staying rural" is reduced or destroyed in the process. Municipal practices for building a "city in the making"; like counting linear feet of paved roads, drains, drinking water pipelines, numbers of streetlights and latrines masks the incremental, socio-spatial adjustments that residents make in anticipation of, and in response to, each improvement. Incremental change in the study area is thus characterized by the ordinary, slow state of being neither one thing nor another. Furthermore, in fragmented, heterogeneous change one slow decision might generate intended or unintended transformative outcomes—diverging pathways in terms of the well-being of all the residents. As such, the moral imagination of this study is motivated by a desire to find incremental ways to improve on or alter these characteristics for the benefit of residents in the area, and for similar lived ecologies in Gangetic West Bengal and Monsoon Asia.

Conceptual Insights

In addition to the empirical contribution noted above, the study offers three conceptual insights. The study contributes to urban theory by highlighting periurban imbroglios with diverse nonhuman agencies like the "graphic entities" of planning documents or the settled-rural, and by carefully describing how these are formed and practiced. Moreover, by focusing on ordinary periurban areas within a relatively recently founded municipality, I have contributed to understandings of actual, and extensive, urban-rural transformations. Furthermore, my commitment to mapping practices and the spatial rendering and re-rendering of Gangetic West Bengal and Monsoon Asia have made a methodological contribution by way of cartography. In the next sub-sections, I substantiate these claims. I first turn to my conceptual contributions to theory before I outline the contribution to methods of research design for practice.

Situated Periurbanization

The goal of a case study is to expand on general theories, usually by adding detailed knowledge of the how and why of processes, identifying patterns and relationships that may either confirm or question accepted understandings. This case study offers interpretative sense-making of periurbanization in place and over time—what Stake (1995), refers to as the "art" of case study research. By selecting a specific instance of periurban Kolkata, this case also contributes to an explanation of periurbanization contextualized within a wider multiscaled logics of urban policy and planning in India, specifically, as well as wider explanations of periurbanization in general. To do this, the study is positioned in relation to both periurban scholarship and situated urban political ecology. I argue that my integration of these two theoretical traditions in an Indian context is a unique contribution, as it is holds explanatory power for understanding ordinary socio-natural transformations taking place through periurbanization. My review of periurban scholarship noted that the present study does not look for a definition of the periurban in relation to a city or through an urban-rural dichotomy lens (see Adell, 1999). Nor does my definition of periurban adopt a flows or linkages approach (see Tacoli, 2011). Rather, it takes a situated approach that acknowledges and takes account of the settled-rural and topological power in Monsoon Asia, showing how the periurban is uniquely realized in this context.

In chapters 1 and 2 of the book, I detailed the multi-scaled policy frameworks in which Maheshtala Municipality and Ward 13 are situated. I showed how periurban areas often must conform to ideas and desires of what counts as urban. I attended in detail to these contextual dimensions because I wanted to chart a diffuse terrain of power—what Allen (2016, p. 153) calls the newfound "reach" of power grounded in an adaptable mix of practices. As noted in the introduction chapter, Allen (2010, p. 1072) starts from a topological account of state spatiality, one that draws attention to the spatial reconfiguration of the state's institutional hierarchies and the ways in which a more "transverse set of political interactions" holds that hierarchy in place, but not in ways conventionally understood through a topographical lens. That is, he says, "topological thinking" suggests that the powers of the state are not so much "above us" as more or less present through mediated and real-time connections, some direct, others more distanced (2010, p. 1072). This is an important contextual dimension of the incremental geography of periurbanization charted in this study, as I have narrated the changing institutional practices for the implementation of national Government of India urban reform initiatives.

As I have shown, Maheshtala Municipality is preoccupied with meeting the controlling compliance requirements of a "maze" (Jha, 2018, p. 15) of central and state-level government initiatives which have little to say about periurban conditions. The support from the state-level government for meeting these directives is inadequate and is hampering the municipality's efforts to meet the requirements of their mandate under the West Bengal

Municipal Act (1993). The promised devolution of power to urban local bodies, as enshrined in the 74th Constitutional Amendment is ever elusive. The resultant lack of financial autonomy means that the municipality is impoverished and financially tied to the central and state governments, which are increasingly enmeshed in "governance by indicators" (Davis et al. 2012) by which standards and pathways of development are realized in and through benchmarking and ranking systems. Ward-level power is similarly diffuse. Residents reluctantly bring issues to the Ward 13 councilors, but as the councilors themselves know, they have limited authority.

A situated approach to periurbanization also takes diverse, nonhuman agencies into account. For instance, the settled-rural in Gangetic West Bengal includes the inherited materiality of village settlements and can be thought of as obdurate. In this obduracy is agency, that is they are accommodating, which allows them to stay in place, and in place they deflect, slow, detour other forces of change. These village settlements are comprised of mud and concrete houses, tree-lined ponds, plantations, and house gardens surrounded by low-lying paddy fields. Furthermore, the settled-rural of Gangetic West Bengal also includes muddy tidal creeks and rivers, and drainage canals, which are crossed and lined with railroad embankments, roadways, and ports. The obduracy of the village-pond-paddy landscape is not simply about its form, but also about deeply embedded senses of inherited responsibility. These can keep residents locked in a settlement logic in which the household may be integrated into urban labor markets or daily routines but retains a sense of one day getting back to the garden, or at some future time attending to the pond, to return them to a state in which it once was. At the same time, there are a range of geographically and temporally distant interventions in the planning and infrastructure of Maheshtala Municipality, over which residents and local political agents have little power, but which have immediate and often irreversible impacts on the locality. The incremental settlement of this particular "kind of urban" can thus happen in multiple dimensions.

A situated approach to periurbanization also considers the agencies of practice. By focusing on property, I have found that the basic, ordinary social relation of being "amicable" is important and has agency. As I have shown, the practices of female home workers, cultivators, middlemen, and associations include much conflict and disagreement. However, a pragmatic need to create and maintain goodwill means that while existing rules and norms about conditions such as jungle and gardens are being replaced, many persist and are respected as newcomers settle into the area. That is, strong human relations with things are not simply "residual" (Williams, 1977), and at the same time, emergent relations with things also have agencies. As I have shown, rules and norms are being invented about road construction and its maintenance, as well as how to live with "infestations" of creatures. What are acceptable or unacceptable compromises in the face of aggressive colony promoters and unwanted waterlogging are also ongoing processes and negotiations.

Overall, the constant effort of, and attention to, creating and maintaining everyday amicability in a context where the settled-rural is dilapidated and misused, and colony infrastructure is scant, can be exhausting. I consider amicability here as a matter of "endurance" (Simone 2014, p. 213). For sociologist Abdul Maliq Simone, endurance is about "bridge building" and by this he does not mean bridges that "conjoin distinct entities into common purposes, resemblances, or mutualities," but rather bridges that "point to breaks and particular procedural frictions" (also see Tsing, 2005). Endurance with keeping amicable relations is thus projective, —or onward-pointing without being teleological. Endurance operates in the manner of fixing broken things that the residents depend upon, but it also defines and expands what it is to be human, here. Thus, amicability is as precious as it is precarious, and creates important socio-spatial conditions for periurban life amid the uncertainty of urbanization and the disrepair of the settled-rural.

Territory

Geographer Jonathan Silver (2014b, p. 790) in writing about incremental infrastructure argues that a focus on ad hoc actions offers important ways to "link micro scales to wider circulations" of people, technologies, and ways of inhabiting cities that diverge from the urban trajectories and futures of Global North cities. I agree with this claim, and in this study, I link my visualizations of micro scale periurban transformations to wider circulations of visualizations of territory, which are also incremental.

Territory is a technique for measuring land and controlling terrain, as well as a process that is continually made and remade (Elden, 2013, p. 36; 2010). My interest in the cartographic and spatial imagination of governmentality is advanced by this critical concept of territory. One mode for reconsidering territory is to think beyond the two-dimensionality of the plan. For some scholars, this is to activate the "volumetric" (Crampton, 2010a) by thinking "through volume, and with volume" (Elden, 2013; also see Graham, 2016). For others, a reconsideration of territory involves thinking about "density" (McFarlane, 2020; Rao, 2014), including how density is measured and evaluated as well as lived. In this study, I draw in both modes, and I also extend the critique of territorial power by thinking anew about the diffuse and situated urban political ecologies of territory.

As shown in chapter 1, various concentric boundaries of Kolkata were defined as an outcome of debates about what to do with a "megacity." The concern was how to manage the populations within the bounded megacity and how to manage the populations that "spill over" the edge of those bounds. The official Kolkata Metropolitan Area is comprised of the various municipal and panchayat territories within that boundary. These territories—the metropolitan, municipal, and panchayat—are produced through perspective and development plans, maps, and an indicator interface. Rather than a two-dimensional map of an area, the territory of the indicator is an interface or portal which visualizes how the effects of urbanization are modulated by initiatives like the Sustainable Development Goals. Governance by indicators can be thought of as a novel territorial strategy created by "calculation" (Crampton, 2010a). In my critical account of these cartographic representations and the frameworks of social and ecological governance they represent, I found that periurban and settled-rural areas were thought of as not much more than neutral, blank spaces for "spill over" populations from the congested and conceptually elevated megacity. I also found that while the "quiet power of indicators" (Merry et al., 2015) signals a shift toward measures other than those of managing population density, the emphasis in periurban areas is nevertheless on "becoming urban." Furthermore, I found that ordinary municipalities are less privileged than so-called "smart ones" with "compact areas."

In response, I then augmented this rendering of Gangetic West Bengal with my own re-rendering, focusing exclusively on periurban conditions. I re-rendered the periphery of the Kolkata Metropolitan Area, selecting Maheshtala Municipality and sampling my one-kilometer-square study area in detail with topographical depth, height, and temporal duration. I highlighted not only the density of people but identified buildings, paddy fields, ponds, and vegetation. Overall, my re-rendering sought to temper the primacy of the megacity as the formative urban element in Gangetic West Bengal.

More specifically, my re-rendering sought to challenge the problems that arise "when space is reduced to a surface" (Elden, 2013, p. 36). Through a sustained critique of a ward-level land-use plan, I showed how other visualization techniques reveal that there are more than either flat "vacant" or all residential areas. For instance, I uncovered accounts of waterlogging, tree-lined ponds, plantations, sawmills, jungle, colonies, middlemen, associations, and infestations within such areas. So, rather than being thought of as not-dense-yet, or not-dense-enough to warrant attention, the study area is thought of as dense along other registers. As McFarlane (2016, p. 644) notes, density is both a "topographical problem of number and measurement" and a problem of "topological politics and space." Thus, I also showed how these lived dense entanglements are also political imbroglios, and shape space and power. In many instances I found that residents' power and nonhumans' diverse agencies are subtle and temporary, but nevertheless present and significant for individuals' everyday lives.

Incremental Practice

Planner Darshini Mahadevia (2011, p. 63) suggests that urban "growth" in India should learn from existing incremental efforts and "go slow." "Let us not glamorize cities and urban development, let us slog it out," she says. While the many ordinary periurban places that I re-rendered through various visualization techniques and described as imbroglios and densities, are not thought of as "territories" in everyday parlance in Gangetic West Bengal, I have brought them forward to prompt such a discussion. My intention is to afford consideration for how they might be better considered within local cultures of governance and inform everyday decision-making by residents. I argue that possible periurban futures can only be interrogated through highly localized conditions, which are molded and controlled by political structures and aspirations shaped in global comparative frameworks. Thus, rather than the area studied being eclipsed by a known future urban, my research argues for the creation of more literacy about, and actions that support, the variable increments of settlement from rural to post-rural, from post-rural to periurban, and importantly, about the ongoing negotiations that maintain an enduring periurban mixity.

My contribution to increasing awareness and appreciation of incremental periurban futures is through mapping, which is itself an incremental practice. Mapping practices link geographic knowledge to power and thus they are political (Crampton & Krygier, 2006). My visualizations that map imbroglios are, therefore, not only a task of representation but also a substantive engagement with mapping as a process of "constant reterritorialization" (Kitchin & Dodge, 2007, p. 331). I described how the rendering of the study area by the State of West Bengal has changed over time, while keeping maps unavailable to the public and producing them as increasingly unreadable. I found that overall, the role of the masterplan map as a guide for the future has diminished over time, being replaced by a database that represents indicator compliance. Maps are things, and they have lives and temporalities of their own (Rossetto 2019, p. 9). If one takes an "object-oriented attitude" such as this, cartographic objects can be seen to have "becomings and 'unbecomings'": that is, a capacity for not only "unceasingly working on the move," but also a capacity for decay, to become disengaged and go dormant

(2019, p. 9).[1] As I have shown, the 2025 vision plan for metropolitan Kolkata has decayed, not due to poor storage in a humid, insect-laden environment, but through poor digital processing and interpretive copying of a confusingly rendered map. Furthermore, the 2025 vision plan had been drafted in 2006, fifteen years before the time of this study and has not been updated since. Overall, the practice of mapping metropolitan Kolkata, first as a problematic megacity, and second as a business-friendly, global city, as evidenced in the 1990s and -2000s, might be thought of as dormant. At the same time, the practice of representing metropolitan Kolkata through an interface managed by the central government, which encourages competition between districts across the whole State of West Bengal, can be thought of as ascendant.

It is not unusual for mapping practices, or "cartographic modes" to change over time (Edney, 2011). Each cartographic mode comprises a set of cultural, social, and technological relationships that determine cartographic practices (2011, p. 305). In his research of the "Western [map] tradition" since the 1500s, Edney (2011, p. 315) finds that various cartographic modes (like topography, charting, geodesy, and chorography) converged and then diverged as new cartographic modes were developed in the 1800s. In the context of Gangetic West Bengal, divergence in cartographic modes can be seen not only with the development of competition between districts, but also with the emergence of the " 'geoweb' and a questioning of expert mapping" (Crampton, 2010b, p. 4)

There are local instances in Kolkata whereby expert mapping is being critiqued.[2] Such unofficial Kolkata-based map projects exist in a complex relationship with state documents and are not "counter to" or resisting the state (Venkataramani, 2015, p. 266). Rather they, augment the states' maps with spaces and expressions of everyday life. The practice of mapping as evidenced in this study is positioned in relation to these "experimental geographies" (Paglen, 2008, p. 31) that take on the production of space in a reflexive way and as integral to their practice. That is, I like to think of the study itself as having agencies, even as I understand that both "potentialities and risks" can emerge when maps move between the "states" of making, publishing, circulating, and revision (Venkataramani, 2015, p. 345). I also understand that periurban settlement is made up of emplaced landscapes that transform over time, leading to untying as much as to stability. Along with unofficial Kolkata-based map-projects, my hope is that many similar projects might afford better recognition of the many types of ordinary periurban territories in Gangetic West Bengal and Monsoon Asia and inform changes that can support their endurance. I thus offer the mapping practice created in this book as an entangled increment in itself—as a "lively thing" (Rossetto, 2019).

Future Directions

There are two directions for future research that have emerged from the findings. First, is a consideration of the reactions by scholars of Indian urbanization to periurban scholarship that emerged from both the Global North and South (see chapter 8). In response to place-based and urban-centered definitions of periurbanization, some Indian scholars have adopted an explicitly process-based approach (see Singh & Narain, 2020), while others have adopted an explicitly agrarian prism (see Gururani & Dasgupta, 2018). This study brings both responses together in an area where the cultivation of paddy has declined since the mid-2000s. What I have shown are situated, multidimensional sequences of events. Overall, the bundle of transformations highlighted might be thought of as a multifaceted image, which prompts an inquiry into the arrangement of the facets of this periurban condition. Must periurban areas emerge through these particular temporal sequences? What other sequences play out in other places? What settled-rural elements are dismantled or are found as obdurate in other places? Following on from this thought, what would be needed to support anticipatory management of the settled-rural landscape by residents in areas deemed for future municipalities? And how might residents and their associations, already deeply embedded in periurban transformations as in this study, be supported in prospering amidst their collective settled-rural? These findings could contribute to and extend "intra-urban comparison" and "inter-urban comparison" (McFarlane et al., 2017): that is, to theorize periurbanization both within cities and across cities.

Second, Lawhon et al. (2014, p. 502) argue that a situated urban political ecology makes the connection between theory and practice explicit. This is because the approach is "rooted in the realities and possibilities of everyday urban practices" (2014, p. 510), rather than an abstract "urban revolution." While much work has been done in this manner by looking at the provisioning and appropriation of infrastructures like water (Truelove, 2019), sanitation (Lawhon et al., 2018), or electricity (Silver, 2014), I have taken a different approach. My study has addressed the connection between theory and practice by thinking through a critique of territorial power and the scholarship on critical cartographies. I have paid attention to the work that maps do, I have analyzed accounts of everyday life through maps and stories, I have represented my findings as maps, and I have positioned the study in relation to cartographic practices past and present. Building on this work, questions that might be asked about a situated urban political ecology of territory could further interrogate map-making, for instance, by further exploring the kinds of landscapes that different types of drawings make possible. What new "graphic entities" can be created? What work do they do; that is, what scales do they constitute and what associations do they build? Alternatively, by looking even more closely at the visualizations that surround topological power, what are indicators doing on the ground, in-place? How does interdistrict, intermunicipal competition work when the city is out of the picture? What ordinary imbroglios are such visualizations creating? Or ignoring? And following on from this, how might those ignored imbroglios be visualized? And for whom or what?

Endnotes

1 Rossetto (2019, p. 9) also studies, “out-of-joint, solitary, vandalized, and half-dead cartographic objects.”

2 While not self-identifying as mapmakers the Kolkata-based visual artists—Shreyashi Chatterjee, Amritah Sen and Sumitro Basak—produce map-like visualizations of periurban-like conditions (CIMA, 2020). In other instances, Kolkata-based artist collaboratives, such as Hamdasti (2020) use mapping and creative events to visualize residents' agencies and to participate in tempering undesirable urban change.

Bibliography

Adell, G. (1999). *Theories and Models of the Peri-urban Interface: A changing conceptual landscape* [Literature review]. The Development Planning Unit.

Ahluwalia, I. J. (2019). Urban governance in India. *Journal of Urban Affairs, 41*(1).

Aijaz, R. (2019). *India's peri-urban regions: The need for policy and the challenges of governance* (Urbanisation and Its Discontents) [ORF Issue Brief No.25]. Observer Research Foundation.

Aitken, S. C., & Michel, S. M. (1995). Who contrives the "real" in GIS? Geographic information, planning and critical theory. *Cartography and Geographic Information Systems, 22*(1).

Allen, A. (2003). Environmental planning and management of the peri-urban interface: Perspectives on an emerging field. *Environment and Urbanization, 15*(1).

Allen, A. (2014). Peri-urbanization and the political ecology of differential sustainability. In S. Parnell & S. Oldfield (Eds.), *The Routledge Handbook on Cities of the Global South* (pp. 522–538). Routledge.

Allen, J. (2016). *Topologies of Power: Beyond territory and networks*. Routledge.

Allen, J., & Cochrane, A. (2010). Assemblages of state power: Topological shifts in the organization of government and politics. *Antipode, 42*(5).

Allen, P., Engelen, G., & Sanglier, M. (1986). Towards a general dynamic model of the spatial evolution of urban systems. In B. Hutchinson & M. Batty (Eds.), *Advances in Urban Systems Modelling* (pp. 199–220). North-Holland / Elsevier.

Andrews, R. B. (1942). Elements in the urban fringe pattern. *Journal of Land and Public Utility Economics, 18*, 169–183.

Angelo, H., & Wachsmuth, D. (2015). Urbanizing urban political ecology: A critique of methodological cityism. *International Journal of Urban and Regional Research, 39*(1).

Arnold, D. (2015). Narrativizing Nature: India, empire, and environment. In E. De Laoughrey, J. Didure, & A. Carrigan, *Global Ecologies and the Environmental Humanities* (pp. 35–50). Routledge.

Ascher, F. (1995). *Métapolis ou l'Avenir des Villes*. Odile Jacob.

Baindur, V., & Kamath, L. (2009). *Reengineering urban infrastructure: How the World Bank and Asian Development Bank shape urban infrastructure finance and governance in India* (pp. 1–53) [Research report]. Bank Information Centre, South Asia.

Balakrishnan, S. (2013). Highway urbanization and land conflicts: The challenges to decentralization in India. *Public Affairs*, *86*(4).

Ball, V. (1880). *Jungle Life in India: Or, the journeys and journals of an Indian geologist.* Thos. De La Rue.

Bandyopadhyay, B. (1976). *Aranyak* (R. Bhattacharyya, Trans.). Mitra and Ghosh.

Bandyopadhyay, B. (2017). *Aranyak: Of the forest* (R. Bhattacharyya, Trans.). University of Chicago Press.

Bandyopadhyay, H. (1990). *The Calcutta Canals, a study of its history in the 19th century* [This paper forms part of Ph.D. dissertation (to be submitted) entitled "Agricultural Marketing in Bengal, 1850 - 1900."].

Bandyopadhyay, K. (2010, April 21). Ring road plan in cold storage. *Times of India.* https://timesofindia.indiatimes.com/city/kolkata/Ring-road-plan-in-cold-storage/articleshow/5838194.cms

Bandyopadhyay, K., & Ray, S. (2018, July 30). Choked canals behind waterlogging in Behala. *The Times of India.* https://timesofindia.indiatimes.com/city/kolkata/choked-canals-behind-waterlogging-in-behala/articleshow/65192737.cms

Banerjee, H. (2018). *History of Canals in Bengal.* Doshor Publication.

Banerjee, T. (2005). Understanding planning cultures: The Kolkata paradox. In B. Sanyal (Ed.), *Comparative Planning Cultures* (pp. 145–163). Routledge.

Banerjee, T. (2009). US planning expeditions to postcolonial India: From ideology to innovation in technical assistance. *Journal of the American Planning Association*, *75*(2).

Banerjee, T., & Chakravorty, S. (1994). Transfer of planning technology and local political economy: A retrospective analysis of Calcutta's planning. *Journal of the American Planning Association*, *60*(1).

Banu, N., & Fazal, S. (2017). A pragmatic assessment of livelihood status in the peri-urban interface: A case from developing India. *Asian Geographer*, *34*(1).

Barua, M., & Sinha, A. (2019). Animating the urban: An ethological and geographical conversation. *Social & Cultural Geography*, *20*(8).

Batterbury, S. P. J., & Bebbington, A. J. (1999). Environmental histories, access to resources and landscape change: An introduction. *Land Degradation & Development*, *10*(4).

Batty, M., & Longley, P. (1994). *Fractal Cities: A geometry of form and function.* Academic Press.

Baud, I. S. A., & de Wit, J. (2008). *New Forms of Urban Governance in India.* SAGE.

Baviskar, A. (2004). Between violence and desire: Space, power and identity in the making of metropolitan Delhi. *International Social Science Journal*, *55*(175).

Behala Flying Club. (2007, September 22). Behala Flying Club to get new lease of life. *The Economic Times*. https://economictimes.indiatimes.com/behala-flying-club-to-get-new-lease-of-life/articleshow/2393678.cms

Benthall, A. P. (1946). *The Trees of Calcutta, and its Neighbourhood*. Thacker, Spink & Co.

Bentick, J. V. (1996). *Brick quarries in Delhi's rural-urban fringe: A model of land degradation in socioeconomic terms*. 28th International Geographical Congress, The Hague.

Bentick, J. V. (2000). Unruly urbanization of Delhi's fringe: Changing patterns of land use and livelihood. *Nederlandse Geografische Studies*.

Berg, B. L. (Bruce L. (1995). *Qualitative Research Methods for the Social Sciences*. Pearson/Allyn & Bacon.

Bhagat, R. B. (2002). Challenges of rural-urban classification for decentralised governance. *Economic and Political Weekly*, *37*(25).

Bhagat, R. B. (2005). Rural-urban classification and municipal governance in India. *Singapore Journal of Tropical Geography*, *26*(1).

Bhan, G. (2019). Notes on a Southern urban practice. *Environment & Urbanization*, *31*(2).

Bhattacharyya, D. (2018). *Empire and Ecology in the Bengal Delta*. Cambridge University Press.

Bhattacharyya, R., & Sanyal, K. (2011). Bypassing the squalor: New Towns, immaterial labour and exclusion in post-colonial urbanisation. *Economic and Political Weekly*, *46*(30–31).

Birkenholtz, T. (2010). Full-cost recovery': Producing differentiated water collection practices and responses to centralized water networks in Jaipur, India. *Environment and Planning A*, *42*(9).

Blomley, N., & Sommers, J. (2019). Mapping urban space: Governmentality and cartographic struggles in inner city Vancouver. In R. Smandych (Ed.), *Governable Places*. Routledge.

Bose, P. S. (2015). *Urban Development in India: Global Indians in the remaking of Kolkata*. Routledge.

Bose, S. (2008). Adaptive and integrated management of wastewater and storm water drainage in Kolkata – case study of a Mega City. In C. Pahl-Wost, P. Kabat, & J. Moltgen (Eds.), *Adaptive and Integrated Water Management: Coping with complexity and uncertainty* (pp. 341–356). Springer.

Braun, B. (2008). Environmental issues: Inventive life. *Progress in Human Geography, 32*(5).

Brenner, N. (2014). Urban theory without an outside. In N. Brenner (Ed.), *Implosions/Explosions: Towards a study of planetary urbanization* (pp. 14–35). Jovis.

Brenner, N., & Schmid, C. (2011). Planetary urbanization. In M. Gandy (Ed.), *Urban Constellations* (pp. 10–14). Jovis.

Brook, R., Purushothaman, S., & Hunshal, C. (Eds.). (2003). *Changing Frontiers: The peri-urban interface Hubli-Dharwad, India.* Books for Change.

Browder, J. O., Bohland, J. R., & Scarpadi, J. L. (1995). Patterns of development on the metropolitan fringe: Urban fringe expansion in Bangkok, Jakarta, and Santiago. *Journal of American Planning Association, 61*(3).

Brush, J. E. (1968). Spatial patterns of population in Indian cities. *Geographical Review, 58*(3).

Brush, J. E. (1977). Growth and spatial structure of Indian cities. In A. G. Noble & A. K. Dutt (Eds.), *Indian Urbanization and Planning: Vehicles of modernization* (pp. 64–93). Tata McGraw-Hill.

Bureau of Applied Economics and Statistics. (2009). *District Statistical Handbook: South 24-Parganas.* Government of West Bengal.

Cadenasso, M. L., Pickett, S. T. A., & Jones, C. (2003). A framework for a theory of ecological boundaries. *BioScience, 53*(8), 750–750.

Cadenasso, M. L., Pickett, S. T. A., & Schwarz, K. (2007). Spatial heterogeneity in urban ecosystems: Reconceptualizing land cover and a framework for classification. *Frontiers in Ecology and the Environment, 5*(2).

Cadenasso, M. L., Pickett, S. T. A., Weathers, K., & Bell, S. (2003). An interdisciplinary and synthetic approach to ecological boundaries. *BioScience, 53*(8).

Cairns, S. (2018). Debilitating city-centricity: Urbanization and urban-rural hybridity in Southeast Asia. In R. Padawangi (Ed.), *Routledge Handbook on Urbanisation in Southeast Asia* (pp. 115–129). Routledge.

Calcutta Metropolitan Planning Organisation. (1966a). *Basic Development Plan for the Calcutta Metropolitan District, 1966-1986.* Calcutta Metropolitan Planning Organisation.

Calcutta Metropolitan Planning Organisation. (1966b). *Master Plan for Water Supply, Sewerage and Drainage, Calcutta Metropolitan District 1966-2001.* Government of West Bengal.

Castree, N. (2002). False antitheses? Marxism, nature and actor-networks. *Antipode, 34*(1).

Cavalieri, C., & Vigano, P. (Eds.). (2019). *HM the Horizontal Metropolis a radical project.* Park Books.

Census Organization of India. (2001). *Census 2001.* Census 2001. http://www.censusindia.gov.in/2011-common/census_data_2001.html

Census Organization of India. (2011). *Census 2011* [Government]. Population Census 2011. http://www.census2011.co.in/

Chakravarty, S., Puri, A., Subba, M., Pala, N. A., & Shukla, G. (2017). Homegardens: Drops to sustainability. In J. C. Dagar & V. P. Tewari (Eds.), *Agroforestry* (pp. 517–527). Springer Natures.

Chakravorty, S. (1996). Let a hundred projects bloom: Structural reform and urban development in Calcutta. *Third World Planning Review, 18*(4).

Charmes, E., & Keil, R. (2015). The politics of post-suburban densification in Canada and France. *International Journal of Urban and Regional Research, 39*(3).

Chatterjee, M. (1970). Regional planning approach to Calcutta Metropolitan Area. *Indian Journal of Regional Science, II*(2).

Chatterjee, M. (2013). *Urbanization Trends and Urban Planning in West Bengal, India. PLA2013-0632.* https://www.atiner.gr/paper-series

Chatterjee, P. (2008). Democracy and economic transformation in India. *Economic and Political Weekly, 43*(16).

Chatterjee, S. P. (1949). *Bengal in Maps: A geographical analysis of resource distribution in West Bengal and Eastern Pakistan.* Orient Longmans Ltd.

Chattopadhyay, S. (2009). *"Bourgeois Utopias"?: The rhetoric of globality in the contemporary suburban landscape of Calcutta.* (No. 30; Working Papers in Contemporary Asian Studies, Issue 30). Centre for East and South-East Asian Studies, Lund University.

Chaudhuri, K. N., Pyne, B., Baidya, P., & Patra, P. (2019). Traditional herbal remedies: Implications for primary healthcare among peri-urban communities in the Southwest of Kolkata. In S. K. Tripathi, K. Upadhyaya, & N. Hegde (Eds.), *Medicinal Plants of India: Conservation and sustainable use* (pp. 77–92). Today & Tomorrow's Printers and Publishers.

Chowdhury, S., & Bhattacharyya, R. (2020, May 24). As Cyclone Amphan flattens rare trees in Kolkata, experts blame poor urban planning. *Indian Express.* https://indianexpress.com/article/india/as-amphan-flattens-rare-trees-in-kolkata-experts-blame-poor-urban-planning-6424578/

Christaller, W. (1966). *Central Places in Southern Germany* (C. W. Bakin, Trans.). Prince Hall.

Christian, J. M., & Dowler, L. (2019). Slow and fast violence. *ACME: An International Journal for Critical Geographies*, *18*(5).

CIMA. (2020). *Centre for International Modern Art* [Art Gallery]. CIMA. https://www.cimaartindia.com/

Clifford, J. (1989). The others: Beyond the 'salvage' paradigm. *Third Text*, *3*(6).

Collard, R.-C., Heynen, N., & Mehta, L. (2018). The antinomies of nature and space. *Environment and Planning E: Nature and Space*, *1*(1–2).

Connolly, C. (2018). Urban political ecology beyond methodological cityism. *International Journal of Urban and Regional Research*. https://doi.org/DOI:10.1111/1468-2427.12710

Cook, I. M. (2015). Link work: Land and housing brokers in Mangaluru, India. *Journal of South Asian Development*, *10*(3).

Corbridge, S., & Hariss, J. (2002). *Reinventing India: Liberalization, Hindu nationalism and popular democracy*. Polity Press.

Corbridge, S., Williams, G., Srivastava, M., & Vernon, R. (2005). *Seeing the State: Governance and governmentality in India*. Cambridge University Press.

Cornea, N. (2020). Territorialising control in urban West Bengal: Social clubs and everyday governance in the spaces between state and party. *Politics and Space C*, *38*(2).

Cornea, N., Zimmer, A., & Veron, R. (2016). Ponds, power and institutions: The everyday governance of accessing urban water bodies in a small Bengali city. *International Journal of Urban and Regional Research*, 395–409. https://doi.org/10.1111/1468-2427.12377

Cowan, T. (2015). Fragmented citizenships in Gurgaon. *Economic and Political Weekly*, *50*(26–27).

Crampton, J. W. (2001). Maps as social constructions: Power, communication and visualization. *Progress in Human Geography*, *25*(2).

Crampton, J. W. (2004). *The Political Mapping of Cyberspace*. University of Chicago Press.

Crampton, J. W. (2010a). Cartographic calculations of territory. *Progress in Human Geography*, *35*(1).

Crampton, J. W. (2010b). *Mapping: A critical introduction to cartography and GIS*. Wiley-Blackwell.

Crampton, J. W., & Krygier, J. (2006). An introduction to critical cartography. *ACME: An International E-Journal for Critical Geographies, 4*(1).

Damodaran, V. (2015). The East India Company, famine, and ecological conditions in Eighteenth-Century Bengal. In V. Damodaran, A. Winterbottom, & A. Lester (Eds.), *The East India Company and the Natural World* (pp. 80–101). Palgrave Macmillan UK.

Das, R. (2015). Contradictions, negotiations, and reform: The story of left policy transition in West Bengal. *Journal of South Asian Development, 10*(2).

Dasgupta, A. (2004). The drainage system of the City of Kolkata and its neighbourhood: The past and present scenario. *Sechpotro (Irrigation Journal), 10*(Oct-Dec).

Dasgupta, B. (Ed.). (1991). *Calcutta's Urban Future: Agonies from the past and prospects for the future.* Government of West Bengal.

Daston, L., & Gallison, P. (2007). *Objectivity.* Zone Books.

Datta, A., & Young, J. (2011). Producing home grown solutions: Think tanks and knowledge networks in international development. *Development Outreach, 13*(2).

Davis, K. E., Fisher, A., Kingsbury, B., & Merry, S. E. (Eds.). (2012). *Governance by Indicators: Global power through classification and rankings.* Oxford University Press.

de Certeau, M. (1984). *The Practice of Everyday Life.* University of California Press.

de la Bellacasa, M. P. (2017). *Matters of Care: Speculative ethics in more than human worlds.* Univ of Minnesota Press.

De Neve, G. (2015). Predatory property: Urban land acquisition, housing and class formation in Tiruppur, South India. *Journal of South Asian Development, 10*(3).

De Neve, G., & Donner, H. (2015). Revisiting urban property in India. *Journal of South Asian Development, 10*(3).

Deleuze, G., & Guattari, F. (1988). *A Thousand Plateaus: Capitalism and schizophrenia.* Bloomsbury.

Department of Planning, Statistics & Programme Monitoring. (2018a, February). *Vision, Mission and Perspective Plan: West Bengal: Project Update* [Powerpoint].

Department of Planning, Statistics & Programme Monitoring. (2018b, December). *Vision, Mission and Perspective Plan: West Bengal* [Powerpoint].

Derickson, K. D. (2014). Urban geography I: Locating urban theory in the 'urban age.' *Progress in Human Geography, 39*(5).

Dillon, L. (2012). Slow violence and the environment of the poor [Review of *Slow violence and the environment of the poor*, by R. Nixon]. *Progress in Human Geography, 36*(6).

Directorate of Animal Resources and Animal Health. (2003). *17th All India Livestock Census, Agriculture Implements and Machinery, Fishery Statistics, West Bengal: South 24 Parganas district*. Government of West Bengal.

Dixit, R. S. (1987). *Glimpses of the Umland of a Metropolis: Vol. 9 Perspectives in Urban Geography* (C. S. Yadav, Ed.; pp. 277–332). Concept Publishing Company.

Dobson, J. E. (1983). Automated geography. *The Professional Geographer, 35*(2).

Dobson, J. E. (1993). The geographic revolution: A retrospective on the age of automated geography. *The Professional Geographer, 45*(4).

Doniger, W. (2015). Sympathy for the Devi: Snakes and snake goddesses in Hinduism. In K. Haq, *The Triumph of the Snake Goddess* (pp. 1–28). Harvard University Press.

Donner, H. (2015). 'Daughters are Just Like Sons Now': Negotiating kin-work and property regimes in Kolkata middle-class families. *Journal of South Asian Development, 10*(3), 318–344.

Douglass, M. (1986). *Population growth and policies in mega-cities: Calcutta* (Population Policy Paper No. 1 ST/ESA/SER.R/61; Issue ST/ESA/SER.R/61). United Nations.

Douglass, M. (1998). A regional network strategy for reciprocal rural-urban linkages: An agenda for policy research with reference to Indonesia. *Third World Planning Review, 20*(1).

D'Souza, R. (2006). *Drowned and Dammed: Colonial capitalism and flood control in eastern India*. Oxford University Press.

Duany, A., & Talen, E. (2002). Transect planning. *Journal of the American Planning Association, 68*(3).

Duncan, O. D., & Reiss, A. J. (1956). Suburbs and urban fringe. In O. D. Duncan & A. J. Reiss, *Social Characteristics of Urban and Rural Communities*. John Wiley & Sons.

Dupont, V. (2004). Urban development and population distribution in Delhi: Implications for categorizing population. In T. Champion & G. Hugo (Eds.), *New Forms of Urbanization: Beyond the urban-rural dichotomy* (pp. 171–190). Ashgate.

Dupont, V. (2007). Conflicting stakes and governance in the peripheries of large Indian metropolises – An introduction. *Cities, 24*(2).

Eaton, R. M. (1993). *The Rise of Islam and the Bengal Frontier, 1204-1760.* University of California Press.

Edney, M. H. (2009). *Mapping an Empire: The Geographical Construction of British India, 1765-1843.* University of Chicago Press.

Edney, M. H. (2011). Cartography without 'progress': Reinterpreting the nature and historical development of map making. In M. Dodge, *Classics in Cartography: Reflections on Influential articles from Cartographica* (pp. 305–329). John Wiley & Sons, Ltd.

Ekers, M., Hamel, P., & Keil, R. (2015). Governing suburbia: Modalities and mechanisms of suburban governance. In P. Hamel & R. Keil (Eds.), *Suburban Governance: A global view* (pp. 19–48). University of Toronto Press.

EKWMA. (2020). *East Kolkata Wetlands Management Authority* [Government]. East Kolkata Wetlands Management Authority. http://ekwma.in/ek/

Elden, S. (2010). Land, terrain, territory. *Progress in Human Geography, 34*(6).

Elden, S. (2013). Secure the volume: Vertical geopolitics and the depth of power. *Political Geography, 34*, 35–51.

Ernstson, H., Lawhon, M., & Duminy, J. (2014). Conceptual vectors of African urbanism: 'Engaged theory-making' and 'platforms of engagement.' *Urban and Regional Horizons, 48*(9).

Express News Service. (2009, April 21). KEIP assures a Behala free of waterlogging. *The Indian Express.* http://archive.indianexpress.com/news/keip-assures-a-behala-free-of-waterlogging/449330/

Fagerholm, N. (2014). Whose knowledge, whose benefit? Ethical challenges of participatory mapping. In Jenny. Lunn (Ed.), *Fieldwork in the Global South: Ethical challenges and dilemmas* (pp. 279–279). Routledge.

Fairhead, J., & Leach, Melissa. (1996). *Misreading the African landscape: Society and ecology in a forest-savanna mosaic.* Cambridge University Press.

Forman, R. T. T. (1995). *Land Mosaics: The ecology of landscapes and regions.* Cambridge University Press.

Forman, R. T. T. (2008). *Urban Regions: Ecology and planning beyond the city.* Cambridge University Press.

Forman, R. T. T., & Godron, Michel. (1986). *Landscape Ecology.* Wiley.

Foster, J. B. (1999). Marx's theory of metabolic rift: Classical foundations for environmental sociology. *The American Journal of Sociology*, *105*(2).

Friedmann, J. (2016). The future of periurban research. *Cities*, *53*, 163–165.

Friedmann, J., & Douglass, M. (1975). *Agropolitan Development: Towards a new strategy for regional planning in Asia*. University of California.

Future Cities Lab. (2020). *Urban-rural Systems: Seeding adaptive infrastructure* [Academic]. Future Cities Lab. https://fcl.ethz.ch/research/archipelago-cities/urban-rural-systems.html

Gandy, M. (2004). Rethinking urban metabolism: Water, space and the modern city. *City*, *8*(3).

Garreau, J. (1991). *Edge City: Life in the new frontier*. Doubleday.

Geertz, C. (1969). *Agricultural Involution: The processes of ecological change in Indonesia*. University of California Press.

Ghertner, A. (2011). Gentrifying the state, gentrifying participation: Elite governance programs in Delhi. *International Journal of Urban and Regional Research*, *35*(3).

Ghertner, A. (2017). When is the state? Topology, temporality, and the navigation of everyday state space in Delhi. *Annals of the American Association of Geographers*, *107*(3).

Ghosh, A. (2021). *Jungle Nama: A story of the Sundarban*. Fourth Estate.

Ghosh, P. (2020). *Making Kantha, Making Home: Women at work in Colonial Bengal*. University of Washington Press.

Glover, W. J. (2012). The troubled passage from 'village communities' to planned new town developments in mid-twentieth-century South Asia. *Urban History*, *39*(1).

Goldstein, S. (2016). Planning the millennium city: The politics of place-making in Gurgaon, India. *International Area Studies Review*, *19*(1).

Gopakumar, G. (2015). Intrusiveness of urban renewal in India: JNNURM as a development fix. *Canadian Journal of Development*, *36*(1).

Goswami, M., & Nautiyal, S. (2020). Transitional peri-urban landscape and use of natural resource for livelihoods. In N. Roy, S. Roychoudhury, S. Nautiyal, S. Agrawal, & S. Baksi (Eds.), *Socio-economic and Eco-biological Dimensions in Resource Use and Conservation* (pp. 435–457). Springer.

Gottmann, J. (1961). *Megalopolis; The urbanized northeastern seaboard of the United States*. Twentieth Century Fund.

Government of India. (1949). *Article 243Q, The Constitution of India.* Government of India.

Government of India. (1988). *Report of the National Commission on Urbanization.* National Commission on Urbanization, Ministry of Urban Development, Government of India.

Government of India. (2007). *Backwards Regions Grant Fund: Programme guidelines.* Ministry of Panchayati Raj.

Government of India. (2008). *Eleventh Five Year Plan (2007-12): Inclusive growth.* Planning Commission, Government of India.

Government of India. (2013). *Twelfth Five Year Plan (2012-17): Faster, more inclusive and sustainable growth.* Planning Commission, Government of India.

Government of India. (2020a). *Census Terms* [Government]. Census Terms. https://censusindia.gov.in/data_products/library/indian_perceptive_link/census_terms_link/censusterms.html

Government of India. (2020b, August 14). *About the Aspirational Districts Programme* [Government]. NITI Aayog. https://niti.gov.in/about-aspirational-districts-programme

Government of West Bengal. (1990). *A Perspective Plan for Calcutta: 2011.* State Planning Board, Development and Planning Department, Government of West Bengal.

Government of West Bengal. (2017). *West Bengal Municipal Act, 1993.* Swastik Books.

Government of West Bengal. (2020a). *West Bengal State Election Commission.* http://www.wbsec.gov.in/

Government of West Bengal. (2020b, January 3). *State Public Policy and Planning Board* [Government]. Department of Planning & Statistics. https://www.wbpspm.gov.in/spppb/menu

Government of West Bengal. (2020c, June 15). *West Bengal State Portal* [Government]. West Bengal State Portal. https://wb.gov.in/index.aspx

Graham, S. (2016). *Vertical: The city from satellites to bunkers.* Verso.

Graham, S., & Marvin, S. (2001). *Splintering Urbanism: Networked infrastructures, technological mobilities and the urban condition.* Routledge.

Graham, S., & McFarlane, C. (2014). *Infrastructural Lives: Urban infrastructure in context.* Routledge.

Grant Thornton. (2011). *Appraisal of Jawaharlal Nehru National Urban Renewal Mission (JnNURM): Final report, volume 1.* Grant Thornton India.

Greenhalgh, J. (2018). *Reconstructing Modernity Space, Power and Governance in Mid-twentieth Century British Cities.* Manchester University Press.

Gupta, B. G., Biswas, J. K., & Agrawal, K. M. (2015). Assessment of water quality of Chatta Canal affected by textile bleaching, dyeing and printing effluents in Maheshtala Region, South 24 parganas, West Bengal, India. *International Journal of Advanced Research, 3*(9).

Gupta, B. G., Biswas, J. K., & Agrawal, K. M. (2017). Air pollution from bleaching and dyeing industries creating severe health hazards in Maheshtala textile cluster, West Bengal, India. *Air, Soil and Water Research, 10*, 1–10.

Gupta, D. (2005). Whither the Indian village: Culture and agriculture in "rural" India. *Economic and Political Weekly, 40*(8).

Gururani, S. (2019). Cities in a world of villages: Agrarian urbanism and the making of India's urbanizing frontiers. *Urban Geography*. https://doi.org/10.1080/02723638.2019.1670569

Gururani, S., & Dasgupta, R. (2018). Frontier urbanism: Urbanisation beyond cities in South Asia. *Economic and Political Weekly, LIII*(12).

Hamdasti. (2020). *Hamdasti* [Non-profit arts]. Hamdasti. https://www.hamdasti.com/

Hann, C. (1998). *Property Relations: Renewing the anthropological traditions.* Cambridge University Press.

Haraway, D. J. (1991). *Simians, Cyborgs, and Women: The reinvention of nature.* Routledge.

Haraway, D. J. (2016). *Staying with the Trouble: Making kin in the Chthulucene.* Duke University Press.

Hardoy, J. E., & Satterthwaite, D. (1986). Shelter, infrastructure and services in Third World Cities. *Habitat International, 10*(3).

Harley, J. B. (1989). Deconstructing the map. *Cartographica: The International Journal for Geographic Information and Geovisualization, 26*, 1–20.

Heynen, N. (2013). Urban political ecology I: The urban century. *Progress in Human Geography*, 1–7.

Heynen, N. (2016). Urban political ecology II: The abolitionist century. *Progress in Human Geography, 40*(6).

Heynen, N. (2018). Urban political ecology III: The feminist and queer century. *Progress in Human Geography, 42*(3).

Heynen, N., Kaika, Maria., & Swyngedouw, E. (Erik). (2006). *In the Nature of Cities: Urban political ecology and the politics of urban metabolism.* Routledge.

High Powered Expert Committee (HPEC). (2011). *Report on Indian Urban Infrastructure and Services*. Government of India.

Hodder, I. (2012). *Entangled. An archaeology of the relationships between humans and things*. Wiley-Blackwell.

Hull, M. S. (2012a). Documents and Bureaucracy. *Annual Review of Anthropology*, *41*, 251–267.

Hull, M. S. (2012b). *Government of Paper: The materiality of bureaucracy in urban Pakistan*. University of California Press.

Hussain, Z., & Hanisch, M. (2014). Dynamics of Peri-urban agricultural development and farmers' adaptive behaviour in the emerging megacity of Hyderabad, India. *Journal of Environmental Planning and Management*, *57*(4).

Huxley, M. (2007). Geographies of governmentality. In J. W. Crampton & S. Elden (Eds.), *Space, Knowledge and Power: Foucault and geography* (pp. 185–204). Ashgate.

Huxley, M. (2008). Space and government: Governmentality and geography. *Geography Compass*, *2*(5).

Iaquinta, D., & Drescher, A. W. (2000, January 1). *Defining the Peri-urban: Rural-urban linkages and institutional connections*. Tenth World Congress of the International Rural Sociology Association, Rio de Janeiro.

Imhof, E. (1982). *Cartographic Relief Presentation*. Walter de Gruyter.

Indovina, F. (Ed.). (1990). *La città diffusa*. Daest.

Ingold, T. (1995). Work, time and industry. *Time and Society*, *4*(1).

Ingram, G. K. (1998). Patterns of metropolitan development: What have we learned? *Urban Studies*, *35*(7).

Institute of Town Planners, India. (1991). *Metropolitan Decentralisation* (39th Annual Town and Country Planning Seminar) [Technical Papers]. Institute of Town Planners, India.

Iqbal, Iftekhar. (2010). *The Bengal Delta: Ecology, state and social change, 1840-1943*. Palgrave Macmillan.

IST. (2019, March 4). *Terrible condition of Budge Budge Trunk Road*. The Times of India Citizen Reporter. https://timesofindia.indiatimes.com/citizen-reporter/stories/terribleconditionofbudgebudgetrunkroad-/articleshow/68248339.cms

Jack, J. C. (1927). *The Economic Life of a Bengal District: A study* (Second). Oxford University Press.

Jacobs, J. M. (2012). Comparing comparative urbanisms. *Urban Geography*, *33*(6).

Jalais, Annu. (2010). *Forest of Tigers: People, politics and environment in the Sundarbans*. Routledge.

Jardine, B. (2017). State of the field: Paper tools. *Studies in History and Philosophy of Science*, *64*(53063).

Jha, G. (2018). *Fragile Urban Governance: Evolution, decline, and empowerment of local self-government in India*. Routledge.

Jones, G. W., & Visara, P. (1997). *Urbanisation in Large Developing Countries: China, Indonesia, Brazil, and India*. Clarendon Press.

Kaviraj, S. (1984). On the crisis of political institutions in India. *Contributions to Indian Sociology*, *18*(2).

Keil, R. (2003). Urban political ecology. *Urban Geography*, *24*(8).

Keil, R. (2005). Urban political ecology. *Urban Geography*, *26*(7).

Keil, R., & Boudreau, J.-A. (2006). Metropolitics and metabolics: Rolling out environmentalism in Toronto. In *In the Nature of Cities: Urban political ecology and the politics of urban metabolism* (pp. 41–62). Routledge.

Kennedy, L. (2007). Regional industrial policies driving peri urban dynamics in Hyderabad, India. *Cities*, *24*(2).

Kennedy, L., & Sood, A. (2016). Greenfield development as tabula rasa: Rescaling, speculation and governance on India's urban frontier. *Economic and Political Weekly*, *LI*(17).

Kirksey, S. E., & Helmreich, S. (2010). The emergence of multispecies ethnography. *Cultural Anthropology*, *25*(4).

Kitchin, R., & Dodge, M. (2007). Rethinking maps. *Progress in Human Geography*, *31*(3).

Kolkata Metropolitan Development Authority. (2005). *Vision 2025, Perspective Plan of KMA: 2025*. Kolkata Metropolitan Development Authority. http://kmdaonline.org/home/land_cell_book9

Kolkata Municipal Corporation. (2018). *IND: Kolkata Environmental Improvement Investment Program (KEIIP)—Tranche 2* (Semi-Annual Social Safeguard Monitoring Report ADB Loan 3413-IND). Kolkata Municipal Corporation.

Kumar, B. (1998). *Urbanization and land use conflict at urban fringes*. A.P.H. Publishing Corporation.

Kundu, A. (1989). National commission on urbanization: Issues and non-issues. *Economic and Political Weekly*, *24*(21.

Kundu, A., Pradhan, B., & Subramanian, A. (2002). Dichotomy or Continuum: An analysis of impact of urban centers on their periphery. *Economic and Political Weekly*, *37*(50).

Kundu, D. (2014). Urban development programs in India: A critique of JnNURM. *Social Change*, *44*(4).

Kundu, D., & Samanta, D. (2011). Redefining the inclusive urban agenda in India. *Economic and Political Weekly*, *46*(5).

Kurtz, R. A., & Eicher, J. B. (1958). Fringe and suburbs: A confusion of concepts. *Social Forces*, *37*, 32–37.

Lahiri, A. C. (1936). *Final Report on the Survey and Settlement Operations in the District of 24-Parganas: For the period 1924-1933*. Superintendent, Government Printing, Bengal Government Press.

Lake, R. W. (1993). Planning and applied geography: Positivism, ethics, and geographic information systems. *Progress in Human Geography*, *17*(3).

Laquian, A. (2005). From Mega-Cities to Mega-Urban Regions. In A. Laquian, *Beyond Metropolis: The planning and governance of Asia's mega-urban regions* (pp. 1–47). John Hopkins University Press.

Latour, B. (1993). *We Have Never Been Modern* (C. Porter, Trans.). Harvard University Press.

Lawhon, M., Ernstson, H., & Silver, J. (2014). Provincializing urban political ecology: Towards a situated UPE through African urbanism. *Antipode*, *46*(2).

Lawhon, M., Nilsson, D., Silver, J., Ernstson, H., & Shuaib, L. (2018). Thinking through heterogeneous infrastructure configurations. *Urban Studies*, *55*(4).

Leaf, M. (2016). The politics of periurbanization in Asia. *Cities*, *53*, 130–133.

Leck, H. (2014). Whose voice? Ethics and dynamics of working with interpreters and translators. In Jenny. Lunn (Ed.), *Fieldwork in the Global South: Ethical challenges and dilemmas* (pp. 279–279). Routledge.

Lefebvre, H. (2003). *The Urban Revolution*. University of Minnesota Press.

Legg, S. (2007). *Spaces of Colonialism: Delhi's urban governmentalities*. Blackwell.

Loftus, Alex. (2012). *Everyday Environmentalism: Creating an urban political ecology*. University of Minnesota Press.

Lorimer, H. (2005). Cultural geography: The busyness of being "more-than-representational." *Progress in Human Geography*, *29*(1).

Lund, C. (2006). Twilight institutions: Public authority and local politics in Africa. *Development and Change*, *37*(4).

Lynch, K. (2005). Understanding the rural-urban interface. In K. Lynch, *Rural-Urban Interaction in the Developing World* (pp. 4–34). Routledge.

MacArthur, R. H., & Wilson, E. O. (1967). *The Theory of Island Biogeography*. Princeton University Press.

Mahadevia, D. (2011). Branded and renewed? Policies, politics and processes of urban development in the reforms era. *Economic and Political Weekly*, *31*, 56–64.

Maheshtala Municipality. (2007). *Draft Development Plan: 2007-2012*. Maheshtala Municipality.

Maheshtala Municipality. (2012). *Draft Development Plan: 2012-2017, Second Generation*. Maheshtala Municipality.

Maheshtala Municipality. (2014). *City Development Plan: 2014-15 to 2018-19*. Maheshtala Municipality.

Maheshtala Municipality. (2015). *Vision Document up to 2015-2016*. Maheshtala Municipality.

Mallik, C. (2016). Sociology of land dispossession: Social capital and livelihoods in transition in Peri-urban Kolkata, India. *World Development Perspectives*, *4*, 38–47.

Marshall, F., & Randhawa, P. (2017). *India's Peri-urban Frontier: Rural-urban transformations and food security* [Working Paper]. International Institute for Environment and Development.

Marshall, F., Waldman, L., MacGregor, H., Mehta, L., & Randhawa, P. (2009). *On the Edge of Sustainability: Perspectives on Peri-urban Dynamics*. STEPS Centre. https://opendocs.ids.ac.uk/opendocs/handle/123456789/2461

Marshall, V. (2014). Ecological Urban Design Visuality and Landscape. *Nakhara: Journal of Environmental Design and Planning*, *10*.

Marshall, V., Cadenasso, M. L., McGrath, B. P., & Pickett, S. T. A. (2020). *Patch Atlas: Integrating design practices and ecological knowledge for cities as complex systems*. Yale University Press.

Massey, D. (2004). Geographies of responsibility. *Geografiska Annaler. Series B, Human Geography*, *86*(1).

McFarlane, C. (2016). The geographies of urban density: Topology, politics and the city. *Progress in Human Geography*, *40*(5).

McFarlane, C. (2020). De/re-densification: A relational geography of urban density. *City*.

McFarlane, C., Silver, J., & Truelove, Y. (2017). Cities within cities: Intra-urban comparison of infrastructure in Mumbai, Delhi and Cape Town. *Urban Geography, 38*(9).

McGee. (1991). The emergence of desakota Regions in Asia. In N. Sydney. Ginsburg, Bruce. Koppel, T. G. McGee, & H. East-West Environment and Policy Institute (Honolulu (Eds.), *The Extended Metropolis: Settlement transition in Asia* (pp. 3–25). University of Hawaii Press.

McGee, T. G. (1989). Urbanisasi or kotadesasi? Evolving patterns of urbanization in Asia. In F. J. Costa (Ed.), *Urbanization in Asia: Spatial Dimensions and Policy Issues* (pp. 93–108). University of Hawai'i Press.

McGee, T. G., & Greenberg, C. (1992). The emergence of extended metropolitan regions in ASEAN: Towards the year 2000. *ASEAN Economic Bulletin, 9*(1).

McGrath, B. (Ed.). (2013). *Urban Design Ecologies*. John Wiley & Sons.

McGrath, B. (2018). Intersecting Disciplinary Frameworks: The architecture and ecology of the city. *Ecosystem Health and Sustainability, 4*(6), 148–159.

McGrath, B., & Gardner, J. (2007). *Cinemetrics: Architectural drawing today*. Wiley.

McGrath, B., Marshall, V., Pickett, S. T. A., Cadenasso, M. L., & Grove, J. M. (2019). Ecological Urban Design: Theory, research, and praxis. In S. T. A. Pickett, M. L. Cadenasso, & J. M. Grove (Eds.), *Science for the Sustainable City* (pp. 307–338). Yale University Press.

McGregor, D., Simon, D., & Thompson, D. (2005). *The Peri-urban Interface: Approaches to sustainable natural and human resource use*. Earthscan.

McKain, W. C., & Burnight, R. G. (1953). The sociological significance of the rural-urban fringe: From the rural point of view. *Rural Sociology, 18*, 109–116.

McLain, R., Poe, M., Biedenweg, K., Cerveny, L., Besser, D., & Blahna, D. (2013). Making sense of human ecology mapping: An overview of approaches to integrating socio-Spatial data into environmental planning. *Human Ecology, 41*, 651–665.

McNeill, J. R. (2003). Observations on the nature and culture of environmental history. *History and Theory, 42*(4).

Merry, S. E., Davis, K. E., & Kingsbury, B. (Eds.). (2015). *The Quiet Power of Indicators: Measuring governance, corruption, and rule of law*. Cambridge University Press.

Ministry of Urban Development. (2005). *Guidelines for Jawahal Nehru National Urban Renewal Mission: Sub-mission for urban infrastructure and governance*. Government of India.

Ministry of Urban Development. (2012). *Jawaharlal Nehru National Urban Renewal Mission: Toolkit for preparation of a City Development Plan (second revision).* Government of India.

Mitra, S. (2018a). A 'peripheries' view of planning failures in Kolkata and Hyderabad in India. In G. Bhan, S. Srivinvas, & V. Watson (Eds.), *The Routledge Companion to Planning in the Global South* (pp. 79–90). Routledge.

Mitra, S. (2018b). Roads to new urban futures: Flexible territorialisation in peri-urban Kolkata and Hyderabad. *Economic and Political Weekly, LIII*(49).

Mohanty, P. (2014). A municipal financing framework. In I. J. Ahluwalia, R. Kanbur, & P. Mohanty (Eds.), *Urbanisation in India: Challenges, opportunities and the way forward* (pp. 119–146). SAGE.

Mohanty, P. (2016). *Financing Cities in India: Municipal reforms, fiscal accountability and urban infrastructure.* SAGE Publications.

Molotch, H. (1976). The city as a growth machine: Toward a political economy of place. *Amercian Journal of Sociology, 82*(2).

Monclús, F. J. (Ed.). (1998). *La Ciudad Dispersa.* Centre de Cultura Contemporania.

Mondal, P. (2020, February 18). West Bengal may opt out of Centre's piped water scheme. *The New Indian Express.* https://www.newindianexpress.com/nation/2020/feb/18/west-bengal-may-opt-out-of-centres-piped-water-scheme-2104984.html

Moore, J. W. (2017). Metabolic rift or metabolic shift? Dialectics, nature, and the world-historical method. *Theory and Society, 46*, 285–318.

Mukherjee, J. (2015a). Sustainable flows between Kolkata and its peri-urban interface: Challenges and opportunities. In A. Allen, A. Lampis, & M. Swilling (Eds.), *Untamed Urbanisms* (pp. 33–49). Routledge.

Mukherjee, J. (2015b). Beyond the urban: Rethinking urban ecology using Kolkata as a case study. *International Journal of Urban Sustainable Development, 7*(2).

Mukherjee, J. (2020a). Disrupted networks. In J. Mukherjee (Ed.), *Blue Infrastructures: Exploring urban change in South Asia* (pp. 125–150). Springer Nature.

Mukherjee, J. (2020b). Untamed Practices. In J. Mukherjee (Ed.), *Blue Infrastructures. Exploring Urban Change in South Asia.* Springer.

Mukhopadhyay, P. (2006). Whither urban renewal? *Economic and Political Weekly*, 879–884.

Nanding, A. M. (2014). *Mosquito Trails: Ecology, health, and the politics of entanglement.* University of California Press.

Narain, V. (2009). Growing city, shrinking hinterland: Land acquisition, transition and conflict in peri-urban Gurgaon, India. *Environment & Urbanization, 21*(2).

Narain, V., Anand, P., & Banerjee, P. (2013). Periurbanization in India: A review of the literature and evidence. *Rural to Urban Transitions and the Peri-Urban Interface, SaciWATERs.*

Nath, S. (2017a). Everyday politics and corruption in West Bengal. *Economic and Political Weekly, LII*(21).

Nath, S. (2017b, July 4). The terror of "syndicate raj" in Bengal. *News18.* https://www.news18.com/news/india/the-terror-of-syndicate-raj-in-bengal-1451411.html

Nath, S. (2018). 'Cultural misrecognition' and the sustenance of Trinamool Congress in West Bengal. *Economic and Political Weekly, LIII*(28), 92–99.

Nijman, J. (2007). Introduction—Comparative urbanism. *Urban Geography, 28*(1).

Nilsson, K., Pauleit, S., Bell, S., Aalbers, C., & Nielsen, T. S. (Eds.). (2013). *Peri-urban futures: Scenarios and models for land use change in Europe.* Springer.

NITI Aayog. (2020). *SDG India: Index and dashboard 2019-20* [Government]. SDG India: Index and Dashboard 2019-20. https://sdgindiaindex.niti.gov.in/#/

Niyogi, S. (2018, July 22). Ride to Batanagar will be a breeze soon as flyover nears completion. *Times of India.* https://timesofindia.indiatimes.com/city/kolkata/ride-to-batanagar-will-be-a-breeze-soon-as-flyover-nears-completion/articleshow/65086888.cms

Niyogi, S., & Mukherjee, K. (2020, January 3). West Bengal: Slight rise in forest cover, larger loss of urban trees. *The Times of India.* https://timesofindia.indiatimes.com/city/kolkata/kolkata-slight-rise-in-forest-cover-larger-loss-of-urban-trees/articleshow/73077748.cms

O'Malley, L. S. S. (1908). *Bengal District Gazetteers: Kulhna.* Bengal Secretariat Press.

O'Malley, L. S. S. (1914). *Bengal District Gazetteers: 24-Parganas.* The Bengal Secretariat Book Depot.

Openshaw, S. (1991). A view on the GIS crisis in geography, or, using GIS to put Humpty-Dumpty back together again. *Environment and Planning A, 23*(5).

Paglen, T. (2008). Experimental geography: From cultural production to the production of space. In N. Thompson (Ed.), *Experimental Geography: Radical approaches to landscape, cartography, and urbanism* (pp. 26–34). Independent Curators International.

Pal, A. (2008). *Planning from the Bottom Up: Democratic decentralisation in action.* IOS Press.

Patel, S. K., Verma, P., & Singh, G. S. (2019). Agricultural growth and land use land cover change in peri-urban India. *Environmental Monitoring and Assessment*, *191*(600).

Pathan, S. K., Jothimani, P., Som, N. N., & Mukherjee, K. (1991). *Urban landuse studies of Calcutta Metropolitan Development Authority area using remote sensing techniques* (RSAM/SAC/MUS/RSAG-LRD/PR/02/91; Issue RSAM/SAC/MUS/RSAG-LRD/PR/02/91). Space Applications Center (ISRO).

Perkins, C., & Dodge, M. (2012). Mapping the imagined future: The roles of visual representation in the 1945 City of Manchester Plan. *Bulletin of the John Rylands Library*, *89*(1).

Phadke, A. (2013). Mumbai metropolitan region: Impact of recent urban change on the peri-urban areas of Mumbai. *Urban Studies*, *51*(11).

Phelps, N., & Wu, F. (2011). *International Perspectives on Suburbanization: A post-suburban world?* Palgrave Macmillan.

Philo, C., & Wilbert, C. (2000). *Animal spaces, beastly places: New geographies of human-animal relations*. Routledge.

Pickett, S. T. A., & Rogers, K. H. (1997). Patch dynamics: The transformation of landscape structure and function. In J. A. Bissonette (Ed.), *Wildlife and Landscape Ecology: Effects of pattern and scale* (pp. 101–127). Springer.

Pickles, J. (1993). Discourse on method and the history of discipline: Reflections on Dobson's 1983 automated geography. *The Professional Geographer*, *45*(4).

Pickles, J. (1995). *Ground truth: The social implications of geographic information systems*. Guilford Press.

Pickles, J. (2004). *A History of Spaces: Cartographic reason, mapping, and the geo-coded world*. Routledge.

Pieterse, E. (2008). *City Futures: Confronting the crisis of urban development*. Zed Books.

Pink, S. (2004). Introduction: Situating visual research. In S. Pink, L. Kurti, & I. Afonso (Eds.), *Working Images: Visual research and representation in ethnography* (pp. 1–10). Routledge.

Pink, S. (2006). *The Future of Visual Anthropology: Engaging the senses*. Routledge.

Pink, S. (2008). Mobilising visual ethnography: Making routes, making place and making images. *Forum: Qualitative Social Research*, *9*(3, Art. 36).

Pousin, F. (2003). Visuality as Politics: The example of urban landscape. In M. Dorrian & G. Rose (Eds.), *Deterritorialisations: Revisioning landscapes and politics* (pp. 161–174). Black Dog Publishing.

Prain, D. (1901). *Bengal Plants: A list of the phanerograms, ferns and fern-allies indigenous to, or commonly cultivated in, the Lower Provinces and Chittagong. With definitions of the natural orders and genera, and keys to the genera and species.* (Vol. 1). Bishen Singh Mahendra Pal Singh.

Press Trust India. (2017, October 6). *Three river bridges in WB to boost trade, highlight culture*. The Indian Express. https://indianexpress.com/article/india/three-river-bridges-in-wb-to-boost-trade-highlight-culture-4877522/

Press Trust Of India. (2014, June 11). West Bengal to have 22 new municipalities. *Business Standard*. https://www.business-standard.com/article/economy-policy/west-bengal-to-have-22-new-municipalities-114061101234_1.html

Priya, R., Bisht, R., Randhawa, P., Arora, M., Dolley, J., McGanahan, G., & Marshall, F. (2017). *Local environmentalism in peri-urban spaces in India: Emergent ecological democracy?* (STEPS Working Paper No. 96; Issue 96). STEPS Centre.

Pryor, R. J. (1968). Defining the rural-urban fringe. *Social Forces*, *47*, 202–214.

Ramaswamy, V. (2011). 'It does not die' – urban protest in Kolkata, 1987-2007: An interview with Ranabir Samaddar. *South Asia Multidisciplinary Academic Journal*, *5*.

Ramsar. (2019). *Ramsar: The Convention on Wetlands* [Government]. https://www.ramsar.org/

Ranganathan, M. (2011). The embeddedness of cost recovery: Water reforms and associationism at Bangalore's fringes. In J. S. Anjaria & C. McFarlane (Eds.), *Urban Navigations: Politics, space and the city in South Asia* (pp. 165–190). Routledge.

Ranganathan, M. (2014). Paying for pipes, claiming citizenship: Political agency and water reforms at the urban periphery. *India Journal of Urban and Regional Research*, *38*(2).

Rangarajan, M., & Sivaramakrishnan, K. (2012). *India's Environmental History*. Permanent Black.

Rao, V. (2014). Infra-city: Speculations on flux and history in infrastructure-making. In S. Graham & C. McFarlane (Eds.), *Infrastructural Lives: Urban infrastructure in context* (pp. 38–51). Routledge.

Rathi, A. (2021). Seeing the Urban from the Agrarian: Emerging forms of agrarian urbanization in India. *South Asia Multidisciplinary Academic Journal*, *26*.

Rauws, W. S., & de Roo, G. (2011). Exploring transitions in the peri-urban area. *Planning Theory & Practice*, *12*(2).

Ravetz, J., Fertner, C., & Nielsen, T. S. (2013). The dynamics of peri-urbanization. In K. Nilsson, S. Bell, C. Aalbers, & T. S. Nielsen (Eds.), *Peri-urban Futures: Scenarios and models for land use change in Europe* (pp. 13–44). Springer.

Ray, M. (2015). *Five Thousand Mirrors: The water bodies of Kolkata. An environmental and social study*. Jadavpur University Press.

Ray, S. (2018, July 14). Kolkata Municipal Corporation: 'Only stalled KEIP drainage upgrade work can save Behala from flooding.' *The Times of India*. https://timesofindia.indiatimes.com/city/kolkata/only-stalled-keip-drainage-upgrade-work-can-save-behala-from-flooding/articleshow/64984928.cms

Ray, S. (2019, December 22). Water relief likely in south Kolkata from March. *The Times of India*. https://timesofindia.indiatimes.com/city/kolkata/water-relief-likely-in-s-kol-from-march/articleshow/72920367.cms

Ray, U. (2009). Aestheticizing Labour: An affective discourse of cooking in colonial Bengal. *South Asian History and Culture*, *1*(1).

Reinemann, M. W. (1960). The pattern and distribution of manufacturing in the Chicago area. *Economic Geography*, *36*, 139–144.

Rigg, J., Salamanca, A., & Thompson, E. C. (2016). The puzzle of East and Southeast Asia's persistent smallholder. *Journal of Rural Studies*, *43*, 118–133.

Robbins, P. (2007). *Lawn People: How grasses, weeds, and chemicals make us who we are*. Temple University Press.

Robinson, J. (2002). Global and world cities: A view from off the map. *International Journal of Urban and Regional Research*, *26*(3).

Robinson, J. (2016). Comparative urbanism: New geographies and cultures of theorising the urban. *India Journal of Urban and Regional Research*, *40*(1).

Robinson, Jennifer. (2005). *Ordinary Cities: Between modernity and development*. Routledge.

Rocheleau, D., Thomas-Slayter, B., & Wangari, E. (2013). *Feminist Political Ecology: Global issues and local experience*. Routledge.

Rondinelli, D. A. (1983). *Secondary Cities in Developing Countries: Policies for diffusing urbanisation*. Sage Publications.

Rose, G. (2014). On the relation between 'visual research methods' and contemporary visual culture. *The Sociological Review*, *62*, 24–46.

Rose, G. (2016). *Visual Methodologies: An introduction to researching with visual materials* (3rd ed.). SAGE Publications.

Rose, G., & Tolia-Kelly, D. P. (2012). Visuality/materiality: Introducing a manifesto for practice. In G. Rose & D. P. Tolia-Kelly (Eds.), *Visuality/Materiality: Images, objects, practices* (pp. 1–11). Ashgate.

Rose, N. (1999). *Powers of Freedom: Reframing political thought.* Cambridge University Press.

Rose-Redwood, R. S. (2006). Governmentality, geography, and the geo-coded world. *Progress in Human Geography, 30*(4).

Rossetto, T. (2019). *Object-oriented Cartography: Maps as things.* Routledge.

Rottenberg, R., Merry, S. E., Park, S. J., & Mugler, J. (Eds.). (2015). *The World of Indicators: The making of governmental knowledge through quantification.* Cambridge University Press.

Routray, S. (2013). Engaging the 'long 1980s': On the emergence of the mission mode of state-fabrication in India. *History and Sociology of South Asia, 7*(2).

Roy, A. (2003). *City Requiem, Calcutta: Gender and the politics of poverty: Vol. 10.* University of Minnesota Press.

Roy, A. (2009). Why India cannot plan its cities: Informality, insurgence and the idiom of urbanization. *Planning Theory, 8*(1).

Roy, A. (2011a). Re-forming the megacity: Calcutta and the rural–urban interface. In A. Sorenson & J. Okata (Eds.), *Megacities* (pp. 93–109). Springer.

Roy, A. (2011b). Urbanisms, Worlding Practices and the Theory of Planning. *Planning Theory, 10*(1).

Roy, A. (2014). Development, land acquisition and changing facets of rural livelihoods: A case study from West Bengal. *Journal of Rural Development, 33*(1).

Roy, A. (2016). What is urban about critical urban theory? *Urban Geography, 37*(6).

Roy, B. (1982). *Calcutta: Marshes to metropolis.* National Council of Education.

Roy, I. (2006). Representation and Development in Urban Peripheries: Reflections on governance in Ahmedabad suburbs. *Economic and Political Weekly, 41*(41).

Roy, S. (2001). *Witness to History.* Manuscript India.

Rudra, K. (2018). *Rivers of the Ganga-Brahmaputra-Meghna Delta: A fluvial account of Bengal.* Springer International Publishing.

Ruet, J. (2009). Thinking the Delhi, Hyderabad, Kolkata, and Mumbai experience: Emerging modes of urban governance and state Intervention. In J. Ruet & S. Tawa Lama-Rewal, *Governing India's Metropolises* (pp. 270–303). Routledge.

Sadoway, D., Gopakumar, G., Baindur, V., & Badami, M. G. (2018). JNNURM as a window on urban governance: Its institutional footprint, antecedents, and legacy. *Economic and Political Weekly*, *53*(2).

Sahana, M., Hong, H., & Sajjad, H. (2018). Analysing urban spatial patterns and trend of urban growth using urban sprawl matrix: A study on Kolkata urban agglomeration, India. *Science of the Total Environment*, *628–629*, 1557–1566.

Sami, N. (2017). Learning by doing: Urban planning in Bangalore. In S. Vidyarthi, S. Mathur, & S. Agrawal, *Understanding India's New Approach to Spatial Planning and Development: A salient shift?* (pp. 90–117). Oxford University Press.

Sangameswaran, P. (2018). Land from wetland: Nature and development in the frontiers of Kolkata, India. *Indian Sociology*, *52*(3).

Scott, A. J. (2001). Globalization and the rise of city-regions. *European Planning Studies*, *9*(7).

Sellers, J. M. (1997). *Governing from Below: Urban regions and the global economy.* John Hopkins University Press.

Sen, S., & Sen, J. (1989). *Evolution of Rural Settlements in West Bengal (1850-1985): A case study*. Daya Publishing House.

Shane, D. G. (2005). *Recombinant Urbanism: Conceptual modelling in architecture, urban design and city theory.* John Wiley & Sons.

Shatkin, G. (2016). The real estate turn in policy and planning: Land monetization and the political economy of peri-urbanization in Asia. *Cities*, *53*, 141–149.

Shaw, A. (2004). *The Making of Navi Mumbai.* Orient Longman.

Shaw, A. (2005). Peri-Urban Interface of Indian Cities: Growth, Governance and Local Initiatives. *Economic and Political Weekly*, *40*(2).

Shaw, A. (2016). The informal sector in Kolkata Metropolitan Area: Appraisal and prospects for local economic development. In A. K. Dutt, A. G. Noble, F. J. Costa, R. R. Thakur, & S. K. Thakur (Eds.), *Spatial Diversity and Dynamics in Resources and Urban Development: Volume II: urban development* (pp. 499–516). Springer Netherlands.

Shaw, A. (2019). Suburbanization in Asia: A focus on India. In B. Hanlon & T. J. Vicino (Eds.), *The Routledge Companion to the Suburbs* (pp. 100–109). Routledge.

Sheppard, E. (1993). Automated geography: What kind of geography for what kind of society? *The Professional Geographer*, *45*(4).

Sheppard, E. (1995). GIS and society: Towards a research agenda. *Cartography and Geographic Information Systems*, *22*(1).

Sheppard, E., Leitner, H., & Maringanti, A. (2013). Provincializing Global Urbanism: A Manifesto. *Urban Geography*, *34*(7).

Sieverts, T. (1997). *Zwischenstadt: Zwischen Ort und Welt, Raum und Zeit, Stadt und Land*. Vieweg.

Silver, J. (2014a). Incremental infrastructures: Material improvisation and social collaboration across postcolonial Accra. *Urban Geography*, *35*, 788–804.

Silver, J. (2014b). Incremental infrastructures: Material improvisation and social collaboration across post-colonial Accra. *Urban Geography*, *35*(6).

Silver, J. (2016). Disrupted infrastructures: An urban political ecology of interrupted electricity in Accra. *International Journal of Urban and Regional Research*, *39*(5).

Simon, D. (2008). Urban environments: Issues on the peri-urban fringe. *Annual Review of Environment and Resources*, *33*(1).

Simon, D., McGregor, D., & Nsiah-Gyabaah, K. (2004). The changing urban–rural interface of African cities: Definitional issues and an application to Kumasi, Ghana. *Environment & Urbanization*, *16*(2).

Simone, A. (2004). People as infrastructure. *Public Culture*, *16*, 407–429.

Simone, A. (2014). *Jakarta: Drawing the City Near*. University of Minnesota Press.

Singh, A. K., & Narain, V. (2020). Lost in transition: Perspectives, processes and transformations in Periurbanizing India. *Cities*, *97*, 1–8.

Sivaramakrishnan, K. C. (2015). *Governance of Megacities: Fractured thinking, fragmented setup*. Oxford Scholarship Online.

Smith, T. L. (1937, November). The population of Louisiana: Its composition and changes. *Louisiana Bulletin*, 293.

Soja, E. (1992). Inside exopolis: Scenes from Orange County. In M. Sorkin (Ed.), *Variations on a Theme Park: The new American city and the end of public space*. The Noonday Press.

Spate, O. H. K., & Learmonth, T. A. (2017). *India and Pakistan: A general and regional geography* (Vol. 12). Routledge.

Spivak, G. C. (1988). Can the subaltern speak? In Cary. Nelson & Lawrence. Grossberg (Eds.), *Marxism and the Interpretation of Culture*. University of Illinois Press.

Sreeja, K. G., Madhusoodhanan, C. G., & Eldho, T. I. (2017). Processes of peri-urban resource – livelihood transitions: Glimpses from the periphery of greater Mumbai city, India. *Land Use Policy*, *69*, 49–55.

Srivastava, S. (2015). *Entangled Urbanism: Slum, gated community and shopping mall in Delhi and Gurgaon*. Oxford University Press.

Stake, R. E. (1995). *The Art of Case Study Research*. SAGE Pubications.

Strang, V., & Busse, M. (2011). *Ownership and Appropriation*. Berg.

Sud, N. (2014). The Men in the Middle: A missing dimension in global land deals. *Journal of Peasant Studies*, *41*(4).

Sudhakar, S., & Raha, A. K. (1993). *Forest cover mapping of West Bengal State through digital image processing of Indian remote sensing satellite data—Procedural manual and inventory* (Manual RRSSC_KGP/1/93; Issue RRSSC_KGP/1/93). Forest Department, Government of West Bengal and Regional Remote Sensing Service, Kharagpur, Indian Space Research Organisation, Department of Space, Government of India.

Sukopp, H. (2002). On the early history of urban ecology in Europe. *Preslie Praha*, *74*, 373–393.

Sundaresan, J. (2019). Urban planning in vernacular governance: Land use planning and violations in Bangalore, India. *Progress in Planning*, *127*, 1–23.

Swyngedouw, E. (1996). The city as a hybrid: On nature, society and cyborg urbanization. *Capitalism Nature Socialism*, *7*(2).

Swyngedouw, E. (2006). Circulations and metabolisms: (Hybrid) natures and (cyborg) cities. *Science as Culture*, *15*(2).

Swyngedouw, E. (2018). *Promises of the Political: Insurgent cities in a post-political environment*. MIT Press.

Swyngedouw, E., & Heynen, N. C. (2003). Urban political ecology, justice and the politics of scale. *Antipode*, *35*(5).

Swyngedouw, E., & Kaika, M. (2014). Urban political ecology: Great promises, deadlock… and new beginnings? *Documents d'Anàlisi Geogràfica*, *60*(3).

Tacoli, C. (1998). Beyond the rural-urban divide. *Environment and Urbanization*, *10*(1).

Tacoli, C. (2011). Links between rural and urban development in Africa and Asia. In *Population Distribution, Urbanization, Internal Migration and Development: An International Perspective* (pp. 110–123). United Nations.

Tarlo, E. (2000). Paper truths: The emergency and slum clearance through forgotten files. In C. J. Fuller & V. Benei (Eds.), *The Everyday State and Society in Modern India* (pp. 68–90). Social Science Press.

The Times News Network. (2014, May 27). Mega corporation proposal cleared. *The Times of India*. https://timesofindia.indiatimes.com/city/kolkata/Mega-corporation-proposal-cleared/articleshow/35624738.cms

Thomas, D. (1974). The urban fringe: Approaches and attitudes. In J. H. Johnson, *Suburban Growth; Geographical process at the edge of the Western city*. Wiley.

Thompson, N. (2008). *Experimental Geography*. Independent Curators International.

Thrift, N. (1996). *Spatial Formations*. SAGE Publications Ltd.

Tolia-Kelly, D. P. (2012). The geographies of cultural geography II: visual culture. *Progress in Human Geography*, *36*(1).

Truelove, Y. (2011). (Re-)Conceptualizing water inequality in Delhi, India through a feminist political ecology framework. *Geoforum*, *42*(2), 143–152.

Truelove, Y. (2016). Incongruent waterworlds: Situating the everyday practices and power of water in Delhi. *South Asia Multidisciplinary Academic Journal*, *14*, 1–25.

Truelove, Y. (2019). Grey zones: The everyday practices and governance of water beyond the network. *Annals of the American Association of Geographers*, *109*(6).

Tsing, A. L. (2005). *Friction: An ethnography of global connection*. Princeton University Press.

Tsing, A. L. (2014). More than human sociality: A call for critical description. In K. Hastrup (Ed.), *Anthropology and nature* (pp. 259–259). Routledge.

TT Bureau. (2019, December 12). *Corporation proposes to turn agriculture land in Calcutta pockets into homestead* [News]. The Telegraph. https://www.telegraphindia.com/west-bengal/corporation-proposes-to-turn-agriculture-land-in-calcutta-pockets-into-homestead/cid/1731120

Tzaninis, Y., Mandler, T., Kaika, M., & Keil, R. (2020). Moving urban political ecology beyond the 'urbanization of nature.' *Progress in Human Geography*, 1–24.

Uchida, H., & Nelson, A. (2009). *Agglomeration Index: Towards a new measure of urban concentration*. World Bank.

UN Habitat. (2016). *UN World Cities Report 2016*. http://wcr.unhabitat.org/

United Nations. (2020, January 3). *Sustainable Development Goals*. Un.Org. https://www.un.org/sustainabledevelopment/sustainable-development-goals/

Unwin, T. (1989). Urban-rural interaction in developing countries: A theoretical perspective. In R. B. Potter & T. Unwin (Eds.), *The Geography of Urban-rural Interaction in Developing Countries: Essays for Alan B. Mountjoy* (pp. 11–33). Routledge.

van Cleef, E. (1941). Hinterland and umland. *Geographical Review*, *31*(2).

van Duijne, R. J., & Nijman, J. (2019). India's emergent urban formations. *Annals of the American Association of Geographers, 109*(6).

Veltz, P. (1996). *Mondialisation, villes et territoires: L'économie d'archipel*. Presses Universitaires de France.

Venkataramani, C. (2015). *Drawn into Life: Mapping, development, and ecological vision in urban India* [Dissertation]. https://jscholarship.library.jhu.edu/handle/1774.2/60570

Venturi, R., Scott-Brown, D., & Izenour, S. (1972). *Learning from Las Vegas*. MIT Press.

Viard, J. (1994). *La société d'archipel*. Editions de l'Aube.

Vidyarthi, S. (2014). Building a "world class heritage city": Jaipur's emergent elites and the new approach to spatial planning. In G. Shatkin, *Contesting the Indian City: Global visions and the politics of the local* (pp. 241–264). Wiley-Blackwell.

Vidyarthi, S. (2017). Rethinking the rural (and the urban). In S. Vidyarthi, S. Mathur, & S. Agrawal (Eds.), *Understanding India's New Approach to Spatial Planning and Development: A salient shift?* (pp. 117–139). Oxford University Press.

Vigano, P. (1999). *La Città Elementare*. Skira.

Vigano, P., Cavalieri, C., & Barcelloni Corte, M. (2018). *The Horizontal Metropolis Between Urbanism and Urbanization*. Springer.

Weinstein, L., Sami, N., & Shatkin, G. (2014). Contested developments: Enduring legacies and emergent political actors in contemporary urban India. In G. Shatkin, *Contesting the Indian City: Global visions and the politics of the local* (pp. 39–64). Wiley-Blackwell.

West Bengal Legislative Assembly. (2016). *Fifteenth Legislative Assembly: Twenty eighth report on study visit to Maheshtala Municipality*. Government of West Bengal.

Westland, J. (1874). *A Report on the District of Jessore: Its antiquities, its history, and its commerce*. Bengal Secretariat Press.

Whatmore, S. (2002). *Hybrid geographies: Natures, cultures, spaces*. SAGE Publications.

Whatmore, S. (2006). Materialist returns: Practising cultural geography in and for a more-than-human world. *Cultural Geographies, 13*(4).

Wilkinson, S. I. (2007). Explaining changing patterns of party-voter linkages in India. In H. Kitschelt & S. I. Wilkinson (Eds.), *Patrons, Clients, and Policies: Patterns of democratic accountability and political competition* (pp. 110–140). Cambridge University Press.

Williams, R. (1977). Dominant, residual, emergent. In *Marxism and Literature* (pp. 121–127). Oxford University Press.

Wissink, G. A. (1962). American cities in perspective: With special reference to the development of their fringe areas. *Sociaal Geografische Studies*.

Wolch, J. (2002). Anima urbis. *Progress in Human Geography*, *26*(6).

Wood, D. (1992). *The Power of Maps*. Guilford Press.

World Bank. (1983). *India—Third Calcutta Urban Development Project* (No. 4310; Issue 4310). World Bank Group. http://documents.worldbank.org/curated/en/940541468267585010/India-Third-Calcutta-Urban-Development-Project

World Bank. (2013). *Urbanization beyond municipal boundaries: Nurturing metropolitan economies and connecting peri-urban areas in India*. World Bank.

Wu, F., & Keil, R. (2020). Changing the geographies of sub/urban theory: Asian perspectives. *Urban Geography*, 1–7. https://doi.org/10.1080/02723638.2020.1712115

Wylie, J. (2007). *Landscape*. Routledge.

Yadav, C. S. (Ed.). (1987). *Rural-Urban Fringe: Vol. 9 Perspectives in Urban Geography*. Concept Publishing Company.

Yengkhom, S., & Ray, S. (2019, August 23). 300 dengue cases in Kolkata; Behala worst hit. *The Times of India*. https://timesofindia.indiatimes.com/city/kolkata/300-dengue-cases-in-kol-behala-worst-hit/articleshow/70795390.cms

Zasada, I., Loibl, W., Berges, R., & Steinnocher, K. (2013). Rural–urban regions: A spatial approach to define urban–rural relationships in Europe. In K. Nilsson, S. Pauleit, S. Bell, C. Aalbers, & T. S. Nielsen (Eds.), *Peri-Urban Futures: Scenarios and models for land use change in Europe* (pp. 45–68). Springer.

Zhou, W., Cadenasso, Mary., Schwarz, K., & Pickett, S. (2014). Quantifying spatial heterogeneity in urban landscapes: Integrating visual interpretation and object-based classification. *Remote Sensing*, *6*(4). https://doi.org/10.3390/rs6043369

Zimmer, A. (2010). Urban political ecology: Theoretical concepts, challenges, and suggested future directions. *Erdkunde*, *64*(4).

About the Author

Victoria Jane Marshall is a Senior Lecturer and Director of the Masters of Landscape Architecture program at the Department of Architecture, National University of Singapore. Marshall has a PhD in geography from NUS, Singapore, a Master of Landscape Architecture and a Certificate in Urban Design from the University of Pennsylvania, USA, and a Bachelor of Landscape Architecture from the University of New South Wales, Australia. Prior to teaching at NUS, Marshall taught in the Urban Studies Program at Yale-NUS College, Singapore and at many highly regarded design schools in the northeast United States and Canada including; The New School, Columbia University, Cornell University, Harvard University, University of Pennsylvania, Pratt Institute, and University of Toronto. She has been a collaborator with ETH–Singapore, Future Cities Laboratory, Urban-Rural Systems and Agropolitan Territories of Monsoon Asia modules since 2016. In 2010 she received a fellowship from the India-China Institute at The New School in New York. Marshall received her professional landscape architecture license in 2008. She joined the American Association of Geographers in 2016, the American Society of Landscape Architects in 2008, and the Australian Institute of Landscape Architects in 1994. Marshall is the founder of Till Design (tilldesign.com), which has been her site for creative design research and professional practice since 2001.

Index

Note: Page numbers in italics refer to figures and captions.